CREATION CONSPIRACY

TRANSFORMING THE BIBLICAL WORLD INTO THE MODERN SOLAR SYSTEM

PETE ORTEGA

CREATION CONSPIRACY

TRANSFORMING THE BIBLICAL WORLD
INTO THE MODERN SOLAR SYSTEM

PETE ORTEGA

Front Cover:

Robinson, George L. *Leaders of Israel: A Brief History of the Hebrews*. The International Committee of Young Men's Christian Associations, 1906, p. 2.

Back Cover:

Vermij, Rienk. "Cosmology in the Renaissance." *Encyclopedia of Renaissance Philosophy*, edited by Marco Sgarbi, Springer, 2022, p. 862.

Table of Contents

I will get a tree. I would be disappointed if we didn't. And I will start over with you.

I'm sorry I flipped out and blurted out what I did. I don't know why I said that, or flipped out. I'm sorry I ruined our evening and weekend.

I'll get a tree if you will. If you want to start over

Preface

Knowing the Conspiracy

Something we all have in common is the impact and influence people have upon our everyday lives—co-workers, friends, children, or the mailman. Right now, I am affecting someone because I said, "Mailman." With today's generation, it is better to say, "Mailperson." Why? It is not about gender. Believe it or not, it concerns the earth's foundation.

We may think people like Eratosthenes of Cyrene, Marsilio Ficino, Nicolaus Copernicus, or Jean Astruc do not affect our everyday life or how we read the Bible. Yet, these people have shaped our beliefs about the "universe" and how we read the Bible. If I am wrong and we are not affected by these people of the past, then we would believe in a solid dome barrier called the firmament that covers the earth (Genesis 1:6–8). If I am wrong, we would believe a heavenly ocean sits above the sun, moon, and stars (Genesis 1:16–17). As Christians, with our modern understanding of the "universe," we do not believe what the Bible tells us. Here is an example of a secular (non-religious) author describing what the Bible plainly teaches (Fig. 1). Ron Miller wrote:

> The authors of the Bible took great pains to describe Earth and its place in the universe. … Giant pillars support [the earth]. Vast waters lie beneath Earth, and a domed sky covers it.[1]

Fig. 1. Biblical view of earth described by modern science.

1

The primary resources I used to write a book about the Bible were not the Bible or Christian sources. My research materials were books, journal articles, videos, and scientists from the secular arena of modern science and academia. Secular scholars or scientists have no problem articulating what the Bible states because they hold to a different standard of truth: modern science.

As this book advances, I will define the terms I am using. When we hear the word "science," we have our preconceived ideas about what that word means. I am not against science. True science is not the problem; modern science is. Science is about knowing the truth. Modern science is about promoting a religious belief. Science and modern science are not the same.

What do the Bible and modern science have in common? The Bible and modern science offer philosophy, history, observations, and the practice of worship. They both offer "truth." The difference between a follower of the Bible and a follower of modern science is that a believer in God's word has learned to reinterpret God's word to fit modern science, and a believer of modern science does not care what the Bible claims. When it comes to believing both the Bible and modern science, Christians have learned to treat God's inspired and infallible word as secondary. The previous sentence was not my original thought but was found in a personal letter written by Galileo on January 15, 1633, just three months before his trial.

There are reasons why we do not believe in the foundations of the earth or a solid firmament. The plot to change our thinking started five hundred years before our Savior, Jesus Christ, was born. It was a plan that took thousands of years to implement, a conspiracy that would attempt to destroy the very authority of God's inspired word.

Knowing their History

Spoiler alert: I am not a theoretical physicist, astronomer, or mathematician. I am a man who loves the Word of God. I also enjoy discussing science because it affects our understanding of God's word. Science is not a typical discussion among Christians or the subject of in-depth Bible studies. We are more comfortable leaving it to the experts.

Let me give an example of why it is challenging to talk about science. If I mention, "We have no evidence that gravity is real," or make a statement like, "Gravity has never been proven," people look at me as if I have lost my mind. People assume I am a nutcase because the whole world knows that gravity is real. The primary approach of this book is not to argue science. I will speak on scientific matters when comparing observation, logical thinking, and God's word. The reader of this book does not need to understand Kepler's laws of planetary motion or Einstein's theory of general relativity. I will explain some scientific theories when required to demonstrate their claims. The primary approach of this book is to learn why we believe what we believe about the "universe." To understand why we changed the heavenly and earthly realms in the Bible into a "universe" incompatible with the Bible.

I do not believe the best approach is to combat the world of modern science with experiments, data, or observations that contradict their claims about the "universe." It has yet to prove helpful in explaining to people the ins and outs of science. Most people do not care. The best approach is to explain how modern science created its "universe." It is easier to decide what to believe if we know how the "solar system" and "universe" came into existence.

I mostly used secular scholarship for this book. I used secular and not Christian scholarship when it comes to what modern science teaches to remove prejudice or bias about the history and foundation of modern science. An example of one of my resources is the *Encyclopedia of Renaissance Philosophy* (ERP). This encyclopedia gives us precise and trustworthy articles on philosophy during the Scientific Revolution (1543–1687). Philosophy is "the use of reason in understanding such things as the nature of the real world and existence."[2]

The ERP is professional scholarship about the historical philosophy during the Renaissance from experts in their fields of study. The ERP is a resource tool that professors and researchers use when they want to learn about the history of philosophy during the Renaissance. The editor of the ERP states:

> The aim of the *Encyclopedia of Renaissance Philosophy* (ERP) is to provide scholars with an easy-access reference work that gives accurate and reliable summaries of the current state of research. It includes entries on philosophers, problems, terms, historical periods, subjects, and the cultural context of Renaissance philosophy. … Understandings and misunderstandings of Renaissance literature, philosophy, art, religion, and science have come to shape European cultures and help shape other civilizations.[3]

The philosophy of the Renaissance period impacted our culture and our understanding of Scripture today. The Scientific Revolution falls within the Renaissance period. The "long" Renaissance is considered to cover the 14th through the 17th century. One of my aims is to show how Greek philosophers (before Christ), the Scientific Revolution (Renaissance era), and modern science (current) have had a dramatic influence on how we understand the "universe" and interpret the Bible. Learning the history of modern science will help us understand why we do not believe what the Bible claims.

Psalm 104:5
He set the earth on its foundations; it can never be moved.

Knowing the Bible

The Bible can stand on its own. We should not have to defend the words found in Scripture against the claims of modern science. The Bible is God's word. It was written by people who heard what the Holy Spirit inspired them to write. The Bible is a book of truth. Jesus Christ claimed, "Your word is truth" (John 17:17).

In our modern times, we are told that we can misinterpret Scripture if we do not know the historical, cultural, and literary context of the authors of the Bible. John Walton, a Christian scholar, reminds us that the Old Testament is an ancient document that is not meant to be understood intuitively. Walton wrote:

> The fact that the Old Testament is an ancient document
> means that we cannot read it as if it were a modern Western
> document. Its words are laden with cultural content that its
> audience intrinsically understood but is often opaque to a
> modern reader.[4]

According to the Bible, Walton is wrong. We do not have to be scholars who know ancient cultures or language experts who speak Hebrew or Greek. Jesus did not place specific qualifications or educational requirements for understanding God's word. Jesus said to ordinary people, "But when he, the Spirit of truth, comes, he will guide you into all the truth" (John 16:13). The apostle John was very sincere when he wrote, "As for you, the anointing you received from him remains in you, and you do not need anyone to teach you." (1 John 2:27).

Can we believe what the Bible teaches? Believing that an iron axe head can float because a prophet threw a stick in the water is one thing (2 Kings 6:6). Believing a virgin woman can have a baby because an angel told her is even more challenging (Luke 1:34). Believing that the earth does not rotate on an axis and is set upon a foundation with our modern understanding of the "universe" is nearly impossible.

Knowing the Bible and believing what it teaches is not impossible. It is easier than we would assume to believe in mornings without a sun, a solid dome, and a motionless earth. Of course, it requires a little faith, but then again, we are people of faith! Can we believe what an ancient, pre-scientific book claims over pictures, videos, and school textbooks? The easy answer is yes. The difficult part is trusting what "God said" (Genesis 1:3, 6, 9, 11, 14, 20, 24, 26, 29).

Knowing this Book

What does a person do when they get a new Bible? If a person were like me, they would first turn to the preface when they opened a new Bible. The Bible does not begin with Genesis but with a preface. The preface introduces a book from the author's perspective and informs the reader about what follows. The preface for the Bible gives us insight into the interpretation mindset and explains the special markings found in the text. I want to point out specific features of this book.

Dates

When dealing with dates, there are different interpretations of when an era ends and a new era begins. Within the Renaissance alone, there is the Pre-Italian Renaissance (1100s), Early Italian Renaissance (1200s–1300s), Early Renaissance (1400s), and High Renaissance (1500s–1600s). There is also the Scientific Revolution (1543–1687), which some historians include with the Renaissance and others place after it.

I am not interested in being a historian, but knowing history and dates is essential to understanding how the Biblical world changed into our modern understanding of the "universe." Technically, the process started in the garden of Eden but climaxed during the Renaissance and Scientific Revolution. This book is not a comprehensive look at the details of the Renaissance or world history. It will only highlight the influential people who helped change the Word of God.

I have listed dates according to the consensus of scholars and historians. When a specific date is known, it will be listed. Dates will be repeated throughout the book. The reason for repeated dates is for future reference or study.

Repeating

Throughout this book, I will repeat subjects, events, and quotes (full or partial). Subjects are repeated with different individuals, examples, or perspectives (secular or Christian). Repeating is intentional. I am not trying to make this book any longer than necessary. The layout of this book deals with three different worlds: the Biblical, Greek, and Modern Christian perspectives. If a person reads the Biblical perspective without dealing with the Greek philosophy, it would be easy to disagree with my arguments. Let me explain.

If I mention that the earth does not rotate (Biblical) or there is no such thing as gravity (Greek), people will dismiss my claim and say, "Whatever. You're crazy." Repeating subjects, events, and quotes contrasts the Bible and modern science no matter what world (perspective) we read about. For the record, the earth not moving is not my claim; the Bible teaches that. Also, for the record, gravity not being real is not my claim; modern science teaches that.

Capitalization and Spelling

When referring to the sun, moon, earth, and "universe," I do not capitalize these words unless they are a part of a title or heading. Nearly all English Bibles do not capitalize those words either. Capitalization of the heavenly lights or the earth is about something other than proper grammar. I do not capitalize the heavenly lights, earth, or the "universe" because they are non-living objects. To modern science, these objects are more than just objects.

When quoting an author, scholar, or scientist, I will not change the capitalization of their quote. It is worth paying attention to how modern science treats the objects in the sky and its theories. Here are several examples of how modern science pays attention to things that are important to it. The following examples are from NASA:

> The ***Moon*** was likely formed after a Mars-sized body collided with ***Earth*** several billion years ago (*emphasis added*).[5]

Webb studies every phase in the history of our ***Universe***, ranging from the first luminous glows after the ***Big Bang***, to the formation of solar systems capable of supporting life on planets like ***Earth***, to the evolution of our own ***Solar System***. Webb launched on Dec. 25th 2021. It does not orbit around the ***Earth*** like the Hubble Space Telescope, it orbits the ***Sun*** 1.5 million kilometers (1 million miles) away from the ***Earth*** at what is called the second Lagrange point or L2 (*emphasis added*).[6]

I also use quotation marks for words like "universe" because I do not believe in modern science's "universe." I believe in a "universe," but not the one people think of when hearing that word. One of my favorite Bible verses reads, "By faith we understand that the universe was formed at God's command" (Hebrews 11:3). The "universe" that the author of Hebrews is speaking about is not the "universe" that modern science created less than five hundred years ago.

Endotes and Links

A friend decided to investigate something I had written in a previous book. The topic was about a Greek philosopher who made something up; now, we all believe it. The friend found a science textbook and learned what I said was correct. A pastor did the same thing. They looked up the information and found that the theories that formed the "universe" have never been proven.

I am going to present information on subjects that may seem utterly ridiculous to the modern thinker and make some extraordinary claims about the "universe." As *Bill Nye the Science Guy*, said, "Extraordinary claims require extraordinary proof."[7] In this book, I want to share the information needed to verify what I state.

I enjoy notes (i.e., footnotes, endnotes, and author's notes). When researching, I like to see the source material the author or scholar uses. I have included endnotes because I do not prefer in-line citations, e.g., Scholars say, "Enjoy the book" (Smith 37). I like the information accessible to verify or explain the subject matter (i.e., page numbers,[8] timestamps, author's notes, etc.). Also, when I cite journal articles, I list the specific page and not the page range to make finding the information faster:

Normal Journal Citation

[347] Allen, George T. "The Egyptian God, Thoth." *The Journal of Religion*, vol. 3, no. 2, The University of Chicago Press, Mar. 1923, ***pp. 207–08*** (*emphasis added*).

Author's Preface

[347] Allen, George T. "The Egyptian God, Thoth." *The Journal of Religion*, vol. 3, no. 2, The University of Chicago Press, Mar. 1923, ***p. 207*** (*emphasis added*).

Typing long website addresses from a printed book is not convenient. When this book is released, I will make the links available in a portable document format (PDF).

Email: info@ortegalife.com

Timestamps

It is not convenient to sit through hours of dialogue when watching a video, trying to find what they say about the subject being researched, even though watching the complete video is recommended. Anyone can be misquoted when taken out of context. That being said, I have included time-stamps in the citation. The format is as follows: hours, minutes, and seconds. The location of the quote could be over an hour into the video (1:25:47), under an hour (6:33), or under a minute (0:18).

Knowing the Reason

Discussing the creation story and modern science is a touchy subject because we want to avoid confronting the possibility that we might be wrong. I am easily disregarded when talking with people: "I don't believe you." "That's not true." "That's not what the Bible meant." "You think the earth is flat?" "The creation story is not to be taken literally."

I will say upfront. I know what I believe. More importantly, I know why I believe it. I know what I believe about the layout of the heavenly and earthly realms, the shape of the earth, and the location of the sun, moon, and stars. I know why I believe the creation story found in Genesis 1 is 100% accurate as to how and what God did when He spoke. I know why I believe in a motionless earth that is set on a foundation. I have given careful thought to what I believe. The Bible warns us that not giving careful thought about what we believe will lead to deception.

Proverbs 14:8
The wisdom of the prudent is to give thought to their ways,
but the folly of fools is deception.

Now I have a question, "Has careful thought been given to the 'universe' we believe in?" Why do we believe in what we believe? What are the reasons for believing in a spherical earth? Why do we believe the earth moves and spins around the sun? Why do we believe the sun's gravity holds "planets" in orbit? Why do we believe modern science over what God said in the Bible?

Modern science claims: "Planet Earth isn't at rest, but continuously moves through space."[9]

The Bible claims: "[God] set the earth on its foundations; it can never be moved" (Psalm 104:5).

The common conclusion to a conversation about modern science and Genesis 1 is, "Well, it doesn't matter. It's not a salvation issue." I will agree. The creation story is not a salvation issue. People do not go to hell because they believe the earth moves. If my goal were to reach the unsaved, my efforts would be in vain. The good news is I am not writing to unsaved people. I am writing to Christians who hold to the Word of God. This book is not about salvation. It is about believing Scripture that we claim to be inspired by a "God, who does not lie" (Titus 1:2).

I would disagree if told, "Well, it doesn't matter." It does matter. The results of modern science's "universe" have impacted many areas of life, not just astronomy. Take, for example, the field of psychology. We live in a culture that believes in mental health, in and outside of the church, that is based upon psychology, that is based upon evolution, that is founded upon a belief that God did not have anything to do with creation because of gravity. The history of modern psychology is long, but it was only after the Scientific Revolution (1543–1687), that psychology became an accepted practice. John D. Greenwood wrote:

As the centuries progressed, critical thinkers continued to speculate about the nature and causes of mind and behavior and to subject their theories to empirical test. The process was accelerated by the scientific revolution in Europe in the 16th and 17th centuries and by the development of experimental physiology and evolutionary theory in the 19th century, which promoted the growth of the institutional science of psychology in the late 19th and 20th centuries.[10]

Psychology is a great example of why we need to know the reason behind why we believe what we believe. The foundation of psychology and the Bible are naturally at odds, just like modern science and the Bible. Dr. Jeffrey H. Boyd is a psychologist affiliated with the Waterbury Hospital in Connecticut whose expertise includes treating depression, anxiety disorders, schizophrenia, and substance abuse. Boyd knows the foundation of psychology is the opposite of the Bible. Boyd, a professional psychologist, wrote:

> The Bible from a Christian perspective offers a God centered view of people. God is the creator, rescuer, and goal of humans. Comparing today's popular psychology with the biblical approach is like comparing a pre Copernican to a Copernican model of the solar system. Popular psychology teaches clients to love themselves and trust their own understanding. The Bible teaches that we should "Trust in the LORD with all your heart and lean not on your own understanding" (Proverbs 3:5). Claudius Ptolemy said that the sun and planets revolve around the earth. Nicolaus Copernicus said that the earth and planets revolve around the sun. We are facing a similar debate in psychology today. Popular magazines, TV and public opinion teach that YOU are the center of the psychological universe: "believe in yourself." The Bible proposes that you revolve around God, meeting or frustrating God's wishes: "believe in God."[11]

This book aims to present the reader with the information needed to make an informed choice. The choice is to believe what the Bible claims or believe in the "universe" modern science presents. For the record, I did not come up with these extreme options; the Bible did, which I will cover later. Either we believe what God said (Biblical World) or what mankind said (Greek or Modern Christian World). We cannot have both. There is no middle ground. Either the earth is motionless, as the Bible states, or we are moving around the sun, as told by modern science. Both cannot be true. The readers of the Bible or the followers of modern science are not given the option to pick and choose what they want to believe is true.

My intention for this book is not to convince the reader to believe what I believe. I aim to provide information to help us understand why we believe what we believe. I know I am biased toward the words found in the Bible, which is why I will use secular (non-religious) scholarship to explain the origin and history of modern science's "universe." May we all make the right choice regarding God's word. I pray that all of us will depend upon the Spirit of truth to lead us "into all the truth" (John 16:13).

— Pete Ortega

The Biblical World

Chapter 1

Don't Talk About It

What comes to mind when we hear "The foundations of the earth"? Most people never think about it, even when we read that phrase in the Bible. Christians marvel at the beauty of God's creation, but we seldom think about the function, layout, and movement of God's creation. We hardly think about the ground beneath our feet or pay attention to the skies above. When we think about our "solar system," we imagine a globe traveling in the vacuum of space being pulled by the sun's gravitational force. The one thing we do not imagine is an earth resting motionless upon a foundation.

Psalm 96:10
Say among the nations, "The LORD reigns." The world is firmly established, it cannot be moved.

Psalm 102:25
In the beginning you laid the foundations of the earth, and the heavens are the work of your hands.

One of the tools we have for studying the Bible is commentaries. They are resources that give us an explanation of what the Bible is trying to tell us. There are different types of commentaries from which we could choose. They range from general commentaries that give us an overview of Scripture to exegetical commentaries that try to provide the author's original meaning or intent. When we search commentaries about the earth's foundation, they usually interpret the passage in two ways. (1) They focus on other parts of creation and not the earth's foundation, or (2) they ignore the foundation altogether. Here are some examples of commentaries dealing with the earth's foundation. The following examples are commentating on the meaning of Psalm 102:25. Daniel J. Estes states:

> In the OT the terms heaven and earth form a merism that uses the extremes of location to refer to the whole universe (cf. Gen 1:1). Everything in the natural world was built by the Lord, so nothing lies outside the scope of the Lord's creation or control (cf. Ps 104:3; Prov 8:27–29; Isa 48:13).

As amazing as the world is, the Lord who created it is even greater and therefore worthy of praise.[1]

Estes does not mention the earth's foundation but focuses on creation as a whole. A. R. Fausset (1821-1910) was an evangelical Bible commentator. Fausset wrote:

> The creation of the heavens and the earth by God is here introduced as the ground on which he rests the statement (v. 26), that 'They shall perish ... and be changed.' What God has made, that He can destroy: heaven and earth, as being things created, shall pass away; but the Lord who created them shall remain. Cf. Heb. 1:10–12, which applies to Messiah what is here said of Jehovah (Heb. 12:26–28).[2]

Fausset does not mention the earth's foundation but focuses on the general act of creation. Kevin R. Warstler stated, "By right of creation, the Lord earned the authority to rule and reign over the cosmos."[3] Warstler does not mention the earth's foundation but focuses on creation and God's rule over the entire "universe." Suppose a commenter mentions the earth's foundation. In that case, it is either described as an archaic idea or labeled poetry or symbolic speech, which allows for a non-literal interpretation.

We do not talk about the earth's foundation because we do not believe the world is motionless and resting upon a foundation. We believe what we have been taught. We believe in the "universe" shown to us since we entered kindergarten. We believe the pictures and videos from government space agencies. We believe the earth rotates on an axis and orbits the sun even though the Bible claims that "the foundations of the earth are the LORD's; on them he has set the world" (1 Samuel 2:8). When we investigate what the Bible states, we find that the Biblical layout of the heavens and the earth is incompatible with our modern understanding of the "universe."

I place quotation marks around "universe" because the word itself is not what we think it is. The word "universe" is commonly used to describe the whole "cosmic system" (e.g., galaxies, planets, black holes, dark energy, other moons, asteroids, etc.). When we use the word "universe" as Christians, we are referring to the heavens and the earth that God created (Genesis 1:1). I occasionally use the word "universe" when talking with people because that is the way they understand the heavens and the earth. One of my favorite Bible verses uses the word "universe" (Hebrews 11:3). I am not against using that word as long as it is understood that I am only talking about the heavens and the earth as described in the Bible. The other stuff in the "universe" (e.g., galaxies, planets, black holes, dark energy, other moons, asteroids, etc.) is all a lie. For the record, I did not call the "universe" a lie. The Bible does. According to the Bible's plain, simple, and natural reading, modern science's "universe" is not what God created.

Modern scholars, professors, and people reading this book may laugh at my naïve and unintelligent approach to Scripture. I would be mocked because I do not understand the creation story's historical, cultural, or literary context. I would be dismissed because I do not understand Hebrew poetry. I would be criticized for how I translate words found in the Bible from their original languages because I am not an expert in Hebrew or Greek. I would be looked down upon because I misinterpret the Biblical author's intent when quoting Scripture. I would be ridiculed for believing an archaic system of the heavens and the earth that was proven false thousands of years ago. I would be corrected in my thoughts because of all the evidence and proof from our modern scientific discoveries.

Several years ago, I would have reacted the same if someone approached me and told me the whole "universe" was wrong. I was just like the scholars, professors, and modern thinkers. I believed in the "universe" as imagined by modern science. I believed in the pictures, videos, and textbooks. I put my faith and trust in modern science.

When I first explored the creation story and modern science, I attempted to find a balance between the two. I hoped that Genesis 1 was accurate while acknowledging modern science's claims. However, it did not take long for me to realize that the Biblical description of the heavens, the earth, and the "universe" were incompatible. How can one reconcile conflicting viewpoints? Scholars have pointed out the incompatibility between Genesis 1 and modern science. Timothy Munyon states:

> If all current attempts to harmonize the Bible and science are plagued with difficulties, why consider them? First, some questions need answering, and we are convinced that because God is a consistent, truthful God (Num. 23:19; Titus 1:2; Heb. 6:18; 1 John 5:20; Rev. 6:10), His Word will agree with His world. Second, the Bible itself seems to call on evidence to support belief (Acts 1:3; 1 Cor. 15:5–8; 2 Pet. 1:16; 1 John 1:1–3); it seems to suggest that one ought to have something intelligent to say about science

and the Bible if asked (Col. 4:5–6; Titus 1:9; 1 Pet. 3:15; Jude 3).[4]

Munyon is correct on two points. First, God's word should align with His creation. If the Bible makes a claim about the natural world, then the Bible should parallel and correspond with what we observe in the natural world. For example, the Bible makes a statement about evaporation.

Ecclesiastes 1:7
All streams flow into the sea, yet the sea is never full. To the place the streams come from, there they return again.

The Bible claims that water from the sea evaporates, returns to the rivers, and eventually returns to the sea. The Bible claims that the water returning to the sea does not flood the sea. Fausset wrote:

> The sun lifts out of the sea as much water as flows into it, which the winds carry as vapour to the dry land, where the hills, with their cold summits, condense it into rain, which having watered the earth, the surplus finds its way to the rivers, and thence into the sea again.[5]

The Bible made a claim in Ecclesiastes thousands of years ago, and it agrees with what we observe today. The Mississippi River does not continue to flow into the Gulf of Mexico, causing it to rise above the borders of Texas or Florida. The river flows into the sea. Evaporation occurs and forms clouds. The clouds become too heavy, and they rain upon the earth. The rain makes its way into the Mississippi River, which flows back into the sea. True science is something we can observe. True science is something that can be tested, proven, and repeated. As William W. Menzies points out, "True science and the Bible are not at odds."[6]

Munyon's second point is also correct. We should have something intelligent to say about science and the Bible. I do not believe that Munyon expects us to explain the second law of thermodynamics, Pascal's law, or Schrödinger's cat. Of course, if we did study these areas of science, we would discover problems with their theories on the atmosphere, gravity, and the origin of the "universe." It is hard to speak out against science because we do not know what we believe. We sound educated when we repeat popular scientific theories or when we can describe the "solar system" in great detail, but we have no clue about the history that made it all up. We do not take the time to investigate the origin of our modern understanding of the heavens and the earth. We have never been taught in school that our current "solar system" was invented by a man who believed the earth sat on a giant crystal ball and rotated around a god called the sun. I did not get my sources from anti-science Christian websites or books. I got my information from secular scientists, historians, and universities. All this information is out there, including how all the theories that hold the "solar system" together have never been proven.

The reason I have "something intelligent to say about science and the Bible if asked"[7] is because I have looked into what the world teaches about the "universe." I studied the "universe" because the Lord asked me in 2020, "What if Genesis 1 was correct?" That is all God said. God did not ask me for my opinion or interpretation of the creation story. He asked me if His words were correct. The definition of "correct" is "in agreement with the true facts."[8] God asked me if Genesis 1 stated the truth as written. Immediately, I went to the world of science to learn what we really believe about the "universe." Again, as Menzies stated, "True science and the Bible are not at odds."[9] I sought information about the sun, moon, and stars and the layout and function of the "universe." If modern science or the Bible were telling the truth, they should align in some form. Truth is truth. Take the origin of human beings, for example. Modern science claims human beings came from the stars[10] and the Bible tells us that God created humanity from dust and the breath of life (Genesis 1:27; 2:7). Who is telling the truth, modern science or God? Both narratives cannot be accurate.

Lawrence Krauss, a theoretical physicist, may not be a common name in the church, but he is an expert in the world of science. Krauss is not a Christian. The former Arizona State University professor "has written more than 300 scientific publications and 10 popular books, including the international best-sellers, 'The Physics of Star Trek,' and 'A Universe from Nothing.' Among his numerous awards are included the highest awards from all three U.S. physics societies and the 2012 Public Service Award from the National Science Board."[11] Krauss accurately states the position of modern science on how human beings came about. In a lecture, Krauss claims that every atom in our bodies came from an exploded star. He tells the university students that we are all stardust. Krauss said:

> "[The atoms in your body were not] created at the beginning of time. They are created in the nuclear furnaces of stars. And the only way they can get into your body is if

the stars were kind enough to explode. So, forget Jesus, the stars died so that you could be here today."[12]

Modern science believes our life comes from the stars. The scientific experts tell us the same thing in a NOVA's *Universe Revealed* episode:

The sun is a creator bringing together atoms forged in generations of ancient stars to create us, beings capable of exploring the cosmos and uncovering our own stellar ancestry. It's a wonderful thing how we share this intimate connection with stars because they are part of our cosmic heritage. We are the children of these stars.[13]

Modern science believes stars created us because of the theory of evolution. Of course, it is easy to dismiss the theory of evolution and claim God created human beings. Ironically, we tend to ignore the theory of evolution because it is opposite to what the Bible teaches. Yet, we hold to a "solar system" that is in direct opposition to God's word. We believe in a "universe" created less than five hundred years ago instead of what the Bible claims. We choose to buy into a "solar system" that does not exist in Scripture. The plot to transform the Biblical world into the modern "universe" is not a conspiracy theory. The creation conspiracy is real. The proof for the creation conspiracy is evident; we believe in modern science's "universe."

Chapter 2

Modern Times

My position is that true science and the Bible do not disagree. What we have been taught about the "universe" is not true science. We have been taught scientism. Scientism is a hyper-belief in the role of science that defends its positions without physical evidence or by applying the scientific method to its claims. It is a belief that science is all we need to gain complete knowledge about the natural world. It is a religious belief in science.

Mikael Stenmark gives an example of a scientist who believes in scientism. Stenmark will cite Richard Dawkins, a biologist, now turned anti-theist (deliberate opposition to God), in his journal article called, "What is Scientism?" Stenmark will explain Dawkins' religious belief in science (scientism). Stenmark wrote:

> Some scientists seem to have an almost unlimited confidence in science – especially in their own discipline – and about what could be achieved in the name of science. Richard Dawkins says that since we have modern biology: "We no longer have to resort to superstition when faced with the deep problems: Is there a meaning to life? What are we for? What is man?" According to him science is capable of dealing with all these questions and constitutes in addition the only alternative to superstition. Science, he says, tells us that: "We are machines built by DNA whose purpose is to make more copies of the same DNA. ... That is EXACTLY what we are for. We are machines for propagating DNA, and the propagation of DNA is a self-sustaining process. It is every living object's sole reason for living."[1]

Scientism does not need God, which Dawkins refers to as a superstition. All we need is a religious belief in science to find all the answers we need. In fact, scientism does not even require evidence or experimental proof.

Michio Kaku is the co-founder of string theory. Kaku is a famous American physicist who regularly appears on CNN, NBC, and FOX. Once, Kaku was being interviewed on C-SPAN2's *BookTV*. Kaku said:

"You're not going to believe this. In science we always say that you make observations, you have a theory, you go make more observations and it's a very, very, tedious process. Wrong. Nobody that I know of in my field uses the so-called 'scientific method.' In our field, it's by the seat of your pants. It's leaps of logic. It's guesswork."[2]

Kaku does not need evidence to promote his eleven or twenty-six dimensions to make string theory work. Kaku only needs to have faith in modern science instead of in the scientific method that is observable, measurable, and repeatable. Kaku does not believe in God's word but in modern science. Kaku does not believe in Genesis 1; he believes in modern science's creation of light (Fig. 2). Kaku said, "In the beginning, God said, 'The four-dimensional divergence of an anti-symmetric second rank tensor equals zero.' And there was light."[3]

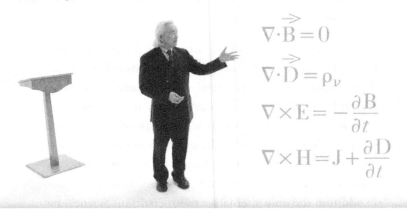

$$\nabla \cdot \vec{B} = 0$$

$$\nabla \cdot \vec{D} = \rho_v$$

$$\nabla \times E = -\frac{\partial B}{\partial t}$$

$$\nabla \times H = J + \frac{\partial D}{\partial t}$$

Fig. 2. Michio Kaku's "In the beginning."

Today, we live in three dimensions: (1) up/down, (2) left/right, and (3) forward/backward. Modern science teaches us that we live in four dimensions, Einstein's spacetime, but this is only a theory. Even though we have no actual evidence that spacetime exists, theoretical physicists promote it as possible because of math and not by the scientific method. Brian Greene, a theoretical physicist and string theorist, was speaking about the imaginary fourth dimension (spacetime). Greene said:

"According to the mathematics well-motivated by these attempts of realizing [Albert] Einstein's dream of unified theory, the math suggests this as a real possibility that there may be more dimensions than the ones that we directly experience."[4]

Notice how modern scientists rely heavily on math rather than objective experimental evidence. Nikola Tesla, a scientist who believed in the scientific method, warned of scientists who only used math and not evidence. Tesla said:

> "Today's scientists have substituted mathematics for experiments, and they wander off through equation after equation, and eventually build a structure which has no relation to reality."[5]

Greene spoke about the possibility of a fourth dimension, but he had to admit that there was no evidence to his claims. Everything Greene states about the "science" of string theory is only a theory written in the language of math with no evidence to prove it. Greene said, "There is no experimental evidence for any of what I'm about to tell you."[6] Modern science is simply a religious belief (scientism). Modern science is founded upon theories that have never been proven. *Forbes* wrote:

> You've heard of our greatest scientific theories: the theory of evolution, the Big Bang theory, the theory of gravity. You've also heard of the concept of a proof, and the claims that certain pieces of evidence prove the validities of these theories. Fossils, genetic inheritance, and DNA prove the theory of evolution. The Hubble expansion of the Universe, the evolution of stars, galaxies, and heavy elements, and the existence of the cosmic microwave background prove the Big Bang theory. And falling objects, GPS clocks, planetary motion, and the deflection of starlight prove the theory of gravity. Except that's a complete lie. While they provide very strong evidence for those theories, they aren't proof. In fact, when it comes to science, proving anything is an impossibility. Reality is a complicated place.[7]

The three foundational theories of modern science (i.e., evolution, big bang, and gravity) have never been proven with experimental evidence. They are theories that state a belief but cannot be validated with proof. The theory of evolution, big bang, and gravity are built upon one single assumption. They all assume the earth moves.

To modern science, reality is complicated because reality must be established on something real. Evolution, big bang, and gravity are not real. *Forbes* informs its readers to trust in unproven theories that formed our "universe." *Forbes* wrote, "So don't try to prove things; try to convince yourself."[8] Modern science has taught people not to trust their intuition. For example, many people do not know that during the winter, the earth is closer to the sun than during the summer (Fig. 3). NASA will explain this to its children. NASA wrote:

> Earth's perihelion (point closest to Sun) = 91,400,000 miles from Sun.
>
> Earth's aphelion (point farthest from Sun) = 94,500,000 miles from Sun.
>
> While that is a difference of over 3 million miles, relative to the entire distance, it isn't much … And, believe it or not, aphelion (when Earth is farthest from the Sun) occurs in July, and perihelion (when we are closest) occurs in January. For those of us who live in the Northern Hemisphere where it's summer in July and winter in January, that seems backwards, doesn't it? That just goes to prove that Earth's distance from the Sun is not the cause of the seasons.[9]

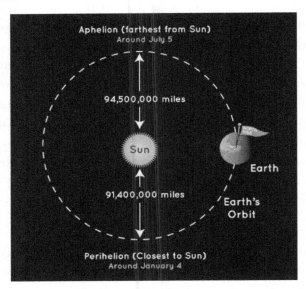

Fig. 3. Perihelion and Aphelion.

It would seem normal to assume that if the earth were 3,100,000 miles closer to the earth, we would expect the earth to be warmer. According to modern science, the answer is no. We are told that the earth is on a 23.4° tilt (1,619 miles),[10] which causes winter and summer, but being 3.1 million miles closer makes no difference in temperature. NASA tells its readers, "Although this idea makes sense, it is incorrect."[11] Modern science teaches us not to rely on our thoughts but on their words.

True science is based on experimental evidence. Modern science is not true science, but a religious belief founded on people's imaginations and mathematical equations. As we will find out, the religious faith of modern science also includes the worship of gods.

What we have been taught about the "universe" is based on scientism and not true science. If we believe in true science (things that are observable, measurable, and repeatable), then we would have to throw out our current belief in modern science's "solar system," "planets," and the "universe," which are all founded on theories that have never been proven. If we suggest anything different from modern science's "universe," we are laughed at and sidelined as a conspiracy theorist, which is synonymous with being an idiot. John Lennox warns Christians about rejecting modern science. Lennox wrote, "We would be very unwise to ignore science through obscurantism or fear, and present to the world an image of a Christianity that is anti-intellectual."[12]

With the continued onslaught of scientism and the promotion of their "universe" for nearly five hundred years, it makes it difficult to speak against modern science. It is easier to go along with the crowd and not talk about the problems with the foundation of the "universe." Instead of asking for evidence, we accept their theories and continue our busy lives. Not paying attention to the origins of modern science has led to our inability to speak with intelligence about the theories of modern science.

When it comes to how we interpret the Bible, many Christian scholars accept modern science and then interpret God's word to work within the framework (context) of the "universe" given to them. They provide their best interpretations, but their understanding is shaped and filtered by the "universe" that modern science has created. They assume modern science's "universe" is correct and proven. Scholars provide answers influenced by a religious belief in modern science, which changes how they understand the Bible.

There is a precise moment when the creation story loses its historical and literal interpretation. Please understand me; God's word has always been under assault since the garden of Eden (Genesis 3:1). The moment in modern history started when the earth began to move less than five hundred years ago. Rienk Vermij, Department of the History of Science, University of Oklahoma, describes that precise moment:

> The world as people had known it for centuries was quickly coming to an end, be it not factually but conceptually. New discoveries and new questions forced people to reconsider their ideas on the universe and in the end led to a completely new view of the world – arguably one of the most important conceptual shifts in human history.[13]

Have we been affected by scientism (religious worship of modern science)? People like to think we, as Christians, are free from any outside influences that could taint the way we read the Bible. After all, we have the Holy Spirit. If that were the case, then we would believe there was water above the sun and moon (Genesis 1:17; Psalm 148:4). We would believe the earth was motionless and placed on a foundation (1 Chronicles 16:30; Hebrews 1:10). We would believe that one day the stars will fall upon the earth (Matthew 24:29; Revelation 6:13).

Jesus Christ believed the stars, the same lights we see in the night sky, would one day fall to the earth. When talking about the end times, Jesus said, "The sun will be darkened, and the moon will not give its light; the stars will fall from the sky" (Matthew 24:29). Jesus did not say the stars will disappear from space. Jesus said the stars would fall from the sky and strike the earth. The word "sky | οὐρανός | ouranos" is defined as the "space above the earth, including the vault arching high over the earth from one horizon to another, as well as the sun, moon, and stars—'sky.'"[14] Remember, according to modern science, one tiny star would destroy the earth, and the closest star would have to travel 24,931,200,000,000 miles just to reach the earth. When God commands the stars to fall, we would have to wait over four years. Modern science teaches:

> The nearest stars to Earth are three stars that lie about 4.37 light-years away in the Alpha Centauri triple-star system. The closest of these stars, Proxima Centauri, is just about 4.24 light-years away (for reference, one light-year is approximately equivalent to 5.88 trillion miles (9.46 trillion kilometers)).[15]

Did Jesus mean that stars (plural) would fall from the sky to the earth? When Proxima Centauri reaches earth, there is no need for other stars to fall since it would destroy the earth. According to modern science, when we compare the size of the earth with a small star, the earth would be destroyed entirely (Fig. 4). If we believe what modern science tells us about stars, it is difficult to take Jesus at His word.

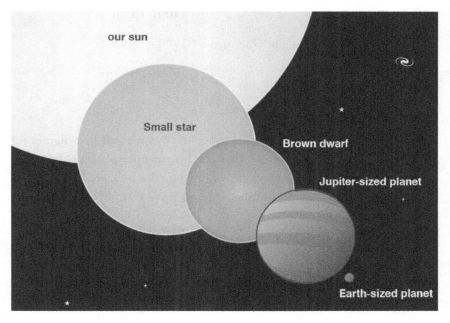

Fig. 4. Size of earth compared to planets and stars.

I believe, as Munyon stated that the Bible should align with the natural world, and we should have something intelligent to say when dealing with modern science. When I mention modern science, I am not talking about true science. True science, things that are observable, measurable, and repeatable, is practiced all the time. I have no problem with true science. This book deals with modern science or scientism (religious belief in science). When I mention modern science, I refer to the theories or so-called "scientific discoveries" from the Scientific Revolution (1543–1687). The following list is a general overview of the history of the world (Table 1).[16] The Scientific Revolution occurred towards the end of the Renaissance.

Name	Date Range
Prescientific Age	?–600 BC
Classical Era	600 BC–500
Middle Ages	500–1300s
Renaissance	1400s–1600s
Age of Reason/Enlightenment	1700s–1800s
Modern Era	1900s–present

Table 1. History of the World.

When an era ends, and a new age begins, it is marked by a significant cultural shift. When the culture changes, how people perceive the world around them changes (e.g., religion, politics, moral values, etc.). The *Understanding Media and Culture* published by the University of Minnesota, states:

> A cultural period is a time marked by a particular way of understanding the world … In the Middle Ages, truth was dictated by authorities like the king and the church. During the Renaissance, people turned to the scientific method as a way to reach truth through reason. … The Modern Age, or modernity, is the postmedieval era, a wide span of time marked in part by technological innovations, urbanization, scientific discoveries, and globalization. … ideals of reason, rationalism, and faith in scientific inquiry slowly began to replace the previously dominant authorities of king and church.[17]

A new culture was formed because of a new faith in scientific theories. That moment was called the Scientific Revolution (1543–1687). The new revolution brought a cultural shift, undermining the authority and trust in the Bible, being replaced by a new religion called science. The revolution started when Nicolaus Copernicus released his thesis on planetary motion, *De revolutionibus orbium coelestium (On the Revolutions of the Heavenly Spheres)* (1543). Less than five hundred years ago, mankind's word became the standard of truth and gained great power and authority because of the cultural shift of humanism during the Renaissance (1400s–1600s).

The results of modern science during the Scientific Revolution can still be seen today. Yuval Noah Harari is considered "one of the world's most influential public intellectuals today."[18] Harari is not a Christian. Harari wrote, "Just 6 million years ago, a single female ape had two daughters. One became the ancestor of all chimpanzees, the other is our own grandmother."[19] Harari is the product of the Scientific Revolution. Harari knows the Scientific Revolution was necessary to turn the lowly human into a powerful divine being. The human being, according to Harari, is not only a god-like figure, but thanks to the Scientific Revolution, humanity now can be just like God. Harari wrote:

> The Scientific Revolution: Humankind admits its ignorance and begins to acquire unprecedented power ... Seventy thousand years ago, *Homo sapiens* was still an insignificant animal minding its own business in a corner of Africa. In the following millennia it transformed itself into the master of the entire planet and the terror of the ecosystem. Today it stands on the verge of becoming a god, poised to acquire not only eternal youth, but also the divine abilities of creation and destruction.[20]

Harari states the effects of the Scientific Revolution. Towards the end of the Renaissance, people believed they could be gods. As Harari articulated, people transformed themselves into the new masters of the world. Harari does not explain how insignificant animals could learn how to become gods with the divine ability to create. To understand the transformation of animals into gods, we must understand the cultural shift that occurred during the Renaissance, which concluded with the Scientific Revolution. Thanks to an ancient god from Egypt, the people during the Renaissance discovered the secrets of becoming divine beings, possessing all knowledge and power.

It may seem that Harari is not a good example of explaining the effects of the Scientific Revolution and the Bible. Harari has nothing in common with Christians. Harari does not believe in the Bible. Harari considers Scripture as imaginary stories written by highly developed animals who use religion for their own advantage. Harari wrote:

> To the best of our scientific knowledge, all these sacred texts were written by imaginative *Homo sapiens*. They are just stories invented by our ancestors in order to legitimise social norms and political structures.[21]

What does an atheist like Harari have in common with a Christian? A lot more than we would imagine. Both Harari and Christians believe in the "universe." Both believe in a moving earth. Both believe what modern science claims over what God's word teaches. The Bible teaches that God "laid the earth's foundation" (Job 38:4). The Bible teaches the earth "cannot be moved" (1 Chronicles 16:30). The common thread that unites Christians with atheists like Harari is the "solar system."

The effect of modern science still plays a role in changing our culture today. Because of modern science, men can be women, babies in the womb are just soulless balls of tissue, and normal anxiety is now a medical disease, all reinforced by "scientific" data. Christians may disagree with modern science and its opinions on gender, abortion, or psychology. Still, the impact of modern science has affected the church since the Scientific Revolution. Modern science has had the most significant influence on our interpretation of the Bible. The creation story found in Genesis 1, once viewed as a literal and truthful record of how God made the heavens and the earth, has now turned into an inaccurate mythological story. The earth's foundation, once believed by people in the Bible, has now disappeared.

Exodus 20:1, 11
And God spoke all these words: [11] For in six days the LORD made the heavens and the earth, the sea, and all that is in them, but he rested on the seventh day.

Job 38:1, 4
Then the LORD spoke to Job out of the storm. He said: [4] "Where were you when I laid the earth's foundation? Tell me, if you understand."

The creation story or the earth's foundation are subjects we do not discuss. It goes against everything we believe. We believe the earth spins every 24 hours and orbits the sun yearly. We believe the earth is in motion and is held by the sun's gravity as we make our way through the vacuum of outer space. We believe the pictures and videos we have seen. We believe in the education we have been taught. The truth is we believe the results of the Scientific Revolution. We believe in a "solar system" created by a false ancient god. Because we have put our faith in modern science, we no longer believe the literal statements found in the Bible. We no longer believe the earth was founded on water.

Psalm 24:1–2

The earth is the LORD's, and everything in it, the world, and all who live in it; ² for he founded it on the seas and established it on the waters.

How can we balance modern science and the Bible? That is where Christian scholarship comes in and helps us overcome the conflict. For example, Leslie C. Allen tells us that people in antiquity believed the earth was motionless and established on the waters (Psalm 24:1–2), but today, we believe that the earth moves and travels around the sun. Allen wrote:

> The modern scientific view of the world is different from that of the ancient Near East, which imagined what might look to us like an oil-rig structure miraculously fixed in the subterranean ocean (cf. Ps 24:2). Yet we moderns, to whom this psalm is ultimately given, are also meant to share in the psalmist's awe and trust, in response to the God who from our viewpoint has fixed the planet earth in its orbit and made it capable of supporting life.[22]

Allen provides a path for the reader to believe in modern science and the Bible. If Allen's interpretation is correct, it will result in three tragic points. (1) God's word made a scientifically false claim. King David, who wrote Psalm 24, said God founded the earth on the seas. The word "founded | יָסַד | yāsad" means "lay a foundation, set a base, i.e., establish a base for a construction."[23] According to modern science, the earth is not on a foundation but moving in the vacuum of space. (2) The Holy Spirit inspired David to write a false claim about the natural world. David wrote that the earth was established on the seas. The word "established | כּוּן | kûn" means "make a foundation, make a support (Ps 24:2)."[24] According to modern science, the earth is resting upon a solid metal ball (inner core), not water. (3) God is a liar. God said He laid the earth's foundation (Job 38:4), but according to modern science, He did not. God said He formed the earth out of water (Genesis 1:9), but according to modern science, He did not. According to modern science, God is a liar.

Allen claims we share the same awe and trust as David, who lived thousands of years ago. Do we? David believed the earth was laid upon a foundation. Do we share the same trust in God's word as David? David thought the world was formed out of water.

Why would the people in ancient times believe the earth was established on the water like an oil rig? It was because of their faith in the creation story. David believed what was written in Genesis 1. The creation story tells us that water was created in the beginning (Genesis 1:2). Then God would separate the water and place water above and below the solid dome barrier called the firmament (Genesis 1:7). On Day 3, God will reveal the land by withdrawing the water (Genesis 1:9). David believed Genesis 1 was correct.

David did not develop his own creation story while writing Psalm 24. He was writing what the Spirit of truth told him to write. David said, "The Spirit of the LORD spoke through me; his word was on my tongue" (2 Samuel 23:2). David believed Genesis 1 was correct and that the earth was formed out of water. Peter, in the New Testament, also believed the earth was founded on water.

2 Peter 3:5
But they deliberately forget that long ago by God's word the heavens came into being and the earth was formed out of water and by water.

David believed what Genesis 1 taught him. David also thought that the "world is firmly established; it cannot be moved" (1 Chronicles 16:30), but Allen tells us to believe, from our modern perspective, that God "has fixed the planet earth in its orbit."[25] What physically changed from David's "solar system" and the modern "solar system"? Nothing. Today, we have the same sun, moon, and earth that God created. The only thing that has changed is the Scientific Revolution, which changed our understanding of the Bible.

I once had a friend who said, "Why can't I read Scripture the way I believe it, and you read it the way you believe it?" Are there two "truths" to the origin of the "universe"? Are there two "truths" to the layout and nature of the sun, moon, and stars? Are there two "truths" regarding the foundations of the earth? No. There is only one truth. There is only one reality. There is only one record of how God made the heavens and the earth.

There are many ways people interpret Genesis 1. There are different theories about what God did and how He did it. Knowing what happened when God spoke the world into existence seems impossible. The good news is it is possible to know. We can understand what happened in the beginning. God wants us to know what happened. The creation story is very important to God. It encapsulates the complete story of the Bible. It provides the foundation for how things began and how it will end. The Bible begins with creation and a garden (Genesis 1, 2), and the Bible ends with a new creation and a new garden (Revelation 21, 22).

People will argue that the creation story is not a salvation issue, meaning that no matter what we believe about Genesis 1, it does not make a difference to the work of Christ. I agree that no one will go to hell because they think the earth moves. So why is the creation story important? The creation story is essential for two reasons. First, believing in the creation story is about faith. It is about our trust in the words that God spoke. Words revealed by God, who "is not human, that he should lie" (Numbers 23:19). The second reason the creation story is important is that the creation story is about knowing the truth. We have a Heavenly Father who speaks the truth. We have an enemy who wants to deceive us. If we are not aware of the schemes of our enemy, we can fall into deception. We can believe things that are not true. Jesus warned us about the last days. Jesus said, "Watch out that no one deceives you" (Matthew 24:4). We will fall for deception if we do not know the truth. If we want to have faith in God's word and see the truth in the Bible, all it requires is to trust and believe what "God said" (Genesis 1:3, 6, 9, 11, 14, 20, 24, 26, 29).

Extreme Nature

I made a promise to God a long time ago. I am not talking about the multiple times at the altar asking Jesus into my heart while growing up. Today, I know I am a child of God, and my loyalty, faith, and desire to seek Him is a journey that will not end until we meet face to face. Things were not always perfect after I promised to give my life to Jesus. I tend to mess up (a polite way to say I sin). The Bible said, "If we claim we have not sinned, we make him out to be a liar and his word is not in us" (1 John 1:10). What was the promise I made to God? The promise was this: "If I find out that You have lied in the Bible, I'm done."

I am serious. I made a vow that if I found out that God lied in the Bible, I would walk away from the faith and never pray or read the Bible again. I meant every word of my statement to Him. That was not a threat or a challenge to God. My declaration was based on sound reasoning. It was not an emotional pledge but a logical conclusion that I arrived at from reading the Bible. Let me explain.

Who is God? The Bible has many titles for God. He is the Most High, Almighty, King of kings, Shepherd, Ancient of Days, and thanks to Jesus' work on the cross, He is our Heavenly Father. The Bible also presents God as someone who is not like us.

Numbers 23:19
God is not human, that he should lie, not a human being, that he should change his mind. Does he speak and then not act? Does he promise and not fulfill?

The Bible tells us that God is not a liar. That means that God cannot, will not, lie. The Bible reveals that His character and nature are based on truth. Jesus promised to send the Spirit of truth (John 16:13). The word "truth | ἀλήθεια | alētheia" found in John 16:13 means "truth, true, sincerity, integrity. Indicates the quality or state of being real or genuine—often in the sense of visible and verifiable reality, demonstrated by facts, actual events, or proven character."[1] The Bible indicates God's proven character only speaks the truth.

The Bible presents us with a "God, who does not lie" (Titus 1:2). When the Bible, God's word, makes such a claim, it is either true or false. The

Bible tells us, "All scripture is given by inspiration of God" (2 Timothy 3:16; KJV). If the Bible is inspired by a God who does not lie, then the Bible as a whole must be true. Either the "word of the LORD is right and true" (Psalm 33:4) or not. Either God inspired the Bible to be accurate, or He did not. Either God speaks the truth, or God speaks lies. There is no in-between or grey area. It is a black-or-white issue.

When it comes to color, black and white are represented by values. Most of us are familiar with RGB colors. RGB (Red, Green, Blue) is used for displays on computer monitors, TVs, handheld devices, cell phones, etc. CMYK (Cyan, Magenta, Yellow; [K] Black) is used in the print industry to make flyers, magazines, cards, brochures, etc. No matter what color system we use, every color has a value. The colors may look the same to the human eye, but colors are not matched by appearance but by a number value. For RGB, if we want black, its value is RGB 0,0,0. If we want white, its value is RGB 255,255,255. The moment we add or subtract to values of black or white, it is no longer true black or true white. The color may appear black if we add just one bit of blue (RGB 0,0,1), but it is not truly black. It is a color that looks black, but it has been tainted with blue.

The moment we add a lie to the truth, it is no longer completely true. The scale of that lie, big or small, does not matter. God's standard is simple. He speaks truth that is not tainted with anything false. Jesus knew God's word to be true and made a statement about it. Jesus said, "Your word is truth" (John 17:17).

We enjoy engaging in the nuances of life. We like to live in a world filled with grey. Unfortunately, the Bible does not see grey. Having grey areas may help us deal with difficult decisions or allow us to believe or do things not in line with Scripture, but the Bible is very extreme regarding our options. Things are good or bad, right or wrong, true or false, or hot or cold. Grey is tepid and lukewarm. Jesus told the church who lived in the grey areas, "So, because you are lukewarm—neither hot nor cold—I am about to spit you out of my mouth" (Revelation 3:16). Jesus did not provide a scale where "less than hot" was acceptable.

The color grey is in the middle of the RGB scale (RGB 128,128,128); it is neither black nor white. Each color has 256 possible choices.[2] We can subtract color and make a dark shade of grey, like Black Leather Jacket (RGB 37,53,41). We can add color and create a lighter shade of grey, like Platinum (RGB 229,228,226). Once the limits of the color values are reached (0 or 255), the only option is either black or white.

The moment when truth becomes tainted with a lie, it is less than true. In the extreme nature of the Bible, a statement that is less than true is called a lie. When we know that truth is tainted with a lie, we call it a half-truth or a white lie. Half-truths or statements that contain 99.9% truth are less than true. The Bible claims that God does not mix lies, untruths, or misrepresentations into His words. When God speaks, He makes statements free from falsehoods and deception. God is not like us. "Let God be true, but every man a liar" (Romans 3:4; KJV).

People would argue that we cannot hold the Bible to this standard (black or white) because the Bible makes claims that are not true. Jesus is not a physical gate or door. Jesus said, "I am a door" (John 10:9; KJV). We do not literally eat Jesus' flesh and drink His actual blood. Jesus said, "Whoever eats my flesh and drinks my blood has eternal life, and I will raise them up at the last day" (John 6:54). This is called a figure of speech. Jesus is speaking in such a way to tell us the truth about Himself. Jesus even said at the time, "I have been speaking figuratively" (John 16:25). The word "figuratively | παροιμία | paroimia" means "a relatively short narrative with symbolic meaning—'parable, figure, allegory, figure of speech.'"[3] The Bible uses poetic and symbolic speech. Jesus spoke the truth but spoke figuratively. We will deal with the historical, cultural, and literary context argument made by scholars, but for now, the point I want to make is the extreme nature of the Bible. Either God's word is true, or it is not.

I was very serious when I said to the Lord: "If I find out that You have lied in the Bible, I'm done." My statement was based on logical thinking. Ted Sundstrom defines what math statements are. Sundstrom wrote:

> A declarative sentence that is either true or false but not both. A statement is sometimes called a proposition. The key is that there must be no ambiguity. To be a statement, a sentence must be true or false, and it cannot be both.[4]

The Bible makes clear and direct statements that are either true or false. No scale or degree is given to the claims made in the Bible. Allowing God to make false claims or misleading statements is not an option. The Bible is simply God's written word inspired by a "God, who does not lie" (Titus 1:2). If God's words are false, then God is a liar and not the God as presented in the Bible. We only have two options regarding the statements made in the Bible. They are: (1) all Scripture is God-breathed and true, or (2) God-inspired Scripture contains lies.

God's word does not make conditional statements (e.g., If *P* then *Q*). God's word does not make claims only when specific criteria are met. It is either an inspired book of truth or a book that is not true. The logical conclusion, based on what the Bible states, is why I decided to put all my hope in God's word that is "right and true" (Psalm 33:4). I decided to put all my trust in someone whose name is "Faithful and True" (Revelation 19:11). I decided to put all my belief in a God who claims that He "is not a man, that He would lie" (Numbers 23:19, NASB).

That may sound extreme, but the Bible made it extreme. The Bible made it extreme when Jesus declared, "Your word is truth" (John 17:17). Leon Morris commented on John 17:17. Morris wrote:

> The divine revelation is eminently trustworthy. It is not only true, but truth. Jesus earlier connected his own "word" with truth, that truth which makes people free (8:31–32). The Father's word, all that he has revealed, is of the same kind. It is truth and may therefore be unhesitatingly accepted and acted on.[5]

The Father's word can be trusted to be true, including specific claims about the natural world. If the Bible made a statement about the heavens and earth, which can be proven wrong by true science, then the Bible made a false claim. That would mean God allowed a false statement to be recorded in the Bible. If God lied or permitted others to lie for Him, then He is no different than the other father who "is a liar and the father of lies" (John 8:44). The Bible is very extreme in its position on God and His truthful nature. There is only one statement that could be made about God's word. The statement is simple: God does not lie.

Chapter 4

Binary Options

The Bible is extreme in its statements, allowing only two options. When it comes to our spiritual father, we only have two decisions, God or the devil (John 1:13; 8:44). When it comes to salvation, we only have two positions, believers or unbelievers (John 1:12; 2 Corinthians 4:4). When it comes to our leader, one leads us to the truth or the other steers us away from the truth (Psalm 23:1–2; John 8:44). When it comes to living, we are either alive or dead (Ecclesiastes 3:2). When it comes to our eternal destination, it is either heaven or hell (John 17:24; Revelation 20:15). When it comes to our status with God, we are either a friend or an enemy (John 15:15; James 4:4). When it comes to allegiance, we are either with Jesus or against Him.

Matthew 12:30
[Jesus said,] "Whoever is not with me is against me, and whoever does not gather with me scatters."

Why is the Bible so extreme? When it comes to truth, there is no in-between; it is either one or the other. Today's culture does not like absolutes. In modern times, "truth" changes depending on the person's ethnicity, age, location, or social conditions. Today's thinking believes in relativism. The *Stanford Encyclopedia of Philosophy* defines relativism by comparing it to absolute truth. Maria Baghramian and J. Carter wrote:

> Traditionally, relativism is contrasted with: Absolutism, the view that at least some truths or values in the relevant domain apply to all times, places or social and cultural frameworks. They are universal and not bound by histori-cal or social conditions. Absolutism is often used as the key contrast idea to relativism.[1]

The Bible does not view things from a relative (not absolute) perspec-tive. It makes claims that are absolute truths, and those claims do not change because of a particular culture, historical moment, or a scientific discovery. For example, the Bible claims that only two genders exist (Genesis 1:27). We may think everyone knows this. Still, to people outside the influence of the

Bible, gender is an internal feeling expressed by the clothing they wear or the way they talk, all based on "scientific" data.

Gender is no longer an absolute truth but relative to a person's subjective thoughts. In 1841, Noah Webster defined gender as " sex, male or female."[2] Today, gender is expressed by internal feelings or external clothing. According to the world-renowned Mayo Clinic Hospital, gender has nothing to do with external genitals but is determined by internal emotions. Mayo Clinic states:

> Gender identity is the internal sense of being male, female, neither, or some combination of both. Gender expression typically involves how gender identity is shown to the outside world by how a person looks or acts. Gender expression may include clothing, mannerisms, communication style, and interests, among other things.[3]

According to the American Psychological Association (APA), gender is left up to society and groupthink. The APA teaches that a person will be told what gender they are, unlike absolute truth, which identifies gender with genitals. The APA states:

> Gender refers to the socially constructed roles, behaviors, activities, and attributes that a given society considers appropriate for boys and men or girls and women.[4]

Gender no longer needs to be an absolute truth since it is determined by the individual's emotions, fashion, or what society decides. Gender identity, approved by medical and psychological experts, uses "scientific" data to validate their claims. No matter how our current scientists, doctors, or psychologists define gender identity, they cannot change the fact that human beings only produce two kinds of humans: male or female. There is no in-between.

God's word makes claims about the heavens and the earth that are either true or not. God's word claims the earth is motionless and set upon a foundation. Either those claims are right, or they are not. Here is where scholars will shout, "You have to understand the historical, cultural, and literary context!" According to scholars, if we do not know the Bible's history, language, culture, or genre, we can misinterpret or misunderstand what the Bible is trying to say. Scholars will tell us that the motionless earth and foundations passages are poetic, symbolic, or phenomenological verses. Scholars will inform us of what the Bible meant to say: the earth moves and is not laid upon a foundation.

I understand scholar's concern about people misreading the Bible. I also understand that we are not required to know the history, language, culture, or even the passage's genre to know the true meaning of Scripture. I did not come up with this rule. The Holy Spirit set the rules when He inspired the apostle John to write a letter to the church.

> **1 John 2:20, 27**
> But you have an anointing from the Holy One, and all of you know the truth. [27] As for you, the anointing you received from him remains in you, and you do not need anyone to teach you. But as his anointing teaches you about all things and as that anointing is real, not counterfeit—just as it has taught you, remain in him.

What is the anointing that we have received from God? It is the Holy Spirit. Colin G. Kruse writes, "the anointing they had received is the Holy Spirit."[5] I. Howard Marshall comments:

> In Old Testament usage anointing was symbolical of the reception of the Spirit (1 Sam. 16:13; Isa. 61:1), and when Jesus is said to have been anointed, it is his reception of the Spirit at his baptism which is meant (Acts 10:38; cf. Lk. 4:18). It is, therefore, not surprising that the majority of commentators think that the anointing here is the Spirit who comes to teach believers and to guide them into all truth.[6]

The Bible tells us that the Holy Spirit will teach us and guide our understanding to "know the truth" (1 John 2:20). Knowing the truth is possible because the Bible said it was possible. It is also possible to believe and know the truth about the creation story in Genesis 1.

I am serious in my position. If the Bible claims something untrue, the only alternative is to say the Bible stated a lie by making a false statement. If the Bible contains lies, then my Heavenly Father, a "God, who does not lie" (Titus 1:2), is not the God of the Bible. If the Bible contains lies, then God hates me. The Bible says, "A lying tongue hates those it hurts" (Proverbs 26:28).

January 2020, the Lord asked me, "What if Genesis 1 was correct?" I did not try to prove science wrong. I believed in modern science. Since 2020, I have come to believe the Bible is more literal than we think. Why would I believe in the firmament? Why would I believe the earth is not turning on its axis? Why would I believe there is water above the stars? I have three reasons why I believe 100% in the claims the Bible makes. (1) God's word tells me to believe it. (2) What the Bible claims about the natural world has never been proven false. (3) Every picture, video, and textbook modern science presents is based on a lie.

Chapter 5

Trust, But Don't Verify

What if someone asked us, "Is Genesis 1 a true and literal story of how God created the heavens and the earth?" What would our answer be? Would we be able to defend our position on the creation story? Literal? Symbolic? Myth? Poetry? No matter what interpretation we believe in, can we defend, Biblically or scientifically, the reasoning for why we believe what we believe? Imagine if we dared to take Genesis 1 as a factual and accurate record of how God created the heavens and the earth. How do we deal with what Genesis 1 claims: mornings without a sun (Genesis 1:5, 8, 13), water above a solid dome that holds the sun, moon, and stars (Genesis 1:7, 17), land that produced the animals (Genesis 1:24), or everything created in 144 hours (Genesis 1:31)? The believers in modern science, both Christian and non-Christian, would laugh at our ignorance or lack of intelligence. For the record, we do not live to please others or live for the "approval of human beings" (Galatians 1:10).

The theories of modern science have changed our understanding of God's infallible, unerring, and Spirit-inspired words written in the Bible. We read the Bible differently because of our modern knowledge. We may not have a good answer for the literal reading of Genesis 1 or the layout of the heavenly and earthly realms because, like most people, we accept what we have been told. Our understanding of the heavens and the earth is the opposite of what the Bible teaches. We have learned to reinterpret the Bible because of the influence of modern science. Gordon J. Wenham explains why we do not believe what we read in the Bible. Wenham explains that we have a "world-view molded by modern science."[1] How we perceive the natural world has been shaped, molded, and predetermined for us. Before we could add one plus one, we were shown the globe and told the earth moves around the sun. No questions asked.

Today, we do not have an answer for the Bible's claims about the natural world and modern science's "universe." We do not have an intelligent response to the firmament or the sun, moon, and stars being placed below water. We have an answer regarding subjects like salvation, marriage, or faith. Concerning the layout and function of the heavens and the earth, we have yet to learn how to respond. If we responded by repeating what Genesis 1 said, we would be mocked and ridiculed for believing in a pre-scientific understanding written in an ancient dead language. That ridicule would come from both inside and outside the church. If we responded by balancing Genesis 1 and modern science, we would create inconsistencies in the Bible. We have no idea how to respond even though we are told all the answers in the Bible.

The Bible and modern science cannot make opposite claims where both are true. Take for example, rainbows. The Bible observes rainbows. The Bible reads, "Like the appearance of a rainbow in the clouds on a rainy day" (Ezekiel 1:28). Is that claim true or false? True science confirms that rainbows appear in the clouds on a rainy day. The *National Oceanic and Atmospheric Administration* (NOAA) wrote:

> A rainbow is caused by sunlight and atmospheric conditions. Light enters a water droplet, slowing down and bending as it goes from air to denser water. The light reflects off the inside of the droplet, separating into its component wavelengths--or colors. When light exits the droplet, it makes a rainbow.[2]

The Bible's claim about rainbows, which can be verified, proved true. The Bible would have stated something untrue if rainbows had nothing to do with clouds or rain (atmospheric conditions). True science and the Bible agree. True science and the Bible can be harmonized because both observations are true.

The Bible makes multiple claims about our natural world, contradicting our modern understanding. The Bible discusses astronomy, geology, phytology, zoology, and biology. The Bible makes scientific claims about these subjects in the first chapter of Genesis. The origin of the "universe" (astronomy; Genesis 1:1). The origin of the earth (geology; Genesis 1:1). The origin of vegetation (phytology; Genesis 1:11). The origin of animals (zoology; Genesis 1:24). The origin of life (biology; Genesis 1:27). Does God's word align with modern science when it comes to the natural world? The answer is no. Remember, Genesis 1 claims three days of morning and evening without a sun (Genesis 1:5, 8, 13). Genesis 1 claims the moon is a light (not a rock), and all three lights (sun, moon, and stars) are in a solid dome barrier with water above it (Genesis 1:7, 17). That is what the plain and natural reading of Genesis 1 tells us.

Munyon said, "One ought to have something intelligent to say about science and the Bible if asked."[3] Unfortunately for us, we are not scientists.

We do not have the intelligence to answer when they speak with big words and even bigger numbers. We cannot explain quantum superposition or understand Einstein's general theory of relativity. Do not worry. We do not need specialized education or to be fluent in a complicated vocabulary to have an intelligent answer for the Bible and modern science. We just have to know the history of modern science.

Familiarizing yourself with modern science's theories (e.g., heliocentric, planetary motion, gravity, etc.) is optional but beneficial. Modern science's theories are the foundation upon which the "universe" was built. Ignoring modern science's theories is only optional if its theories do not influence how we read the Bible. If we believed the earth was motionless (1 Chronicles 16:30; Psalm 104:5), our belief in modern science's "solar system" would never have occurred. If modern science has influenced our interpretation of Scripture, then getting familiar with their theories would be of value.

How do we believe in a literal creation story and the earth's foundation? There is an easy answer. There is a challenging answer as well. Here is the easy part. We must believe what "God said" (Genesis 1:3, 6, 9, 11, 14, 20, 24, 26, 29). This answer sounds like the old song, *God Said It, I Believe It, That Settles It*, by the Heritage Singers:

> God said it, and I believe it, and that settles it for me.
> Though some may doubt that His word is true,
> I've chosen to believe it, now how about you?[4]

It is that simple: "God said it and I believe it." Now comes the more challenging part: we must trust what "God said" (Genesis 1:3, 6, 9, 11, 14, 20, 24, 26, 29). Claiming we believe the Bible is one thing, but trusting God's words is another issue. Can we trust the Bible's creation story over what we have been shown in pictures or videos and what we have been educated to believe? Can we trust what God said about the earth's foundation even though we cannot verify what God said? Believing in the literal creation story and the earth's foundation requires us to "Trust in the LORD with all your heart and lean not on your own understanding" (Proverbs 3:15). It is challenging when we want to hold on to modern science's "solar system" and the Bible's claims about a motionless earth. It requires us to put aside our modern understanding and trust in the simple words found in the Bible. It requires us to believe that what God said about the heavens and the earth is factual and accurate. Either what God said was true, or it is not true.

I believe in the creation story as presented in Scripture. I believe the earth is resting on a foundation that God Himself said He laid. I wish I could say that my belief in God's word came about because I trusted what I read in Genesis 1. My belief in Genesis 1 came about because the "universe" I believed in crumbled beneath my feet. What started my questioning of the "universe"? It was gravity. The one thing that was supposed to hold the "universe" together was the one theory no one could explain. I found professionals who could not explain something that everyone thinks they know. Let me walk us through how a scientist explains gravity to five individuals, ranging from a child to a physics expert.

Dr. Janna Levin, PhD in theoretical physics and astrophysicist, is a professor of Physics and Astronomy at Barnard College of Columbia University, NY. Levin was asked to explain gravity on five different levels of complexity. The problem with gravity is that it is very complicated. Why is gravity so complicated? It is because gravity is not real, and scientists are trying to invent solutions to convince people that it is. Levin will start by confirming to a child that gravity is a force but then changes to the bending of spacetime, and then, according to the expert, we are told there is no gravity. However, with another unproven theory, modern science will eventually prove gravity. As for now, according to the expert, modern science has yet to find answers as to what gravity is. Levin begins her opening dialogue:

> "Gravity seems so familiar and so every day, and yet it's this incredibly esoteric abstract subject that has shaped the way we view the universe on the larger scales, has given us the strangest phenomena in the universe like black holes, that has changed the way we look at the entirety of physics. It's really been a revolution because of gravity."[5]

Levin is correct in saying that gravity is an esoteric (knowledge that is understood only by the few) and an abstract (thoughts about complex ideas without a connection to reality) subject. Levin explains to a child that gravity is a force theorized by Isaac Newton. According to Newton, the mass of an object determines its amount of gravity. Next, Levin explains to a teenager that gravity is like the string on a yo-yo. The string keeps pulling the yo-yo towards the hand, which is Newton's centripetal force (Fig. 5). Newton's gravity is a force.

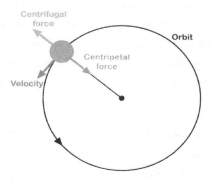

Fig. 5. Force diagram of rotational motion.

Levin then introduces a high school teenager to general relativity, Albert Einstein's theory of gravity. After Levin explains general relativity, the teenager laughs and says, "I don't even know what to say to that."[6] Levin now explains gravity to a college student. Levin said:

> "Even though the earth is three stories below us, it's not as though it's pulling at us from a distance. We're actually interacting with the field at this point and there's a real interaction right here at this point. And that's nice, because people were worried that if things acted at a distance, that the way that old-fashioned inverse-square force law de-scribes it, that it was a spooky as mind-bending a spoon, that it was like telekinesis. If you don't touch something, how do you affect it? And so the first step was to start to think of gravity as a field that permeates all of a space."[7]

Levin said Newton's old-fashioned inverse-square force law, gravity, was spooky. Remember the yo-yo string? Newton's gravity relied upon a string that he never could define. He called it a force. When people started to look into Newton's gravity, they discovered it was flawed. Then comes Einstein, who will remove the string (force) and create a new concept, spacetime (field). The force is unnecessary, thanks to Einstein, and objects now follow the bending of spacetime. I will cover more about gravity and provide the source material for my statements, including personal letters from Newton and Einstein.

Next, Levin will speak to a graduate student pursuing a PhD in theo-retical high-energy physics. The graduate student is studying neutron stars, the remains of a supernova (collapsed star). The neutron star is so dense it would have the sun's mass that could fit into an average city in the United States. One teaspoon of a neutron star could weigh about a billion tons on earth. Then Levin starts to discuss black holes. Modern science tells us that black holes are created when a neutron star cannot hold itself together and collapses on itself. The student then asks Levin what is inside a black hole. Leven responded:

> "There isn't a sensible way to talk about it yet, and that probably means that's where Einstein's theory of gravity as a curved spacetime is beginning to break down and we need to take the extra step of going to some kind of quantum theory of gravity. And we don't have that yet."[8]

When Newton's gravity failed, Einstein came along to help us believe in gravity. When Einstein's gravity failed, we turned to quantum gravity. According to the leading particle physics lab in the United States, Fermi National Accelerator Laboratory (Fermilab), its scientists state, "There is no confirmation of quantum gravity."[9] Modern science must save gravity even if it has to rely on more unproven theories (quantum gravity).

Finally, Levin talks to an expert about gravity. The expert is the chair of the Department of Physics at New York University, NY. Levin mentions that the current views of gravity may be wrong, gravity may not exist, or gravity is just an illusion. The expert said:

> "We've got two sides, which are actually secretly the same. On one side there's definitely no gravity. On the other side, well, it's a quantum theory of gravity, whatever that means … there's so many open questions. The fact that there are all these fundamental issues that we really don't understand … But ultimately what is gonna emerge from that, what structure is lying under it, we just don't know. … the fact that there are so many fundamental questions that we just don't know the answer to, that is an opportunity that's exciting, it's great."[10]

The expert told us the secret. According to the expert, (1) there is definitely no gravity, and (2) there is quantum gravity. The secret is that both points are the same, meaning there is no experimental evidence to prove gravity, Newton's/Einstein's, or quantum gravity. Even after the Laser Interferometer Gravitational Observatory (LIGO) announced that it had proved

Einstein's gravity (spacetime) on February 11, 2016, the expert in 2019 said the secret was, "There's definitely no gravity."[11]

Gravity is confusing because nearly 350 years after Newton reported the discovery of gravity, scientists still have not answered what gravity is. Yes, we can drop an apple and watch it fall, but that does not mean the earth is orbiting the sun because of a "spooky" force that Newton never defined. Yes, we can imagine the sun bending spacetime, but it does not mean the earth moves in the curvature of space because Einstein had "thought" experiments instead of actual experiments. Everything in modern science depends on gravity being real. We will come back to gravity and learn from the experts that nobody knows what gravity is.

The only thing Newton got right was his words to Richard Bentley. When Newton released his theory, Bentley questioned gravity. As *Big Think* states, Newton responded in a letter to Bentley and told him, "Any competent thinker shouldn't believe his theory [of gravity]."[12]

I do not believe scientists purposely lie to us when talking about gravity. They think they know what gravity is and it has unquestionably been proven. Even now, people may not believe what I am saying. Scientists may understand the problems with gravity, but they do not doubt it for a second.

According to modern science, gravity is a fundamental force of nature. Gravity is central to modern science and is one of the four fundamental forces that created the "solar system." NASA wrote:

> Why does Earth stay in orbit around the Sun? How does light travel? What holds atoms and nuclei together?
>
> For centuries, scientists have sought to describe the forces that dictate interactions on the largest and smallest scales, from planets to particles. They understand that there are four fundamental forces — gravity, electromagnetism, and the strong and weak nuclear forces — that are responsible for shaping the universe we inhabit.[13]

Just recently, Levin was interviewed by Neil deGrasse Tyson on *StarTalk*. Tyson was wondering if Levin thought that gravity did not exist. Levin replies, "I am saying that gravity might not exist as a fundamental thing in the universe."[14] Levin will then explain that there is a thing called gravity, but it is not the gravity of Newton or Einstein. It is not the gravity that built modern science's "universe." It is not the gravity that makes the earth orbit the sun.

What would happen if the scientific world discovered that gravity was not real? Nothing. *Big Think* informs how the scientific community responds to an incomplete (false) theory like gravity. *Big Think* wrote:

> Regardless, [Newton's gravity] worked. Astronomers used his equations to predict the motions of planets and comets, as well as the location and timing of solar eclipses. (And, one day, NASA used them to land on the Moon.) No matter how philosophically unsatisfying, gravity seemed to be a force of some sort.[15]

The response from the scientific community is, "It doesn't matter." That is how modern science works. Someone proposes a theory, and someone else confirms it without experimental evidence. Nicolaus Copernicus (1543) said the earth moved on a giant crystal ball. "It doesn't matter." Johannes Kepler (1609) said the earth moves around an imaginary point in space. "It doesn't matter." Isaac Newton (1687) could not define the force of gravity. "It doesn't matter." Albert Einstein (1905) said that while we are on earth, we cannot prove the earth moves. "It doesn't matter."

There is a conspiracy to make gravity work no matter the cost. It must work. If gravity is not real, then the foundation on which modern science is built would fail. What is the foundation of modern science? The earth is moving. When modern science tries to provide experimental evidence (e.g., Airy, Michelson, Morley, Hubble, NASA, etc.), the results show the earth is not moving. Everything depends on gravity to keep the world moving. That is why modern science is not interested in proving gravity but "confirming" it.

After discovering that the theory of gravity was not real, the whole "universe" I believed in fell apart. After learning that gravity could not be proven, I started researching the Scientific Revolution (when gravity was discovered). In 144 years, the Scientific Revolution would change the world. To understand the philosophy of the Scientific Revolution (1543–1687), one has to understand the philosophy of the Renaissance (1400s–1600s). The Renaissance was not about music or art. The Renaissance was a rebirth of an ancient religion. The Renaissance was a humanistic movement that taught people how to become gods. The ancient religion discovered during the Renaissance was the same religion the apostle Paul warned the church in Corinth about 1,400 years earlier. The apostle Paul knew "the philosopher of this age" (1 Corinthians 1:20) and the religion they practiced.

Chapter 6

Before the Beginning

The Bible does not use a zero-based numbering system. We do not have Genesis 1:0. In the Bible, our numbering system starts with the number one. The first verse in the Bible, "In the beginning" (Genesis 1:1), has nothing before it. According to the Bible, certain things occurred before the first verse. I am not arguing about changing the numbering in the Bible or adding text before Genesis 1:1. God's inspired word is complete. From within Genesis, we are given the story of creation. Outside of Genesis, reading the other books found in the Bible, we can see that God did some things before the creation of the heavens and the earth.

The Bible does not always provide the full details of its stories. Take, for example, Adam and Eve. When the first couple disobeyed God's word in the garden, something instantly happened to them: they died spiritually.

Genesis 3:7
Then the eyes of both of them were opened, and they realized they were naked; so they sewed fig leaves together and made coverings for themselves.

The Bible tells us they knew something was wrong, which is why they "hid from the Lord God among the trees of the garden" (Genesis 3:8). We are given a hint that something happened, but we are not given the full details. We know that Adam and Eve could see before "the eyes of both of them were opened" (Genesis 3:7). We can make this assumption because Adam had to see the animals to name them (Genesis 2:20), and the fruit was pleasing to the eye before Eve ate it (Genesis 3:6). Adam and Eve could see before they disobeyed God's command. After they disobeyed God's word, their eyes opened (Genesis 3:7). What eyes? They could already see. The reader is not explicitly told that they died spiritually. We are only told what happened as the result of their disobedience. It is from the New Testament that we learn about their spiritual death and the reason why we need Jesus. The last Adam, Jesus, would come to restore our spiritual life.

1 Corinthians 15:45
So it is written: "The first man Adam became a living being"; the last Adam, a life-giving spirit.

Paul tells the church that they are made "alive with Christ" (Ephesians 2:5). We can assume that Paul is writing to people who are alive. Paul was writing to the people who lived and breathed before they came to Christ. Paul understood that when Adam and Eve sinned, they died spiritually. Paul knows that life apart from Jesus means we are just like Adam and Eve, dead spiritually. Paul reminded the living people who are now followers of Christ, "As for you, you were dead in your transgressions and sins" (Ephesians 2:1). We no longer live a dead spiritual life but now live in the Spirit. The Bible tells us, "You, however, are not in the realm of the flesh but are in the realm of the Spirit" (Romans 8:9). We are not told about our spiritual death in Genesis. We learn about our dead spiritual life when we read outside of Genesis and look at other parts of Scripture.

If Genesis 1:0 did exist, what would we learn? Genesis 1:0 would explain several things. We would know that before the creation of the heavens and the earth, Jesus was there (John 1:1, 17:24; Colossians 1:16). Before the creation of the heavens and the earth, we would learn that God had a plan of salvation for His people (Ephesians 1:4; Matthew 25:34; Revelation 13:8). Before the creation of the heavens and the earth, we would also learn that God would prepare the earth's foundation (Job 38:4, 1 Samuel 2:8, Psalm 104:5). There was much happening before Genesis 1:1. For the focus of this chapter, we will only focus on one thing: the foundations of the earth.

Psalm 102:25
In the beginning, you laid the foundations of the earth,
and the heavens are the work of your hands.

The idea of a foundation for the earth is nowhere in Genesis. Moses never mentioned it in the Torah, the Bible's first five books. The first mention of the earth being established on a foundation is found in 1 Samuel 2:8. Hannah prayed to the Lord and mentioned the earth on a foundation.

1 Samuel 2:1, 8
Then Hannah prayed ... [8] "He raises the poor from the dust and lifts the needy from the ash heap; he seats them with princes and has them inherit a throne of honor. For the foundations of the earth are the Lord's; on them he has set the world."

Hannah was a woman who prayed often. She was Samuel's mother, who, for the longest time, could not have a child. Hannah would often go to the house of the Lord and pray. Hannah vowed that if God gave her a son, she would dedicate him to the Lord. E. Michael Rusten and Sharon Rusten wrote:

> She vowed that this son would be dedicated to God. Hannah's prayer was so desperate that Eli at first mistook it for drunken babbling. Soon after this, in about 1105 BC, Hannah conceived and bore a son.[1]

The Lord gave Hannah a son whom she dedicated to the Lord just as she promised. Hannah said, "So now I give him to the LORD. For his whole life he will be given over to the LORD" (1 Samuel 1:28). In Hannah's prayer, she said, "The foundations of the earth are the LORD's" (1 Samuel 2:8). How did she know this? Samuel was born 300 years after Moses' death (1406 BC).[2] Moses never wrote about the earth's foundation. The Bible records Hannah's prayer, which claims that God set the earth on a foundation or pillars. Where did this information come from? It came from the Book of Job.

According to scholars, the oldest book written in the Bible is the Book of Job.[3] Walter A. Elwell and Barry J. Beitzel point out that the lack of priesthood and the description of wealth indicate the early date of the Book of Job. Elwell and Beitzel wrote:

> The internal evidence points to a very early setting for the book. There are no levitical institutions cited. Job sacrifices for his family as in the period before the priesthood (1:5). The wealth of Job, given in terms of cattle, seems to reflect the patriarchal milieu (1:3).[4]

Traditionally speaking, Job was considered one of the oldest books written in the Bible. H. L. Ellison notes the lack of history and the covenants, indicating that the Book of Job was written before Moses wrote the Torah. Ellison wrote:

> The evidence for a very early date lies mostly in the non-mention of any of the details of Israelite history, but this is sufficiently explained by the author's wish to discuss the central problem outside the framework of the covenant. Other evidence, such as the mention of the Chaldeans as nomadic raiders (1:17) and of the archaic qeśîṭâ (42:11), point merely to the antiquity of the story and not to that of its present written form.[5]

The evidence from the Book of Job suggests that it was written before Moses' time. The covenant and God's chosen people are mentioned frequently in the Old Testament, which revolved around Abraham, Moses, the chosen people, and the Law. In the Book of Job, these subjects are never mentioned.

The Book of Job was also known to the prophets. When God's word came to the prophet Ezekiel, God told him, "Even if these three men—Noah, Daniel and Job" (Ezekiel 14:14). Job was a real historical person that God Himself mentions. The story of Job was also known to the New Testament audience. James wrote, "You have heard of Job's perseverance and have seen what the Lord finally brought about" (James 5:11).

When Hannah prayed, she mentioned the earth's foundation as if it were something people would understand. The Book of Job would have been the most likely source for the earth's foundation. What does Hannah mean when praying "the foundations of the earth" (1 Samuel 2:8)? David Tsumura wrote:

> The phrase always appears in poetic texts, used idiomatically. However, the reference to the foundation or support ("pillars") of the earth is meaningful here, for the Lord is the one who upholds the place where we live as well as the moral order of this world.[6]

Tsumura said that the phrase always appears in a poetic sense. Classifying 1 Samuel 2:8 as poetry is a common way for scholars to handle passages that deal with conflicts between the Bible and modern science. Hannah's song of praise was based on truth. Ralph W. Klein wrote, "[Hannah's] song is usually classified form-critically as a hymn, though elements from the Psalm of Thanksgiving genre are also present."[7] Hannah was singing a song of praise that reflected what she believed to be accurate. By claiming something is poetry, scholars permit themselves to change the meaning of the verse since no modern person thinks the earth is set upon pillars or a foundation. Let us look at an example of poetry from King David.

Psalm 6:6 (KJV)
I am weary with my groaning; all the night make I my bed
to swim; I water my couch with my tears.

David said that he was so upset that he became weak from all his grieving. David said that he cried so much that he saturated his bed with tears, and his couch became wet from his sobbing. When we read David's poetry, we know he is being descriptive with his words. We do not believe David's bed could swim or David put tears in a watering can and watered his couch. Since this is poetry, do we have the right to change the meaning of the text? Can we change what David intended to tell us? Can we read Psalm 6:6 and say that David was filled with joy and laughed? No. Just because David wrote something in poetry does not allow us to change the intent of his words.

The same standard must apply to Hannah's prayer. Can we read 1 Samuel 2:8 and say there is no foundation for the Lord to set the earth upon? No. Passages written in poetry do not permit us to change the meaning of what the person is trying to communicate to the reader.

Hannah's song may have been written in Hebrew poetry, but her words intend to convey what she believes to be true, a concept that is repeated in the Old and New Testaments. Joyce G. Baldwin comments on Hannah's prayer. Baldwin wrote, "The exact meaning of 'pillars' (Heb. *mĕṣuqê*) is not so clear, because the noun occurs only here and in 1 Samuel 14:5, where it is translated 'crag' in the RSV."[8] Baldwin is correct that "foundations | מְצֻקֵי | *māṣûq*" is also found in 1 Samuel 14:5 and is translated, "the one crag was (as) a pillar from the north 1 S 14:5."[9] In 1 Samuel 2:8, Hannah is not talking about a cliff or crag but the pillars (foundation) upon which God set the earth. In 1 Samuel 2:8, Hannah said, "foundations | מְצֻקֵי | *māṣûq*," which means "*pillars of the earth* 1 S 2:8."[10] According to Baldwin, the meaning of foundations may be unclear in 1 Samuel 14:5. Still, it is evident in her prayer that Hannah is praising God for the pillars (foundations) of the earth where God "has set the world" (1 Samuel 2:8).

What does "foundations | מְצֻקֵי | *māṣûq*" mean? According to James Swanson, "foundations | מְצֻקֵי | *māṣûq*," the word Hannah used in 1 Samuel 2:8, means "pillar, i.e., an upright foundational support shaft for a construction (1Sa 2:8+)."[11] William D. Mounce translates "foundations | מְצֻקֵי | *māṣûq*" as "foundation, pillar, support."[12] *The Dictionary of Classical Hebrew* translates "foundations | מְצֻקֵי | *māṣûq*" as "*pillars of the earth* 1 S 2:8."[13] Hannah was giving praise for the foundation (pillars) that God had made. The foundation that God set the earth upon.

What did Hannah intend to say when she prayed, "For the foundations of the earth are the LORD's; on them he has set the world" (1 Samuel 2:8)? Hannah meant that the Lord placed the earth on a foundation. Not only did Hannah pray these words, but King David also taught his men to praise the Lord similarly. David wanted his men to praise the Lord for the earth's foundation.

1 Chronicles 16:7, 30

That day David first appointed Asaph and his associates to give praise to the LORD in this manner: [30] Tremble before him, all the earth! The world is firmly established; it cannot be moved.

When we search scholarly commentaries, there is not much said about 1 Chronicles 16:30. Verse-by-verse commentaries usually include 1 Chronicles 16:30 with other verses and then refer to God's overall kingship. For example, David A. Hubbard et al. wrote:

This psalm is a psalm of praise to Yahweh the king, a summons to worship him on the basis of his superiority over all the peoples of the earth and their gods, which are in fact only idols (v 26), and in view of his coming judgment (v 33).[14]

Hubbard et al. did not comment on David's thoughts about the earth being "firmly established; it cannot be moved" (1 Chronicles 16:30). The concept of the world not moving was important to David. According to David's perspective, the earth was "established | כּוּן | *kûn*." Strong defines "established | כּוּן | *kûn*" as "to be set up, be established, be fixed."[15] David taught his men to praise God because the earth was fixed and "cannot be moved" (1 Chronicles 16:30).

David is letting his men know that God should be praised because of "what he has done" (1 Chronicles 16:8). David told his men to remember "his miracles" (1 Chronicles 16:12). David wants his men to praise the Lord because of "the covenant he made with Abraham" (1 Chronicles 16:16). David directs the men to sing to the Lord and to "proclaim his salvation day after day" (1 Chronicles 16:23). David reminds them to "bring an offering and come before him" (1 Chronicles 16:29). David also wants the men to praise the Lord because "The world is firmly established; it cannot be moved" (1 Chronicles 16:30). Notice we do not have a problem with David's instructions. We praise God for what He has done (1 Chronicles 16:12). We know God performs miracles (1 Chronicles 16:12) and keeps His covenants (1 Chronicles 16:15). We know that God saves His people (1 Chronicles 16:23). We know that God is worthy of our offerings (1 Chronicles 16:29). When praising God for a fixed and non-moving earth, we claim it is poetry and state that David did not mean what he said.

How did David know the earth did not move? Where did David get this information from? Moses never wrote about the earth being set on a foundation in Genesis. Moses never mentioned it in Exodus, Leviticus, Numbers, or Deuteronomy. How could David know the earth was on a foundation? How did David know the earth did not move? It is the same reason Hannah knew. The knowledge of the earth's foundation came from the Book of Job. How did Job know the earth was set upon a foundation? God told him.

Job 38:1, 4
Then the LORD spoke to Job out of the storm. He said: [4] "Where were you when I laid the earth's foundation? Tell me, if you understand."

Chapter 7

Learning from Job

The purpose of covering the Book of Job in this book is not about the meaning or message of Job. Is God just? Why does God never address Job's suffering? Is Job just a pawn in the story between God and the adversary? Plenty of books cover the meaning or message of the Book of Job. The purpose of discussing the Book of Job is to understand how the heavenly and earthly realms were viewed before Moses wrote the Pentateuch (the first five books of the Bible). The heavenly and earthly realms would be what many people refer to as the "universe." Job and his friends will make statements about the heavens and the earth that will provide a framework for others to follow (e.g., Hannah, David, Jeremiah, etc.). These statements will develop people's understanding of how things function in the heavenly and earthly realms. Not only will Job and his friends comment about the natural world, but God Himself will make certain claims about how things function in the heavenly and earthly realms.

The Book of Job has traditionally been considered the oldest book written in the Bible. It would have been written or spoken before Moses wrote Genesis (mid-15th century). *Nelson's Complete Book of Bible Maps & Charts* wrote:

> Although it is not possible to determine the precise date of the events described, several factors argue for a patriar-chal date (2000–1800 B.C.): the absence of references to Israelite history or biblical law; Job's long life of over 100 years (42:16); Job's role as priest for his family, which was prohibited by Mosaic law (1:5); and the measurement of Job's wealth in terms of livestock (1:3).[1]

Since the Book of Job does not mention the Law, priesthood, or God's chosen people, it is widely accepted that it was written before Genesis. That would mean that no one would have known the details of creation and how God brought this realm into existence.

Inside the dialogue of the Book of Job, we learn about the function of the sun, moon, stars, and the great sea monster that Genesis 1 speaks about.

We learn about the foundations of the earth that Moses never wrote about but is found elsewhere in Scripture, including the New Testament.

Different Realms

We first learn that the heavenly and earthly realms are separate dominions. Spiritual beings (God and angels) are in one location, and people are in another. We learn this in chapter 1. The Bible tells us that the angels and the adversary (Satan) were on the earth. The angels and Satan had to leave this world to present themselves before the Lord. We understand that Satan's location (earth) was different from God's location (heaven). Satan had to leave the earth to be in God's presence.

> **Job 1:6–7**
> One day the angels came to present themselves before the LORD, and Satan also came with them. [7] The LORD said to Satan, "Where have you come from?" Satan answered the LORD, "From roaming throughout the earth, going back and forth on it."

We learn that God's dwelling place and earth are two different locations, and we also learn something about angels and people. We understand that angels can visit the earth, and we, as human beings, cannot leave it. If we read the Book of Job for the first time, we would know from our personal experience that we cannot go to God's dwelling place. We are people of the earth. We cannot present ourselves before the Lord like the angels or Satan could. Satan, our enemy who is a "murderer from the beginning" (John 8:44), was allowed to go before God, who is "seated on his holy throne" (Psalm 47:8). Because of Jesus' resurrection, our enemy would lose his right to go past the firmament. Why Satan was allowed to enter God's holy presence is a subject discussed in my previous book, *The Story of the Bible*.[2]

In the Book of Job, we have two realms, the heavenly and the earthly. The spiritual beings have access to heaven and earth, but humans are limited to just earth. Job's audience understands that the heavenly and earthly realms are two different dwelling locations.

> **Job 16:18–19**
> [Job said,] "Earth, do not cover my blood; may my cry never be laid to rest! [19] Even now my witness is in heaven; my advocate is on high."

Location of Realms

We also learn that the location of heaven, God's home, is above us. God's house is above the clouds and stars. It is God who lives in the highest part of heaven. We learn that God walks on the vaulted dome of heaven.

> **Job 22:12–14**
>
> [Eliphaz said,] "Is not God in the heights of heaven? And see how lofty are the highest stars! [13] Yet you say, 'What does God know? Does he judge through such darkness? [14] Thick clouds veil him, so he does not see us as he goes about in the vaulted heavens.'"

Job's friend Eliphaz makes a statement about the layout of the heavens and the earth. Eliphaz claims that God is in the heights of heaven. The word "heights | גֹּבַהּ | gōbah" means "tallness, height, i.e., a lofty spatial dimension."[3] Eliphaz believes God's location is in heaven, far above all things. Eliphaz believes that God is even higher than the stars above. To see the stars, we have to look up. John E. Hartley comments, "God is more distant than even the farthest stars."[4] Not only is God higher than the stars, but God walks upon the vaulted dome that is over the earth. The vaulted dome is located up (opposite our feet). William D. Reyburn wrote:

> Vault of heaven is not an expression that is currently used in English. Vault is sometimes used to refer to an arched ceiling or roof, and as applied to heaven it suggests the dome-like appearance of the sky rising above the horizons.[5]

David J. Clines wrote:

> It is rather the vault of heaven, "that inverted Bowl we call The Sky" ... The vault or firmament of heaven, pictured in Gen 1 as a thin but solid covering (רקיע 'thing beaten out'), thus separates God from his creation.[6]

Eliphaz believes God is located in heaven, far above the stars. Eliphaz also believes that over the earth is a vaulted-dome-like structure. Eliphaz's belief was confirmed later when God spoke to Moses about the vaulted dome (firmament; Genesis 1:6–8). The prophet Amos also mentions the vaulted dome over the earth.

Amos 9:6 (NASB)

The One who builds His upper chambers in the heavens
And has founded His vaulted dome over the earth, He who
calls for the waters of the sea And pours them out on the
face of the earth, The LORD is His name.

The Underworld

We learned about the heavenly and earthly realms. We are also told
about the underworld, translated as grave or Sheol. The word "Sheol | שְׁאוֹל
| *she'ôl*" means "the Underworld, Hades, the Grave, i.e., a place under the
earth where the dead reside, the realm of death."[7] The word "Sheol | שְׁאוֹל |
she'ôl" means "the Underworld. The name for the place where the dead are
… it is not always clearly distinguished from the physical grave (e.g., Psa
141:7)."[8] Sheol, the realm of the dead, was first mentioned in Job.

Job 7:9

As a cloud vanishes and is gone, so one who goes down to
the grave (Sheol) does not return.

The location of the underworld is also mentioned in the Book of Job.
Sheol is located below our feet. It is down. In the oldest written book of the
Bible, we are told of the layout of the entire "universe." The simple layout of
the heavens, the earth, and the underworld will be followed throughout the
entire Bible. We learn that heaven is above our heads, the earth is where we
stand, and the underworld (Sheol) is below our feet.

Job 11:8 (ESV)

It is higher than heaven—what can you do? Deeper than
Sheol—what can you know?

The standard model for the rest of the Bible (heaven, earth, underworld), is the only layout the Bible recognizes. The Bible does not reference
any other layout. Even after Jesus' resurrection from the cross, the authors of
the Bible understood that the heavenly and earthly realms did not change.

Philippians 2:9–10

Therefore God exalted him to the highest place and gave
him the name that is above every name, [10] that at the name
of Jesus every knee should bow, in heaven and on earth and
under the earth.

Sun, Moon, and Stars

The Book of Job speaks about the nature of the sun, moon, and stars. We learn the sun is responsible for the growth of plants. Bildad the Shunhite said, "They are like a well-watered plant in the sunshine, spreading its shoots over the garden" (Job 8:16). We learn the moon moves in the heavenly realm. Job said, "the moon moving in splendor" (Job 31:26). We learn the stars are lights in the vaulted heavens. Job said, "he seals off the light of the stars" (Job 9:7).

According to the Book of Job, the sun, moon, and stars are all lights. Job said, "He speaks to the sun and it does not shine; he seals off the light of the stars" (Job 9:7). Bildad said, "The moon is not bright" (Job 25:5). The word "bright | אָהַל | 'āhal" means "be bright, shine (moon)."[9] Bildad said the moon could shine. Jesus would later confirm Bildad's statement and tell us that the moon has its own light.

> **Mark 13:24**
>
> [Jesus said,] "But in those days, following that distress, 'the sun will be darkened, and the moon will not give its light.'"

There is also the mention of the morning stars in the Book of Job. What are morning stars? E. W. Maunder states, "The last stars to appear in the east before sunrise, were the 'morning stars,' the heralds of the sun."[10] The most famous morning star is the wandering star called Venus. Fraser Cain of *Universe Today* said, "One of the nicknames of Venus is 'the Morning Star.'"[11] The Book of Job does not refer to Venus as a "planet" but a star that is so bright that it could be seen when the dawn first appears. Venus, the wandering star, would announce the coming of a new day.

When Job first speaks after the tragedy of losing everything, Job curses his birth and wishes things were different. Job does not want a new day to come because of the loss he has suffered. The morning stars would be visible at the dawn of the morning just before the sun would rise. Job does not want the morning stars to appear because he cannot bear another day after losing everything.

> **Job 3:9**
>
> [Job said,] "May its morning stars become dark; may it wait for daylight in vain and not see the first rays of dawn."

In the Book of Job, the sun, moon, and stars all shine because they are lights. Sun: "Now no one can look at the sun, bright as it is in the skies" (Job

37:21). Moon: "If even the moon is not bright" (Job 25:5). Stars: "The light of the stars" (Job 9:7). Not only are they lights, but the Book of Job tells us the moon moves. Job said, "the moon moving in splendor" (Job 31:26). Of course, the moon's movement is evident to Job's audience and us today since we see it moving across the night sky. I point out the obvious movement of the moon because if Job or his friends said something false about the natural world, then God's word and His world would not match up. We will discuss the compatibility problems caused by the sun, moon, and stars. The Bible makes specific claims about the heavenly lights that we do not believe today. In the Book of Job, the sun, moon, and stars are simply lights in the heavenly realm.

Foundation

The audience to the Book of Job would have understood the heavenly and earthly realm, along with the underworld, sun, moon, and stars. Job and his friends mentioned these subjects as if the audience had some knowledge of them. Remember, Job's pre-Moses audience would not know the details of the creation story nor have access to the writings of David, Jeremiah, or any other author of the Bible since it would have been written before Moses or the other Bible authors were even born. The Book of Job will reveal something about the earth that no one knew beforehand. Something that would be repeated throughout Scripture. How did the audience learn about the foundation that the earth was set upon? The person responsible for disclosing this information is God.

> **Job 38:1, 4**
> Then the LORD spoke to Job out of the storm. He said: [4] "Where were you when I laid the earth's foundation? Tell me, if you understand."

Initially, I was going to leave the subject of Leviathan out of this book. I wanted to focus the attention of this book on astronomy. The reason I decided to include the topic of Leviathan is twofold. First, sea monsters are mentioned in the creation story (Genesis 1:21), which has been influenced by modern science. Second, Leviathan is an excellent example of how our modern understanding has changed how we read the Bible. Thanks to the Scientific Revolution (1543–1687), Leviathan changed from a real creature into a mythological fairytale. Since this will be the only mention of Leviathan, I will include commentary from other books of the Bible outside of the Book of Job.

Leviathan

Job is the first to bring up the sea monster in his opening statement. The name of the sea dragon was called Leviathan. Job had some understanding about this monster since he mentioned it by name. "Leviathan | לִוְיָתָן | *livyāṯān*," means, "dragon, i.e., a reptile, serpent-like creature of the sea that takes on mythological proportions."[12] The *New American Standard Hebrew-Aramaic and Greek Dictionaries* defines "Leviathan | לִוְיָתָן | *livyāṯān*" as "'serpent,' a sea monster or dragon:—Leviathan."[13] When Job hears the news of his calamity and tragedy, including the loss of his children, Job begins to curse the day he was born. During Job's opening remarks, he will speak of Leviathan, the dragon.

Job 3:8

[Job said,] "May those who curse days curse that day, those who are ready to rouse Leviathan."

John E. Hartley said that Leviathan was "the monster that inhabits the sea and that is the personification of all forces that resist God's rule."[14] Robert L. Alden believes "Leviathan is the mythological monster."[15] David Guzik commented, "Usually Leviathan is considered to be a mythical sea-monster or dragon that terrorized sailors and fishermen."[16] Victor Harold Matthews et al. state, "Leviathan appears in the Bible as a sea monster representing the forces of chaos."[17] Job's audience would understand the idea of a great sea monster or dragon.

At the end of Job, Leviathan will reappear. This time, Job does not mention the creature; God does. God speaks to Job and explains that Job has no idea how to run this world. God will discuss the natural world, animals, justice, and Leviathan (Job 41:1–34). After God brings up the great dragon, Job repents.

Job 42:4–6

[Job said:] "You said, 'Listen now, and I will speak; I will question you, and you shall answer me.' ⁵ My ears had heard of you but now my eyes have seen you. ⁶ Therefore I despise myself and repent in dust and ashes."

Scholars are quick to point out the mythical nature of Leviathan. Today, we do not believe in a creature that haunts the sea or a monster covered in a coat of armor with fearsome teeth. We do not believe in an enormous creature that could spit fire from its mouth. By the way, this is not my description of the dragon but God's description of Leviathan.

Job 41:12–14, 19–21

[God said,] "I will not fail to speak of Leviathan's limbs, its strength and its graceful form. ¹³ Who can strip off its outer coat? Who can penetrate its double coat of armor? ¹⁴ Who dares open the doors of its mouth, ringed about with fearsome teeth? ¹⁹ Flames stream from its mouth; sparks of fire shoot out. ²⁰ Smoke pours from its nostrils as from a boiling pot over burning reeds. ²¹ Its breath sets coals ablaze, and flames dart from its mouth."

Was God speaking about a mythical creature? According to the Bible, no. Leviathan was a real sea monster that we would identify as a dragon. When Moses was inspired to write Genesis 1, Moses did not write his own words but was "carried along by the Holy Spirit" (2 Peter 1:21). Moses was writing what was being revealed to him by God. It was God who claimed that He made sea monsters.

Genesis 1:21

So God created the great creatures (sea monsters) of the sea and every living thing with which the water teems and that moves about in it, according to their kinds, and every winged bird according to its kind. And God saw that it was good.

The word "creatures | תַּנִּין | *tannin*" means "very large, impressive-looking creatures of the oceans, including very large fish and large marine mammals … note: possibly referring to a sea monster."[18] The word "creatures | תַּנִּין | *tannin*" means "*sea-* (or river-) *monster.*"[19] The word "creatures | תַּנִּין | *tannin*" means "sea monster … sea-dragon."[20] The word "creatures | תַּנִּין | *tannin*" means "*serpent, dragon, sea monster:—dragon.*"[21] Genesis 1 tells us that God made sea monsters. "Creatures | תַּנִּין | *tannin*" is in the plural form. I believe the creation story found in Genesis 1 is 100% factual and accurate, including sea monsters. One of those sea monsters was called Leviathan.

The word "Leviathan | לִוְיָתָן | *livyāṯān*" means "dragon, i.e., a reptile, serpent-like creature of the sea that takes on mythological proportions … may be a large sea creature."[22] The word "Leviathan | לִוְיָתָן | *livyāṯān*" means "serpent, dragon, leviathan."[23] The word "Leviathan | לִוְיָתָן | *livyāṯān*" means "Leviathan, sea-monster."[24] Leviathan is classified as a sea monster or dragon.

I am not talking about "dinosaurs." The creatures we are taught to believe in by modern science are fictional creatures. Plenty of Christian-based ministries would argue that "dinosaurs" existed. Some claim Behemoth (Job 40:15) refers to a "dinosaur." God compares Behemoth to animals, "which feeds on grass like an ox" (Job 40:15) and not a sea monster like Leviathan. Commentators will insist Behemoth is a "dinosaur" because its tail is as long as a cedar tree. God never said the tail is as long as a tree but said its tail hangs or "sways like a cedar" (Job 40:17).

"Dinosaurs" were invented from a hand-drawing of a giant man's thigh bone and iguana teeth by a scientist in 1841 who came up with the idea to invent a new class of species (Fig. 6). No feet. No arms. No ribs. No skin. No skull. No skeleton. All the scientist had was a hand drawing of a giant's thigh bone and iguana teeth. Then the scientist "came to realize" that the two objects belonged together and turned the drawing of one bone and teeth into a full-blown new creature called "dinosaur" (Fig. 7). "Came to realize" is another name for speculated, made-up, or guessed. *Scholastic* will explain the history of the created "dinosaur" in an article adapted from one of their professional books designed for grade school. *Scholastic*[25] explains:

> Way back in 1676, Robert Plot, the curator of an English museum, described and drew a thigh bone that he believed belonged to a giant man. Although that fossil disappeared without a trace, the surviving illustration suggests that it may well have been part of a "Megalosaurus." Later, in 1822, large teeth discovered in England by Mary Ann Mantell and her husband, Gideon, were thought to be the remains of a huge and extinct iguana. It wasn't until 1841 that British scientist Richard Owen *came to realize* that such fossils were distinct from the teeth or bones of any living creature. The ancient animals were so different, in fact, that they deserved their own name. So Owen dubbed the group "Dinosauria," which means "terrible lizards" (*emphasis added*).[26]

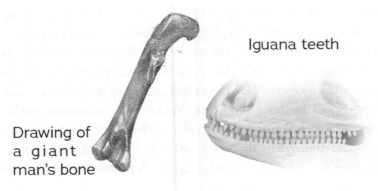

Iguana teeth

Drawing of
a giant
man's bone

Fig. 6. Items used to create Megalosaurus.

Fig. 7. Megalosaurus.

According to the Bible, Leviathan was a real sea monster that existed. Genesis 1 told us God made the sea monsters on Day 5. Today, people would mock me for believing in sea monsters. It is comforting to know that I am not alone in my belief of a real creature that exists in times past. Job believed in "Leviathan" (Job 3:8). The psalmist believed in "the heads of Leviathan" (Psalm 74:14). Isaiah believed in "Leviathan the gliding serpent, Leviathan the coiling serpent" (Isaiah 27:1). Ezekiel believed in "a monster in the seas" (Ezekiel 32:2). John believed Jesus when Jesus told John about "an enormous red dragon" (Revelation 12:3).

In modern times, we are praised by the world if we believe in "dinosaurs." If we claim to believe in a sea monster that Genesis 1 talks about, we are stupid and unsophisticated individuals. Before the 19th century, no one talked about "dinosaurs." What people did talk about was sea monsters. The following illustration is from Olaus Magnus' 1539 *Carta Marina* map (Fig. 8). The sailors from Norway would not understand "dinosaurs," which would not be invented until 300 years later. They would understand sea monsters resembling Isaiah's "coiling serpent" (Isaiah 27:1).

Fig. 8. The Sea Serpent (1539).

Where are the "dinosaurs" today? According to secular scientists, the only remaining "dinosaurs" today are birds. The famous velociraptors of *Jurassic Park* (1993) should have had feathers. Stephen Brusatte, a professor at the University of Edinburgh, Scotland, wrote:

> Tens of millions of people have flocked to theatres this summer to see Jurassic World … What I didn't like, however, was that the Velociraptors were depicted as big, drab-coloured, scaly brutes. That's because the real Velociraptor was a lapdog-sized predator covered in feathers.[27]

In 1996, the bird "dinosaur" was first said to be discovered in Liaoning, China. Paleontologists looking for evidence of a bird "dinosaur" found their evidence in Liaoning. A few years later, the bird "dinosaur" evidence was found to be a hoax. The *Guardian* reported:

> After months of scrutiny involving x-rays and scans, [Stephen] Czerkas' bird dinosaur was proclaimed a new

species, Archaeoraptor liaoningensis, by none other than the prestigious National Geographic journal. The magazine heralded the find as a crucial "missing link", representing conclusive proof that birds were the last living descendants of the dinosaurs. But weeks later, archaeoraptor was unveiled as a hoax, wedged together with bits and pieces from at least two animals by canny Chinese farmers with a feel for what palaeontologists were looking for. It now appears to have been the dinosaur version of Piltdown Man, the notorious fossil hoax put together in Sussex in 1911 to provide the missing link between man and ape predicted by Charles Darwin.[28]

Nearly 30 years ago, the bird "dinosaur" was proposed. Nearly 25 years ago, the evidence for the bird "dinosaur" was found to be a fraud. Nearly 5 years ago, all "dinosaurs" are birds. The *Smithsonian Magazine* wrote, "Birds are the only dinosaurs left."[29] That is how modern science works. When scientists want to prove their big bang, evolutionary, or bird "dinosaurs," they will.

Where are the "dinosaurs" today from a Christian perspective? Some Christians believe that God created "dinosaurs" with the other animals, either in a literal 24-hour day or over time. Most scholars assume the flood would have changed everything for the "dinosaurs," causing their extinction. *Creation* says, "Even though there are occasional stories of dinosaurs, it's really unlikely that there's a population of dinosaurs somewhere we haven't looked."[30]

Could the flood cause the "dinosaurs" to become extinct? To believe Noah's flood could have changed everything, we must first believe in the Biblical account of the flood. Let me explain. We are taught the earth is moving because of the sun's gravity (accepting gravity is required for modern science's "solar system"). Let us examine what the Bible claims about the flood.

Genesis 7:11–12

In the six hundredth year of Noah's life, on the seventeenth day of the second month—on that day all the springs of the great deep burst forth, and the floodgates of the heavens were opened. [12] And rain fell on the earth forty days and forty nights.

The Bible tells us that water came from the great deep. The same deep waters "the earth was formed out of" (2 Peter 3:5). According to modern science, silicate rock is beneath the earth's crust. The Bible tells us that water came from heaven's floodgates (windows). The Bible tells us that God placed water "above the firmament" (Genesis 1:7, KJV). The same firmament where the sun is located (Genesis 1:17). According to the Bible, water flooded the earth from above the sun. According to modern science, the sun is sitting in the emptiness of space.

Finally, the flood included water from the clouds. Scholars like to combine the floodgates of heaven and rain as one water source. The Bible said, "And rain fell" (Genesis 7:12). Rain only comes from the clouds. The clouds are located in the atmosphere. The atmosphere is located below the sun. The sun is in the firmament. The firmament has water above it. That is what the Bible teaches. Could there be a canopy over the earth, and all the water was gone when the flood was finished? No. The psalmist will praise God for the water above our sky (atmosphere) and not the water in clouds. The psalmist wrote this verse, inspired by the Holy Spirit, after Noah's flood.

Psalm 148:4
Praise him, you highest heavens and you waters above the skies.

If we believe the Bible in its literal sense, the flood account is easy to understand. Water came from below (great deep), water came from above (firmament), and water came from our atmosphere (clouds). If we believe in modern science's "solar system," the flood account is impossible.

If water were above the sun, as the Bible claims, it would have to travel at least 93,000,000 miles to reach the earth's surface. The water would have to travel over a month because "forty days the flood kept coming on the earth" (Genesis 7:17). In forty days, the sun would have moved 432,000,000 miles, and the earth would have orbited 63,957,120 miles while spinning over 1,000 mph. Time is another factor. How early did God start the flood so that the water could reach the surface of the earth? If the water traveled from the sun at the speed of light, it would take 8 minutes. Unfortunately, we must include the stars since the Bible says they are located in the same "space" as the sun (Genesis 1:17). Now the water would take 4.25 years to reach the surface of the earth (closest star) if the water was traveling at the speed of light (186,000 miles per second). The Biblical account of the flood does not make sense when trying to make it work in modern science's "solar system."

Scientists invented "dinosaurs" to remove God from His creation. Since God created sea monsters, people were determined to invent land monsters. Leviathan is an excellent illustration of how we turn actual Biblical claims about sea monsters into nothing more than Greek mythology or fantasy— the moment when Leviathan turned into myth happened during the 19th century. After the Scientific Revolution (1543–1687), Bible scholars had to deal with modern science's moving earth. We will talk about mythology in, "The Modern Christian World."

I have been asked if I believe in sea monsters or Leviathan. My answer, without hesitation is yes. Do they still exist today? That is a good question. The only answer I can give with confidence is this. I do not have to worry about Leviathan because God destroyed him.

> **Psalm 74:13–14**
> It was you who split open the sea by your power; you broke the heads of the monster in the waters. [14] It was you who crushed the heads of Leviathan and gave it as food to the creatures of the desert.

Chapter 8

Statements Made In Job

General Statements

The Book of Job contains statements about the "universe" made by Job and his friends. Job said the earth had pillars. Job declared that God could shake "the earth from its place and makes it pillars tremble" (Job 9:6). Job also believed in the "pillars of the heavens" (Job 26:11). Stephen M. Hooks wrote:

> Beneath this cosmic dome the pillars of the heavens, known elsewhere as the "pillars of the mountains" which were believed to support the huge canopy of the sky, are said to quake before the sound of God's rebuke (cf. Ps 18:8[7] = 2 Sam 22:8).[1]

The sky was thought to be a dome-shaped vault over the earth. It was on this solid dome that the heavens were stretched over like a tent. Job's friend Elihu said, "Can you join him in spreading out the skies, hard as a mirror of cast bronze?" (Job 37:18). John E. Hartley comments, "Elihu asks Job if he could assist God in *spreading out* (lit. hammering out) the solid sky."[2] Job also observes the stars.

Job 9:9
He is the Maker of the Bear and Orion, the Pleiades and the constellations of the south.

Scholars are unsure what constellations Job sees, but the text tells us that Job could recognize specific patterns the stars made. David J. Clines wrote, "These three constellations, although they cannot be identified with certainty, were undoubtedly recognized in the ancient world as outstandingly splendid."[3] The audience of the Book of Job knew about stars that formed specific patterns or shapes.

Constellations were recognized in ancient Babylon and Egypt. Constellations were known to the prophet Isaiah. "The stars of heaven and their constellations will not show their light" (Isaiah 13:10). In the Book of Isaiah, "constellations | כְּסִיל | *kĕsîl*" is thought to be Orion. A. R. Fausset wrote,

"[Constellation is] applied to the constellation *Orion*, who was represented as an impious giant (Nimrod deified, the founder of Babylon) chained to the sky."[4]

The constellation Orion is still known to us today. It is incredible to know that the simple pattern of Orion or any constellation has remained the same in our night skies even though we are taught that the earth has traveled more than 92,808,119,250,000,000 miles since Isaiah saw Orion in the night sky. How can Orion never lose its shape relative to each other as we have traveled 92.8 quadrillion miles? Stars have been relied upon because they never changed their patterns or shape for thousands of years because of their fixed location in the firmament.

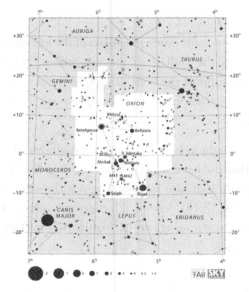

Fig. 9. Orion.

Job and his friends made their observations without the tools of science that we have today. They formed their thoughts by using what God gave them: their eyes. Job and his friends' observations were correct and still are consistent with what we see today.

We know that daylight comes because the sun is about to appear in the sky (Job 3:9). We still see sunshine (Job 8:16). We know that the day is brightest at noon (Job 11:17). We know that we can get a tan because of the sun (Job 30:28). We understand the moon is not as bright as the sun (Job 25:5). We know there are different phases of the moon (Job 26:9). We know the moon moves across the night sky (Job 31:26). We see the morning stars shine at dawn (Job 3:9). We know the stars are located above the clouds and atmosphere (Job 22:12).

Eliphaz's observation about the vaulted dome over the earth is still what we observe today. Eliphaz said that God "goes about in the vaulted heavens" (Job 22:14). The word "vaulted | חוג | ḥûg" means "a vast celestial domed or circular throne room in the sky (Job 22:14; Isa 40:22+)."[5] Today, if we observe the night sky, we see a vaulted dome.

Neil deGrasse Tyson, astrophysicist, author, and popular TV science communicator, wrote about the celestial dome in the night sky. In his book, *Death by Black Hole: And Other Cosmic Quandaries*, Tyson claims that we cannot trust what our eyes tell us. Tyson admits that from common observation, using just our eyes, it is hard to imagine us living on a spherical "planet." In the chapter called "Seeing Isn't Believing," Tyson wrote, "Without satellite imagery, it's hard to convince yourself that the Earth is anything but flat, even when you look out of an airplane window."[6] Tyson admits that with the naked eye, the earth seems flat, even when we look out of the curved windows of an airplane flying 36,000 feet in the air. Tyson also admits the sky looks like a giant dome resting over the earth:

> Now look up. Without a telescope, you can't tell how far away the stars are. They keep their places, rising and setting as if they were glued to the inside surface of a dark, upside-down cereal bowl.[7]

Tyson tells us to imagine a large dome (upside-down cereal bowl) to make sense of the night sky. Tyson did not invent this illustration. Astronomers know the night sky resembles a solid dome barrier covering the earth. Arthur Berry (1899), a believer in modern science, said that from our observations, we see a dome (celestial sphere), and we are at the center of the universe. Berry does not believe in the firmament (solid dome barrier) or that everything revolves around the earth, but Berry tells his readers that it only appears that way. Berry wrote:

> If an observer looks at the stars on any clear night he sees an apparently innumerable host of them, which seem to lie on a portion of a spherical surface, of which he is the centre. This spherical surface is commonly spoken of as the sky, and is known to astronomy as the celestial sphere. The visible part of this sphere is bounded by the earth, so that only half can be seen at once.[8]

Tyson is trying to convince his readers that seeing is not believing. Tyson wants us to consider something other than what Eliphaz observed thousands of years ago about the celestial dome. Tyson knows that if we believe anything the Bible tells us about the natural world, we are a fool who has no idea how things work. Tyson said:

> "If you knew nothing about science, and you read, say, the Bible, the Old Testament, which in Genesis, is an account of nature, that's what that is, and I said to you, 'Give me your description of the natural world based only on this,' you would say the world was created in six days, and that stars are just little points of light much lesser than the sun. … To even write that means you don't know what those things are. You have no concept of what the actual universe is. So everybody who tried to make proclamations about the physical universe based on Bible passages got the wrong answer."[9]

Tyson must prevent us from believing what the Bible teaches about the earth not moving and the location of the stars. Tyson said we would get the wrong answers if we held to what the Bible teaches. The Bible and Ptolemy (Greek philosopher) suggest that the earth is at the center of creation, and everything revolves around us. Tyson wrote:

> For millennia, people understandably thought of stars as "fixed,'" a concept evident in such influential sources as the Bible ('And God set them in the firmament of the heaven,' Genesis 1:17) and Claudius Ptolemy's *Almagest*, published circa A.D. 150, wherein he argues strongly and persuasively for no motion.[10]

Tyson wants to convince us that what we see is untrustworthy. We must trust in what modern science claims and not believe in the celestial dome that we naturally see in the night sky—the same celestial dome that Eliphaz saw thousands of years ago. Tyson must ensure that his readers do not rely upon the Bible or what they observe. Tyson wrote, "And of course there is no bowl."[11] Eliphaz's observation about the celestial dome, the solid sky, will be confirmed later when God reveals to Moses what He did on Day 2 of creation (Genesis 1:6–8).

Job and his friends made observations about the natural world, which are still true today. They also made statements about things that they could not verify. They commented on the underworld even though Job and his friends never visited the grave (Sheol or the realm of the dead; Job 7:9). Job believed God was watching from heaven even though Job had never been there (Job 16:19). Job also makes a statement about the earth. A statement that God would not let slide. A statement that God described as "words without knowledge" (Job 38:2).

Job's Statement

Bildad the Shuhite finished his comments to Job (Job 25:1–6). In response, Job said the earth was suspended mid-air over nothing. This verse is significant to believers in modern science. It is the only verse in the Bible that speaks about the earth not being on a foundation.

> **Job 26:7**
> [Job said,] "He spreads out the northern skies over empty space; he suspends the earth over nothing."

Here is how modern scholars who believe in modern science interpret this verse. Robert Alden wrote, "Job's assertion that the earth hangs on nothing is amazingly accurate and certainly counters the charge that the Bible's writers held that the earth stood on something else."[12] Stephen Hooks will also comment on how Job's statement aligns more with our modern understanding of the "solar system" than Job's contemporaries:

> When Job says that God suspends the earth over nothing, he is more in tune with the cosmology of the modern scientific age than he is with the teachings of his own time. In the ancient Near Eastern world the earth was thought to stand on "pillars" (perhaps mountains) anchored in the watery depths (cf. 9:6; Ps 75:4[3]; 104:5; 1 Sam 2:8). Job's poetic description of an earth suspended in empty space (lit., "nothing"; בְּלִימָה, bəlîmāh) anticipates by centuries what science will later discover.[13]

David Guzik wrote, "Job remarkably understood this. In contrast to ancient mythologies that said the earth was held up on the backs of elephants or giant turtles, Job knew that He hangs the earth on nothing."[14] Albert Barnes would also assert Job's belief that the earth is not on a foundation.

Barnes wrote his commentary in 1847. Barnes believes in modern science (theories from the Scientific Revolution [1543–1687]). Barnes wrote:

> There is no certain evidence here that Job was acquainted with the globular form of the earth, and with its diurnal and annual revolutions. But it is clear that he regarded it as not resting on any foundation or support; as lying on the vacant air, and kept there by the power of God.[15]

Warren W. Wiersbe wrote, "Job began his hymn of praise with a statement about God's power in the heavens (vv. 7–9), and he described the earth with remarkable scientific accuracy (v. 7)."[16] Roy B. Zuck said, "God sustains the skies (cf. v. 13) over empty space and supports the earth on nothing—statements amazingly in accord with facts not known or agreed on by scientists till a few hundred years ago."[17] J. Vernon McGee will also explain how Job's word confirms what modern science teaches. A belief that ancient astronomers did not believe. McGee stated:

> He "hangeth the earth upon nothing." Who in the world told Job that? Remember that Job lived back in the age of the patriarchs, and yet this man knew that this earth is hanging out in space. That God suspends the huge ball of earth in space with nothing to support it but His own fixed laws is a concept unknown to ancient astronomers. Job understood that He "hangeth the earth upon nothing." There is no foundation under it.[18]

Commentators use Job's statement, "He suspends the earth over nothing" (Job 26:7), as evidence of the earth orbiting the sun. It is important to keep in mind that Job made this comment without any observation to back up his claim. A. R. Fausset (1821–1910) tells us the reason the earth is suspended is because of the laws of motion and gravity:

> The law of attraction and gravitation, whereby the globular form of the earth and the heavenly bodies is maintained, is a beautiful instance of the sublime simplicity, universality, and efficiency of God's working in nature. … Though the Bible was not designed to unfold physical science, yet the germ of the discoveries of modern science is often found in hints which it affords—as in v. 7,"He hangeth the earth upon nothing."[19]

Fausset passed away in 1910. Fausset is referencing Isaac Newton's gravity (1687). Fausset claimed that Job is describing Newton's "law of attraction and gravitation." Unfortunately, Fausset died just before Einstein told the world that Newton's gravity was wrong. According to Fausset, Job is describing gravity as the reason for the "planets" to maintain their orbit. If Fausset had been correct, the Bible would have contained a false statement since Einstein would have proved God's word wrong in 1915.

Fausset believed in gravity because he trusted modern science. We believe in gravity because we trust modern science. The question remains, "What is gravity?" Isaac Newton never defined gravity in his book *Philosophiae Naturalis Principia Mathematica* (*The Mathematical Principles of Natural Philosophy*) (1687). Besides, when talking about gravity, we must first determine what gravity we are speaking about, Newton or Einstein. Sean Carrol will inform us that Newton's theory of gravity was replaced by Albert Einstein's theory of general relativity. Carrol said, "GR [general relativity] is a theory of gravity, so we can begin by remembering our previous theory of gravity, that of Newton."[20] Einstein proved Newton wrong. Ethan Siegel wrote, "Newton's theory predicted an instantaneous force, again violating relativity. In 1915, Albert Einstein put forth a new alternative theory of gravity: General Relativity."[21] A new alternative theory is a nice way of saying Newton was wrong.

Today, no one knows what gravity is. It is hard to imagine Job in the Bible being in tune with Newton's theory of gravity, which has yet to be proven. What is gravity? John Lennox, a Christian author and professor of mathematics at Oxford University, England, said, "Do you realize that no one knows what gravity is, still today. And if you don't believe that you better read Richard Feynman and he worked at the University of California, so you better check before you disagree with him."[22]

God's Statement

Job and his friends made several statements about the earth based on their observations of the natural world. God did not correct Eliphaz about his statement of the domed sky or "vaulted heavens" (Job 22:14). God did not bring up Elihu and his description of the sky that was "hard as a mirror of cast bronze" (Job 37:18). When Job made a statement about the earth being suspended over nothing (Job 26:7), God was going to correct Job's misunderstanding.

The Book of Job is a long conversation between Job and his friends, and it finishes with God speaking but never addressing why Job had to suffer.

The first two chapters of the Book of Job give the readers insight into what is happening in the unseen realm. Then, in thirty-five chapters, the Book of Job covers Job's dialogue with his friends. Finally, God will speak to Job and eventually address Job's friends. The Bible says, "The LORD spoke to Job out of the storm. He said: ³ 'Brace yourself like a man; I will question you, and you shall answer me'" (Job 38:1, 3). John E. Hartley wrote:

> For clarity it is specifically stated that Yahweh addresses *Job*. After the Elihu speeches the person addressed needs to be identified. This fact means that Yahweh's words are primarily spoken to Job, not to the comforters or to the audience at large.[23]

After God addresses Job, He turns to Job's friends. God will correct Eliphaz, Bildad, and Zophar for not speaking the truth about Him. God does not address their observations about the earth. Why would God correct Job's observation about the earth? God was pleased with Job, who had "spoken the truth about [Him]" (Job 42:7). God was not pleased when Job spoke about something that was not true about His creation. God will inform Job that the earth is not suspended over empty space but is set upon a foundation. A foundation that God Himself prepared for the earth.

Job 38:4–7

[The LORD said,] "Where were you when I laid the earth's foundation? Tell me, if you understand. ⁵ Who marked off its dimensions? Surely you know! Who stretched a measuring line across it? ⁶ On what were its footings set, or who laid its cornerstone— ⁷ while the morning stars sang together and all the angels shouted for joy?"

Job 38:4 states that God laid the earth's foundation. Job 38:4 is translated in English Bibles as the "earth's foundation" or "foundation(s) of the earth." When the Hebrew scribes wanted to translate the Hebrew Bible into Greek (Septuagint; LXX), they translated it as the "earth's foundation."[24] When scholars interpret this verse, trying to tell us the meaning of what God said, things are not that simple.

Reaction to God's Statement

Scholars have different reactions to God's statement: "I laid the earth's foundation" (Job 38:4). If we took God at face value, then the earth is set on a base (foundation). That would go against everything we have been taught and everything we believe about the "solar system." On the one hand, we read in the Bible that the earth "cannot be moved" (Psalm 96:10). On the other hand, when we read, the earth "cannot be moved" (1 Chronicles 16:30), we believe the earth is moving. Let us examine how scholars handle the foundation of the earth, as mentioned in Job 38:4.

John Hartley's solution is to shift our attention from the earth's foundation and put it on wisdom. Commentators commonly group multiple subjects into a single topic. Hartley said:

> Job is asked to make known his knowledge of the initial stages of the creation of the world as though he were the primordial man who had witnessed the laying of the earth's foundation (cf. 15:7). From an OT perspective, however, wisdom was God's sole companion present at creation (ch. 28; Prov. 8:22–31). Therefore, since Job lacks this essential knowledge, how could he expect to dispute successfully with God?[25]

Hartley does not address the central issue God had with Job. God wanted Job to know there was a foundation underneath the earth. Francis I. Andersen will not focus on the foundations of the earth either. Andersen will tie verses 4 and 7 together and suggest that God is reminding Job that he was not at creation, unlike the "divine" beings that witnessed it (angels; sons of God). Andersen wrote:

> As in Psalm 24, Isaiah 40, and other passages, the world is described as a vast edifice whose designer and maker is God, who *laid the foundation of the earth*. The figure is developed with material details, including a trench for footings, cornerstone, etc. This makes it possible that *bînāh* in verse 4 is not *understanding*, but a noun based on *bānāh*, "build." The *when*-phrase in verse 7 links with the *when*-phrase in verse 4 to complete the strophe. God was not solitary when he started this world. His world was already populous with creatures: "divine" beings (literally *sons of God*), the angels of later theology, whom we have already met in assembly in chapters 1 and 2."[26]

Andersen arrives at his conclusion by concentrating on the word "under-stand | בִּינָה | bînâ." The word "understand | בִּינָה | bînâ" means "understand-ing, insight, discernment, i.e., a good sense or wisdom to respond properly to the LORD."[27] Andersen focuses on God who revealed to Job that angels or morning stars were present when He created the earth (Job 38:7). Who are the morning stars? Hooks states, "Here, as the poetic parallelism suggests, [morning stars] are used figuratively to refer to the 'sons of God,' i.e., the angels."[28]

Andersen is correct that angels (morning stars) were present, but this is not what God wanted Job to know at first. God wanted Job to know that the earth was not hanging in mid-air but resting upon a base. Robert Alden will also concentrate on the wisdom present when the earth was created. Alden will correctly point out that wisdom was there in the beginning when God created the heavens and the earth. The Book of Proverbs, which would have been written after Job lived, tells us that wisdom was "formed long ages ago, at the very beginning, when the world came to be" (Proverbs 8:23). Wisdom will also testify that God was the one who "marked out the foundations of the earth" (Proverbs 8:29). Even though Alden cites Proverbs 8, he does not address the meaning of the earth's foundation which is mentioned in both Job and Proverbs. Alden, like Andersen, will concentrate on Job not being there in the beginning. Alden wrote:

> Unlike personified Wisdom, who was present at the creation (Prov 8:22–31), Job was a creature of time. When God "laid the earth's foundation," Job simply was not yet born. Not even Adam and Eve, the first couple, were present at this inaugural event that marked our planet's birth. Job could not answer because he was not there and could not know.[29]

When scholars explain the earth's foundation, they interpret the passage within the "solar system" and "universe" designed by modern science. Scholars repeat the phrase, "laid the earth's foundation," but then move on to the next subject. Because scholars believe in modern science, they interpret the earth's foundation as a "virtual" foundation. A. R. Fausset will comment on wisdom's account of the earth's foundation in Proverbs 8. Fausset wrote:

> [God] made it as stable as a building resting on solid *foun-dations*. The earth's centre is its virtual foundation, as all bodies and parts of the earth, by the centripetal force of

attraction, gravitate towards it. Job 26:7 hints at the true theory of the earth's foundation.[30]

Fausset uses Job's "suspends the earth over nothing" (Job 26:7) to explain the earth's foundations in Proverbs 8:29 as Biblical evidence for the theory of gravity. The theory of gravity is just as important to people in and outside the church. Without gravity, the earth could not orbit the sun. Without gravity, people could not live on the bottom of the earth. Without gravity, the ocean's water could not stay on a spinning globe. Why does modern science continually push a theory that has never been proven? Without gravity, we would realize we were deceived into believing in a "solar system" made by pagan philosophy, math, and magic.

The Gravity of God's Claim

Fausset mentioned Isaac Newton's centripetal force of attraction. Newton defined centripetal force in Book I of his *Principia* (1687). Newton wrote:

Definition V.

A centripetal force is that by which bodies are drawn or impelled, or any way tend, towards a point as to a centre. Of this sort is gravity, by which bodies tend to the centre of the earth magnetism, by which iron tends to the load-stone; and that force, whatever it is, by which the planets are perpetually drawn aside from the rectilinear motions, which otherwise they would pursue, and made to revolve in curvilinear orbits.[31]

Newton will give the example of a stone being held in a sling that "orbits" the hand holding the sling. Without the sling (gravity), the rock would fly off in a straight line. It is the sling that continues to draw the stone back to the hand that creates the "orbit." What is the sling, the force that holds the "planets" in its orbit around the sun? It is the force of gravity. How did Newton define this force? Newton wrote, "that force, whatever it is."[32]

Everyone assumes that the theory of gravity is proven. When I tell people that the inventor of gravity did not know what gravity was, they look at me like I am crazy. Some people try to correct my claim by quickly dropping an object before me. They proudly say, "See, it's gravity." We all have witnessed things falling, yet the physics experts tell us, "There is no gravity." The problem is that no one knows what gravity is.

Richard Panek, author of the book *The Trouble With Gravity: Solving the Mystery Beneath Our Feet*, wrote an article for the Washington Post newspaper in 2019. Panek, who believes in modern science, will tell us what the average person's response would be if they were told that we do not know what gravity is:

> Say that to the average person ["We don't know what gravity is"], and the answer you'll probably get is some version of: "What are you talking about? Gravity is the force of attraction that makes things fall straight down." But say it to a physicist, and the answer you'll get is, "That's right." I know, because those are the two answers I've been getting for the past few years, ever since I figured out that nobody knows what gravity is ... nobody knows that nobody knows what gravity is. The exception is physicists: They know that nobody knows what gravity is, because they know that they don't know what gravity is."[33]

How is the theory of gravity, one of the four fundamental forces that created the "universe," still unknown? How can experts not define things we supposedly learned in elementary school? Scientists today do not know what gravity is. Why is gravity so crucial to modern science and promoted as if it is verified? Without gravity, it was difficult for people to accept Copernicus' idea that the earth orbited the sun (1543). Copernicus believed the earth was on a giant transparent sphere circling the sun. *History* tells us, "With no concept of gravity, Earth and the planets still revolved around the sun on giant transparent spheres."[34] Still, to this day, no one knows what gravity is. Dr. Allan Chapman "teaches the history of science at Oxford University. His specialist areas are the history of astronomy and medicine."[35] Chapman said:

> It seemed to many scientists that what Newton was doing was bringing back magic. Newton didn't know what gravitation was. He admitted it. We don't know what gravity is today.[36]

Chapman mentioned that Newton was accused of "bringing back magic." When we discuss the history of modern science, I will explain why Chapman's comment about magic was correct.

Neil deGrasse Tyson, astrophysicist and science communicator, was interviewed on the *StarTalk* radio show. When asked, "What is gravity?" Tyson responded, "We have no idea."[37] Tyson continued, "We can describe gravity, we can say what it does to other things, we can measure it, predict with it, but when you start asking like 'what it is?', I don't know."[38] Tyson, who served as a presidential advisor for President George W. Bush (2001), cannot tell us what gravity is but expects us to trust science and accept gravity because they said so.

Tyson believes that modern science is the only standard of truth. My intention in this book is not to pit religion against science. The intention of modern science is to destroy our religious beliefs. Modern science wants to force its religious views on us, and if we do not accept the doctrines it teaches, we will be labeled ignorant and stupid.

In 2006, David Paszkiewicz, a New Jersey history teacher, told his class that evolution and the big bang were not scientific, and that Noah had dinosaurs on his ark. Paszkiewicz was sued because his comments became known when a 16-year-old student recorded him. Tyson wrote a letter to the New York Times editor about the lawsuit against Paszkiewicz. Tyson wrote:

> To the Editor:
>
> People cited violation of the First Amendment when a New Jersey schoolteacher asserted that evolution and the Big Bang are not scientific and that Noah's ark carried dinosaurs.
>
> This case is not about the need to separate church and state; it's about the need to separate ignorant, scientifically illiterate people from the ranks of teachers.
>
> Neil deGrasse Tyson.[39]

In today's society, we do not have the option to believe the claims of the Bible. According to Tyson, if we reject their teachings, we are ignorant. To modern science, the Bible is nothing more than an ancient philosophy book written by the scientifically illiterate.

As Christians, we can reject the big bang and the theory of evolution. Still, we unquestioningly accept the theory of gravity, which made the big bang and the theory of evolution possible. For modern science to succeed, the authority of God's word must be destroyed. Tyson would comment on his letter to the editor when giving a presentation called "Religion vs.

Science." Tyson explains why the New Jersey school teacher is an ignorant fool. Tyson said:

> "If he wants to believe Jesus is a savior, that's not synonymous with being scientifically illiterate because 40% of American scientists pray to a personal God. What is identical with being scientifically illiterate, is that if Noah was a human being, he did not have dinosaurs on his ark cause humans and dinosaurs did not co-exist. Every scientist knows that even the 40% that pray to God."[40]

Today, the "solar system" and "universe" result from a theory proposed by Copernicus, held together by gravity. The theory of gravity is why modern science does not need our Creator. To modern science, gravity is god. Steven Hawking was considered to be a genius and highly esteemed scientist. Hawking argues that the creation of the "universe" does not need a divine being to intervene in the "universe" because they have a creator, gravity. Hawking wrote:

> Because there is a law like gravity, the universe can and will create itself from nothing in the manner described in Chapter 6. Spontaneous creation is the reason there is something rather than nothing, why the universe exists, why we exist. It is not necessary to invoke God to light the blue touch paper and set the universe going.[41]

Panek, the author of *The Trouble With Gravity*, made an honest assessment of gravity. Panek told us the secret that scientists do not know what gravity is. Panek wrote:

> Nobody knows what gravity is, and almost nobody knows that nobody knows what gravity is. The exception is scientists. They know that nobody knows what gravity is, because they know that they don't know what gravity is.[42]

No one knows what gravity is, yet we believe it is real. Even with quotes and sources from modern science, we do not doubt gravity. The theory of gravity is central to the world of modern science. Without gravity, their "universe" could not exist. Gravity is how modern science explains the creation of everything. Hawking describes how their god created their "universe." Hawking wrote:

As time went on, the hydrogen and helium gas in the galaxies would break up into smaller clouds that would collapse under their own gravity. As these contracted, and the atoms within them collided with one another, the temperature of the gas would increase, until eventually it became hot enough to start nuclear fusion reactions.[43]

Modern science teaches, "In the beginning, gravity created the sun (nuclear fusion)." Gravity is needed to explain how we orbit the sun, why the earth has an atmosphere, why people are grounded to the earth, and how 317 million trillion gallons of water can stay on a globe spinning over 1,000 mph.[44] If the theory of gravity would fall, their house of cards would collapse. If the theory of gravity would fail, then people's trust in modern science would crumble.

For modern science to become the standard of truth for people to believe in, it must prove God wrong. The way to prove God wrong required one thing: a moving earth. The conspiracy to change people's perception of the natural world was not easy. It would require a revolution and the resurrection of an ancient religion. It would require the transformation of human beings into gods. It would also require the removal of the earth's foundation—the very foundation that God made.

Job 38:4
[The LORD said,] "Where were you when I laid the earth's foundation? Tell me, if you understand."

The Greek World

Chapter 9

The Unreal Universe

No matter how we feel about science, it is necessary to talk about the history of modern science and the formation of our current understanding of the "universe." When I write "universe," I use quotation marks. "Universe" is what people think of when trying to describe "the heavens and the earth" (Genesis 1:1). The word "universe" is a modern word that was invented in the late-16th century to describe everything above the clouds. NASA defines what they are talking about when they use the word "universe":

> The universe is everything. It includes all of space, and all the matter and energy that space contains. ... Earth and the Moon are part of the universe, as are the other planets and their many dozens of moons. Along with asteroids and comets, the planets orbit the Sun. The Sun is one among hundreds of billions of stars in the Milky Way galaxy ... The Milky Way is but one of billions of galaxies in the observable universe — all of them, including our own, are thought to have supermassive black holes at their centers. All the stars in all the galaxies and all the other stuff that astronomers can't even observe are all part of the universe. It is, simply, everything. [1]

Many Christians use the word "universe," and even one of my favorite Bible verses uses that word. The Bible states, "By faith we understand that the universe was formed at God's command" (Hebrews 11:3). Scholars define "universe" to mean everything that exists under time and space or everything that exists in the heavens (outer space) and the earth. Before the invention of the word "universe," another word was used. Here are some examples of how the "universe" in Hebrews 11:3 was translated starting in the 14th century.

Hebrews 11:3 (Wycliffe; 1382-1395) [2]
Bi feith we vndirstonden the worldis for to be schapun, 'or maad, bi Goddis word...

Hebrews 11:3 (Tyndale; 1536)[3]

Thorow fayth we understande that the worlde was ordeyned by the worde of God...

Hebrews 11:3 (Geneva Bible; 1560)[4]

Through faith we understand that the worlde was ordeined by y worde of God...

Hebrews 11:3 (KJV; 1611)[5]

Through faith we understand that the worlds were framed by the word of God...

Hebrews 11:3 (Wesley's Notes on the New Testament; 1755)[6]

Through faith we understand that the worlds were framed by the word of God...

The word "universe | αἰών | aiōn" occurs in Hebrews 11:3 in the plural form. That is why the previous examples of old translations of the English Bible translated "universe" as "worlds." In current English Bibles, "universe" is translated as worlds, the universe, the entire universe, or the world. What was the intention of the author of Hebrews when he wrote, "universe | αἰών | aiōn"? The author wanted to focus our attention on the creation story. Gareth Lee Cockerill comments on Hebrews 11:3:

> These words take the hearers back to the first chapter of Genesis. There God created the physical world and arranged its parts in a harmonious whole by merely speaking his word. But the term translated "worlds" also means "ages." It is by the word of God that the "ages" of the world have been ordered and will be brought to their climax (cf. 1:2).[7]

Willilam L. Lane stated, "The formulation in v 3a clearly refers to Gen 1:1 and its sequel (Gen 1:3–2:1), where the creative word of God has performative power in calling forth and ordering the visible universe."[8] David L. Allen said, "The author speaks of the creation of the universe as 'by [means of] the word' (rhēmati, dative of means). This alludes to the seven times in Genesis 1 where God's speech is connected with creation."[9] Scholars agree that the author of Hebrews intended to point us back to the creation story.

Genesis 1 is the official narrative of the creation of the "universe." Today's understanding includes items not found in God's account of creation. Those items include "planets, galaxies, black holes, or moons (including the earth's moon)." The earth's moon, according to the person "molded by modern science,"[10] believes it is a rock circling the earth and reflects the sun's light. According to God's word, the moon is a light, just like the sun, except it is not as bright.

Genesis 1:16

God made two great lights—the greater light to govern the day and the lesser light to govern the night. He also made the stars.

I do not mind when people use the word "universe." It is how we have come to understand the heavenly and earthly realms God created. The heavenly and earthly realms God has created are much different than the pictures we have grown accustomed to seeing. Then again, the images we are shown by modern science do not make sense either. Here is an example of an actual image from NASA, where the earth is suspended over nothing, floating in their "universe" (Fig. 10).

Fig. 10. Blue Marble 2012.

There are two major problems with this image from NASA. The first is that it is not an actual photo, which I will explain in just a moment. The second is the size of the globe. How big is the earth? According to modern science, the circumference of the globe is 24,873.9 miles. To find the circumference of a sphere, we multiply 2 times Pi times radius ($C = 2\pi r$). We are told the earth's radius is 3,958.8 miles.[11] If this number changes, then other numbers will change (e.g., rotational speed, mass, volume, etc.). Here is an image of several globes from NASA's Flickr page (Fig. 11). Notice that the Blue Marbles, the name NASA uses for its images of earth, all have the same circumference size.

Fig. 11. Blue Marbles (1972–2012).

The globe in the lower left (Fig. 11) is the Blue Marble 2012. The following image is the Blue Marble 2012 (Fig. 10), which is highlighted to show the size of the United States and Mexico (Fig. 12).

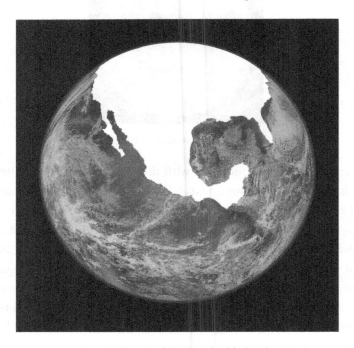

Fig. 12. Blue Marble 2012 (highlighted).

The apparent problem with NASA's globe in space is space. The problem is not outer space but space on their globe. The image they released shows all the Blue Marbles are the same size (Fig. 11). Where will we fit the rest of the continents? Here is NASA's worldview from March 2024 (Fig. 13). How can we fit the rest of the earth on their globe? Fig. 12 is not big enough to fit Canada, Russia, Africa, China, India, Antarctica, Europe, or Australia. Fig. 12 cannot even fit the entire Americas (North and South) on one side of the globe.

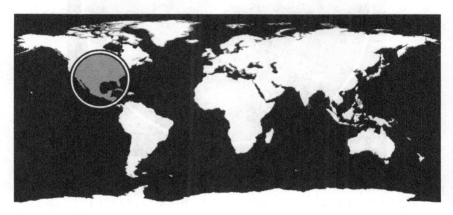

Fig. 13. Worldview (highlighted).

Realizing the problem with their January Blue Marble 2012 (Fig. 10), NASA released another image a few months later, the Black Marble 2012, uploaded on December 5, 2012. NASA wanted us to know why they released their Black Marble 2012 (Fig. 14). NASA said, "The new data was mapped over existing Blue Marble imagery of Earth to provide a realistic view of the planet."[12] Why would NASA produce unrealistic pictures of the earth? When we search online for "images of earth from space," the Blue Marble images, if not the first, will be included in our search results.

The Black Marble 2012 (Fig. 14) is highlighted to show the Americas easier. Thanks to NASA's lead data visualizer and information designer, we are now shown a more realistic image of earth that can fit the rest of the landmasses on their globe.

Fig. 14. Black Marble 2012 (highlighted).

NASA Earth Observatory produced the Black Marble 2012 image (Fig. 14). The man who is credited with creating the Black Marble 2012 is Robert Simmon.[13] We will come back to Simmon in a moment. The problem with their Blue Marble images is that none are genuine.[14] The images of earth that people believe are from space are nothing more than data, photo editing, and imagination. The visualizers for NASA take data from low-orbit satellites and stitch a flat map on a sphere. They even include a specular highlight to imitate the sun reflecting off a sphere.

NASA tells us that the Blue Marble 2012 (Fig. 10) was captured by Suomi NPP. NASA states, "Suomi NPP is NASA's next Earth-observing research satellite. It is the first of a new generation of satellites that will observe many facets of our changing Earth."[15] The Suomi NPP did not capture an image; it recorded data. Then, the visualizers for NASA take the data, photoshop it, add clouds, water, and land, and finally wrap a flat image on a ball. The Blue Marble 2012 (Fig. 10) is a composite of different wavelengths, temperature, and radiation readings. Adobe, the makers of Adobe Photoshop, defines a composite image:

> The use or combination of two or more different images to
> create a new one. Although it sounds simple, the creation
> of a new image using the composite method is a process

that can take hours — it's something that requires constant practice in order to create believable compositions.[16]

NASA informs us about their Blue Marble 2012 composite image (Fig. 10). NASA said, "This composite image uses a number of swaths of the Earth's surface taken on January 4, 2012."[17] The problem is the Suomi NPP satellite does not have a camera to take pictures. The satellite has five instruments on board that record data, but a camera is not one of them. Even if the satellite could record an image, it would be too close to the earth to take a full picture of the globe. According to NASA, NPP (the NPP satellite was renamed 'Suomi NPP' on January 24, 2012),[18] flies just over 500 miles above the surface of the earth. NASA's brochure tells us, "NPP flies 512 miles (824 kilometers) above the surface in a polar orbit, circling the planet about 14 times a day. NPP sends its data once an orbit to the ground station in Svalbard, Norway." [19] NASA does not receive images taken by video or image cameras; instead, it receives raw data from sensors that are converted into an earth image using computer software and creativity. It is no wonder that NASA's visualizers must imagine what the earth looks like.

Robert Simmon created the original Blue Marble 2002. His Blue Marble became famous in 2007 when Apple used his image on their first iPhone. Simmon wrote a blog explaining how he created his earth. Simmon designed the earth from data and his imagination:

> To make the Earth look realistic, or at least how I imagined the Earth would look, I needed to do some work. First of all, the satellite images weren't usable over deep water (it collects data, but there's no automated process to detect clouds and correct for the atmosphere), so I needed to add some color into the water. … Throw in a map of clouds stitched together from 200 satellite scenes, and a global topographic map to add some texture in the landscape, and I was ready to bring everything into my 3D software (Electric Image at the time). Wrapping a rectangular image onto a sphere and rendering out images was probably the simplest and fastest part of the entire process. … Compositing separate images into a convincing whole is (of course) easier said than done.[20]

The images from NASA are not actual photos of the earth. They are composites made of data and artistic license. According to Simmon, the image of the earth is influenced by how the visualizer imagines what the world looks like. Helen-Nicole Kostis is another NASA visualizer. Here is an article that has been removed from NASA's old website. Thanks to the Internet Archive's *Wayback Machine* and *Phys.org*, this article is still available. Kostis is the featured visualizer in the article titled "Behind-the-Scenes View Shows How NASA Science Visualizer Creates Earth from Hundreds of Images." The article states:

> At NASA Goddard Space Flight Center's Scientific Visualization Studio (SVS), Kostis works as part of a team of visualizers who take raw scientific data and translate that data into visual imagery. ... Many Earth views we see in print and video are created by artistically splicing together various images from different satellite instruments, taken at different times and heights, in different wavelengths of light, and at different pixel resolutions. Using image-blending techniques, photo artists create a realistic-looking two-dimensional flat view from these disparate images. They then wrap this image layer, called a 'texture,' onto a sphere in a software program to create a view of Earth. While it makes for stunning imagery, the Earth depicted in these views is fictional -- a hodge-podge of different images created from a great deal of artistic license. ... The final view is both science and art. And it was captured not by a satellite, but by a scientific instrument infinitely more sophisticated -- the human mind.[21]

When people think about the earth, they imagine a blue globe floating in endless space while orbiting the sun at the center of the "solar system." That concept is not what the Bible describes. The Bible clearly describes the layout of the entire "universe": the heavens, the earth, and the underworld. According to the Bible, the heavens consist of three parts: God's abode, the firmament, and the atmosphere. I believe in a "universe" as described by the Bible, but not the "universe" presented by modern science.

The purpose of modern science's "universe" was to destroy our understanding and trust in what the Bible said. The enemy's attempt to undermine God's word is a tactic that our enemy has used from the beginning. The "ancient serpent called the devil" (Revelation 12:9) wants us to mistrust what God said. Our enemy's first words were, "Did God really say?" (Genesis 3:15).

When it comes to modern science, they know what the Bible teaches. Modern science states what the Bible claims about the heavens and the earth more accurately than most Bible scholars. They also know the Bible and modern science's "universe" cannot co-exist. Neil deGrasse Tyson was asked if faith and science can be joined together. Tyson responded, "I don't think they're reconcilable. ... All efforts that have been invested by brilliant people of the past have failed at that exercise."[22] The Bible and modern science's "universe" are entirely incompatible. Secular scholars honestly portray how the authors of the Bible perceived the "universe" of the Bible. Ron Miller, a secular author, summarized what the Bible teaches about the "universe":

> The authors of the Bible took great pains to describe Earth and its place in the universe. They said Earth is flat, square or rectangular in shape, with four corners. Giant pillars support it. Vast waters lie beneath Earth, and a domed sky covers it. Water lies above the dome. Sometimes windows in the dome open, and rain pours through. Earth lies motionless at the center of the universe. Everything else circles Earth. The Bible also explains how God created Earth specifically for humans as a unique place in the universe.[23]

Secular scholars and historians know the Bible teaches a geocentric (earth at rest; sun moves) system instead of Copernicus' heliocentric (sun at rest; earth moves) theory. Secular textbooks recognize that for most of history, people believed what the Bible described: a non-moving earth. *Fundamental Astronomy* wrote:

> Astronomical research has changed man's view of the world from geocentric [earth at center], anthropocentric [people at center] conceptions to the modern view of a vast universe where man and the Earth play an insignificant role.[24]

The Scientific Revolution (1543–1687) changed our perspective of the heavens and earth. The results of modern science's "universe" not only impacted our understanding of the heavenly and earthly realms but also changed our perspective of who we are as people. As Christians, we know that we are "fearfully and wonderfully made" (Psalm 139:14). We recognize that it is God "who gives breath to its people" (Isaiah 42:5). Our lives are essential to God, who created us.

Thanks to modern science, people are now insignificant and meaningless. We now live in a time when a mother or doctor can decide whether a baby, a living soul, should live or not. We live in a time when a man can identify as a woman based on personal preference. We live in a time when everyone is a racist but excludes the people who are racist. These are not cultural issues. These are not current issues. The problems we face today are not the result of a political party controlling Congress. They are the result of the greatest conspiracy of all time. It has been the plan of our enemy, a simple plan. The devil's strategy is to deceive people.

Deception is not about tricking people. Deception is about getting people to believe something that is not true. It is dangerous when someone falls into deception because they do not know they are deceived. When someone falls for deception, even if presented with the truth, they will not believe it. They will purposely reject the truth. Deception is a dangerous game. Jesus warned us, "Watch out that you are not deceived" (Luke 21:8). Deception happens when we doubt God's word. Deception occurs when we believe something that is not true. Falling for deception is easy. Getting out of deception is much more difficult.

The "universe" was designed for a purpose. The purpose for modern science's "universe" was to deceive people. Once modern science became the standard of truth, people would no longer believe what God said. Without the truth (God's word), people would fall for deception and never think twice about it. For example, people outside the church do not know that we are "fearfully and wonderfully made" (Psalm 139:14). The people who believe in the deception of modern science consider their lives nothing more than highly evolved animals that came from the sun. Tyson states the human race is now "emotionally fragile, perennially gullible, hopelessly ignorant masters of an insignificantly small speck in the cosmos."[25]

Christians can also fall into deception when they start to doubt what God said. Deception is not about trickery; it is about our destruction which begins when we reject God's truth. The purpose of the "universe" was to get God's people to doubt God's word. Because of the "universe" and "solar system" created by modern science, we have learned to reject God's truth found in the Bible. God's word tells us that the earth is set on a foundation and is motionless, but we believe it is suspended over nothing and is in constant motion.

Psalm 104:5

He set the earth on its foundations; it can never be moved.

I was deceived. I believed in the entire "universe" and "solar system" that modern science had to offer. Many factors caused me to wake up to the truth. It was not an easy process nor was it pleasant. It does not have to be that way for everyone. There is a simple way to know the truth about the heavenly and earthly realms. There is a simple way to avoid deception regarding the "universe." We can prevent many deceptions if we adhere to Paul's advice. What was Paul's advice? The apostle Paul told us not to listen to the pagan Greek philosophers because they "are always liars" (Titus 1:12).

Chapter 10

Unseen Reality

Satanic worship has been normalized, especially to the younger generation. Anton LaVey, the founder of the church of Satan and author of the satanic bible, said, "Young people now have been exposed to Satanic symbols all their lives."[1] The worship of Satan is real. The followers of Satan are many. The children of Satan are abundant. The practice and worship of Satan is happening now. The problem is that we have not paid attention to the dark spiritual world we cannot see. Satanic worship is very real. The servants of Satan can fool us into believing they are on our team. I am not saying everyone who does not follow Jesus Christ is a Satan follower. Jesus said it.

Matthew 12:30
[Jesus said,] "Whoever is not with me is against me, and whoever does not gather with me scatters."

According to the Bible, there are only two choices regarding our allegiance. It is either God or the devil. Let me be clear: God and the devil are not equal. God is the Most High, and the devil is a created being. The Bible is clear about our choice for our allegiance; it is either God or the devil. Our allegiance demands a choice; there is no middle ground. The Bible tells us there are only two options: part of God's family or the devil's offspring.

Genesis 3:15
[God said,] "And I will put enmity between you and the woman, and between your offspring and hers; he will crush your head, and you will strike his heel."

Today, the children of the devil are alive and plentiful. The Bible warns us that the devil's children can even fool us into believing they are Christians or servants of God. Paul warns us that the devil's "servants also masquerade as servants of righteousness" (2 Corinthians 11:15). Jesus told us about people who could prophesy, cast demons out, and perform miracles. Yet, these people were not going to enter the kingdom of heaven. Jesus told the people who called Him Lord, "Away from me, you evildoers!" (Matthew

7:23). Jesus is sincere and direct. People are evildoers when they do not align with "the will of my Father who is in heaven" (Matthew 7:21).

The war over God's creation and the devil's servants has been raging since the garden of Eden. That war did not stop because Jesus rose from the dead. We do not tend to reflect on the unseen world in our modern times because we are reasonable, enlightened, and educated. The authors of the Bible knew the battle we are in. Paul wrote (after Jesus rose from the dead), "The weapons we fight with are not the weapons of the world. On the contrary, they have divine power to demolish strongholds" (2 Corinthians 10:4). We have been living in this war since birth. Once we decide to join God's family, our enemy seeks to destroy us. Our enemy wants us to fall for his deception because he is "a liar and the father of lies"(John 8:44).

Why did I start to talk about satanic stuff? I brought up the subject of our enemy to keep in context what has been going on from the beginning and up to our current time. Recently, a pastor commented about a state legislative session that attacked the church. The pastor said, "The Church is not getting political, politics has become religious!" That is not true. Politics has always been religious. While the church was trying to stay neutral in politics, our enemy was focused on the destruction of God's people, even if we did not engage in politics. Our enemy will use politics, education, entertainment, or whatever he can utilize for the sole purpose of destroying the people in God's family.

The creation of our "universe" had a purpose. When the Scientific Revolution (1543–1687) began, it was not about scientific discoveries but about starting a revolution. A revolution that would revive an old pagan religion, reject the authority of the Bible, and produce many children who would promote the lies of their father, the devil.

The followers of the devil have always been present in our world. When Jesus walked here on earth, He dealt with the offspring of the enemy (Genesis 3:15). The Bible states, "When evening came, many who were demon-possessed were brought to [Jesus], and he drove out the spirits with a word and healed all the sick" (Matthew 8:16). To be an offspring of the devil, a child of the devil, a person does not have to be demon-possessed. Jesus dealt with Satan's children, who were not under demonic possession.

John 8:42, 44, 47

Jesus said to them, "If God were your Father, you would love me, for I have come here from God. I have not come on my own; God sent me. ⁴⁴ You belong to your father, the devil, and you want to carry out your father's desires. He was a murderer from the beginning, not holding to the truth, for there is no truth in him. When he lies, he speaks his native language, for he is a liar and the father of lies. ⁴⁷ Whoever belongs to God hears what God says. The reason you do not hear is that you do not belong to God."

Who was Jesus speaking to? Jesus was talking to non-demon-possessed religious people who claimed, "The only Father we have is God himself" (John 8:41). Jesus was speaking to people who knew the Law. Jesus was talking to people who observed the Torah. Jesus was speaking to children of the devil. As I said, the Bible is very extreme regarding allegiance. What qualifies a person to be an offspring, a child of the devil? A child of the devil is a person who does not obey and follow God.

Demon possession is not a qualification for being a child of the devil. When Elymas opposed Paul, Paul said, "You are a child of the devil and an enemy of everything that is right!" (Acts 13:10). Why was Elymas a child of the devil? Because Elymas "opposed them and tried to turn the proconsul from the faith" (Acts 13:8). Paul did not try to cast out an evil spirit from Elymas. Paul understood Elymas was a child of the devil because Elymas opposed the gospel message. When Paul did encounter a child of the devil who was demon-possessed, Paul's reaction was different.

Paul and his friends were going to pray, and a woman was there shouting, "These men are servants of the Most High God, who are telling you the way to be saved" (Acts 16:17). Paul, after a few days, realized that this woman was not a child of God but was a child of the devil who was possessed by an evil spirit. Paul turned to her and said, "In the name of Jesus Christ I command you to come out of her!" (Acts 16:18). A person does not need to be possessed by an evil spirit to be a child of the devil. According to the Bible, according to Jesus, an offspring of the devil is someone (possession or not) who wants to carry out the desires of the devil (John 8:44). A child of the devil is someone who listens to the devil's voice.

John 8:38

[Jesus said,] "I am telling you what I have seen in the Father's presence, and you are doing what you have heard from your father."

Our world today has millions of people who are the offspring of the devil. People that are nice and friendly. People that we call relatives, coworkers, and neighbors. People the Bible warns us about because they "masquerade as servants of righteousness" (2 Corinthians 11:15). We live in a world filled with people listening and obeying what their father, the devil, desires. Those people include the founders of our modern "universe" during the Scientific Revolution.

Once the new "universe" was established as truth, we started to transform the Bible's creation story into mankind's created story. Thanks to modern science, we no longer believe that it was God who "laid the foundations of the earth" (Isaiah 48:13). Thanks to modern science, we no longer believe the earth is motionless (Psalm 104:5). Thanks to modern science, we no longer believe in what God said He created in 144 hours (six 24-hour days; Exodus 20:11) but in what mankind created in 144 years (Scientific Revolution [1543–1687]).

John Lennox explains how modern science has helped us rethink what the Bible says. Lennox, a Christian author, admits that we changed God's word because of modern science. Lennox wrote:

> The vast majority of Christians are therefore perfectly happy with a metaphorical interpretation of the foundations and pillars of the earth. They do not regard it as contrived or subservient to science, even though science has helped them refine and adjust their interpretation.[2]

Lennox is correct. Modern science has helped many Christians adjust how they read the Bible. Lennox admits that our new interpretation does not come from studying the Bible. As Lennox wrote, this new "interpretation relies on scientific knowledge."[3]

Establishing a new "solar system" did not happen on its own. The theories that changed how we read the Word of God did not come about by chance. There has been an orchestrated attempt to undermine the authority of God's word. I am not talking about a conspiracy theory. I am not referring to the Illuminati, The Olympians (Committee of 300), Bohemian Grove, Freemasons, or any other secret society trying to rule the world. I am talking about one entity, one being, that is the "father of lies" (John 8:44). An enemy that has enough talent to deceive everyone in this world. The Bible tells us that the devil is the one who "leads the whole world astray" (Revelation 12:9). The Bible says the whole world. The only way to escape the devil's words of deception is to know the truth. The truth of God's word will set us free from the devil's lies. The truth of God's word will keep us from falling for the deception of our enemy.

John 8:32
[Jesus said,] "Then you will know the truth, and the truth will set you free."

Chapter 11

Visible and Invisible

Paul Harvey talked about how the United States could be destroyed by the prince of darkness in his famous speech, "If I were the devil" (1965).[1] Harvey was not a prophet, but his words ring true today. Harvey said:

> So I'd set about however necessary to take over the United States. I'd subvert the churches first. I'd begin with a campaign of whispers. With the wisdom of a serpent, I would whisper to you as I whispered to Eve: "Do as you please."

> To the young, I would whisper that, "The Bible is a myth." I would convince them that man created God instead of the other way around.[2]

Whether we like it or not, we have been influenced by modern science's "universe." If we say "No," then we would believe God "set the earth on its foundations; it can never be moved" (Psalm 104:5). When did the shift happen? When did the war against God's word begin? The visible answer is in 1543, at the start of the Scientific Revolution. The invisible answer started the day when the devil knew that it was predetermined that he would be defeated.

Genesis 3:14–15

So the LORD God said to the serpent, "Because you have done this, "Cursed are you above all livestock and all wild animals! You will crawl on your belly and you will eat dust all the days of your life. [15] And I will put enmity between you and the woman, and between your offspring and hers; he will crush your head, and you will strike his heel."

God promised to the "ancient serpent called the devil" (Revelation 12:9) that one day, a child would come from the line of the woman who would defeat the devil. Now that the mystery of Christ is revealed (resurrection from the cross), we know that it was Jesus who crushed the head of our enemy.

1 John 3:8

The one who does what is sinful is of the devil, because the devil has been sinning from the beginning. The reason the Son of God appeared was to destroy the devil's work.

What about before the cross? What would the devil's options be before Jesus came? The devil's only option was to destroy the one who would destroy him. How could the devil accomplish this? If the devil could stop the "seed" from coming into this world, then God's promise would not come true. If there is no "seed" to destroy him, then God's spoken words are not accurate. If God speaks words that are not accurate or true, then God is a liar. If God is a liar, then God is not God (Numbers 23:19). This was the devil's only option to defeat the one who could not be defeated. Remember that the devil only had one motivation before the cross: to rule like God.

Isaiah 14:13–14

You said in your heart, "I will ascend to the heavens; I will raise my throne above the stars of God; I will sit enthroned on the mount of assembly, on the utmost heights of Mount Zaphon. [14] I will ascend above the tops of the clouds; I will make myself like the Most High."

The devil did not care about Eve. He wanted to rule. The devil did not care about Noah, Abraham, Job, Moses, the chosen people of God, or anyone else who had the breath of life. The devil was solely focused on being like God Most High and ruling over creation. Once Christ defeated his work on the cross, the devil realized he would never rule on high like the Most High. Now that the devil's hopes of ruling were over, our enemy has a new focus. The devil is now highly motivated to "steal and kill and destroy" (John 10:10).

The devil wants us to fall for his deception, hoping we will fall, just like Eve. Paul warned us, "But I am afraid that just as Eve was deceived by the serpent's cunning, your minds may somehow be led astray from your sincere and pure devotion to Christ" (2 Corinthians 11:3). The devil knows that Jesus, the Word, living inside of us is greater. The only way to defeat us is to make us doubt God's word. Where would the devil start in his goal of making us doubt God's word? Our enemy started with the first chapter, Genesis 1. As Paul Harvey said, "To the young, I would whisper that, 'The Bible is a myth.' I would convince them that man created God instead of the other way around."[3]

Chapter 12

In the Beginning, Pythagoras Said

Have you ever wondered where our modern-day understanding of the "universe" came from? If you are normal, the answer is, "Who cares?" We have kids to feed, jobs to work, games to watch, homes to repair, and lawns to cut. When things do not affect us personally, subjects like Kepler's laws of planetary motion do not matter. When talking to Christians, their response can be summed up as: "It doesn't matter. I know God created the heavens and the earth. The creation story has nothing to do with salvation. Stick to Jesus." Besides, why should we learn about the "universe" when we have pictures and videos that show us what it looks like? If we do not investigate what we believe, we are in jeopardy of believing things that are not true. We are in danger of being deceived. I am not an expert in quantum entanglement or stellar parallax. I am not a scientist. What I am is curious.

In 2020, the Lord, knowing I am curious, asked me, "What if Genesis 1 was correct?" The whole day the Lord did not speak again. As I sat there and pondered His question, I decided to accept God's challenge. I knew the creation story (at least I thought I did) so I decided to investigate how the "universe" functioned. I spent day and night looking into everything that modern science taught. I read, watched, and listened, trying to learn everything I could from secular scientists about the "universe." What I discovered were a few themes that were repeated in my research.

The first theme I noticed was modern science's deep hatred of God. A person reading a few journal articles or watching some videos will not notice this. When research is done into the prophets of modern science (e.g., Tyson, Cox, Nye, Carroll, Hawking, Sagan, etc.) the hostility between faith and modern science becomes evident. Modern science hates God. Modern science hates people who believe in God's word.

Richard Dawkins, a biologist and author of *The God Delusion*, explains why modern science hates religion. Modern science is about the removal of God from His creation. Modern science is hostile to God and is anti-God. Belief in God's word is destructive to their religion of science (scientism), which is why modern science must destroy God's word. Dawkins said:

> "Evolution is fundamentally hostile to religion. … I believe
> a true understanding of Darwinism is deeply corrosive to

religious faith. Now it may sound as though I'm about to preach atheism and I want to reassure you that that's not what I'm going to do. … Instead, what I want to urge upon you is militant atheism. … If I was a person who was interested in preserving religious faith, I would be very afraid of the positive power of evolutionary science, and indeed science generally … because it is atheistic."[1]

What is the proper understanding of Darwinism? The actual point of evolution is mankind's rejection of God's word. Dawkins is like Giordano Bruno (1548–1600). Bruno was too honest about the nature of Copernicus' heliocentric (earth moves) theory, which cost him his life. Dawkins said that science, in general, is purely atheistic at its core.

Modern science (religious belief in theories from the Scientific Revolution) opposes the truth found in the Bible. Modern science is opposed to Jesus, the one who is "the truth" (John 14:6). Because we hold to the Bible, the Word (John 1:1), modern science hates us.

John 15:19

[Jesus said,] "If you belonged to the world, it would love you as its own. As it is, you do not belong to the world, but I have chosen you out of the world. That is why the world hates you."

The second theme in modern science is the worship of the sun. This worship is central to modern science's heliocentric (Helios: sun god; centric: placed at the center) theory. Sun worship will be covered.

The third theme I found was the lack of evidence for their theories about the "universe." For example, why do we believe the earth is a sphere? Let me ask this question differently. When was the earth determined to be a sphere? Modern science tells us the spherical earth was established as a fact five centuries before Jesus was born.

Modern science tells us that the round earth was discovered around 500 BC. What if someone just made up a round earth? What if someone assumed the earth was a sphere because the sphere was the perfect shape? That is precisely what happened.

Over 2,500 years ago, the Greek philosopher and mathematician Pythagoras just made it up. Pythagoras did not give any experimental evidence for his claim. Pythagoras thought the earth should be a sphere because it is the perfect shape of the gods. Janet Henriksen wrote a journal article about how our earth became a sphere:

> Pythagoras (500 bc)—put forward the idea that the earth was round, but not on the basis of observation; rather he, like many ancient philosophers, believed that a sphere was the perfect shape and the gods would have therefore created the Earth in this form.[2]

Pythagoras was famous for the Pythagorean or Pythagoras' theorem ($a^2 + b^2 = c^2$). Pythagoras was also renowned for his belief in transmigration (reincarnation). Pythagoras was a follower of the teachings from Hermes, the god of medicine, astronomy, and magic. The philosophy of Pythagoras and the teachings of Hermes are so closely linked that it is hard to tell them apart. Peter Kingsley wrote:

> On the surface, Pythagoreanism and Hermetism [writings attributed to Hermes] are two quite distinct and different movements: the one formally acknowledging its origin in Pythagoras, the other in Hermes. But, as noted earlier in this chapter, the overlap between them in interests and concerns was at times immense.[3]

Hermes, a false god, shaped modern science's "universe." Pythagoras believed in Hermes, a false god, who we know to be the devil, who promises his followers "all the kingdoms of the world" (Luke 4:5). Alex Long wrote, "According to the fourth-century Academic Heraclides of Pontus, Pythagoras claimed to have been offered by the god Hermes anything except immortality."[4] As we will soon find out, the teachings of this ancient pagan god, Hermes, will rise again to take center stage in constructing a new sun system we know as the "solar system."

Pythagoras, a follower of pagan gods, a believer in reincarnation, and a mathematician suggested that the earth was a sphere. Not by evidence or proof but by reason and thought. Since the Greeks believed the sphere was the perfect shape, the gods who created the earth would choose a sphere. Michael M. Woolfson was a physicist and scientist who researched the origins of "planets" and stars. Woolfson "was elected a fellow of the Royal Society in 1984, and received the Royal Society Hughes Medal in 1986."[5] Woolfson will inform us on how Pythagoras will transform the shape of the earth into a globe. Woolfson wrote:

> There were early suggestions that the Earth and the Sun were flat but Pythagoras (572–492 BC) suggested that all bodies were spheres, mainly for the reason that the sphere was regarded by the Greeks as the "perfect" shape.[6]

At the Ohio State University (OSU), Todd A. Thompson's bio reads, "Professor of Astronomy and Physics (Courtesy), University Distinguished Scholar."[7] Thompson goes by, "he/him/his." I point out Thompson's pronouns to remind us of modern science's influence on our world and how seriously they hold to their religious belief in modern science (scientism). The OSU's Office of Institutional Equity provides guidance for pronouns on its *LGBTQ at Ohio State* webpage:

> Pronouns indicate how the outside world should recognize and address us. Being referred to with the wrong pronouns can be detrimental to one's sense of well-being, especially for those who are transgender and gender-nonconforming.[8]

Our secular world religiously believes in modern science as truth. Modern science has taught its followers that they can identify as any gender they choose instead of recognizing the observable truth that we only have two genders: "male and female" (Genesis 5:2).

In 2011, Thompson posted his lecture notes for the class *Astronomy 161: An Introduction to Solar System Astronomy*. In his fourth lecture, he discusses the history of how we could measure the earth. Thompson starts by informing his students about the ancient beliefs about the earth. He said that the most common way people viewed the earth was similar to Eliphaz's observation of the "vaulted heavens" (Job 22:8). People in antiquity believed in a "dome" over our sky. Thompson then leads the students into the age of the Greeks and their love of geometry, arrangement, and balance. Thompson explains how the earth became a sphere. Thompson's lecture notes read, "500 BC: Pythagoras proposed a spherical earth purely on aesthetic grounds."[9]

Our earth took shape because Pythagoras, who sought the knowledge of pagan gods, assumed the earth would be better if it were a sphere. Pythagoras was uninterested in the Hebrew Bible and learning about Israel's God. He was more interested in learning the secret arts of magic from his teacher, Hermes, a god important to the architects of the "universe" during the Scientific Revolution.

Kingsley mentions how people spoke about Pythagoras. It was said that as Pythagoras "went around from town to town the word got about that Pythagoras was coming–not to teach but to heal."[10] The type of healing Pythagoras offered was not about holistic or natural remedies. Kingsley said the "type of healing and medicine involved had a great deal to do with the world of incantation, magic, and ritual."[11]

History has painted a different picture of Pythagoras. Today, he is known as a great philosopher and mathematician. When we push all the praise about Pythagoras aside, what we have is a man who was a pagan. A man who was seeking the hidden and secret arts of magic, rituals, and numbers. A Greek philosopher who believed the earth was a sphere because it was the perfect shape of the gods—a man who did not provide any evidence for his claim. Thompson's lecture notes end with how the church viewed Pythagoras' spherical earth. Thompson wrote that over five hundred years after Pythagoras died, the church resisted the round earth because of "the 'pagan absurdity' of a spherical earth."[12]

Chapter 13

Trouble with the Curve

This book will not cover all the details that created the modern "universe." It will cover the key players. I started my investigation into science because I wanted to know what the "universe" was and how it functioned. From the recent James Webb Space Telescope images to inflation theory, I started from the end and worked my way backward.[1] I was not trying to prove science wrong, but I wanted to know how the "universe" operated.

My research began with simple questions. What is the earth? I found out it was a "planet." What is a "planet"? The definition of a "planet" according to the International Astronomical Union (IAU), must meet three requirements. The IAU requirements are:

1. It must orbit a star (in our cosmic neighborhood, the Sun).

2. It must be big enough to have enough gravity to force it into a spherical shape.

3. It must be big enough that its gravity has cleared away any other objects of a similar size near its orbit around the Sun.[2]

Once I learned about what a "planet" was, I asked more questions. Why do we orbit? What is gravity? How does gravity make every "planet" into a sphere? How do we know the earth is a sphere? Who took the first picture to determine if the earth was a sphere? According to NASA, the first detection of the earth's curvature was documented in 1935. NASA states, "The highest pictures ever taken of the Earth's surface were from the Explorer II balloon, which ascended 13.7 miles in 1935, high enough to discern the curvature of the Earth."[3] According to NASA, at 13.7 miles is when we can detect the earth's curve. Before we get too excited, scientists now tell us that at 13.7 miles, the earth is flat.

Neil deGrasse Tyson was the keynote speaker at the 2014 South by Southwest (SXSW) conference. Tyson explained to the audience why the earth looked flat because Felix Baumgartner had decided to jump higher than 13.7 miles. In 2012, Baumgartner performed the "highest freefall from a distance of 127,852 feet [24.2 miles]"[4] known as the Red Bull Space Dive. When viewing the footage of his jump, people noticed how curved and brown the earth looked (Fig. 15). The earth is said to be 70% covered with water, but Baumgartner's video did not show any ocean water.

Fig. 15. Jumping from Space.

Tyson had to explain why the spherical earth we saw in Baumgartner's video was not an accurate view of the earth. Tyson points out that Baumgartner used a unique lens to create the earth's curvature. Tyson said:

> "They make sure to photograph him standing there with a really wide-angle lens, which curves horizontal lines, so in the photo you see this curvature of Earth's surface ... at that height you don't see the curvature of the Earth. ... That stuff is flat."[5]

Tyson explained to the audience that at 24.2 miles, the earth is flat. In 1935, we were told we could see the earth's curve at 13.7 miles. Today, we are told the earth looks flat since curvature cannot be detectable until 40 miles. *USA Today* reported:

> But experts also note the Earth is so large that people can't directly observe the curvature from Earth's surface. The curvature only becomes visible from a vantage point that is at least 40 miles above the Earth's surface.[6]

When can we see the curvature of the earth? People have told me they have seen the earth's curvature while looking out curved airplane windows. Even if we could fly in the military SR-71 Blackbird, which can reach 80,100 feet (15.2 miles), we are told we cannot see the earth's curve.

It is fascinating to know that people were able to determine the shape of the earth all before we could go into outer space to even see for ourselves. It is even more impressive that Pythagoras guessed the earth's shape without any tools or evidence to prove it. Universe Films (today known as Universal Studios) knew the earth was a sphere even before we sent up any satellite to confirm it. Here is their logo from 1914 (Fig. 16).

Fig. 16. *The Boy Mayor*. Universal Films, 1914.

How would we prove the earth is a globe? What would be our answer? What would be our evidence? How could we prove it? We are told the earth's shape has been settled for 2,500 years. How do we know we live on a round earth? In a few chapters, I will explain how modern science claims it has been proven for centuries about the earth's shape. In this chapter, I am interested in "Why do we believe what we believe about the earth?" The most popular way for modern science to prove the earth is round is with the ocean.

Bill Nye's bio page states that he is a "scientist, engineer, comedian, and inventor. He holds a B.S. in Mechanical Engineering from Cornell University."[7] Nye is mainly known for his PBS/Discovery Channel show *Bill Nye the Science Guy*. The description for his episode called "Pseudoscience" reads, "People once thought that the world was flat or nearly flat. It was considered a bit crazy to think of it as a big ball. But it is. You can prove it."[8] Nye will explain how we can prove the earth is round. Nye said:

"As ships sail away, they don't disappear all at once. Now first the bottom will disappear. See the bottom of the ship is gone, now you can see mid-way up, and then the whole thing disappears. Now ships came back, they did not fall off the table. So people realized that the world is curved."[9]

Popular Science, like Nye, explains how to prove the earth is round by observing ships:

Approaching ships do not just "appear" out of the horizon like they should have if the world was flat, but rather seem to emerge from beneath the sea. ... The reason ships appear as if they "emerge from the waves" is because the world is not flat: It's round.[10]

How can we see the curvature with our eyes from the earth's surface while scientists tell us we cannot see the curve 24.2 miles high? According to scientists, the earth's curve is too big to see at 24.2 miles above the earth's surface, but then we are told we can prove the earth's curvature by standing on the earth's surface and looking at ships disappear around 3 miles away. Modern science is okay with adjusting its language to prove its theories. When Felix Baumgartner opened his door at 127,852 feet, the earth had no exaggerated spherical shape. As Tyson said, the horizon looked flat (Fig. 17).

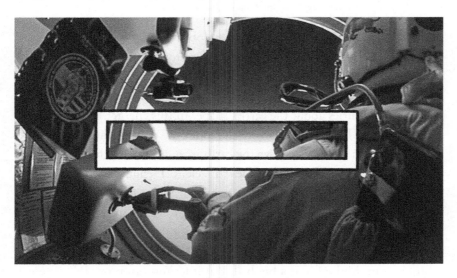

Fig. 17. Flat Horizon.

What do we believe? Is the earth round or flat? The question is a fair question, but it is not the right question. If I were asked what I believe, I would respond that I believe the layout that the Bible gives us: the heavens, the earth, and the underworld (Philippians 2:10; Revelation 5:3). I would respond that I believe in the foundations of the earth (Job 38:4; Hebrews 1:10). I would respond that I believe the earth does not move (Psalm 104:5; 1 Chronicles 16:30). I have reasons for my belief. As Munyon said, "One ought to have something intelligent to say about science and the Bible if asked."[11] I have something to say about what I believe based on observation, science, Scripture, and common sense.

My aim is not to convince someone to believe what I believe. My goal is to present information to help others make an informed choice. I am not a globe earther, flat earther, or social media conspiracy theorist. The earth's shape is less important than knowing and trusting God's word. I will explain more in the chapter "Dealing with Flat Earth." Knowing and trusting God's word includes believing what the Bible says about the heavens and the earth. I care about the truth found in God's word. I believe what my denomination believes, "The Scriptures, both the Old and New Testaments, are verbally inspired of God and are the revelation of God to man, the infallible, author-itative rule of faith and conduct."[12] My belief about God's word is non-ne-gotiable. God's word is infallible. R. C. Sproul defines infallibility as "The truthfulness and reliability of all matters that Scripture addresses."[13] *Concise Oxford English Dictionary* defines infallible as "Incapable of making mistakes or being wrong."[14] C. Stephen Evans defines infallible as "The characteristic of being completely trustworthy, incapable of erring or failing to accom-plish an intended purpose."[15] I believe without a doubt in the infallibility of the Bible and its claims about the heavens and the earth. I believe the Bible, a book translated for thousands of years, is reliable, incapable of error, non-misleading, free of lies, and trustworthy. How do I know this to be true? Where is my proof? What is my evidence? Easy—it is called faith.

Hebrews 11:1
Now faith is confidence in what we hope for and assurance
about what we do not see.

"What do we believe?" That is not the right question. "Why do we believe what we believe?" That is the better question. Why do we believe what we believe about the earth's shape, the layout of the "universe," or the sun's location? The question "Why?" is harder. The question "Why?" deals with our reasoning for believing something. It clarifies what we consider factual and how we arrive at our conclusions. It explains our reasoning for the position we take on a subject. It clarifies what we perceive to be the facts about the matter we think to be true.

What we believe is easy to answer. Let me ask, "Is the earth set on a foundation?" It is easy to answer yes or no. Let me ask another question, "Why do we believe we move around the sun?" People may think this is easy to answer. Our answer would be, "Science said." That answer relies upon trust in the people who told us the earth moves. Another question is, "If God told us the earth is set on a foundation, why do we believe the earth moves?" Answering this question requires us to give a reason for not believing what God said.

Job 38:4

[God said,] "Where were you when I laid the earth's foundation? Tell me, if you understand."

The "Why?" question forces us to consider and reflect on how we arrived at our conclusions. We have no observation to tell us the earth moves. Everyone sees the sun, moon, and stars move. We have no physical sensation that confirms we are moving. People only believe the earth moves because modern science tells them it moves.

Why do I believe the earth does not move? Easy, the Bible says, "The world is firmly established, it cannot be moved" (Psalm 96:10). My reasoning for trusting in what God said is because I know how our "universe" was invented and the theories that formed it. I know their theories do not hold up to scrutiny or everyday observations. I know the reason the "universe" was formed and the god who was behind it. How do I know all this? It was because the Lord asked me one morning, "What if Genesis 1 was correct?" That morning, as I thought about that question, I finally asked myself, "Why?"

Since that morning in January 2020, I have asked myself, "Why do I believe what I believe?" Why do I believe the earth orbits the sun? Why do I believe the sun is traveling 450,000 miles per hour? Why do I believe in gravity? The answers I found only led to more questions.

Today, I believe in the Bible's teachings about the heavenly and earthly realms. Today, the creation story, as plainly stated in Genesis 1, is accurate and factual. Today, the earth is set on a foundation, just like God said, "My own hand laid the foundations of the earth" (Isaiah 48:13). Why do I believe what I believe? The answer is easy: I trust in my "God, who does not lie" (Titus 1:2).

Chapter 14

Scientific Fortunetelling

Predicting the future is what modern science does best. A theory is presented, and then someone comes along and confirms what was predicted. I am not talking about the scientific method, where we test someone's hypothesis. I am talking about modern science, which tells us its theories are proven because someone confirmed them. Modern science is not true science. Modern science is a religious belief in the idea of science, called scientism.

In our Christian belief, there are things we cannot explain. It is called faith.[1] As Christians, we are reasonable and knowledgeable people. There are times when reason and knowledge are set aside, and we trust in God (Proverbs 3:5). We believe in God's supernatural ability to make the impossible happen. We believe in miracles—unexplainable experiences such as healing, provision, or opportunity. It takes faith to believe in miracles; to believe we have "the evidence of things not seen" (Hebrews 11:1).

To modern science, they also have faith in their religious beliefs. They believe in their theories and models that have built their "universe." Modern science wants to avoid testing its claims while telling us they are true—like gravity. According to modern science, gravity is the reason the stars were created. Gravity is why water and people do not fly from earth into space. Gravity is the reason we orbit the sun. The problem is their expanding "universe" defies the laws of gravity. Instead of testing to see if gravity was wrong, they invented things that cannot be seen, like dark matter, which Fritz Zwicky (1933) created to save the theory of gravity.

Zwicky noticed that a cluster of galaxies lacked the mass needed for gravity to work, so he speculated dark matter was the reason (unobservable matter that has gravity). Now, modern science believes in something that cannot be seen to save gravity. CERN will confirm Zwicky's imaginary dark matter.

CERN is a large scientific organization located in Switzerland. The Higgs boson particle was discovered at CERN which is also known as the "god particle." CERN uses "the world's largest and most complex scientific instruments to study the basic constituents of matter – fundamental particles."[2] CERN is also infamous for its demonic ritual opening ceremony in

June 2016. CERN will inform us why we can still believe in gravity even though it does not work in their expanding "universe":

> Galaxies in our universe seem to be achieving an impossible feat. They are rotating with such speed that the gravity generated by their observable matter could not possibly hold them together; they should have torn themselves apart long ago. The same is true of galaxies in clusters, which leads scientists to believe that something we cannot see is at work. They think something we have yet to detect directly is giving these galaxies extra mass, generating the extra gravity they need to stay intact. This strange and unknown matter was called "dark matter" since it is not visible.[3]

The creation of dark matter is more science fiction than reality. Modern science's knowledge of dark matter is based on someone's thoughts, "They think …" If they were serious about science, they would follow the scientific method, but they do not. As mentioned earlier, Kaku, a theoretical physicist and co-founder of string theory, said, "Nobody that I know of in my field uses the so-called 'scientific method.'"[4]

Ó

The world's view has changed since the Old Testament authors walked upon the earth. The prophet Jeremiah wrote, "This is what the LORD says: 'Only if the heavens above can be measured and the foundations of the earth below be searched out'" (Jeremiah 31:37). Newman and Stine comment about the earth's foundation. Newman and Stine wrote, "This reflects the world-view of Jeremiah's day, according to which the earth was a flat, pancake-like mass supported by tall pillars."[5] The prophet Isaiah wrote, "the four quarters of the earth" (Isaiah 11:12). The *Nelson's New Illustrated Bible Dictionary* commented on Isaiah 11:12. They wrote, "To the people of Bible times the earth was flat and square. They knew nothing of a spherical earth which orbited the sun."[6] The *BibleProject* is a popular Christian website that helps people understand the story of the Bible. The *BibleProject* explains how the people in the Bible viewed the earth:

> The earth was a flat, disc-shaped piece of land floating on deep cosmic waters, which is why if you dig deep enough, you eventually hit water. This is "the deep" in Genesis 1:2,

so they believed the land must be suspended, or "floating" above the deep by pillars (you've maybe heard the biblical phrase, "pillars of the earth"). The land, surrounded by waters, is where humans and land animals lived, and the waters around the land was "the sea," where all the sea creatures lived. Ancient Israelites also observed that the sky was a dome shape and that the sun, moon, and stars were embedded into the dome.[7]

Scholars tell us that the Bible's audience thought the earth was flat. For people in ancient times who were non-scientific, it was natural to assume the earth was flat. Then again, engineers in modern times assume the earth is flat and motionless. John S. Preisser submitted his findings on gyroscopes and radar data to NASA (Fig 18). Preisser wrote, "The method is limited, however, to application where a flat, nonrotating earth may be assumed."[8]

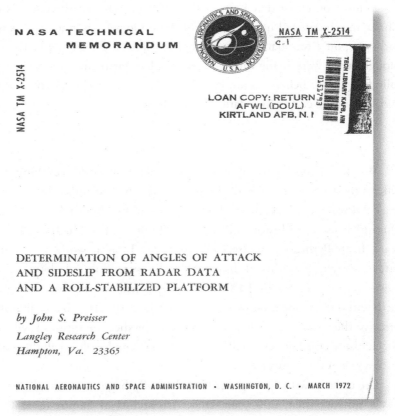

Fig. 18. Determination of angles of attack and sideslip
from radar data and a roll-stabilized platform.

The people in the Bible believed the earth was flat, and according to scholars, people in the Bible thought it rested on a foundation or pillars. *Nelson's New Illustrated Bible Dictionary* wrote about the pillars of the earth:

> [Pillars of the earth:] a phrase found in 1 Samuel 2:8: "For the pillars of the earth are the LORD'S, and He has set the world upon them." A pillar is a support for holding up a building. The idea that the earth is supported by pillars, or upon foundations of some sort, is found often in the Old Testament (Ps. 18:15; Jer. 31:37; Mic. 6:2).[9]

It is not a hidden secret that the authors of the Bible believed in a simple layout: the heavens, the earth, and the underworld. When it came to the earth, they thought it was flat because the earth was on a foundation (pillars). The Bible authors believed the earth had a solid dome barrier that supported the celestial seas above the sun, moon, and stars.

Before you claim that I am a "flat earther," I did not invent this idea. Christian scholars tell us the people of the Bible believed the earth was flat and set upon a foundation. According to scholars, the people in the Bible thought they were living on a flat, motionless earth that was laid upon a solid base. Their belief was not based on science. It was based on what God said, "I laid the earth's foundation" (Job 38:4).

Ó

When we leave the world of the Bible, the Greek world sees things much differently. I will not cover all the people who helped build the "universe" (e.g., Aristotle, Euclid, Hipparchus, etc.). I will highlight the main players. Our quick survey of history will start in 500 BC and end in 1687. In 2,187 years, from Pythagoras to Isaac Newton, the Biblical world of a domed, flat, non-rotating earth will disappear, and a water-covered globe will now move around the sun. In 2,187 years, people will change their view of the earth without anyone leaving the surface of the earth. The change in how we perceive the world was due to the ability to predict the future. I will cover Greek history first and later talk about the pagan gods behind all the magical discoveries of the "universe."

Let us start with Pythagoras (500 BC). Pythagoras assumed the earth was a sphere. Then, 230 years later, Aristarchus of Samos (c. 270 BC) suggests that the earth moved around the sun. A few years later, Eratosthenes of Cyrene (c. 235 BC) would measure the earth and confirm Pythagoras' original guess that the earth was round. Greek philosophers continued to develop their thoughts about the earth. Then, 385 years later, Claudius Ptolemais (150 AD) said the earth did not move and was at the center of the known "universe." The belief in a motionless earth stayed the same for nearly 1,400 years.

According to *the World History Encyclopedia*, Ptolemais (Ptolemy for short) was "an Alexandrian mathematician, astronomer, and geographer. His works survived antiquity and the Middle Ages intact, and his theories, particularly on a geocentric [earth at center] model of the universe."[10] Ptolemy believed that the earth was fixed (unique location) and everything revolved around a non-movable earth. The famous astronomer Carl Sagan wrote:

> Ptolemy believed that the Earth was at the center of the universe; that the Sun, Moon, planets and stars went around the Earth. This is the most natural idea in the world. The Earth seems steady, solid, immobile, while we can see the heavenly bodies rising and setting each day.[11]

Ptolemy's view of a non-moving earth stuck, and people held on to it for centuries. A non-moving earth was easy to believe because every observation we see to this day informs us that we are not moving. Ptolemy was a Greek philosopher. Keep in mind that we left the world of the Bible and entered the Greek world. Greek philosophers did not think like the Biblical world. King David was inspired because God made the stars and set them in place (Psalm 8:4). When Ptolemy looked at the stars, he believed he was standing with Zeus and eating with the gods:

> When I trace at my pleasure the windings to and fro of the heavenly bodies, I no longer touch the earth with my feet: I stand in the presence of Zeus himself and take my fill of ambrosia, food of the gods.
>
> – *Almagest* Book I[12]

Ptolemy, a Greek astronomer, believed he was eating the food (ambrosia) that Zeus ate. Ptolemy did not believe in God Most High but in Zeus, the god of the sky. Ptolemy did believe, like the people in the Bible, that the earth was motionless. Ptolemy's geocentric (motionless earth) model would last for centuries. Finally, a new theory will come on the scene. When Martin Luther (1539) began to hear of a new astronomer (Copernicus) and his idea that the earth moves, Luther said, "The fool will turn the whole science of Astronomy upside down."[13]

In 1543 Nicolaus Copernicus released his theory, using the tools of his eyes and math, and claimed that the earth was moving around the sun. He was not a Greek philosopher. Copernicus was a man seeking Greek philosophy. He did not discover anything new but brought back the teachings of the Greek philosopher, Pythagoras.

Copernicus thought the earth moved on transparent spheres. His theory was not widely accepted. Later, Johannes Kepler (1609) came along to help Copernicus by showing the world how the "planets" moved and removed the giant transparent spheres. Kepler said the earth, and all "planets" orbit the sun in an ellipse.

To make an elliptical orbit, we need two focal points. Kepler's first law requires two focal points to make his orbit idea work. What two focal points make the earth move in an ellipse? One is the sun, and the other is a theoretical point. Theoretical meaning, "related to an explanation that has not been proved."[14] The second focal point (f_2) is just some imaginary point out in space (Fig. 19).

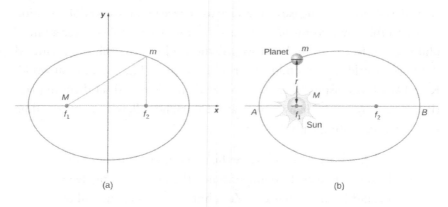

Fig. 19. Kepler's Laws of Planetary Motion.

What focal point in space causes the earth to perform an elliptical orbit around the sun? An imaginary, unproven point, somewhere out in space, makes the earth move in an ellipse. Here is NASA's explanation of Kepler's first law:

Kepler's First Law: each planet's orbit about the Sun is an ellipse. The Sun's center is always located at one focus of the orbital ellipse. The Sun is at one focus. The planet follows the ellipse in its orbit, meaning that the planet to Sun distance is constantly changing as the planet goes around its orbit.[15]

NASA never addresses the second focal point (Fig. 19, f_2). They mention the sun twice as one of the focal points (Fig. 19, f_1). NASA does not mention the second imaginary point in space to make Kepler's first law work. After Kepler had released all three laws of planetary motion, no one knew what force was making them orbit. The biggest question people had about Kepler's laws was, "How do planets obey Kepler's law?" Thankfully, Isaac Newton (1687) could explain the "planet's" obedience to Kepler's laws: the universal law of gravitation. Newton could never define what the force of gravity was, but that did not matter. Once Newton's law of gravitation became accepted, Copernicus' heliocentric (earth moving) theory would become the accepted model of our modern "universe." Our modern understanding, "molded by modern science,"[16] was in the making for over 2,500 years.

Modern science is built upon fortunetelling (predictions). When God speaks in the Bible, He does not make predictions about the natural world. University of California, Berkeley, defines prediction as "A possible outcome of a scientific test based on logically reasoning about a particular scientific idea (i.e., what we would logically expect to observe if a particular idea were true or false)."[17] God does not speak and then requires a test to validate His claims. God does not make predictions. God makes statements. Ted Sundstrom wrote, "A statement, a sentence must be true or false, and it cannot be both."[18]

The Bible makes statements about the earth that directly contradict modern science and their "universe." Statements that God makes are either true or false. God is not asking us to validate His claims. God is asking us to trust His words. The Bible claims a solid dome is over the earth (Genesis 1:6–8). The Bible claims the sun, moon, and stars are located underwater (Genesis 1:17). The Bible claims the earth is on a foundation and does not move (Psalm 104:5). These statements are either true or not. God is not a fortune teller. God does not make predictions but statements that are completely, without fail, accurate and true.

Chapter 15

Making the Earth Round

If we search for when we knew the earth was round, our answers would be about the same. Scholars would inform us, "We have known the earth is round for thousands of years!" In Creation Ministries International's children's book, *Creation Astronomy for Kids*, it reads, "Let's start with our own planet, the earth. For at least 2,500 years, we have known that this is a huge ball."[1] *History* tells us, "Humans have known the earth is round for thousands of years."[2] *Reuters* tells us, "Humans have known that Earth is round for more than 2,000 years, a spokesperson for NASA's John F. Kennedy Space Center said to Reuters in an email."[3] We are told the earth is round, which has been known for thousands of years.

When we look at what they cite as proof about the round earth, the same "proof" can be used to prove the earth is flat. Who was it that proved the earth was a sphere? Remember, Pythagoras said it was a sphere but provided no evidence for his claim. Pythagoras thought a sphere was the perfect shape, and the gods would have used a sphere for the earth. The man responsible for confirming Pythagoras' guess was the Greek astronomer Eratosthenes of Cyrene (276 BC–194 BC). According to world history, Eratosthenes had a simple way of determining the shape and size of the earth with water wells. He knew that on the summer solstice in Syene, the sun was directly overhead at noon, and the bottom of the well was no shadow. On the same day, he knew shadows appeared in Alexandria when the sun was directly overhead. From this observation, Eratosthenes predicted the earth was 25,000 miles in circumference, and the shape of the earth was a sphere. The following diagram illustrates his experiment (Fig. 20).

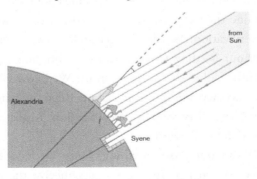

Fig. 20. Eratosthenes' method.

When we hear that people have known for thousands of years that the earth is curved, it comes from Eratosthenes' work. Carl Sagan was an astronomer and promoter of modern science. Sagan was famous for his TV series called *Cosmos*. Sagan wrote:

> But how could it be that at the same instant there was no shadow at Syene and a substantial shadow at Alexandria? The only possible answer, [Eratosthenes] saw, was that the surface of the Earth is curved. Not only that: the greater the curvature, the greater the difference in the shadow lengths. The Sun is so far away that its rays are parallel when they reach the Earth.[4]

Sagan held Eratosthenes in high regard even though some of Eratosthenes' friends did not think so. Sagan states, "One of his envious contemporaries called him 'Beta,' the second letter of the Greek alphabet, because, he said, Eratosthenes was second best in the world in everything."[5] Modern scientists do not always give us the complete picture. While scientists love to credit Eratosthenes for the round earth, they never mention that he thought the sun was smaller than the earth and that the "universe" was tiny. Dennis Rawlins wrote:

> Eratosthenes was pretending that the Sun was 12 times smaller than the Earth ... This discovery widens our basis for appreciating how Eratosthenes climbed to academic eminence in Ptolemaic Alexandria, promoting a cozy universe trillions of times smaller than that already proposed by Aristarchos of Samos.[6]

I understand science may not be a favorite subject for many, but the details on how modern science's "universe" came about are essential. When we do not examine their claims, we are forced to accept what they say as truth without verification. We do this naturally as Christians. We accept God's word without needing to validate its truthfulness because we have "the Spirit of truth" (John 16:13) living in us. We know what God says is true. Modern science depends on people giving them the same level of trust, blindly accepting what they say without objection. Modern science is not God's word; it is mankind's word.

Eratosthenes did not prove anything. Since we have been preconditioned to believe the earth is round, we preconceive the earth is round.

Naturally speaking, a round earth is counterintuitive to our natural senses. James Hannam wrote *The Globe: How the Earth Became Round*. Hannam believes in modern science and a round earth. Hannam makes the point that the round earth is not a natural experience:

> I am not trying to convince you that we really inhabit a disc, only that the planet's true shape is far from evident. Level ground corresponds to our everyday experience and there are rarely reasons to question it. Science messes with our instincts and shows us that the world doesn't work in the way we think it ought to. It seems obvious that the Earth isn't moving ... Once upon a time, everyone assumed the world was flat. Many continued to do so right up until the twentieth century. A few still do.[7]

Hannam states that modern science is why we think counterintuitively about the earth. Our experience and our instincts tell us the earth is not moving and everything is flat. Hannam states that our common sense is ignored because of modern science, and we trust what scientists have told us. Hannam also knows that the globe is a hard sell if we believe what the Bible says about the natural world:

> As the rest of the world drew together into a sphere in the nineteenth century, there were some who looked back to simpler times, when the Bible could be taken to contain a full description of nature. ... Our modern world picture is not obvious and we shouldn't be too hard on those who still won't swallow it. ... As for us, we don't believe the planet is round because we're more clever or rational than the people who came before us; we're just lucky enough to live in a society that takes it for granted.[8]

Hannam makes two valid points. First, people do not trust the Bible. Hannam wrote, "When the Bible could be taken to contain a full description of nature."[9] The effect of modern science has changed our trust in the Bible's statements about the natural world, inside and outside of the church. The second point Hannam makes is that people do not question science. People do not investigate why we believe what we believe about the "universe." We live in a culture that does not seek out the "truth" beyond a few internet searches. These searches are filtered by companies with their best interests, not ours.

Hannam states that society takes a round earth for granted. I cannot entirely agree with Hannam that people take a round earth for granted. Our society merely trusts what modern science tells them. Our culture believes in the spinning globe shown to them all their lives. Since we trust what we have been told, we carry on with our daily lives without even questioning if we are orbiting the sun at 66,622 mph.[10]

Hannam also brings up Eratosthenes in his book. Eratosthenes supposedly proved the curvature of the earth thousands of years ago. Hannam points out two crucial points about Eratosthenes and his experiment:

> Eratosthenes didn't set out to prove that the Earth is a sphere. It was just one assumption that lay behind his calculations. Another was that the Sun is a very long way away. This meant that he could assume that the curvature of the Earth was entirely responsible for the difference in shadows between Alexandria and Syene.[11]

Hannam lists two assumptions that Eratosthenes made when determining his test results. The first assumption was that the earth was a sphere. When Pythagoras determined without scientific proof that the earth was a sphere, other Greek astronomers, including Eratosthenes, accepted it.

The second assumption was the sun's distance from the earth, causing the sun's rays to be parallel to the earth. If we believed the sun was located 93,000,000 miles from the earth, we would imagine its light to be parallel. When modern science wants to claim Eratosthenes was right, it claims the sun's rays are parallel (Fig. 21). When it wants to explain solar eclipses, it claims the sun's light is extended and now causes light to be non-parallel (Fig. 22).

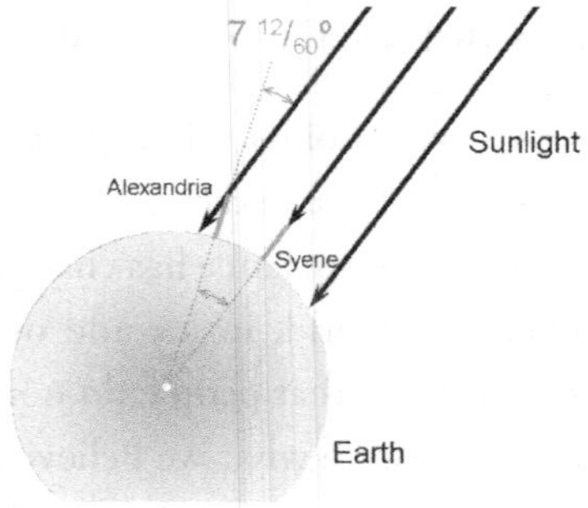

Fig. 21. Shadowless in Syene.

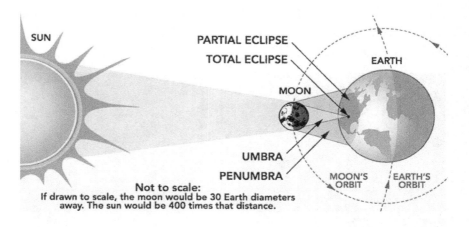

SUN

PARTIAL ECLIPSE

TOTAL ECLIPSE

EARTH

MOON

UMBRA

PENUMBRA

MOON'S ORBIT

EARTH'S ORBIT

Not to scale:
If drawn to scale, the moon would be 30 Earth diameters
away. The sun would be 400 times that distance.

Fig. 22. Solar Eclipse Guide.

The angle of the light is essential. Does the sun (point source) cause parallel light rays (Fig. 21), or does the sun (extended light source) cause objects to produce an umbra and penumbra shadow (Fig. 22)? For Eratosthenes experiment to work, the light must be parallel. Again, Sagan wrote, "The Sun is so far away that its rays are parallel when they reach the Earth."[12] If Sagan was right, then our model for the solar eclipse is wrong (Fig. 22). For this chapter, we will assume the light is parallel to the earth, as described in Eratosthenes' experiment. After this chapter, the light can be a point (parallel) or an extended (non-parallel) source, depending on what modern science tries to prove.

Neil deGrasse Tyson, the Hayden Planetarium director and astrophysicist, has been quoted and will continue to be mentioned throughout this book. Many Christians who are familiar with Tyson dismiss him as an atheist, anti-Bible scientist. Tyson is not the sole scientist who believes what he believes about the "universe." He is just one of many who repeat what modern science teaches. Tyson is a "spokesperson" for modern science. Inside the world of the church, Tyson is an unbeliever. Outside the church, Tyson is a highly respected expert in modern science.

Tyson was dealing with the issue of the round earth on his podcast, *StarTalk*. Within the first ten seconds, Tyson claims we have videos of the earth from space that show a spherical earth, proving the earth is round. For example, NASA released a video of the earth spinning in space from their Galileo spacecraft (1990).[13] It was a video of a time-lapse of the earth rotating in space for over five and a half hours (Fig. 23). Who created this video of the earth's rotation? It was created by an animator named Horace

Mitchell, who works in their visualization department. The same imagery studio that produced the "not-real" images of earth from space called "The Blue Marble" (Fig. 10).

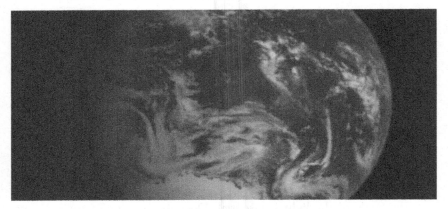

Fig. 23. Earth Rotation from Galileo.

Tyson goes on to explain how moon observations prove the earth is round. Tyson's illustration of the sun does not use parallel light since the earth is casting a larger shadow than the earth's diameter (Fig. 24). In a few minutes, Tyson will make sure to use parallel light when talking about Eratosthenes. According to Tyson, observing a lunar eclipse is evidence that the earth is curved (Fig. 24). Tyson's reasoning is based upon the assumption that the earth orbits the sun. This assumption is the opposite of what the Bible teaches. Tyson's example also assumes that the moon orbits a spherical earth. Again, this assumption is nowhere to be found in the Bible.

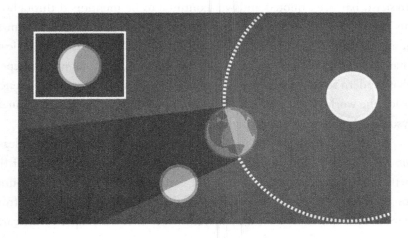

Fig. 24. Lunar Eclipse.

Next, Tyson will use Eratosthenes to show how we know the earth was round thousands of years ago. Tyson uses water wells, like Eratosthenes, to show how light and shadows work on a flat surface (Fig. 25). Tyson said:

> "How could we use this observation to see if the earth's surface is curved? We need another well. Turns out we can't see the bottom of both wells at the same time. What might explain this? Well, there are two possible explanations. First, we could have a flat earth with a Sun that's small and close by so that the light hits the second well at an angle."

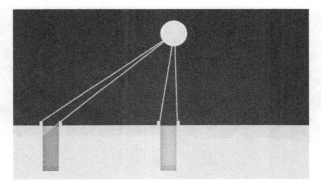

Fig. 25. Flat Plane.

Tyson now explains light and shadows on a curved surface (Fig. 26). Tyson continues:

> "Or, second, we could have a curved earth with a Sun that's big and far away so that all the light comes in parallel but only one well at a time is lit all the way to the bottom."

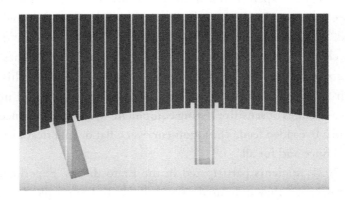

Fig. 26. Curved Surface.

Tyson explains that Eratosthenes' experiment can work on both a flat and curved surface (Fig. 27). Then Tyson, like a magician, claims that the flat earth model is wrong. Tyson said:

> "Turns out with just two wells, there's enough wiggle room for both explanations to fit our observations. Eratosthenes only had two wells, but what if he added a third? With a third well, it doesn't matter where the Sun is. No flat earth model can explain the angles of all three shadows, but the spherical model explains it all."[14]

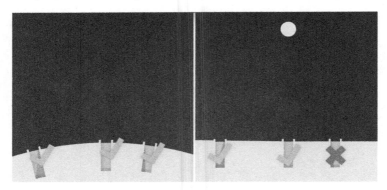

Fig. 27. Three Wells.

If the sun were smaller and closer or larger and farther from the earth, the results would be the same. There is a way to prove the earth is flat or round. Tyson told us all we need is a third well. With three wells, we can confirm the surface of the earth. Tyson reaffirms that only a globe can explain the shadows in all three wells. There is a problem with Tyson's statement. As Tyson said, "Eratosthenes only had two wells."[15]

Eratosthenes' experiment did not prove anything. Assuming the earth is flat, we can make Eratosthenes' experiment work. Assuming the earth is spherical, we can make Eratosthenes' experiment work. The only thing we need to change is the size and location of the sun. If Eratosthenes' experiment proves the earth is round, why do scientists not repeat this simple test with a live video stream for all the world to see? We would not need expensive satellites or sensitive testing equipment. We would only need three sticks and a live video feed. The argument over a flat or spherical earth could be settled once and for all.

In 2021, students participated in the Eratosthenes' Experiment. Just like Eratosthenes, they only used two "wells."[16] Today, people do not need experiments to prove anything because we have pictures and videos. Tyson knows that people believe what they see. Tyson also admits that without video, no one would naturally think the earth was a sphere. In his book, *Death by Black Hole: And Other Cosmic Quandaries*, Tyson wrote, "Without satellite imagery, it's hard to convince yourself that the Earth is anything but flat, even when you look out of an airplane window."[17]

How did Eratosthenes know the sun was far away and the light was parallel? We do not know. The problem with Eratosthenes' history is that none of his work survived. Thompson states, "Eratosthenes' work was lost, except for a description of his method in an obscure source."[18] Thompson states that the "obscure source" was written hundreds of years after Eratosthenes died, "1st or 4th century AD."[19]

Why do we believe the earth is a sphere? Observation is not the answer. Tyson said that if the sun were closer, we would have the same results because of the angle of the light. Do we observe parallel light coming from the sun, supposedly 93,000,000 miles away? No. We observe a sun that produces angled sun rays, just like Tyson's example (Fig. 25). We see a sun that appears closer than what modern science tells us. When the sun shines through the clouds and when we trace the angle of the sun's light back to its source, we see what looks like a sun that is much closer to the surface of the earth (Fig. 28).

Fig. 28. Sun rays.

After Tyson explains Eratosthenes' method, he offers another proof of why the earth is a globe (Fig. 29). Tyson said that his next example should be obvious to any critical thinker. Okay, let us think about what Tyson said:

> "If you send a ship straight to the horizon, eventually it begins to disappear until it's no longer visible beyond your horizon and you should ask yourself, 'What kind of surface would produce that kind of result?'"[20]

Fig. 29. Over the horizon.

What kind of earth would produce a ship disappearing over the horizon? According to Tyson, a globe, unless we are 24.2 miles above the surface, then it is flat. In 2014, Tyson said, "At that height [24.2 miles], you don't see the curvature of the Earth. ... That stuff is flat."[21] Now, in 2018, Tyson wants us to believe that while we are standing on the earth's surface, we can see the earth's curvature because a ship sails beyond our ability to see (approx. 3 miles).[22]

According to Tyson, earth's curvature starts to make a ship disappear in just 3 miles, but Marc Bret Gumá took a photo that could see France from Spain which is the current Guinness World Record of the longest line of sight photograph at 275 miles.[23] According to earth curvature calculators, the mountain Gumá photographed, Pic Gaspard, France (12,740 ft), should have been below the earth's curvature by 3,707 feet (0.7 mile) from his elevation (Pic de Finestrelles, Spain; 9,272 ft). Modern science tells us that the earth's curvature is visible in 3 miles because of ships, but the earth's curvature is not detectable if jumping from a balloon 24.2 miles above the surface.

Why do we believe the earth is a sphere? The honest answer is that we have been told what to think. Observations do not line up with modern science's description of the natural world. From the moment we are born, we are flooded with images and videos of a round earth. When we enter school, we are shown the globe and taught about the "universe." One of the purposes of education and school is to get us to believe in the "universe" modern science has created.

Education is designed to train us on how to think. Benjamin Bloom wrote a book called *All Our Children Learning: A Primer for Parents, Teachers, and Other Educators*. According to the University of Chicago Chronicle, Bloom's book "showed from evidence gathered in the United States and abroad that virtually all children can learn at a high level when appropriate practices are undertaken in the home and school."[24] Bloom believed that all children could learn. How do they learn? Through education and school.

What is the purpose of education and school? According to Bloom, education and school are designed to train us on how to think. Bloom wrote, "The purpose of education and the schools is to change the thoughts, feelings and actions of students."[25] This quote was taken from the chapter titled "The Role of Educational Sciences in Curriculum Development." Modern science does not line up with observations. That is why modern science needs to train us on how to think. Modern science wants to change our thoughts so that we believe what they say and not what we see.

Bloom is not alone on his thoughts about education. Tyson will conclude with two reasons why people are questioning the round earth. His first reason is that we live in the United States where free speech is protected. Tyson does not elaborate on his free speech comment. The second reason Tyson suggests has to do with the failed educational system that has not been able to train people to think the right way. Tyson said:

> "We live in a country with a failed educational system. Our system needs to train you not only what to know but how to think about information and knowledge and evidence. If you don't have that kind of training, you'd run around and believe anything."[26]

Tyson, who "has served on presidential commissions studying the future of the U.S. aerospace industry,"[27] tells us that the purpose of the educational system is to tell people what they need to know. According to Tyson, people need to be trained not only on "what to know" but on "how to think." Free thinkers are not allowed in modern science. We are not allowed to question the movement or the shape of the earth.

Tyson knows modern science must convince us to believe in their "universe." Tyson knows that their claims about the earth's shape are easier to believe with education and pictures. Tyson wrote, "Without satellite imagery, it's hard to convince yourself that the Earth is anything but flat."[28]

If we were allowed to think for ourselves, Tyson worries that we would be at risk of believing untrue thoughts about the earth. Without their pictures and videos, without their system of education, we could be in danger of believing false ideas. According to Tyson, we could end up believing hazardous things like God setting "the earth on its foundations; it can never be moved" (Psalm 104:5).

Chapter 16

Believe What You Don't See

Pythagoras (500 BC) guessed the earth's shape, and Eratosthenes (c. 235 BC) measured it, but the world would have to wait over 2,000 years before we finally figured out the earth moved. The problem was people could not feel movement. Stacy Palen, professor of astronomy at the University of Washington, wrote:

> Since there is no sensation of movement associated with being on the Earth it seemed natural to accept that the Earth was at rest and that every other astronomical body moves relative to it. This was the basis of the geocentric model of the Solar System put forward by Ptolemy (c. 150 AD), another Alexandrian Greek, which was to be dominant for the next 1400 years.[1]

Common sense told people that the earth did not move. It was normal and reasonable to assume the ground did not move because no one felt movement. Andreas Athanasakis, from the University of Athens, wrote:

> Ptolemy laid the foundations of medieval astronomy. His system was sufficiently accurate to remain in use for approximately 1500 years. The first two introductory books contain his fundamental assumptions: that the earth is spherical endorsing the Aristotelian eclipse argument (*De Caelo* 297b30–34); that the heavens are spherical turning round a fixed axis and that the earth is in the center of the heavens, without motion.[2]

Ptolemy, the Greek philosopher who thought he stood with Zeus and ate with the gods, believed the earth was a sphere located at the center of the entire "universe." Ptolemy believed that the earth was fixed and motionless and did not spin on an axis, but the heavens revolved around the earth. There was no reason to argue the earth's motion because people could not sense motion. Pietro Daniel Omodeo, from the Max Planck Institute for the History of Science, Berlin, Germany, wrote why people rejected any theory that stated the earth moved, including Copernicus' heliocentric theory

(1543). The rejection was over the fact that no one can feel the earth move. Omodeo wrote, "The motion of the Earth, in spite of its velocity, is not perceived by our senses."[3]

The real task was to convince people that the earth was moving. It was a legitimate claim before satellites and pictures. Is the argument that we cannot perceive movement a valid argument today? Yes. That is why it took thousands of years to convince people not to believe what their senses told them. People like Tyson and Miller say it is hard to believe in their "universe" without pictures. It took thousands of years for people to believe in a system not supported by any observation or experimental evidence. N. M. Swerdlow, "a distinguished historian of science and the world's foremost expert on Ptolemy and Copernicus,"[4] points out why the lack of motion is a valid argument against the earth moving. Swerdlow states that Copernicus' heliocentric (sun at the center; earth moves) theory is not supported by any observation or detection of the earth moving, which is a powerful argument. According to Swerdlow, the geocentric (earth at the center; sun moves) theory is supported by observation, and the heliocentric theory is not:

> They are very strong arguments since they are supported by every observation that could be made, and they placed a great burden on supporters of the heliocentric theory, such as Copernicus, Kepler, and Galileo Galilei (1564–1642), to argue that, even though supported by observation, the geocentric theory is false, and even though not supported by observation, the heliocentric theory is true.[5]

The late theoretical physicist Stephen Hawking (1942–2018) knew that observation made believing in the Copernican system difficult. Our observations of the "universe" tell us that the earth is at rest. Hawking, who lived during the time of satellites and pictures, tells us that Ptolemy's model still works today because that is what we naturally observe:

> So which is real, the Ptolemaic or Copernican system? Although it is not uncommon for people to say that Copernicus proved Ptolemy wrong, that is not true. As in the case of our normal view versus that of the goldfish, one can use either picture as a model of the universe, for our observations of the heavens can be explained by assuming either the earth or the sun to be at rest.[6]

At this very moment, we do not feel the earth moving 66,622 mph around the sun. When a moving earth was proposed, people resisted it because of our God-given senses. Copernicus was not the first astronomer to assume the earth moved; it was Aristarchus of Samos (270 BC). Omodeo writes, "A proper heliocentric theory had to wait until the third century BC, when Aristarchus of Samos developed and defended it as a viable astronomical thesis."[7] Because of observations, Aristarchus' theory (sun at the center; earth moves) did not hold up. When Ptolemy presented his ideas (150 AD), people naturally understood his theory because it made sense.

Ó

Remember that the history I am presenting, starting with Pythagoras (500 BC), is what happened outside the Bible. What did the New Testament authors believe? We know that Paul did not believe in a heliocentric (earth moving) ideal. Paul did refer to Greek or pagan philosophers (Acts 17:28; 1 Corinthians 15:33; Titus 1:12) in his letters, but he never mentions their "universe" as a valid system to believe in. Paul rejected the teachings of Greek philosophy because they were not from God. Paul warned Titus about the Greek philosophers: "Cretans are always liars" (Titus 1:12). John Walton, a Christian scholar, knew Paul did not believe in Greek astronomy. Walton wrote, "After all, Paul would have believed in a geocentric universe like everyone else around him."[8]

Paul did not believe in Greek astronomers and what they said about the "universe." Paul did not trust pagan philosophers to tell him about the heavenly and earthly realms. Paul had the Old Testament. Paul believed in a non-moving earth because that is what the Old Testament taught. The Scriptures taught the earth was on a foundation and did not move. Paul believed in the Biblical layout of the heavens, the earth, and the underworld, as the Word of God said, not in a "universe" designed by Greek philosophers and their gods.

Philippians 2:9–10

Therefore God exalted him to the highest place and gave him the name that is above every name, [10] that at the name of Jesus every knee should bow, in heaven and on earth and under the earth.

Ó

Outside of the world of the New Testament, the Greek astronomers were creating a new "universe" to believe in. Unfortunately, they would have to wait until the time was right. They would have to wait for the right culture. Then, thousands of years later, the conditions were just right in Europe during the 15th century. The European culture was now beginning to experience the revival of occult practices and esoteric knowledge once hidden. The renewed interest in magic and secret knowledge was making a comeback. During the 1400s, magic and the secret arts became commonplace thanks to a man who would translate ancient Greek philosophy into Latin.

Chapter 17

Preparing the Way

How do we convince people to believe in the opposite of what we see or feel? Math. That is how Nicolaus Copernicus (1543) convinced the world the earth was moving. Copernicus used math as evidence for his theory. If a high school or college student needed to know how Copernicus proved his earth-moving theory, they could turn to McGraw-Hill Education Professional *Schaum's Outlines*. The student would learn that math, not experimental tests or evidence, was the sole reason that caused people to believe the earth was moving. *Schaum's Outline of Astronomy* wrote, "[Copernicus] published *De Revolutionibus Orbium Coelestium* in which he provided mathematical evidence for the heliocentric theory of the Universe."[1] Copernicus did not provide physical or observable evidence to reinforce his theory, but numbers and equations. Math was an acceptable proof for Copernicus, Kepler, and Newton during the Scientific Revolution (1543–1687) because the cultural conditions were perfect for a new creation story to begin. Math was the numbers of the gods.

After Constantinople fell, the capital of the Byzantine Empire, to the Ottoman Empire (1453), many refugees, including Greek scholars, fled to Italy. When they arrived in Italy, there was a new interest in ancient math from the Greeks. The influx of new information from ancient Greek mathematics set the stage for astronomers in the field of mathematics to convince people of their new "universe." Omodeo wrote, "During the Renaissance, astronomy was one of the so-called mixed sciences. Like optics, mechanics, and music, it used mathematical demonstrations to account for physical phenomena."[2] The new way of describing the world was with math. Isaac Newton (1687) could not prove the "magical" force of gravity. Still, he could convince everyone with a "mathematical" force of gravity (Fig. 30).

$$F = G\frac{m_1m_2}{r^2}$$

Fig. 30. Newton's universal law of gravitation.

At the end of the Middle Ages (500–1300s), western Europe was introduced to ancient Greek mathematics as scholars fled the Ottoman Empire takeover. Once Constantinople fell, the Greek scholars fled to the west. That marked the end of the Middle Ages and the beginning of the Renaissance era. Renaissance is a French word that means "rebirth." The new era was about the rebirth of ancient literature, including math, coming from Constantinople. Emily Grosholz, History and Philosophy of Mathematics at Pennsylvania State University explains the importance of mathematics to the Renaissance:

> The historical conditions for this flowering include the fall of Constantinople in 1453, which created a diaspora of scholars from Asia Minor to western Europe, some of whom were learned in the Greek and Arabic mathematical traditions. This stream of scholars (and manuscripts) arrived in Italy about the same time as the invention of the printing press and the Renaissance fascination with classical antiquity.[3]

Not only did a new wave of math hit western Europe, but other fields of study would soon follow suit. During the 15th century, "new" ancient literature and religious teachings would return. The flood of Greek literature from Constantinople would bring about a rebirth in secret ancient wisdom and magic.

Magic and esoteric (knowledge understood only by a few) practices have existed since Moses' times. The Bible tells us, "The Egyptian magicians also did the same things by their secret arts" (Exodus 7:11). Their secret arts were only hidden from us, but their knowledge of spells and rituals was known to the magicians. Throughout history, magic and secret practices have been performed. Today, hexes, rituals, spells, and secret occult sorcery and witchcraft continue. Magic has never disappeared from this world; it is only hidden from us. The German philosopher Georg Wilhelm Friedrich Hegel (1770–1831) said in a lecture on philosophy, "Magic has existed among all peoples and in every period."[4]

In 1453, the fall of Constantinople would have dire consequences when the scholars of the Byzantine Empire fled west to Italy. Ancient Greek literature made its way west, and so did their culture. The humanist movement of the east would soon invade the west. The *Encyclopedia Britannica* defines humanism:

> Any belief, method, or philosophy that has a central emphasis on the human realm. The term is most commonly applied to the cultural movement in Renaissance Europe characterized by a revival of Classical letters, an individualistic and critical spirit, and a shift of emphasis from religious to secular concerns.[5]

A new movement of secularism (removal of religion) and the increase of ancient Greek literature would change the culture of western Europe. It would influence the arts, music, astronomy, architecture, philosophy, and even theologians. The rebirth of ancient wisdom would also bring a renewed interest in the human body. The culture of the Renaissance glorified the human being and the mind. Human beings were enlightened through the study and illumination of "classical letters" (ancient Greek literature from the east). During the Renaissance, the human body was adored and worshipped, as evident in the artwork of Michelangelo's *The Last Judgment* (Fig. 31). Artists would remove the clothing to reveal the now-glorified human body. Michelangelo's painting can be found at the pope's official residence in Vatican City.

Fig. 31. The Last Judgment.

The introduction of classical literature from the ancient past and a new culture of secular humanism transformed western Europe. The west was no longer interested in the God of the Scriptures. They were interested in their new god, the human being. They wanted to explore, minus God, everything this world had to offer. The Renaissance was about the human being and their attempt to become the gods of this world. Robert Wilde wrote:

> The Renaissance was a cultural, scholarly, and socio-political movement which stressed the rediscovery and application of texts and thought from classical antiquity. It brought new discoveries in science; new art forms in writing, painting, and sculpture; and state-funded explorations of distant lands. Much of this was driven by humanism, a philosophy that emphasized the ability for humans to act, rather than simply rely on the will of God.[6]

After the fall of Constantinople (1453), there was a problem. When eastern literature arrived in Italy, the primary language people read was Latin. The Greek scholars from Constantinople were bringing documents written in ancient Greek. Thanks to Marsilio Ficino (1433–1499), the writings of the ancient past and the secret knowledge of magic would rebirth during the Renaissance (1400s–1600s). The *Encyclopedia of the Scientific Revolution from Copernicus to Newton* gives us a timeline of when ancient wisdom and occult practices would return and the god who would teach them:

> 1469: Initial Latin translation of the *Corpus Hermeticum*, an influential series of tracts on theology and the occult, believed to have been written by Hermes Trismegistus, an ancient Egyptian sage.[7]

Chapter 18

Reading Ancient Greek

Marsilio Ficino was instrumental in the return of ancient texts from an old god. While working on other projects, Ficino quickly began to pour all his interests into translating the ancient texts known as Hermetic or Hermetica (writings attributed to Hermes Trismegistus). Denis J.-J. Robichaud, from the University of Notre Dame, wrote, "Ficino turned his attention to translating Hermetic dialogues into Latin, which he published under the title *Pimander*."[1] Ficino not only translated Hermes Trismegistus' works but also published his own theories.

Ficino's personal books included topics on medicine and magic. Robichaud said, "Ficino's early translation of Hermetic texts also signals his long-standing interest in pagan religious sapiential texts, which he understood as parts of traditions of ancient theologies."[2] Ficino's work gave people in the 15th century a way to learn about the esoteric practices taught in Hermetic literature. Ficino's translations would transform the Renaissance and bring a renewed interest in magic. Laura Sumrall, History and Philosophy of Science, University of Sydney, Australia, wrote:

> Marsilio Ficino (1433–1499), a scholar and physician in the employ of the Florentine Medici, produced and translated seminal works for this Renaissance transformation of magic. The famed corpus of Hermes Trismegistus … were introduced to the Latin West through Ficino's translations. In addition, Ficino explicated his own theory of magic in his medical treatise *De vita libri tres* (1489), a text that would receive nearly 30 editions by the mid-seventeenth century.[3]

The culture was changing in the 15th century. People were no longer insufficient humans coming out of the Middle Ages (500–1300s). Human beings were evolving even before Charles Darwin (1859) published his theory of evolution. During the Renaissance, people had a new divine purpose. David A. Lines, Professor of Renaissance Philosophy and Intellectual History at the University of Warwick, Coventry, UK, wrote that "life came to be identified much more strongly with 'the knowledge and contemplation of the divine mind and the divine ideas.'"[4] People now became their own creators and gods. Timothy Kircher, Guilford College, noted that humanity "discovered itself [during the Renaissance] as the maker of itself and its world."[5]

Where did all this divine knowledge and humanistic philosophy come from? The *prisca theologia*. An ancient theology that was once lost but now was found. Ovanes Akopyan, Centre for the Study of the Renaissance, University of Warwick, UK, writes:

> Marsilio Ficino, the first translator of the entire Platonic corpus, the *Corpus Hermeticum*, Plotinus' *Enneads*, and Iamblichus' *De Mysteriis Aegyptiorum* into Latin, was responsible for enlarging the astrological discourse with new sources. He ascribed the previously unknown knowledge to the *prisca theologia* tradition, which stated there existed a single wisdom transmitted over times through various ancient theologians, spreading from Egypt and Persia to Greece and Rome ... [Ficino's] intention was to revive the legacy of *prisca theologia* and supplement it with Christian teaching. Given that most of these texts abound in magical and astrological elements, it opened the door for magical speculation in Ficino's and his contemporaries' thought.[6]

Ficino believed there was one single source of all wisdom called the *prisca theologia* (ancient theology). The wisdom from the *prisca theologia* was superior and was the knowledge of the gods given to mankind. The god responsible for revealing the true theology of the gods was named Hermes Trismegistus, the first of the great teachers. Stanton J. Linden, from Washington State University, wrote:

> Found in Hermes an embodiment of religious and moral authority that placed him at or near the beginning of the so-called *prisca theologia* or ancient theologians: [Hermes Trismegistus] is called the first author of theology.[7]

The god Hermes Trismegistus was believed to be the sage who gave the world its true religion. Hermes Trismegistus was the first theologian to explain all spiritual and ethical standards. The religious practices of Christianity were believed to be an offshoot of Hermes Trismegistus' teachings. Wouter J. Hanegraaff, from the University of Amsterdam, Netherlands, wrote:

> For religious philosophers during the Renaissance, the Platonic-Orientalist framework implied that Christianity was the inheritor of an extremely ancient tradition of universal wisdom that had reached the Christians through Platonic sources, and Christian doctrine could therefore be harmonized with the most profound teachings of pagan philosophy and religion. According to a first perspective, known as *prisca theologia* and represented notably by Marsilio Ficino, the original purity and perfection of the ancient wisdom had been contaminated and lost through a long process of historical degeneration, and a restoration or revival was therefore needed.[8]

Ficino's work on translating ancient theology affected the religious theologians at the time and influenced the upcoming Scientific Revolution (1543–1687). A scientific revolution rooted in a renaissance (rebirth) of an age-old theology (*prisca theologia*). Stephen A. McKnight, University of Florida, wrote:

> In the fifteenth and sixteenth centuries, interest in and respect for the *prisca theologia* increased dramatically, and *prisca theologia*'s effect on some of the most important theologians and philosophers of the period made it a seminal influence on the Renaissance and the Scientific Revolution.[9]

Ficino believed it was his responsibility to teach the world a genuine wisdom hidden from the world. That wisdom was divine and could illuminate the mind to understand the secret truth often hidden from the masses. Ficino would translate the *prisca theologia* (ancient theology) for all to read. Gianluca De Candia, University of Münster, Germany, wrote:

> Ficino, who showed himself well aware of being the heir and protagonist of this wisdom, provides a good example of what philosophy was meant to be in this age: a divine wisdom underlying the entire history of thought and bringing philosophy and religion together (*prisca theologia*). In fact, to Ficino the origin of philosophy is an illumination of the human mind by a real divine revelation that has shone the light of a single truth throughout the world, although along paths that are often hidden and in need of unveiling.[10]

Ficino's influence on his generation and the generations to come was truly remarkable. The readers that would be impacted by Ficino's love of Hermes Trismegistus and magic would influence some of the greatest minds of all time. One of his readers would include an astronomer who would change everything. Robichaud wrote:

> The huge impact of Ficino's Platonic scholarship and philosophical writings, especially on metaphysics, cosmology, psychology, and theology, is difficult to assess in few words. Ficino's famous early modern readers include ... Copernicus.[11]

The cultural shift in the 15th century, thanks to Ficino's translation of ancient literature, did not just impact the people into the secular arts but also affected the church. The influence of magic and the secret arts in the church was necessary to prepare the way for the next major historical shift. This movement changed how people read the Bible, which undermined its authority. The shift happened when a man named Nicolaus Copernicus released his book.

People have falsely claimed that Copernicus rejected his own theory in the forward of his book *On the Heavenly Realms*. Copernicus' book was released on his deathbed (1543). Andreas Osiander, a Lutheran theologian, wrote the forward to Copernicus' book. Many historians believe Osiander wrote the forward without permission after Copernicus' death. Osiander wrote:

> For these hypotheses need not be true nor even probable … So far as hypotheses are concerned, let no one expect anything certain from astronomy, which cannot furnish it, lest he accept as the truth ideas conceived for another purpose, and depart from this study a greater fool than when he entered it.[12]

Osiander was associated with Martin Luther. Osiander's intentions are unknown, but his words indicated that he believed the astronomy Copernicus presented was a guess, which may be incorrect. Osiander felt no one should expect to learn the truth from astronomy. Arthur Koestler wrote:

> The *Book of the Revolutions of the Heavenly Spheres* was and is an all-time worst-seller. … Few people, even among professional historians of science, have read Copernicus' book. … Not even Galileo seems to have read it.[13]

Copernicus' book did not convince the world to change their opinion about the earth moving. The book offered no proof or evidence. Owen Gingerich wrote, "*De revolutionibus* was branded 'the book that nobody read.'"[14] Copernicus' book did not promote scientific discovery; its purpose was to promote the idea that the earth moves. That being said, Osiander wrote a correct statement in his forward that no one should expect to learn anything from Copernicus' theory.

For Copernicus' theory to work, the church needed to lower its stance on God's word about the natural world. The only way Christians would change their commitment to the literal reading of the Bible was to ruin the authority of the Bible. The church needed to forget about the motionless earth and believe in a theory that teaches the earth moves. Some Christians resisted. Others surrendered. Today, people no longer believe God set the earth on a foundation. Today, people believe in an earth that moves. I would say their plan worked.

How did Christians, people of the Word, change their position on the foundations of the earth? As the old saying goes, "If you can't beat them, join them." Many leaders in the Christian faith during the 16th and 17th centuries combined the teachings of Christ with the wisdom of Hermes Trismegistus. It was a time of religious synchronization. Then, in the 18th century, Christian scholars invented their own theories, which changed the history and story of the Bible.

Chapter 19

Thrice Great

Let us take a moment to answer the question, "Who was Hermes Trismegistus?" Hermes Trismegistus was a godlike figure who was believed to be a great teacher or sage. Hermes Trismegistus was not a new god but a new name for the ancient Egyptian god Thoth, sometimes pronounced "thought." It was believed that Hermes Trismegistus held the secrets of the "universe." Keith Hutchison wrote, "The traditional Egyptian god Thoth … became identified with the Greek god Hermes (also identified with the Roman god Mercury)."[1] Trismegistus means "the great, the great, the great" or "thrice great." Hermes Trismegistus taught his ancient wisdom to his followers about the secrets of astronomy and alchemy (magic). Hanegraaff wrote:

> In the Hellenistic culture of late antiquity, the legendary figure of Hermes Trismegistus ("thrice greatest Hermes") emerged from a fusion between the Egyptian god Thoth and the Greek Hermes. As a semidivine teacher of ancient spiritual wisdom and a supreme authority on the secrets of the universe, his name appears in many textual materials that are either attributed to him directly or were believed to be based upon his knowledge.[2]

One of the most influential philosophers of the Renaissance was Giordano Bruno (1548–1600). Bruno believed in Copernicus' "universe," magic, and Hermetic texts (writings attributed to Hermes Trismegistus). Fabrizio Meroi, Department of Literature and Philosophy, University of Trento, Italy, wrote:

> But we must also recall that Bruno was greatly influenced by Hermetic texts, that is, by the corpus of writings of the Hellenistic period on magical-astrological and religious-philosophical subjects, that Renaissance thinkers – and Bruno with them – believed to be the work of Hermes Trismegistus, a legendary figure of wisdom, with almost divine traits, whose authority was considered equal, if not superior, to that of the greatest sages of the ancient world.[3]

Bruno's promotion of Copernicus' heliocentric (sun at rest; earth moves) theory was more about promoting the teachings of Hermes Trismegistus than about science. People like Marsilio Ficino, the translator who introduced the writings of Hermes Trismegistus to the western world, believed that the writings of Hermes Trismegistus were older than Christianity. Bruno rejected the teachings of Christianity and held to Hermes Trismegistus as the true teacher of religion. Bruno also believed that everything, whether it was alive or not, had a living spirit or soul (animism). Ingrid Merkel and Allen G. Debus wrote:

> Ficino had taught that the Hermetic texts had forecast the coming of Christianity, but Bruno simply accepted the pseudo-Egyptian religion of the Hermetics as the true religion. ... Bruno saw signs of a return of this true religion all around him.[4]

The belief in Hermetism or Hermetic texts (writings attributed to Hermes Trismegistus) was valuable to the Renaissance. A new treasure trove of Greek literature that was believed to be from the ancient Egyptian god Thoth was now available to western Europe. The writings of Hermes Trismegistus, the giver of this ancient wisdom, were believed to be older than the writings of Moses from the Bible. Salaman et al. wrote:

> A codex containing fourteen treatises [was] attributed to Hermes Trismegistus, an ancient Egyptian sage. This work's arrival caused a great stir, because Hermes, identified with the Ibis god Thoth, was held to be older than that of Plato and Moses and the underlying inspiration of all philosophy and religion that followed him ... Along with some astrological and alchemical works, also named after Hermes, these tracts became the fundamental writings of the Renaissance, together called Hermeticism, whereas the doctrine of the *Corpus Hermeticum* is called Hermetism.[5]

In 1614, Isaac Casaubon proved that the *Corpus Hermeticum* was younger than Renaissance readers believed. That did not matter. People during the Renaissance (1400s–1600s) and the Scientific Revolution (1543–1687) thought it was ancient wisdom and held to its teachings about the "universe" and occult (hidden) knowledge. From the writings of Hermes Trismegistus, the worship of the sun and a "solar system" (sun-centered) would make a comeback. Pamela O. Long, a visiting professor at the Harvard University Center for Italian Renaissance Studies, wrote:

> Ficino's translations included the dialogues of Plato (ca. 428–348 B.C.E.) and a group of third-century writings known as the *Hermetic Corpus* that were believed to have been written by an Egyptian, Hermes Trismegistus, who lived before Moses ... Hermetic writings pointed to sun worship and a Sun-centered universe.[6]

Bruno recognized the importance of Copernicus' heliocentric theory. However, Bruno did not see heliocentricity as a breakthrough in astronomy. Instead, Bruno saw it as a sign of what it was: sun worship. Hermes Trismegistus' writings were about worshiping a visible god called the sun. Initially published in 1988, Timothy Ferris, emeritus professor at the University of California, Berkeley and "'the best science writer of his generation' by *The Washington Post*,"[7] wrote:

> Copernicus was influenced by Neoplatonic sun worship as well. This was a popular view at the time—even Christ was being modeled by Renaissance painters on busts of Apollo the sun god—and decades later, back in the rainy north, Copernicus remained effusive on the subject of the sun. In *De Revolutionibus* he invokes the authority of none other than Hermes Trismegistus, "the thrice-great Hermes," a fantastical figure in astrology and alchemy who had become the patron saint of the new sun-worshipers: "Trismegistus calls [the sun] a 'visible god.'"[8]

The Renaissance was about coming out of the Dark Ages (the beginning of the Middle Ages) into the rebirth of sun worship. Constantine decriminalized Christianity in Rome when he became emperor (306–337). The result would be God's exaltation and the sun's rejection. Some have said the Dark Ages was the result of Christianity and the killing of sun worship. Ferris, a fellow of the American Association for the Advancement of Science, wrote:

> One could write a plausible intellectual history in which the decline of sun worship, the religion abandoned by the Roman emperor Constantine when he converted to Chris-

tianity, was said to have produced the Dark Ages, while its subsequent resurrection gave rise to the Renaissance.[9]

The Roman emperor Constantine, who claimed to have converted to Christianity, discarded the act of sun worship. Then, 1,200 years later, Copernicus would return sun worship to the center stage again. Copernicus would remove the earth from the center of the "universe" and place the sun god called "sol" (Latin for sun) in the center. Copernicus was honoring the sun god by creating a "sun/sol(ar) system" for people to believe. Bruno knew the ancient practice of sun worship was making a rebirth (Renaissance means "rebirth"). Ingrid Merkel and Allen G. Debus wrote:

> Bruno saw signs of a return of this true religion all around him; an important aspect was Copernicus' heliocentric theory, itself quoting Hermes Trismegistus on the sun as a visible god ... [Bruno] said that Copernicus was just a mathematician who had not understood the true meaning of heliocentrism. Bruno asserted that Copernicus' theory portended a return to magical insight into a living nature, a magical animism.[10]

Bruno saw the opportunity to promote the teaching of Hermes Trismegistus because he knew Copernicus was promoting sun worship with the heliocentric theory. According to Copernicus' *De revolutionibus orbium coelestium* (*On the Revolutions of the Heavenly Spheres*), the sun was a visible god that deserved to be seated in the middle of the "universe." Copernicus believed the sun was a god seated upon a royal throne, ruling over the earth, "planets," and stars. Copernicus was following the teachings of Hermes Trismegistus. In Book 5 of the *Corpus Hermeticum*, it reads:

> The sun is the greatest god of the gods in heaven, for whom all heavenly gods give way as to a king and master. He, who is so great, greater than the earth and the sea, supports the turning stars. He has them above him although they are smaller than himself.[11]

Remember that Copernicus did not provide evidence for his theory that the sun was at the center of the "universe." Copernicus provided math as proof the earth was moving. He also used the teachings of Hermes Trismegistus as a way of justifying the sun being placed in the center of the entire "universe." Copernicus talks about the sun just below his illustration of the new sun system (Fig. 32). Copernicus wrote:

> At rest, however, in the middle of everything is the sun. For in this most beautiful temple, who would place this lamp in another or better position than that from which it can light up the whole thing at the same time? For, the sun is not inappropriately called by some people the lantern of the universe, its mind by others, and its ruler by still others. [Hermes] the Thrice Greatest labels it a visible god … Thus indeed, as though seated on a royal throne, the sun governs the family of planets revolving around it.[12]

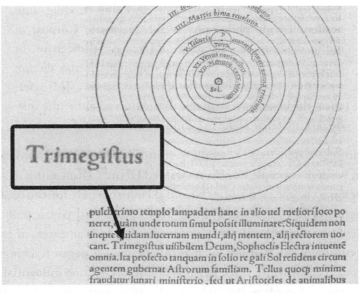

Fig. 32. *De revolutionibus* (Trismegistus highlight).

Copernicus was not interested in the "universe" as much as in restoring the ancient wisdom from the east. Copernicus made the same observations that people made for thousands of years. Observations that convinced people that the earth did not move. The same observations we have today that instinctively tell us the sun moves, and the earth does not. Copernicus did not discover new observations or experimental evidence. Copernicus discovered the ancient teachings of an Egyptian god named Thoth, who now goes by Hermes Trismegistus. Copernicus wanted to restore the wisdom that ancient Greek philosophers like Pythagoras learned. Thomas W. Africa, who was a professor of history at Binghamton University, wrote:

Few would question the existence of the Copernican Revolution for good or ill, but Copernicus was no revolutionary and fancied himself the restorer of ancient wisdom, rather than the discoverer of a new astronomy. Whatever his thesis meant to others, [Copernicus] saw it as the foundation of a Pythagorean Restoration.[13]

The new theory of Copernicus (1543) was acceptable to the Renaissance audience because of the fall of Constantinople (1453). In one hundred years, waves of Greek literature brought a renewed interest in ancient wisdom, including astronomy and magic. Paul Larson, at the Chicago School of Professional Psychology, wrote:

Another stream from classical antiquity feeding into modern occult philosophy is the Hermetic Corpus, or group of writings attributed to Hermes Trismegistus, or thrice-great Hermes; especially important is the dictum from the *Emerald Tablet*, "as above, so below." This references the basic tenet of magic that action on either the spiritual or material plane can influence the other.[14]

During the Renaissance, people were interested in occult knowledge and ancient wisdom—people like Bruno wanted Hermes Trismegistus' teachings on religion to be the standard of worship. Unfortunately for Bruno, he was too aggressive in promoting Hermes Trismegistus and pagan philosophy. Eventually, he would be burned at the stake. Bruno is an excellent example of the culture of the Renaissance that sought ancient pagan teachings from false gods. Larson wrote, "The hermetic tradition became influential in the Renaissance ... Giordano Bruno (1548–1600) went too far and was burned at the stake for his promotion of hermetic ideas."[15]

The "universe" was created from ancient pagan wisdom and magic. The "universe" was built without any experimental evidence or observations during a time when people idolized the human body and mind. The sun-centered "universe" was built on the teachings of Hermes Trismegistus. Despite the culture of the Renaissance, when Copernicus released his new theory, it was not readily accepted. People could not feel the ground beneath their feet move. People also had objections because of the Bible. Nevertheless, Copernicus' theory would continue to be pushed until the world accepted that the earth moved.

Chapter 20

Fusion of Faith

During the Renaissance (1400s–1600s), the church was not immune from the pagan impact on theology and interpretation of Scripture. The influence of magic was a part of the people's culture, in and outside the church. Mixing faith in Jesus and witchcraft was nothing new. In the Bible, when Paul went to Ephesus, some Jews tried to cast out demons in the name of Jesus. The demons did not recognize the authority of the Jews, and the demons ended up beating up the Jews, and "they ran out of the house naked and bleeding" (Acts 19:16).

The Bible tells us that the fear of the Lord came upon the church, and the Christians now deeply respected the name of Jesus. Then, the Bible tells us that the believers were in such fear of the name of Jesus that they "came and openly confessed what they had done" (Acts 19:18). What did the Christians confess? They confessed to mixing their faith in Jesus with occult (hidden) knowledge of witchcraft and magic.

Acts 19:19
A number who had practiced sorcery brought their scrolls together and burned them publicly. When they calculated the value of the scrolls, the total came to fifty thousand drachmas.

The Christians were mixing faith in Jesus and the practice of witchcraft and magic. The word "sorcery | περίεργος | *periergos*" means "witchcraft, sorcery, black magical arts."[1] Followers of Jesus were also followers of demonic-powered sorcery. I. Howard Marshall wrote, "They therefore brought the various magical handbooks and compilations of invocations and formulae to which they were still clinging and made a final break with them by publicly burning them."[2] Mixing faith and pagan practices is nothing new.

During the Renaissance, there was a blending of Christianity and pagan philosophy, which included witchcraft or magic. The desire to reject paganism in the church was not as great as the desire to make Christianity "co-exist" with other practices. The Bible is true, "What has been will be again, what has been done will be done again; there is nothing new under the sun" (Ecclesiastes 1:9). Today, there is still a movement trying to unify all religions of this world (Fig. 33).

Fig. 33. Original Coexistence Sign.

During the Renaissance, a blending of pagan and Christian theology was typical in western Europe. Once the ancient teachings of the east invaded the west, the rise of humanistic philosophy, pagan practices, and magic was now being merged with the church. The *prisca theologia* (ancient theology), an ancient Egyptian religion, was believed to be the uncontaminated religion that would unify all religious practices. Ovanes Akopyan is "an Andrew W Mellon fellow at Villa I Tatti - the Harvard University Center for Italian Renaissance Studies, the most idyllic place to dedicate one's time to the study of Renaissance culture."[3] Akopyan wrote:

> First developed in early patristics in order to demonstrate the compatibility of Christianity with pagan thought, the *prisca theologia* concept was popular among Renaissance thinkers of the late fifteenth and sixteenth centuries, who considerably renewed the meaning and significance of the term. The doctrine claimed that a single, true wisdom was transmitted over time through various ancient theologians, spreading from Egypt and Persia to Greece and Rome. Its roots were often dated back to the figures seen as legendary magicians and theologians of the past, such as Zoroaster, Hermes Trismegistus, Orpheus, and others.[4]

William Hamblin, a professor of history at Brigham Young University, explains the *prisca theologia* and its importance to the Renaissance period. Hamblin speaks about the fusion of Christianity with the teachings of Thoth, the ancient Egyptian god who was now called Hermes Trismegistus:

> In its strictest sense, *Prisca Theologia* is a Latin phrase meaning "the old/ancient theology." It is a technical term probably first used in the early Renaissance by Florentine scholar Marsilio Ficino (1433-1499) which refers to the belief that a lineage of ancient philosophers taught a philosophical wisdom that parallels and complements the biblical Hebrew and Christian revelations. It was funda-

mentally a movement by para-pagan Renaissance philosophers and magicians to attempt to legitimize and Christianize a series of pagan books that they believed contained authentic philosophical and magical wisdom. Although the list of the philosophers and texts of the *Prisca Theologia* varies, it generally includes Zoroaster (Chaldean Oracles), Hermes (Corpus Hermeticum), Orpheus, Pythagoras (Golden Verses) and Plato. The essence of the movement was the syncretistic Christianization of pagan philosophy, magic, astrology, alchemy ...[5]

During the Renaissance, the Bible was being harmonized with the teachings of Hermes Trismegistus. Angels and demons also underwent a change during the Renaissance. Good or bad, angelic beings were the lower gods that interacted in our world. The lower gods were astral, meaning "relating to the stars or outer space."[6] In the Bible, angelic beings are at times poetically compared or alluded to as being stars (Job 38:7; Isaiah 14:12; Revelation 9:1). The Bible is clear that stars are just lights created on Day 4 of creation (Genesis 1:16; Psalm 8:3). According to the Bible, angels and demons are not stars. Manuel De Carli, at the Renaissance Centre for Higher Studies, Université de Tours, France, explains that during the Renaissance, angels and demons are connected to the stars:

> The "worldly gods," Ficino continues, serve the ideas of all things that exist in the divine mind, while the demons fulfill the function of intermediaries between the gods and the inferior things, to which they hand the divine gifts bestowed by the angels and the celestial souls. Therefore, the demons – that are evidently related to astral [from the stars] influences – perform the duty of establishing and strengthening the divine gifts and the original endowments.[7]

The Renaissance's lower gods (angels and demons) influenced theology and the natural world. Mattia Geretto, Ca'Foscari University of Venice, Italy, wrote about the nature of angels and demons during the Renaissance with the aid of Hermeticism (writings from Hermes Trismegistus):

> Angels and demons belong to the Renaissance period in many ways: from philosophy to theology, from medicine

to cosmology, to art and literature, these figures appeared regularly enough to make them an essential element of this age. ... New perspectives emerged with the development of hermetic, magical, and cabalistic thought, thanks also to the immense work of the translation of the classics on Hermeticism and Neoplatonism undertaken by Marsilio Ficino.[8]

From the translations of Ficino to the work of Giovanni Pico della Mirandola, also known as Pico (1463–1494), the fusion of Christianity and paganism would continue to be merged. Pico was a friend and associate of Ficino and promoted the Christian Kabbalah (becoming one with "God" through mystic teachings). Pico believed in blending Christianity and mystical knowledge from Hermes Trismegistus.

Shelia J. Rabin, emeritus professor of history at Saint Peter's University, New Jersey, wrote, "Pico's continuing interest in Jewish mysticism led to the beginnings of Christian Kabbalism, and in 1487 he published a kabbalist interpretation of the Creation story titled *Heptaplus*."[9] The fusion of faith continued throughout the Renaissance. With the arrival of ancient Greek literature from the east, people were motivated by ancient Egyptian religious wisdom. Thanks to translators like Ficino and philosophers like Pico, the idea of mixing Christianity with pagan practices and esoteric knowledge became the norm. Also, the interest in the teachings of Hermes Trismegistus brought about a new passion for magic. Grantley McDonald, University of Oxford, UK, wrote:

> Marsilio Ficino (1433–1499) attempted to create a workable synthesis of Christianity and Neoplatonism. Through his reading of such ancient philosophers as Plotinus, Iamblichus, and pseudo-Hermes Trismegistus, Ficino became interested in magic. ... The thought of Giovanni Pico della Mirandola (1463–1494) was driven by the urge to find common religious themes between Christianity, Judaism, Islam, and the esoteric "Ancient Theology" of Hermes Trismegistus. ... Pico also recommended magic.[10]

Magic and the Scientific Revolution go hand in hand. We cannot separate the two. The magic from the Renaissance was not stage magic by an illusionist. Magic was a demonic, supernatural power. In the Bible, God made a stick turn into a snake, water into blood, and frogs come up from the sea, but so did the sorceress who knew the secret arts (Exodus 7:11, 22; 8:7). Jesus warned us about magicians who would "perform great signs and wonders to deceive, if possible, even the elect" (Matthew 24:24). In the Book of Acts, Simon was one of those magicians who deceived people with his supernatural power.

Acts 8:9–11

Now for some time a man named Simon had practiced sorcery in the city and amazed all the people of Samaria. He boasted that he was someone great, [10] and all the people, both high and low, gave him their attention and exclaimed, "This man is rightly called the Great Power of God." [11] They followed him because he had amazed them for a long time with his sorcery.

According to the Bible, "sorcery | μαγεύω | *mageuō*" is defined as "to practice magic, presumably by invoking supernatural powers—'to practice magic, to employ witchcraft, magic.'"[11] The magic during the Renaissance was not about card tricks or making objects disappear. The magic sought after during the Renaissance was supernatural power that came from the teachings of Hermes Trismegistus.

Isaac Newton considered one of the most influential scientists of all time and the founder of the laws of motion and universal gravitation, was not interested in gravity but in alchemy (magic). Newton was interested in sorcery and the ability to transform base metals into gold with the philosopher's stone. Newton had a personal handwritten copy of the *Emerald Tablet* in his library, which was believed to be from Hermes Trismegistus. The *Emerald Tablet* taught about the magic of alchemy. In 1855, Newton's first biographer David Brewster wrote:

In so far as Newton's inquiries were limited to the transmutation and multiplication of metals, and even to the discovery of the universal tincture, we may find some apology for his recaches; but we cannot understand how a mind of such power; and so nobly occupied with the abstractions of geometry, and the study of the material world, could stoop to be even the copyist of the most contemptible alchemical poetry, and the annotator of a work, the obvious production of a fool and a knave. Such, however, was the taste of the century in which Newton lived.[12]

Newton's fascination with the philosopher's stone (alchemy) would be mocked today. As Brewster wrote, people who sought the magic of alchemy would be considered a fool and a knave (an old word for a dishonest or deceitful person) for believing we could create a stone that would magically turn cheap metal into gold. That is the fantasy stuff Harry Potter is known for. When J. K. Rowling released her first book, she named it *Harry Potter and the Philosopher's Stone*. The same stone Isaac Newton was trying to make through magic. Later, Rowling released her book in the United States, which she called *Harry Potter and the Sorcerer's Stone*, ensuring her readers understood that her books were about magic. The *Encyclopedia Britannica* wrote:

> Philosopher's stone, in Western alchemy, an unknown substance, also called "the tincture" or "the powder," sought by alchemists for its supposed ability to transform base metals into precious ones, especially gold and silver. Alchemists also believed that an elixir of life could be derived from it.[13]

The renewed interest during the Renaissance of alchemy came from the esoteric knowledge from the east after the fall of Constantinople (1453). Magic, witchcraft, or sorcery was a fundamental practice throughout the Renaissance. The secret knowledge of turning metal into gold and elixir of immortality came from the teachings of Hermes Trismegistus. People like Michael Maier, a German physician, normalized the practice of alchemy. The University of Oxford's *Cabinet* wrote:

> Seventeenth-century alchemists were eager to confirm the ancient lineage of alchemy and to show that it had be practiced by great men and women of every nation. In this work [Fig. 34], the German alchemist Michael Maier crafted a lineage through twelve nations, stretching from Hermes Trismegistus himself ...[14]

Fig. 34. Hermes Trismegistus.

There were attempts by scientists like Francis Bacon (1561–1626) who wanted to separate science from magic. During the start of the Scientific Revolution, science was not concerned with experimental evidence. Bacon knew that if science were to be taken seriously, evidence from testing would be needed. Doina-Cristina Rusu, University of Groningen, Netherlands, wrote:

> Throughout the history, Bacon was considered to be the first promoter of experimental philosophy and of the inductive method. Bacon criticized the Aristotelian-Scholastic philosophy, which was a prevalent view of the universities in the beginning of the seventeenth century. In doing so, he emphasized the importance of studying nature through experimentation, and not through mere observation or analysis of ancient philosophical texts.[15]

Bacon was considered to be the father of the scientific method (observe, question, hypothesis, experiment, analysis, and conclusion)—the same scientific method that is taught today in school and that modern-day theoretical physicists do not use. Michio Kaku, a theoretical physicist, said, "Nobody that I know of in my field uses the so-called 'scientific method.' In our field, it's by the seat of your pants. It's leaps of logic. It's guesswork."[16] Despite Bacon's philosophy on magic, he did not dismiss magic completely. Rusu wrote:

> On the one hand, magic was using the natural powers of bodies to bring about practical ends; on the other hand, the only way to discover those powers was through trials and experiments. Both these ideas stay at the basis of the Baconian method.[17]

Magic in the Renaissance was closely connected to witchcraft and demonic supernatural power. Magic was about the secret arts of hidden knowledge. Occult knowledge and the practice of sorcery drove the Renaissance and Scientific Revolution. Bacon knew he had to separate his natural (good) magic from normal (evil) magic. Bacon believed his natural magic was better than normal magic because it was not from demonic sources. Rusu wrote:

> Because of the unpopularity of magic and its connection to witchcraft and demonology ... Bacon was at pains to distinguish his own conception of natural magic from the common use. For him, magic is the supreme knowledge of nature, which is used in transforming natural bodies.[18]

The Bible is clear. All forms of magic are not acceptable. God does not operate with secret knowledge. God's wisdom has been written for all to read. God does not hide supernatural power with hidden words, symbols, or rituals waiting to be discovered. God's power is available to His followers. Actual power, signs, and wonders are done "through the power of the Spirit of God" (Romans 15:19). The followers of God are not allowed to use magic to gain knowledge or power.

Deuteronomy 18:14
The nations you will dispossess listen to those who practice sorcery or divination. But as for you, the LORD your God has not permitted you to do so.

Blending Christianity and pagan knowledge (magic) was common during the Renaissance. For example, John Everard (c. 1584–1641) was a preacher who held a Doctor of Divinity from Cambridge. Everard was also a part of the movement that fused Christianity and occult philosophy. Ariel

Hessayon, co-head of the Department of History, University of London, UK, wrote that Everard "had a deep interest in alchemical, mystical, Hermetic, philosophic, and Rosicrucian texts."[19] Mixing Christianity and paganism was common in western Europe during the Renaissance. Allison Coudert, professor emerita of Religious Studies, University of California, Davis, wrote:

> Everard was also a Neoplatonist, an alchemist, and a Hermeticist. He made the first English translation of the *Corpus Hermeticum* and of the *Asclepius*, which was published after his death in 1657. His sermons are heavily influenced by neoplatonic and Hermetic ideas. In his first sermon, Christ is identified as Nous, or Mind. Everard also translated the *Emerald Table* of Hermes Trismegistus and the alchemical works of Basil Valentine.[20]

The mixing of Christianity and secret pagan knowledge did not start during the 15th century, and the Renaissance humanistic movement did not start because of the ancient Greek literature that flooded the western world. The desire to know secret knowledge started in the garden of Eden. Eve wanted secret knowledge so she could be like God. The serpent, the devil, tempted Eve by suggesting, "You will be like God, knowing good and evil" (Genesis 3:5).

Henry More (1614–1687) is another example of how people mixed faith and paganism. More lived during the late Renaissance and Scientific Revolution. More was not what we would think of as a Bible conservative. He believed the soul existed before the body and came from God as immortal, but they degrade from their immortal status when they join up with the body. Andrea Strazzoni, assistant professor for the Department of Historical Studies, Università di Torino, Italy, documented More's philosophy:

> Souls become individuated from a unique world ... degrade from their original perfection as they are joined to three elements (ethereal, aerial, and terrestrial): therefore, souls cannot have been created by God, as this would imply that He is responsible for their degradation."[21]

More did speak out against some of his contemporaries. More realized that the philosophy of his day relied too much on "ancient wisdom" and its mysticism and magic. Levine writes about More's stance on his cultural moment. Levine writes, "All the best things in modern times seemed to [More] mere revivals of the ancient wisdom: Copernicus had restored the hypothesis of Pythagoras about the motion of the earth."[22] More knew that Copernicus was repeating ancient religion that taught the earth moved.

During the Renaissance, there was a desire to be like God. The way for people to achieve godlike status was to be a god. Hermes Trismegistus taught people that they had great power to become gods. Hermes Trismegistus discovered people's ability to become a god from Nous, the universal mind. Coudert wrote:

> [Trismegistus was told about mankind,] "See what power, what swiftness you possess. It is so that you must conceive of God; all that is, he contains within himself like thoughts, the world, himself, the All. Therefore unless you make yourself equal to God, you cannot understand God. ... Believe that nothing is impossible for you, think yourself immortal and capable of understanding all, all arts, all sciences, the nature of every living being."[23]

One final example of fusing Christianity and occult knowledge is Heinrich Cornelius Agrippa von Nettesheim (1486–1535). Agrippa believed in the Christian Kabbalah. Rossella Pescatori, professor at El Camino College, CA, defines kabbalah during the Renaissance:

> Kabbalah, or Cabala from the Hebrew בָּלָה, means "that which has been received" ... Italian Kabbalah, both Jewish and Christian was much more universalist, more inclined to magic ... Christian readers were eager to read more, and they were looking for Latin translations, and recruited Jewish scholars to teach them Hebrew and to help them to understand the hidden meaning of the holy writings. ... Agrippa (1486 ca–1535) wrote in three books the *De Occulta Philosophia* (*Three books of Occult Philosophy*), where Kabbalah is exposed in book 3. Agrippa's focus is placed in Kabbalah's esoteric powers.[24]

Agrippa, a proclaimed Christian and occultist, desired esoteric knowledge and magic. Agrippa was very open about his desire for magic in his books, *De occulta philosophia* (*Three books of occult philosophy*). That is why scientists like Bacon (1561–1626) wanted to separate science from magic, as the use of magic (witchcraft) was widespread. Strazzoni wrote:

> Agrippa was the main expounder of the occult philosophy, which is the knowledge of the hidden causes of things and is finalized to their manipulation by magic. Magic, in turn, is the highest form and the end of philosophy. According to his *De occulta philosophia*, magic is threefold: natural (concerning sublunar world), celestial (concerning stars and heavenly intelligences), and divine (concerning God and higher angels).[25]

Where did Agrippa's knowledge about magic come from? It came from Hermes Trismegistus, the author of the Hermetic philosophy of the Renaissance. Agrippa's desire was not to live as a Christian according to the Bible but to realign Christianity according to the ancient Egyptian god Thoth, who was known as Hermes Trismegistus during Agrippa's time. Strazzoni wrote:

> Agrippa's overall aim was to purify magic from its necromantic and irrational components: this would enable the restoration of the prelapsarian condition of man (in accordance with the Hermetic ideal of deification) and a Christian reform of culture.[26]

Agrippa is a model for the mindset of the Renaissance and Scientific Revolution. Agrippa was a man who wanted the ancient teachings of a god to be restored. Agrippa wanted to restore Christianity by returning to *prisca theologia* (ancient theology). The author of that ancient work was Hermes Trismegistus, the old Egyptian god known as Thoth. The *Stanford Encyclopedia of Philosophy* reads:

> Agrippa provides a clear demonstration that the eagerness of Renaissance humanists to recover the works of the ancients included not only authors regarded as "respectable" by modern classical scholars but also a vast body of ancient (or pseudo-ancient) texts that claimed to offer wisdom going back to the very origins of human civilization, the so-called "ancient theology" (*prisca theologia*), such as the Hermetic texts from ancient Egypt.[27]

The Renaissance played a significant role in causing Europe to undergo a cultural shift with the introduction of humanism and pagan literature. The Renaissance prepared people to be persuaded, without any evidence, by scientists who provided no proof for their theories. The Renaissance also led to the mixing of Christianity and mysticism. Not all was lost during the Renaissance. The self-centered humanistic philosophy of the Renaissance would play a significant factor in the Protestant Reformation. The Protestant Reformation was about returning to the original teachings of the Bible. For example, Martin Luther spoke out against the earth moving because the earth moving was contrary to what the Bible declared. While there is always a remnant of God's people who hold to the Scriptures, the results of the Renaissance (1400s–1600s) and the Scientific Revolution (1543–1687) did influence theologians and scholars within the church. Those effects can still be felt today in how we interpret the Bible.

The Renaissance and Scientific Revolution did not just happen. It was a conspiracy, a plot to destroy our confidence in God's written word. The master conspirator behind this scheme was not Hermes Trismegistus but the devil. Our enemy, whose sole ambition was to be "like the Most High" (Isaiah 14:14), had a plan from the very beginning. Our enemy is not an idiot but is described by the Bible as "full of wisdom" (Ezekiel 28:12). He knows precisely what he is doing. The devil is not alone in this conspiracy. He has many people helping him who pretend to be "servants of righteousness" (2 Corinthians 11:15). With the help of his servants, the earth that God created would be transformed into a moving "planet" that now bows to the visible god, the sun.

Chapter 21

Greek Philosophy

Life today is different than yesterday. We tend to forget life before children, smartphones, TV remotes, GPS, microwaves, and the internet. We naturally forget about the details of the past. Through the writings of historians, we can remember the days of old. Thanks to Andrew Dickson White, we can remember why we no longer believe what the Bible tells us.

Andrew Dickson White (1832–1918) was a "distinguished scholar, lecturer, and writer. His major work, *A History of the Warfare of Science with Theology in Christendom* [1896], was published in at least six languages during his lifetime."[1] White taught at the University of Michigan and later was the first president of Cornell University. White also served as the president of the American Historical Association. White will explain how the men of the Scientific Revolution (1543–1687) convinced the people to reject the Bible and to believe in the new prophets, the "greatest men" of modern science. White wrote:

> For there came, one after the other, five of the greatest men our race has produced—Copernicus, Kepler, Galileo, Descartes, and Newton—and when their work was done the old theological conception of the universe was gone. 'The spacious firmament on high'—'the crystalline spheres'—the Almighty enthroned upon 'the circle of the heavens,' and with his own hands, or with angels as his agents, keeping sun, moon, and planets in motion for the benefit of the earth, opening and closing the 'windows of heaven,' letting down upon the earth the 'waters above the firmament,' 'setting his bow in the cloud,' hanging out 'signs and wonders,' hurling comets, 'casting forth lightnings' to scare the wicked, and 'shaking the earth' in his wrath: all this had disappeared. These five men had given a new divine revelation to the world; and through the last, Newton, had come a vast new conception, destined to be fatal to the old theory of creation ... But, more than this, these men gave a new basis for the theory of evolution as distinguished from the theory of creation.[2]

White wrote that Copernicus, Kepler, Galileo, Descartes, and Newton gave the world "a new divine revelation." The divine revelation came from the Scientific Revolution. White knew that since people believed the earth was now moving, God was no longer seated on His throne directly above a motionless earth (Isaiah 40:22; Psalm 104:5). White knew that since people no longer believed in the firmament as recorded in God's word, the heavens did not open because of doors and windows (Revelation 4:1; Genesis 7:11). White, a man of science, knew what the Scientific Revolution was all about. The purpose of the revolution was to destroy the authority of the Bible. White knew that if people believed in modern science (theories from the Scientific Revolution), it would be fatal to the creation story found in the Bible. White was right.

The collapse of the literal reading of God's word did not start during the Scientific Revolution. As mentioned, it began in the garden of Eden when the serpent asked, "Did God really say?" (Genesis 3:1). Throughout history, theologians and scholars have pushed for a non-literal reading of the Bible. The non-literal reading of Scripture is often related to scientific matters (e.g., creation story, flood account, foundations of the earth, etc.). Throughout history, theologians and scholars have suggested not to read or interpret the creation story as literal. Benjamin Wormald, the senior researcher at the Pew Research Center's *Forum on Religion & Public Life*, tells us how Augustine of Hippo viewed the creation story:

> Augustine of Hippo [354–430], a Catholic theologian and philosopher, argues that certain events depicted in the Bible, notably the creation story in the book of Genesis, should not necessarily be interpreted literally.[3]

Less than 300 years from when the last book of the Bible was written, Revelation, "church fathers" told people not to take the creation story as a factual and accurate account of history. On another note, it is also encouraging to know that nearly 1,800 years after Moses walked the earth, people still took the creation story literally, believing what "God said" (Genesis 1:3, 6, 9, 11, 14, 20, 24, 26, 29).

Most Christians read the Bible and take things very literally. We believe a woman had a baby without a husband (Luke 1:31), a man died and was raised to life because someone spoke his name (John 11:43), and a man could float up to heaven (Acts 1:9).

We literally believe Mary was a virgin. We literally believe Lazarus was dead for four days. We literally believe Jesus ascended into heaven. We would classify those things as miracles or supernatural events. We tend to believe in miracles or supernatural events. Was the creation of the heavens and the earth or setting the earth on a foundation a miracle or supernatural event? Yes. The creation story was a miracle because the Miracle Maker spoke the heavens and earth into being. The laying of the earth's foundation was a supernatural event because a supernatural God did it. Why do we choose what miracle or supernatural event to believe in? Subjects dealing with the earth or "universe" are more challenging to accept as factual or accurate because of pictures, videos, education, and the Scientific Revolution.

I have learned over these last few years that subjects like the earth's foundation, the shape of the earth, or the layout of the "solar system" cannot be touched. The moment I speak against the theories from the Scientific Revolution, I am immediately called a fool, flat-earther, conspiracy theorist, or ignorant by Christians and non-Christians. The fact is, I speak against modern science because the "universe" was created by scientists rooted in ancient Greek pagan philosophy, built upon theories that cannot be proven. The information is available to anyone who wants to look.

The reason I started to research secular (non-religious) material is because both Christians and non-Christians share the same sun, moon, and stars. Our observations are the same. Our mornings and evenings are the same. Our seasons are the same. Christianity and modern science may disagree about the origin of the "universe" and life, but we share the same objects in the sky: sun, moon, and stars. When I started looking into the history of our "universe," I discovered that our knowledge of the current "solar system" came from ancient Greek wisdom. The very same ancient Greek wisdom that Bible authors had to deal with.

Ó

The apostle Paul was in the same dilemma we are in today. Paul had to decide what to believe. The options for Paul are the same for him as they are for us. The choice for us today is whether we will believe in the wisdom of the Greeks, the pagan literature that came to the west after the fall of Constantinople (1453), or the wisdom found in Scripture. Paul (c. 5–65 AD) had to decide if he was going to follow the wisdom of the Greek philosophers, men like Pythagoras (c. 500 BC), Plato (c. 390 BC), Aristotle (c. 350 BC), or Eratosthenes (c. 235 BC). For Paul, it was not a hard choice. He chose the wisdom of God found in Scripture over the ancient and current Greek wisdom of his day.

Paul was writing a letter to the people of Corinth, who were very familiar with the philosophy and religion of the Greeks. The *Holman Illustrated Bible Dictionary* says, "Although the restored city of Paul's day was a Roman city, the inhabitants continued to worship Greek gods."[4] Corinth would also have been occupied by Greeks. William M. Ramsey tells us it would have had "a large Greek population."[5] Paul makes it clear to the audience of Corinth that God will "destroy the wisdom of the wise" (1 Corinthians 1:19). Paul will ask his readers who live in a Greek-influenced culture to ponder and think about what wisdom, what teacher, what philosophy will they put their faith in.

1 Corinthians 1:20

Where is the wise person? Where is the teacher of the law?
Where is the philosopher of this age? Has not God made
foolish the wisdom of the world?

Paul is direct with his audience, "The foolishness of God is wiser than human wisdom" (1 Corinthians 1:25). Paul is not interested in the "wisdom of this age" (1 Corinthians 2:6). Paul decided to hold to the Scriptures that contain the wisdom and words of God. Paul knows that believing in the teachings of the ancient Greek philosophers will only lead us astray from God's word. Paul warns the church that they could fall for the deception if they seek ancient Greek philosophy.

1 Corinthians 3:18

Do not deceive yourselves. If any of you think you are wise
by the standards of this age, you should become "fools" so
that you may become wise.

For Paul, the Greek philosophers like Pythagoras and Eratosthenes were not the standard of truth. The wisdom that Paul chose to seek was found in the Scriptures. For Paul, ancient Greek philosophy was not wisdom but words from people whose "wisdom" was designed to lead people astray.

Today, the same choice is presented to us. The pictures, videos, education, and theories from the Scientific Revolution are not based on God's word but on ancient Greek philosophy. The same Greek philosophy that said the earth was a sphere because it was the perfect shape of the gods— Pythagoras (c. 500 BC). The same Greek philosophy that taught that no god hears the people's prayers—Aristotle (c. 350 BC). Otfried Hoffe commented on Aristotle's view of God from the Old Testament. Hoffe wrote, "There is no place for ideas of creation, [or] a personal god ... Nor is Aristotle's god the recipient of prayers or the object of meditation."[6] The same Greek philosophy that said the earth moved around the sun—Aristarchus of Samos (c. 270 BC). The same Greek philosophy that claimed the earth had a curve—Eratosthenes (c. 235 BC). When given a choice, Paul rejected the wisdom of this world and chose to hold to God's wisdom. Paul decided to "declare God's wisdom" (1 Corinthians 2:7).

Paul knew the "Greeks look for wisdom" (1 Corinthians 1:22). Paul also knew that Greek philosophy was not wisdom. Paul's advice to the church of Corinth, living in Greek culture, was to stick to God's wisdom because the Greek's wisdom was foolish, based on deception (craftiness), and void of actual content (futile).

1 Corinthians 3:19–21

For the wisdom of this world is foolishness in God's sight. As it is written: "He catches the wise in their craftiness"; [20] and again, "The Lord knows that the thoughts of the wise are futile." [21] So then, no more boasting about human leaders!

Paul said the Lord knows that the wisdom of this world is futile (1 Corinthians 3:20). The word "futile | μάταιος | *mataios*" means "pertaining to being useless on the basis of being futile and lacking in content—'useless, futile, empty, futility.'"[7] Paul knew the philosophy from pagan wisdom was empty and lacking content. Paul also said that God "catches the wise in their craftiness" (1 Corinthians 3:19). The word "craftiness | πανουργία | *panourgia*" means "trickery involving evil cunning—'craftiness, treachery.'"[8] The Bible tells us that God will expose the lies of deceit that come from the wisdom of this world; the very deceit and trickery that led the first person astray because she did not trust what God said.

2 Corinthians 11:3

But I am afraid that just as Eve was deceived by the serpent's cunning [craftiness], your minds may somehow be led astray from your sincere and pure devotion to Christ.

The church did not take the warning given nearly 2,000 years ago by Paul in his letter to Corinth. We have chosen to believe in ancient Greek wisdom and philosophers over what the Bible teaches. Our faith in God's word has been fused with pagan ideas. We believe God created the heavenly lights, but ancient Greek philosophy is why we do not think a solid dome barrier holds water above the sun, moon, and stars. We believe God created the earth, but ancient Greek philosophy is why we do not think the earth is motionless and fixed. We believe in God's power to sustain the earth, but ancient Greek philosophy is why we do not believe "the foundations of the earth are the LORD's; on them he has set the world" (1 Samuel 2:8).

No one believes they are deceived. That is the power of deception. It causes us to believe things (half-truths, bending of truth, false statements) that are untrue. For example, someone is deceived if they think they can go to heaven by rejecting Christ. The Bible tells us, "Jesus answered, 'I am the way and the truth and the life. No one comes to the Father except through me'" (John 14:6). The reason we know a person is going to hell if they reject Christ is because we know the truth. We know that "Whoever believes in the Son has eternal life, but whoever rejects the Son will not see life, for God's wrath remains on them" (John 3:36). Because we have accepted Jesus Christ as our Lord, the blinders that once covered our eyes have been removed and now we know the truth.

2 Corinthians 4:4

The god of this age has blinded the minds of unbelievers,
so that they cannot see the light of the gospel that displays
the glory of Christ, who is the image of God.

Has ancient Greek wisdom deceived us? How would we know? Deception is powerful and convincing until we discover the truth. Children believe in Santa Claus until they discover the truth. Children believe in the Tooth Fairy until they find out the truth. Children believe in the earth's shape, pictures of the "solar system," and books about dinosaurs until …

Children start to figure out that their home does not have a chimney for Santa to come down. They question how Santa could deliver all the gifts to everyone in one night. Eventually, children learn the Tooth Fairy is not real, especially when a child starts requesting large bills or plastic (parents will help them discover the truth). The deception presented to children about the "universe" does not end. The theories and pictures are constantly shown to us. The deception of the "universe" will continue to last until we "know the truth, and the truth will set you free" (John 8:32).

Chapter 22

The Bible Deceives

Before 2020, I believed in the "universe" and "solar system" as presented by modern science. I believed in the shape of the earth, black holes, and gazillions of stars that filled the cold, empty blackness of space. I thought the earth rotated and orbited the sun. I believed in galaxies, dark matter, and "planets." I also took a bold stance against the false teachings of the big bang and evolution. I trusted God's word regarding the origin of the "universe" and the creation of life; for everything else, I trusted modern science.

After researching the history of modern science and its unproven theories based on ancient Greek wisdom, I chose to be deceived by the Bible. The word "deceive" means "to persuade someone that something false is the truth."[1] People think I am deceived when I mention that I believe the earth is set upon a foundation and the earth is motionless. People think I am being led astray in untruths about the natural world. My deception comes from the plain and natural reading of the Bible.

Was the author of Hebrews deceived because he believed in the foundations of the earth (Hebrews 1:10)? Was King David deceived because he believed the earth never moved (1 Chronicles 16:30)? If a person wants to believe what the Bible teaches about the natural world, are they deceived? Here is a table to compare the difference between modern science and Biblical point of view (Table 2).

Modern Science	The Bible
Mornings happen because of the sun.	First three mornings without a sun (Genesis 1:5, 8, 13).
The sun, moon, and stars are located in open space.	The sun, moon, and stars are in the firmament (Genesis 1:17).
The sun was created before the earth and water.	Earth and water were created before the sun (Genesis 1:1–2).
The moon reflects light.	The moon is a light (Genesis 1:16; Revelation 21:23).
Earth sits in the vacuum of space.	Earth rests underneath a solid dome barrier (Genesis 1:6–7, 9).
Earth is floating in space.	Earth is laid upon a foundation (Job 38:4; Hebrews 1:10).
Earth is rotating on an axis.	Earth is motionless (Psalm 104:5; 1 Chronicles 16:30).

Table 2: Who is Deceived?

What about the historical, cultural, and literary context of the Bible? What about passages that are poetic or figures of speech? We will deal with these issues in the following chapters and discuss how church scholars and theologians came up with ways of changing the literal reading of the Bible into figurative and mythological passages. Bible scholarship has a history, too. New Bible interpretation techniques came about after the Scientific Revolution (1543–1687).

How do we know if we are deceived? How do we know if what we believe is a lie? We must know the truth. Without the truth, deception is inevitable. Paul warns the church to "Put on the full armor of God, so that you can take your stand against the devil's schemes" (Ephesians 6:11). Many people do not think about what the devil's schemes are. The word "schemes | μεθοδεία | *methodeia*" means "crafty scheming with the intent to deceive."[2] Paul tells us the devil wants to deceive the church. The devil intends to cause Christians to believe something that is not true. The only protection is God's armor, which includes "the belt of truth" (Ephesians 6:14).

How do we know if we are deceived? We must know the truth, and according to Jesus, God's "word is truth" (John 17:17). Only truth can be found in God's word because it was inspired by a "God, who does not lie" (Titus 1:2). Things that are not true come from "the father of lies" (John 8:44). Our enemy is the one who schemes to deceive us. Our enemy is the one who wants us to believe in something that is not true. The "solar system" did not come from wise astronomers or ancient Greek philosophers; it came from our enemy, who is "full of wisdom" (Ezekiel 28:12). It came from the devil—our enemy who has been scheming to trick us into believing something that is not true. Our enemy is the one who wants us to disagree with what "God said" (Genesis 1:3, 6, 9, 11, 14, 20, 24, 26, 29).

Our enemy is real, our enemy is on the prowl, and our enemy is defeated. The Bible tells us, "The reason the Son of God appeared was to destroy the devil's work" (1 John 3:8). It was Jesus who would fulfill the very first promise God made to our enemy: "He will crush your head" (Genesis 3:15). After Jesus rose from the dead, the New Testament authors knew that the devil's plot to destroy us was not over. Peter warned us, "Be alert and of sober mind. Your enemy the devil prowls around like a roaring lion looking for someone to devour" (1 Peter 5:8). Peter is not giving this warning to the unbelievers but to the church.

If the devil could steal from us, he would. If the devil could kill us, he would. If the devil could destroy us, he would. Jesus told us our enemy's job is to "steal and kill and destroy" (John 10:10). Yet, we are protected by "the good shepherd" (John 10:11). The devil cannot take our life on his own. Jesus told the disciples, "Satan has asked to sift all of you as wheat" (Luke 22:31). The devil has to ask. While living here on earth, we are not free from trials and tribulations. We will face persecution and hardship. Our Shepherd allows our suffering for a reason, but know that the good Shepherd is with us. The reason for suffering is so that we do not lack anything.

James 1:2–4

Consider it pure joy, my brothers and sisters, whenever you face trials of many kinds, ³ because you know that the testing of your faith produces perseverance. ⁴ Let perseverance finish its work so that you may be mature and complete, not lacking anything.

Even under the protection of our Lord, we are in danger while living here on earth. Jesus knows the danger, especially as the end times draw near. When His disciples asked about the end times, the first thing Jesus said was, "Watch out that no one deceives you" (Matthew 24:4). Deception is the weapon the devil uses against God's protected children. Our enemy does not want us to believe God's word. Our enemy wants us to believe what he speaks.

Chapter 23

The Moon Landing

On January 4, 1983, a band called Eurythmics released an album called *Sweet Dreams (Are Made Of This)*. On the B-side (second side of a vinyl album), the song *Sweet Dreams (Are Made Of This)* was the first track. Eurythmics would later release a music video for their number-one hit. The song's opening lines are:

> Sweet dreams are made of this.
> Who am I to disagree?
> I travel the world and the seven seas.
> Everybody's looking for something.

The Eurythmics music video of *Sweet Dreams (Are Made Of This)* opens with the band's lead singer, Annie Lennox, dressed in a business suit. The scene shows a globe of the earth sitting on a conference table and a video screen playing the launch of the Apollo 11 rocket being sent towards the moon (Fig. 35). I think the Eurythmics correctly displayed NASA's moon landing mission as a dream.

Fig. 35. Sweet Dreams (Are Made Of This).

After a few seconds into the video, Lennox begins to sing. When the opening line, "Sweet dreams are made of this," is sung, the video switches to a view of the earth from space (Fig. 36). Then Lennox, using a magician's wand, points to the globe on the video screen. Could the view of the earth be just a dream or an illusion by a magician? Could it be a deception? Let us talk about the moon landing.

Fig. 36. Sweet Dreams (Are Made Of This).

Many people believe the moon landing was real because they saw a video, learned about it in school, or heard an astronaut speak about it. Was the moon landing real, or was it just a sweet dream? I will list four reasons why the moon landing did not occur. I will not go into depth with the first three. In making brief statements about the Apollo moon landing (the first three reasons), everything can be verified. Talking about the moon landing is important because if we choose to believe it, we must also believe in the systems that took them there.

Before I list my arguments, I understand people's position when they say the Bible should not be used as a science book. With that reasoning, my first two points could be easily dismissed. What is science? Science is about knowledge. The Bible is an excellent source of knowledge. The Bible tells us, "All Scripture is God-breathed and is useful for teaching" (2 Timothy 3:16) us knowledge about the things God created: "the heavens and the earth" (Genesis 1:1). People are correct. The Bible is not a science book, but the Bible does speak about scientific matters. The Bible is also not a history book but speaks about historical events. When the Bible talks about subjects of science or history, we can trust that His word is always "right and true"

(Psalm 33:4). Here are four reasons why the moon landing was just a sweet dream.

I do not believe in the Apollo moon landing because the Bible teaches that (1) the moon is a light (Genesis 1:16; Isaiah 60:19; Matthew 24:29). Light is not an object we could land on. Another reason I do not believe in the moon landing is (2) the location of the moon. According to the Bible, the moon is located in the "firmament | רָקִיעַ | *rāqîa'*," which means:

> Expanse, firmament, i.e., an area of atmospheric space, either relatively close to the ground or in the upper limit of the sky and heavens … note: though to the modern mind the expanse of the sky is a void of empty space, it is perceived as a "solid" space (hence firmament) and is so a kind of base to hold up highly heavenly objects such as water or a throne.[1]

The "firmament | רָקִיעַ | *rāqîa'*," means "plate, firmament (i.e., vault of heaven, understood as a solid dome) Gn 1:6."[2] The "firmament | רָקִיעַ | *rāqîa'*," means "the vault of heaven, or 'firmament,' regarded by Hebrews as solid, and supporting 'waters' above it, Gn 1:6, 7."[3] According to the Bible, the moon is in a solid dome barrier separating God's home and the earth.

Ó

There has been much debate on what the firmament means. Scholars define it using the verb form, meaning "hammer out" or "spread out." For example, *A Handbook on Genesis* defines firmament as:

> As used in Ezek 6:11; 25:6, the related verb in Hebrew means "to stamp with the feet," and in Exo 39:3 it means "to hammer out, beat flat" with reference to hammering or flattening metal into sheets.[4]

Using the verb form of firmament is the reason many scholars believe "expanse" is the best way to translate "firmament | רָקִיעַ | *rāqîa'*." Paul Kissling will also use the verb form to translate firmament:

> The word translated "expanse" (רָקִיעַ, *rāqîa'*) comes from a Hebrew verb meaning "to stamp or spread," sometimes of beating out metal into thin sheets. The word is translated as "firmament" in the KJV because of the Latin Vulgate's

firmamentum implying something firm or solid. But the word only occurs eight times outside of this chapter and always elsewhere in poetic contexts.[5]

When "firmament | רָקִיעַ | *rāqîa*" is translated using the verb form, it allows for the firmament to become the vastness of outer space (expanse). Using the verb form also allows the possibility to state that it is the sky. For example, *Got Questions* tells its readers, "In short, the 'firmament' is a vast expanse, specifically the atmosphere or sky."[6]

God did not give Moses the verb form but the noun, which is not something that is spread out or an expanse. God told Moses the firmament (noun) was a solid dome barrier to hold the celestial waters above the sun, moon, and stars. Changing the meaning of the firmament is an excellent example of how the Bible becomes secondary to modern science's "solar system" and "universe." Scholars must change the meaning of the words of the Bible to fit an earth that is not on a foundation.

Kissling mentioned that outside of Genesis, firmament is always used in a poetic sense. What is the point of stating that it is in a poetic context? Scholars claim passages as poetic to inform their readers that a different meaning is intended. King David said, "The heavens declare the glory of God; and the firmament sheweth his handywork" (Psalm 19:1, KJV). David said the heavens declare God's glory, and the firmament, the solid dome barrier, displays God's creative power. David meant what he wrote. David praised God for creating the firmament on Day 2 (Genesis 1:6–8).

Ezekiel also mentions the firmament (noun). The Bible says, "And above the firmament that was over their heads was the likeness of a throne, as the appearance of a sapphire stone" (Ezekiel 1:26, KJV). Over the heads of the living creatures was the appearance of a sapphire stone. That is the same language used when Moses and the seventy elders ate with God. Underneath God's feet was the sapphire stone as blue as the sky.

Exodus 24:10 (KJV)
And they saw the God of Israel: and there was under his feet as it were a paved work of a sapphire stone, and as it were the body of heaven in his clearness.

Ezekiel's vision fits into Genesis' description of the firmament. Ezekiel said God's throne was high above the solid dome barrier (firmament). Ezekiel said, "high above on the throne was a figure like that of a man" (Ezekiel 1:26). Ezekiel's vision matches what Stephen saw. When Stephen was being stoned, he saw the solid dome barrier open up and saw a figure like that of a man, Jesus, standing next to God. Stephen said, "I see heaven open and the Son of Man standing at the right hand of God" (Acts 7:56). Stephen saw the solid dome barrier open just like John. When Jesus invited John to come up to heaven, John saw the solid dome barrier open. John wrote, "I looked, and there before me was a door standing open in heaven" (Revelation 4:1). An expanse or space does not need windows and doors to open; a solid dome barrier does.

Scholars like to use the verb form of firmament, but the Bible uses the noun, which means a solid dome barrier. The firmament created in Genesis 1 is a solid dome barrier that rests over the earth. Whatever scholars call it (vault, sky, expanse), its function is to hold the waters of heaven above the sun, moon, and stars. Moses did not write his observation of the sky. He wrote what God inspired him to write: the solid dome called the firmament (noun).

Genesis 1:8 (KJV)
And God called the firmament (noun) Heaven. And the evening and the morning were the second day.

Ó

Another reason I do not believe in NASA's moon landing is because of (3) technical difficulties. One technical difficulty would have been the deadly Van Allen radiation belt the astronauts had to travel through. During an interview, Allen Bean, Apollo 12, was asked if he suffered any side effects from the Van Allen belt. Bean responded that he did not even know he went through the Van Allen belt. The most significant technical difficulty is we do not have any technical information. All the telemetry data has been lost or erased. We do not have any original evidence of the moon landing. NASA released a report called *The Apollo 11 Telemetry Data Recordings: A Final Report* (2009). NASA reported:

> Perhaps there are no clear answers. All that can be said with any certainly is that NASA and the Goddard Space Flight Center followed all procedures in storing the Apollo telemetry tapes, the search team has concluded. After reviewing their content and determining that Apollo program managers no longer needed the data, Goddard personnel

shipped the telemetry tapes to WNRC for storage. Over the ensuing years, Goddard recalled them and either reused the one-inch tapes to meet a network shortage in the early 1980s or disposed of them because of the high cost of storing them. At no time did anyone recognize the unique content on roughly 45 tapes containing the actual moonwalk video.[7]

The report released by NASA states that they do not have any original video footage of the moonwalks, which makes it seem like only the moonwalk video is missing. That is not true. NASA is missing voice communications, data from sensors, video, and guidance computer information. NASA used its Unified S-Band System (USB) for the Apollo moon missions. NASA informed us, "the USB system will be the only means of tracking and communicating with the spacecraft."[8] All the data from the Apollo missions went through one stream of data. NASA's *Apollo Lunar Surface Journal* wrote:

> The system employed was known as the "Unified S-Band System" (USB). This system combined tracking and ranging; command, voice and television into a single antenna. S-Band frequencies were minimally attenuated by the Earth's atmosphere and were suitable for both Earth orbit and Lunar use. A USB-equipped antenna could transmit and receive simultaneously. Voice, telemetry and television were all received together.[9]

The technical problem is we have no data from the moon landing. NASA tells us the moon landing was one of the greatest moments in modern science history, but we do not have any recorded information because it was destroyed. Astronaut Don Pettit said it best to explain why we cannot return to the moon. Pettit said, "I'd go to the Moon in a nanosecond. The problem is we don't have the technology to do that anymore. We used to, but we destroyed that technology, and it is a painful process to build it back again."[10] Houston, we have a problem!

Last but certainly not least, I do not believe in the Apollo missions because (4) the moon landing is based upon a heliocentric (earth moving) theory. To believe in the moon landing, we would have to believe the moon is a solid sphere that is tidally locked (a scientific term to explain why the moon's face never changes). We would have to believe in an earth that is orbiting the sun. When Copernicus released his theory, he provided no evidence to prove the earth was moving. To this day, the heliocentric theory presented by Copernicus has never been proven. A journal article called *A General Test of the Copernican Principle* by Chris Clarkson et al. wanted to test Copernicus' model of a moving earth:

> To date, there has been no general way of determining if the Copernican principle—that we live at a typical position in the Universe — is in fact a valid assumption, significantly weakening the foundations of cosmology as a scientific endeavor.[11]

The article recognizes that for nearly five hundred years, there has been no observational proof of Copernicus' assumption that the earth has moved. All observations tell us the earth is fixed and motionless. The journal article's authors wanted to come up with an independent test to prove that Copernicus was right. Clarkson et al. wrote, "We have presented a new, straightforward, test of the Copernican assumption which may play an important role in our understanding of dark energy."[12] How did the authors of the article provide proof that Copernicus was right? They used the Friedmann-Lemaître-Robertson-Walker (FLRW) model and Edwin Hubble's theory on redshift. Clarkson et al. wrote:

> We present a new test for the CP [Copernican principle] which relies on a consistency relation of the homogeneous and isotropic Friedmann-Lemaître-Robertson-Walker (FLRW) models between distances and the Hubble rate, both as a function of redshift.[13]

The problem with Clarkson et al.'s method to test the earth's movement was that they relied upon two models that assume the earth moves. FLRW, developed during the 1920s–1930s, is a model that assumes we live in an expanding (or contracting), homogeneous (uniformly distributed), and isotropic (looks the same in all directions) "universe." Scientists like Einstein did not believe the "universe" was expanding. Clarkson et al. wrote, "Einstein erroneously imposed the [Copernican Principle] in both space and time by demanding a static Universe."[14] According to the FLRW metric, the universe was expanding. One of the authors, Georges Lemaître, believed in an expanding universe and wrote the big bang theory (the source of the earth's movement). Christians may reject the big bang theory, but they accept the results of the big bang: the earth moves.

The other model Clarkson et al. used was from Edwin Hubble's redshift observation. Hubble wrote about his observation and theory in his book, *The Observational Approach to Cosmology* (1937):

> Such a condition would imply that we occupy a unique position in the universe, analogous, in a sense, to the ancient conception of a central earth. The hypothesis cannot be disproved but it is unwelcome and would be accepted only as a last resort in order to save the phenomena ... But the unwelcome supposition of a favoured location must be avoided at all costs ... Such a favoured position, of course, is intolerable; moreover, it represents a discrepancy with the theory, because the theory postulates homogeneity. There-fore, in order to restore homogeneity, and to escape the horror of a unique position, the departures from unifor-mity, which are introduced by the recession factors, must be compensated by the second term representing effects of spatial curvature. There seems to be no other escape.[15]

What did Hubble see when he looked through his telescope? Accord-ing to Hubble, what he saw was unwelcome, intolerable, and horrifying. Hubble saw an earth that was motionless and located at the center (unique position) of the "universe." Hubble stated that modern science did not welcome a geocentric (ancient conception of a central earth) model. Hubble wrote that a motionless earth was not something the scientific community could tolerate or accept. According to Hubble, a motionless earth cannot be proven false. The old ancient model, like the one presented in the Bible, had to be destroyed.

The only way Hubble could save his "phenomena" (things moving away; redshift) was with math. He did not have evidence to prove his theory. What Hubble saw was the opposite of his theory. The only solution for saving the earth's movement was with numbers. Like Copernicus, Hubble relied upon math, "There seems to be no other escape."[16]

The journal article *A General Test of the Copernican Principle* by Clarkson et al. wanted to prove Copernicus right by using two models that believed Copernicus was right. That is circular reasoning. Modern science is trying to prove the earth is moving by starting with the premise that the earth moves. Modern science does not provide evidence. Modern science offers circular reasoning. Copernicus presents his theory. Others who believe Copernicus was right will confirm that Copernicus was right.

Nothing has changed in modern science. For example, NASA believes in the big bang and then launches the James Webb Space Telescope to prove the big bang theory. NASA states:

> Webb is the premier observatory of the next decade, serving thousands of astronomers worldwide. It studies every phase in the history of our Universe, ranging from the first luminous glows after the Big Bang, to the formation of solar systems capable of supporting life on planets like Earth, to the evolution of our own Solar System.[17]

Modern science has no evidence that the big bang is how everything started, yet they confirm it is true. Copernicus moved the sun to the center without evidence; others will confirm it is true. Kepler would confirm Copernicus. Newton would confirm Copernicus. Einstein would confirm Copernicus. Lemaître would confirm Copernicus. Hubble would confirm Copernicus. Hawking would confirm Copernicus. James Webb Space Telescope would confirm it all. All of this "confirmation" is based upon an assumption that has never been proven. According to the Bible, modern science's "universe" is all a lie, being confirmed by more lies.

Psalm 104:5

He set the earth on its foundations; it can never be moved.

If we are to believe that NASA landed on the moon, we would have to believe in modern science's "universe." We must accept the earth is moving around the sun-centered "solar system." When tests were performed to detect the movement of the earth, the data showed that the earth did not move (e.g., Airy's failure and Michelson–Morley experiment). Even the famous Albert Einstein admitted that from earth, we cannot prove the earth moves. For Einstein, a man who put his faith in Copernicus' sun-centered "solar system," evidence was not needed to believe the earth moved. At Kyoto University, Japan, Einstein was giving a lecture called "How I Created the Theory of Relativity" (1922). Einstein said:

> "Therefore, I wanted somehow to verify this flow of ether against the earth, namely, the movement of the earth. When I posed this problem to my mind at that time, I never doubted the existence of ether and the movement of

the earth. ... While I had these ideas in mind as a student, I came to know the strange result of Michelson's experiment. ... Since then I have come to believe that, though the earth moves around the sun, we cannot perceive this movement by way of optical experiments."[18]

Einstein, who we are told is a genius, knew the earth's motion could not be detected, but in his mind, the earth moved. George Airy failed to prove the rotation of the earth (1871), and Albert Michelson and Edward Morley could not prove the earth's motion (1887). Einstein pushed data aside that confirmed a motionless earth and held to a theory that said the earth moved. The experiments of Airy and Michelson–Morley were not failures. They just produced results that modern science did not like. The experiments told the world of science what the Bible claimed thousands of years before Copernicus released his theory: the earth is motionless.

Why would scientists not tell us the truth about the earth or the "universe" we live in? Why would scientists not believe the data that showed the earth did not move? The simple answer is pride. I am not talking about arrogance. I am talking about Biblical pride:

Pride: I am god; You are not.

Humility: You are God; I am not.

If Einstein would admit that the earth did not move, his theory of general relativity would be pointless. If Hubble admitted the earth was fixed, then his theory on expansion would produce a null result. If Newton had revealed that the earth did not move, his law of universal gravitation would have been useless. If Kepler admitted the earth was at the center of the "universe," then his laws of planetary motion would be thrown out. If Copernicus knew the earth did not move, then the teachings of Hermes Trismegistus, the ancient Egyptian god Thoth, would be wrong. The Bible warns us about listening to gods. God said, "You shall have no other gods before me" (Exodus 20:3).

People do not investigate the origin of the modern "universe" created in 1543 by Copernicus. We simply believe what we are told and trust the pictures shown to us. When someone starts questioning the "universe," we rely upon groupthink and the majority to back us up. We say, "Everyone knows the earth rotates," "Everyone knows the earth is a globe," "Everyone knows what the solar system looks like because we have pictures from space," and "Everyone knows we went to the moon."

When evidence is presented, like the Michelson–Morley experiment that proved the earth did not move, we ignore it and invent ways to disbelieve the data and trust what we are told. Why would scientists not speak about the possibility of a motionless earth? The simple answer is pride. Albrecht Fölsing stated the reason why no one wants to tell the truth. In *Albert Einstein: A Biography*, Fölsing wrote:

> But no one wanted to go back to before Copernicus, to a geocentric view, or conclude from the Michelson–Morley experiment that the Earth was resting motionless in the ether. Instead, brilliant theories were designed to prove that it was impossible to observe a movement relative to the ether.[19]

Another way of saying, "No one wanted to go back to before Copernicus," is to say, "Copernicus was wrong." Instead of reporting the facts and telling the world the earth was motionless, it was easier to ignore the evidence, create new theories, and say that the earth moves. When Einstein published his general relativity theory, it was the "brilliant" theory they needed to nullify the Michelson–Morley experiment, which proved the earth did not move.

For Einstein's relativity theory to work, we must accept an assumption (unexamined belief). We must assume there is no such thing as absolute motion or rest. Let me explain. If we are standing on the side of the road and see a car pass by, we are not actually standing still watching the car move because the earth, the sun, and the "universe" are moving. According to classic relativity, motion cannot be detected because everything moves.

Einstein said we cannot detect the earth moving from earth because the earth is moving (circular reasoning). People during Einstein's day thought his relativity theory was wrong and a quick attempt to cover for the Michelson–Morley results. In a letter to Arnold Sommerfeld, a German physicist (1908), Einstein wrote:

> If the Michelson–Morley experiment had not brought us into serious embarrassment, no one would have regarded the relativity theory as a (halfway) redemption.[20]

What was Einstein trying to redeem? The motion of the earth. The Michelson–Morley experiment (1887) gave concrete evidence that the earth did not move, and now people like Einstein had to come along and save their heliocentric (sun at center; earth moving) theory. When Copernicus released his theory, others had to come along and save the earth-moving theory; scientists like Kepler (1609), Galileo (1610), and Newton (1687) had to come along and save Copernicus' sun-centered theory.

Einstein was a prideful man, the kind of pride that God opposes (James 4:6; 1 Peter 5:5). Einstein had no room for a personal God. When Einstein received a telegram from Lorentz, who confirmed Einstein's theory on the deflection of light, Einstein showed the telegram to Ilse Rosenthal-Schneider, a doctrinal student. After Rosenthal-Schneider read the letter, she wondered how Einstein would have felt if his theory was wrong. Einstein told her, "In that case I'd have to feel sorry for God, because the theory is correct."[21] Einstein had no need for the God of the Bible. Einstein assumed the role of creator. Fölsing wrote:

> Except for a brief phase during his adolescence, he never
> had any use for the personified God of the Judeo-Christian
> tradition. ... Einstein would attempt to slip into the role of
> the creator of the world and its laws.[22]

On March 24, 1954, Einstein wrote a personal letter to a man in New Jersey, explaining his thoughts about God. The New Jersey man was an atheist, and Einstein wanted to set the record straight about his position on God. In the letter, Einstein wrote:

> It was, of course, a lie what you read about my religious
> convictions, a lie which is being systematically repeated. I
> do not believe in a personal God and I have never denied
> this but have expressed it clearly. If something is in me
> which can be called religious then it is the unbounded ad-
> miration for the structure of the world so far as our science
> can reveal it.[23]

Scientists like Einstein do not need God because they make up their own laws of nature. Scientists like Einstein are not interested in the God who created this world but choose to tell us about their creation, the "universe." Of course, Einstein is not unique regarding scientists and their pursuit of building a "universe" that is absent of God. Richard Dawkins wrote, "Pierre-Simon Laplace (1749-1827), [the] mathematician that took Newton's theory of gravity further, was asked why he never mentioned God in his calculations. His response was, 'I had no need of that hypothesis.'"[24] Scientists who created our "universe" did not need God.

The Bible claims the moon is a light. Modern science cannot define what light is. The subject of light has yet to be settled. Light is described as waves, particles, or sometimes as both. Arthur H. Compton, who taught physics at the University of Chicago and winner of the Nobel Prize in Physics (1927), wrote:

> From the time that the ancient Greeks told each other about the shafts of light shot by Apollo, men have concerned themselves with what light is. Together with its sister problem, the nature of matter, this question presents the fascination of a fundamental mystery. During the last generation a rich mine of new information regarding light has been worked ... Yet in spite of this new information light remains as perhaps the darkest of our physical problem.[25]

I do not believe in the moon landing because I do not believe in a theory that claims the earth moves. I do not believe in the moon landing just because NASA, a government agency, tells me they did it while destroying all their evidence and data. Most importantly, I do not believe in the moon landing because the Bible tells me the moon is a light located in the solid dome barrier called the firmament, a place that does not belong to humanity. The Bible tells us, "The highest heavens belong to the LORD, but the earth he has given to mankind" (Psalm 115:16).

Chapter 24

Observation

Before we continue, let us review the motion of the "universe." The following numbers are based on "scientific data." It is important to remember the following information when talking about the heavenly and earthly realms. The numbers presented are what secular and Christian education teaches. Christian schools (home or private) may not promote the theories like the big bang or evolution, but they do use the numbers supplied to them by the experts of modern science. Here is a quick review of the motion of the "universe."

Ó

The Earth

The earth is presumably moving through the vacuum of space, orbiting around the sun at "66,622 mph."[1] While the earth is making its way around the sun, the earth is also spinning on its axis every "23.934 Hours."[2] The earth's rotation is just over 1,000 mph. *Space* states, "If you estimate that a day is 24 hours long, you divide the circumference by the length of the day. This produces a speed at the equator of about 1,037 mph."[3]

The Sun

When we envision our "solar system," we place the sun at the center with all the "planets" orbiting it. The sun is also in motion according to modern science. NASA states:

> The Sun orbits the center of the Milky Way, bringing with it the planets, asteroids, comets, and other objects in our solar system. Our solar system is moving with an average velocity of 450,000 miles per hour (720,000 kilometers per hour). But even at this speed, it takes about 230 million years for the Sun to make one complete trip around the Milky Way.[4]

The Milky Way Galaxy

Lister Staveley-Smith, professor at University of Western Australia estimates the speed of the Milky Way Galaxy to be around "2.2-million kilometers an hour"[5] or 1,367,017 mph. The earth and sun are also moving with the Milky Way Galaxy. According to modern science's data, our "galaxy" is moving at the speed of 1.4 million mph through an ever-expanding "universe."

$$Ó$$

According to *Fundamental Astronomy*, the science of astronomy is built upon observations, theories, and logic. *Fundamental Astronomy* tells us that if things do not align with observations, we must reconsider our theories and try again. *Fundamental Astronomy* states:

> Modern astronomy is fundamental science, motivated mainly by man's curiosity, his wish to know more about Nature and the Universe. Astronomy has a central role in forming a scientific view of the world. "A scientific view of the world" means a model of the universe based on observations, thoroughly tested theories and logical reasoning. Observations are always the ultimate test of a model: if the model does not fit the observations, it has to be changed, and this process must not be limited by any philosophical, political or religious conceptions or beliefs.[6]

The previous statement about astronomy sounds reasonable. The problem is that our modern "universe" does not match any observation or sensation that we see or feel. Our God-given senses are extremely important since they are the only way we connect to reality. David Harriman, a physicist and speaker on the Scientific Revolution, wrote, "The senses provide our only direct contact with reality."[7] Modern science's "universe" was built on math and not observations of reality. Nikola Tesla (1856–1943) said, "Scientists have substituted mathematics for experiments, and they wander off through equation after equation, and eventually build a structure which has no relation to reality."[8] As *Fundamental Astronomy* said, observation should be the ultimate test of how we approach the world around us.

What do we observe? What do we sense? The earth feels motionless. We see the sun moving. We see the moon moving. We see the fixed stars making perfect circles every twenty-four hours around Polaris, the North Star. The fixed stars never change course or shape unlike the wandering stars. A wandering star might be better understood if I used the word "planet."

A "planet" today is considered a spherical object (rock or gas) that orbits a star. They were not always thought to be reflectors of light. In the past, "planets" were stars that followed a different path from fixed stars. In the Bible, the "planets" were also known as "wandering stars" (Jude 13). The International Astronomical Union (IAU) states, "The word 'planet' originally described 'wanderers' that were known only as moving lights in the sky."[9] The IAU confirms what the Bible teaches. All objects in the sky are lights: the sun, moon, and stars (fixed or wandering).

Genesis 1:16–17 (KJV)
And God made two great lights; the greater light to rule the day, and the lesser light to rule the night: he made the stars also. [17] And God set them in the firmament of the heaven to give light upon the earth.

The "planets" that we can see (Mercury, Venus, Mars, Jupiter, and Saturn) were known to be stars that moved just like the sun and moon. The wandering stars would come and go like the sun and moon. Since their path was different from the other fixed stars, astronomers called them wanderers. The Merriam-Webster Dictionary explains the history of the word "planet":

Planet goes back to ancient Greek *planēt-* (literally, "wanderer"), which is derived from *planasthai*, a Greek verb which means "to wander." The word was originally applied to any of seven visible celestial bodies which appeared to move independently of the fixed stars—the sun, the moon, Mercury, Venus, Mars, Jupiter, and Saturn.[10]

One of the observations we can all see is the unchanging pattern of the fixed stars. When NASA posted their *Astronomy Picture of the Day*, they used a timelapse photo that displays the fixed stars rotating around the North Star (Fig. 37). The North Star remains at the center of the picture while supposedly the earth, sun, and the Milky Way were moving. The photographer said the timelapse photo took over four hours to create.[11] According to modern science, the following table shows the distance the earth, sun, and Milky Way would have traveled during a four-hour timelapse photo (Table 3).

Movement	Distance
Earth's orbit	266,488 miles
Sun's orbit	1,800,000 miles
Milky Way's travel	5,468,068 miles

Table 3. The Motion of "Universe" in Four Hours

According to modern science, the earth, sun, and Milky Way would have traveled unimaginable distances in four hours. Yet, the fixed stars make perfect circles, day after day, around the North Star (Fig. 37). NASA must reinforce the moving "universe" idea because natural observations make it seem like the stars are rotating around a non-moving earth. NASA wrote, "As the Earth spins on its axis, the sky seems to rotate around us."[12]

Fig. 37. Star Trails Over Oregon.

If observation is so essential to astronomy, as *Fundamental Astronomy* states, how could anyone believe the earth is moving? When Aristarchus of Samos (270 BC) introduced his earth-moves theory, people did not believe him. The reason was because of simple observation. As *Fundamental Astronomy* stated, people rejected Aristarchus' idea because it did not match observation. When Ptolemy (c. 150 AD) introduced a geocentric model, it matched people's observations, and it would continue to be the model that was supported for nearly 1,400 years until Nicolaus Copernicus.

When Copernicus presented his theory that the earth moved, he did not present any observation to show the earth moved. How was Copernicus able to change the world simply by a drawing and no proof (Fig. 38)? The Renaissance was conditioned to accept new ideas founded on Hermetic writings (attributed to Hermes Trismegistus). Long wrote, "Hermetic writings pointed to sun worship and a Sun-centered universe."[13] Copernicus' drawing was accepted because it taught the philosophy of Hermes Trismegistus: sun worship.

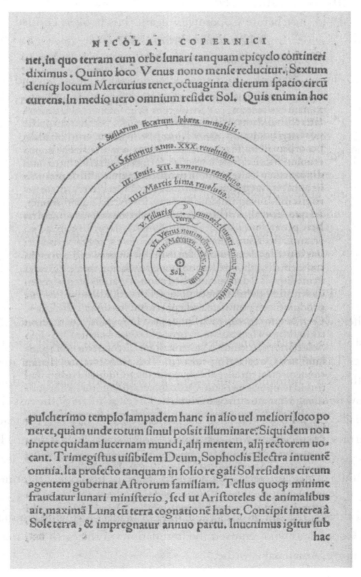

Fig. 38. *De revolutionibus.*

Historically speaking, 1543 was the defining moment when everything changed inside and outside the church. Historians debate when the Middle Ages (500–1300s) ended and the Renaissance began (1400s–1600s). Most historians agree that the Scientific Revolution (1543–1687) started with Nicolaus Copernicus and ended with Isaac Newton. The revolution began when Copernicus said the earth was moving. John Freely, a historian of science, wrote:

> The heliocentric theory, as it was called, was published in 1543, just before Copernicus' death. His book is entitled *De revolutionibus orbium coelestium libri VI* (*Six Books Concerning the Revolutions of the Heavenly Spheres*), a truly revolutionary work whose reverberations were felt far beyond the realm of astronomy. During the first century after its publication, the Copernican theory was accepted by only a few astronomers, most notably Kepler and Galileo, but their new sun-centred astronomy sparked the seventeenth-century Scientific Revolution that climaxed with the new world system of Isaac Newton, the beginning of modern science. ... Though his *De revolutionibus* has been called 'the book that nobody read,' it changed our view of the universe forever, breaking the bounds of the finite geocentric cosmos of antiquity and opening the way to the infinite and expanding universe of the new millennium.[14]

There was only one moment in history when the movement of the earth started to be seriously considered, at a time when an ancient god named Hermes Trismegistus was being reborn. The Renaissance (literal meaning "rebirth") was a humanistic movement in the hunt for ancient wisdom that was now flooding western Europe from the Greek scholars of the east. Thanks to Marsilio Ficino who translated the ancient Greek literature, the teachings of Hermes Trismegistus would become center stage. It was from Hermes Trismegistus where Copernicus would label the sun as a god to be seated in the middle of the "universe." Copernicus wrote in his book, "[Hermes] the Thrice Greatest labels it a visible god ... Thus indeed, as though seated on a royal throne, the sun governs the family of planets revolving around it."[15] It was Copernicus who removed the foundations of the earth and made the world move. Athanasakis wrote:

Nicolaus Copernicus (1473–1543) – astronomer, mathematician, physician, and Catholic clergyman – was one of the most important contributors of the Scientific Revolution due to the formulation of the heliocentric model of the universe, according to which the earth revolved around the stationary mean sun.[16]

When Copernicus released his theory, some major obstacles had to be addressed. People questioned celestial (sun, moon, and stars) movement that seemed to revolve around the earth and the lack of motion experienced by humans. Omodeo listed one of the problems with the heliocentric theory: "The motion of the Earth, in spite of its velocity, is not perceived by our senses."[17] People instinctively knew the earth did not move. However, another pressing obstacle had to be overcome: the Bible.

Chapter 25

Two Approaches to Astronomy

Nicolaus Copernicus' theory faced opposition because of observation and people's commitment to the Word of God. For those who held to the literal reading of Scripture, it was not readily accepted that the earth moved. How do we resolve what Copernicus proposed to the statements found in the Bible that taught the earth was motionless? Omodeo wrote:

> Theological difficulties: Several Biblical passages refer to the immobility of the Earth and the motion of the Sun (e.g., Joshua 10.12–14 and 2 Kings 20:8–11). In order to reconcile Copernican theory and the Bible, one ought to abandon a literal exegesis of these passages and therefore to dismiss the interpretations of the Fathers of the Church and of the most credited theologians.[1]

There is no compromise when it comes to modern science and the Bible. If we try to mix the two, we find ourselves abandoning God's literal words and adjusting our interpretation to fit modern science. Martin Luther (1483–1546) was one theologian who refused to surrender a literal interpretation of the Bible. Even before Copernicus released his theory (1543), Luther spoke out against Copernicus and held to a literal reading of the Bible. Professor Richard Pogge, from the Ohio State University's Department of Astronomy, tells us Luther's response to Copernicus' new astronomy that taught the earth moved:

> [Luther's remarks:] "There is talk of a new astrologer who wants to prove that the earth moves and goes around instead of the sky, the sun, the moon, just as if somebody were moving in a carriage or ship might hold that he was sitting still and at rest while the earth and the trees walked and moved. But that is how things are nowadays: when a man wishes to be clever he must needs invent something special, and the way he does it must needs be the best! The fool wants to turn the whole art of astronomy upside-down. However, as Holy Scripture tells us, so did Joshua bid the sun to stand still and not the earth."[2]

Luther believed Copernicus was a fool for suggesting the earth moves, an idea opposite to what Scripture teaches. The passage Luther was referring to is found in the Book of Joshua. According to Luther and the Book of Joshua, the sun and moon move, not the earth.

Joshua 10:12–13

On the day the LORD gave the Amorites over to Israel, Joshua said to the LORD in the presence of Israel: "Sun, stand still over Gibeon, and you, moon, over the Valley of Aijalon." [13] So the sun stood still, and the moon stopped, till the nation avenged itself on its enemies, as it is written in the Book of Jashar. The sun stopped in the middle of the sky and delayed going down about a full day.

For Luther, the Bible was not just a holy book; it was God's word that made truthful statements about the earth being motionless. Miller comments on how much Luther respected God's written words. Miller wrote, "Copernicus' idea of a moving Earth contradicted the Bible. Luther believed the Bible was the ultimate authority, so he felt Copernicus must be wrong."[3]

There were also other theologians like John Calvin (1509–1564) who wanted to avoid joining in on the fight. Calvin held to the authority of the Bible but also believed what the modern astronomer was teaching about "planets." E. C. Lucas commented on John Calvin's approach to science and the Bible:

> Calvin held strongly to the Reformation doctrine of the perspicuity of Scripture, its accessibility to everyone. This led him to what has been called the doctrine of accommodation. The language of the Bible is 'adapted … to common usage' because the Holy Spirit 'would rather speak childishly than unintelligibly to the humble and unlearned.' … Because the Bible is 'a book for laymen', he says, 'He who would learn astronomy and other recondite arts, let him go elsewhere'. He therefore refused to join those who used the Bible to attack the newly emerging astronomical ideas of his day. … the findings of science in interpretation might be to determine when the language of the Bible is 'adapted to common usage'. This will prevent some statements being taken in a woodenly literal way when they should not be.[4]

Christians who hold to modern science like to quote Calvin's famous, "He who would learn astronomy and other recondite arts, let him go elsewhere." Calvin thought astronomy was just another field of study to learn. Gingerich wrote:

> Given the wide distribution of *De revolutionibus*, it seems likely that John Calvin saw the book. But he probably also joined many of his devout contemporaries in viewing it as a mathematical device for calculation rather than a real description of nature.[5]

Calvin did not understand that astronomy during the Scientific Revolution was not about math or the stars but faith in a false god. Calvin yielded to the science of his day and changed the Bible's meaning. Lucas wrote:

> An example of this use of science is found in Calvin's comment on Gn. 1:16. Some exegetes of his day insisted that this verse teaches that the sun and moon are the two largest heavenly bodies. Against this Calvin argues that since the astronomers had shown that Saturn is larger than the moon, and only *looks* smaller because of its distance from us, the language here is simply that of appearance.[6]

According to Calvin, the moon was no longer the largest light in the night sky; it was Saturn. Calvin did not learn this from the Bible but from modern science. Calvin's philosophy was that the Holy Spirit spoke to the authors of the Bible so that the ordinary person could understand. God's word does not need accommodation or adjusting because a scientist claims Saturn is larger than the moon. According to the naked eye, Saturn is just a tiny dot of light in the sky. If a person during Calvin's day claimed Saturn was a "planet" larger than the moon, then it was just a guess and not based on scientific data. Remember, no one during Luther's or Calvin's day had a telescope since it was invented in the 17th century. Every human being, including Luther and Calvin, in the 16th century, saw that the moon was the great light in the night sky and the wandering star (Saturn) was a small point of light, just like the Bible said.

The "universe" was shaped by scientists who did not believe what the Bible said. The "universe" was developed outside of the influence of the Bible. A "universe" that is rooted in ancient Greek philosophy that was opposed to the God of Moses, King David, and Paul. During the Scientific Revolution, astronomy was not about understanding the stars but about worshiping the sun.

Chapter 26

New Meets Old

Does the Bible teach a heliocentric or geocentric model? If we search popular Christian ministries, the quick answer we will get is, "No, the Bible does not teach a geocentric model." Here are two examples of online Christian ministries that handle the debate between a moving or motionless earth model. *Answers in Genesis* writes, "Contrary to what many believe, the Bible doesn't teach geocentrism. It's not that the Bible teaches heliocentrism either."[1] *Got Questions* writes, "Does the Bible teach geocentrism? ... The short answer to this question is 'no.' Nowhere in the Bible are we told that the earth is at the center of the universe."[2] Despite the Christian ministry's stance that the Bible does not teach geocentrism (earth not moving), they will teach their readers why heliocentrism (earth moving) is correct.

The previous ministries explain that Ptolemy's geocentric model was believed until Nicolaus Copernicus presented his heliocentric theory in 1543. They will also inform their readers that the heliocentric theory was proven not by Copernicus but by others like Galileo.

Mark Galli and Ted Olsen confirm what the Christian websites suggest. Galli and Olsen wrote, "It wasn't until Galileo (1564–1642) that Copernicus' ideas were seen for what they were—a revolution in how humankind conceived of itself."[3] The *Pocket Dictionary of Church History* also teaches that Galileo was the evidence needed to confirm Copernicus:

> Although living before the invention of the telescope, Copernicus noted several anomalies in the motion of the planets that were not accounted for by the Ptolemaic theory of a geocentric universe (with the Earth at the center, standing still, and everything rotating around it). He developed an alternative model, the heliocentric (sun-centered) view, and delineated it in *On the Revolution of Celestial Spheres*. Published in 1543, the year he died, this work was not seen as a threat by the church until Galileo's observations of the heavens with a telescope confirmed it a half century later.[4]

Most scholars attribute the heliocentric (sun-centered) theory to Copernicus, but the "earth moving" theory is linked to Pythagoras. William Shedd wrote:

> The heliocentric theory was known to the ancients. It was ascribed to Pythagoras and also to Philolaus, one of his disciples ... Aristotle recognized the existence of the doctrine by arguing against it.[5]

Aristotle promoted a geocentric model, but like Pythagoras, Aristotle also believed the earth was a sphere. Hoffe wrote, "Aristotle represents his geocentric conception of the world: according to this, the relatively small Earth ... is situated, spheric and immobile, in the middle of the world."[6]

The men of the Renaissance and the Scientific Revolution were not discovering new things but reviving an ancient Greek philosophy. They were linked to Aristotle (384–322 BC), Plato (c. 427–348 BC), and Socrates (c. 470–399 BC). They were tied to ancient Greek philosophy as far back as Pythagoras (c. 570 BC–500 BC). Copernicus did not invent a theory that made the earth move; he just brought it back to life. Edward Knight wrote:

> The heliocentric theory was held by the ancient Egyptians, and taught by them to Pythagoras. The theory did not flourish in Greece. Plato mentions it. A few scholars, like Nicolas (probably of Laodicea, fourth century A. D.), entertained it during the vast intervening period, and it was eventually revived by Copernicus.[7]

Old Egyptian teaching was fundamental to the Scientific Revolution. After the fall of Constantinople (1453), Greek scholars fled to Italy and brought with them Greek literature. Then Marsilio Ficino would translate the Greek writings into Latin, which was believed to be the lost wisdom of Hermes Trismegistus. The ancient teacher, Hermes Trismegistus, was just a new name for the ancient Egyptian god named Thoth (Fig. 39). Copernicus, who sighted Hermes Trismegistus as his reasoning for calling the sun a visible god, wanted to restore the *prisca theologia* (ancient theology). What Copernicus revived was what Pythagoras learned from the Egyptians. Christoph Riedweg wrote:

> Pythagoras of Samos, too, was said to have visited Egypt, in order to be initiated by the priests there into the local customs and cultural achievements. ... But Pythagoras

eagerly and steadfastly observed all their rules, and this won him such great admiration that he, as the only ever foreigner, was also granted the privilege of sacrificing to the Egyptian gods and taking part in their worship.[8]

Fig. 39. Carving of Thoth.

Pythagoras was a Greek mathematician who sought the wisdom from the Egyptian gods. He was interested in one Egyptian god named Thoth (pronounced like "oath" with "th" or "thought"). Who is Thoth? Thoth was the god of philosophy, magic, theology, astronomy, and math. He taught humanity their true wisdom and geometry.

Geometry was not just about points and angles. Geometry was important because it was about measuring the earth. Geometry means "'measurement of earth or land; geometry,' from combining form of *gē* 'earth, land' [and] *metria* 'a measuring of.'"[9] The god Thoth would teach Pythagoras how to measure the earth. Pythagoras would learn geometry, and then later, Eratosthenes (c. 235 BC) would use it to measure the earth. Thoth was responsible for humanity's wisdom in science, religion, astronomy, and geometry. Markus Carabas wrote:

> It was Thoth's calculations that set in motion the universe, its orbs, and laws, and his female counterpart Maat ensured its continued function ... Thoth dedicated himself to revealing and producing knowledge for humankind. He gave his name to all advances in knowledge, from science to magic and all aspects of philosophy and theology in

between. Since he set the universe in motion he was also the natural patron of astronomy and astrology. ... Thoth became the god of mathematics and geometry too.[10]

Pythagoras sought knowledge, and the one god to reveal that knowledge would be Thoth, the "All-knowing One." Pythagoras, a man seeking esoteric (known only to a few) and occult (hidden) knowledge, would learn from the god of understanding and reason. Patrick Boylan, who was a professor of eastern languages and Scripture, wrote:

> Thoth appears in Egyptian texts — especially in those of the later period — as the All-knowing One, as the dispenser of every kind of strange and mysterious gnosis. To him is assigned the invention of language and script. He is regarded as the patron of the sciences. He can read the secrets of men' hearts. He is the "one who knows" in every direction. In the end he comes to be looked on as Understanding (or Reason) itself personified.[11]

Thoth was the god who created astronomy, religion, and math. Boylan wrote, "Thoth, the wisest of the gods ... god of literature, and of science, of theology, and of ritual, as the fountain and source of all knowledge and wisdom, Thoth, 'the knowing one.'"[12] During the Renaissance, Thoth would be known as Hermes Trismegistus, whose writings were written in ancient Greek and were brought to the west after the fall of Constantinople (1453). The secret wisdom of Hermes Trismegistus was known as Hermetic or Hermetica writings. T. George Allen wrote:

> [Thoth] is one of the oldest and most highly developed figures in the Egyptian pantheon. His worship can be followed in Egyptian religious literature from the Pyramid Texts, with their reflection of beliefs of the third and even of the fourth millennium before Christ, all the way down to the Ptolemaic and Roman temple inscriptions. ... Thoth became identified with Hermes and was thus involved in the speculation of the Hermetic writings.[13]

As mentioned earlier, Africa, from Binghamton University, acknowledges Copernicus' desire to restore the ancient wisdom that Pythagoras (500 BC) had learned. Copernicus was interested in the secret knowledge that came from ancient Egypt. Africa said Copernicus wanted a "Pythagorean Restoration."[14]

George Grote wrote about Pythagoras' life and travels. Grote mentions that Pythagoras was said to have traveled for nearly thirty years to the Arabians, Syrians, Phoenicians, Chaldeans, and Indians. Grote tells us that Pythagoras just "really visited Egypt."[15] Grote informs us that Pythagoras was a believer in reincarnation (transmigration). Grote will give an example of Pythagoras claiming he heard the voice of his friend trapped inside the body of a dog:

> The spectacle of Egyptian habits, the conversation of the priests, and the initiation into various mysteries or secret rites and stories ... impressed the mind of Pythagoras, and given him that turn for mystic observance, asceticism, and peculiarity of diet and clothing ... [Pythagoras] believed in the metempsychosis or transmigration of the souls of deceased men into other men as well as into animals, we know, not only by other evidence, but also by the testimony of his contemporary, the philosopher Xenophane's of Elea: Pythagoras, seeing a dog beaten and hearing him howl, desired the striker to desist, saying—"It is the soul of a friend of mine, whom I recognised by his voice."[16]

The "universe" was created during the Scientific Revolution, which sought the teachings of Hermes Trismegistus, the new name for an old god, Thoth. The false god Thoth gave his seekers the secret wisdom of magic, astronomy, and math. The information I have shared is not a reinterpretation of history or a modern point of view. I am not presenting a narrative to prove an agenda. I have repeated history as taught by historians and scholars. I have shared information about a god that is still sought after today.

$$Ó$$

Pursuing secret knowledge to gain power is nothing new and is not absent from modern times. I wanted to include a current example of people who believe in the esoteric teachings of the Egyptian god Thoth, who would become Hermes Trismegistus. The following are two men who sincerely believe in Hermetic teachings. They think they are real gods and kings walking in this world, enlightened by the wisdom of the one who started it all, Hermes Trismegistus.

Aubrey Marcus has a podcast that interviews people like Aaron Rogers, Joe Rogan, Matthew McConaughey, Jamie Foxx, and Robert F. Kennedy Jr. On September 24, 2022, Marcus spoke to Robert Edward Grant, who is knowledgeable about mystic and esoteric principles. Marcus was sharing how people with the secret knowledge were called wizards because of what they could manifest within themselves, the ability to make things happen in this realm (magic). Grant interrupts to explain what Marcus is talking about. Grant said:

> "Actually, what you're bordering into now are the next stages. You know, if you go back and look at what was, first historical reference to astrology, it was the Epic of Gilgamesh, and it was almost identical to the western astrology we have today. So, who started this? Because it does seem like remarkably accurate on so many levels … So, when you start digging into it, you're like, who established all this stuff? … Where did all this stuff come from? You're going to find that literally all of it, this esoteric wisdom that seems to have withstood the passage of time, all came through Hermes Trismegistus."[17]

Chapter 27

All For One and One For All

When Nicolaus Copernicus released his sun-centered system, which we know as the "solar system," according to Copernicus, it was the entire "universe." Later in history, scientists will change Copernicus' "universe" into a local "solar system." Copernicus also believed the earth traveled on a giant crystal ball. Once again, scientists will help. Copernicus' giant celestial spheres will change into an imaginary dot in an imaginary point out in space.

Johannes Kepler (1609) would explain the "planet's" movement around the sun. Kepler gets rid of the giant celestial spheres or crystal balls. Pietro Daniel Omodeo, who works for an institute that specialize in the history of science (Max Planck Institute for the History of Science, Berlin, Germany), states that Kepler was the one who removed the medieval idea of crystal balls:

> The astronomical work of Kepler deserves particular mention as the substitution of a kinematic treatment of planetary motions through geometrical modeling for physical astronomy, that is, the explanation of celestial motions as resulting from the action of forces. After the dissolution of the celestial spheres of the medieval tradition in the 1580s, the question about the causes of the celestial motions was raised.[1]

If the earth was not sitting on a celestial sphere, how did it move? Thanks to Kepler, people now had an answer. Kepler invented his three laws of planetary motion. How did Kepler make his theory work without experimental evidence? Kepler injected a theoretical or imaginary point out in space that caused the earth to orbit in an ellipse (Fig. 40). Even with Kepler's mathematical model, people wondered how the earth or any other "planet" obeyed his laws without a force or something acting upon it.

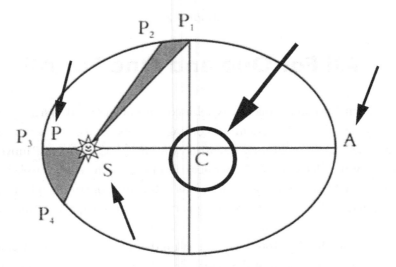

Fig. 40. Kepler's first law (arrows added).

The following illustration shows Kepler's explanation for how the "planets," including earth, move around the sun (Fig. 40). P$_1$ through P$_4$, located on the elliptical path, are the positions of the "planet's" orbit. Highlighted with arrows are points S, A, P, and C. Voelkel explains what each letter represents. S is the sun. A is the aphelion when the "planet" is the farthest from the sun. P is the perihelion when the "planet" is closest to the sun. Voelkel explains Kepler's first law. What is not explained is point C.

Voelkel explains the need for two focal points for an elliptical orbit. Voelkel wrote, "The planets move in elliptical orbits, with the sun at one focus."[2] What about the other focal point? Voelkel never explains point C. Two focal points are needed to make an elliptical path. No one can explain Kepler's first law because it is some imaginary point in space invented to prove Copernicus' sun-centered system. That is why, in the 17th century, when Kepler released his laws, people asked, "How do the planets obey Kepler's laws?" This was a valid question then and now.

People needed more than just an imaginary point in space to make Copernicus' system work. The answer was Galileo Galilei, usually referred to as Galileo (1610). When Galileo pointed his new telescope into the night sky, he discovered something that no one else had ever seen before: the moons of Jupiter (Fig. 41). At first, Galileo thought the "moons" were just stars. Miller explains:

> When Galileo turned his telescope toward Jupiter, he made
> more surprising discoveries. "There were three little stars,"

Galileo wrote on January 7, 1610, "small but very bright, near the planet." At first he thought the objects were stars. But when he looked at Jupiter again on the following night, the three little stars had moved! He realized that Jupiter's "stars" are actually moons.[3]

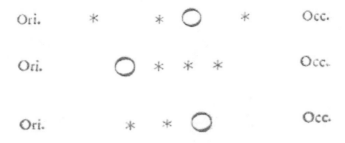

Fig. 41. Galileo's drawing of the moons of Jupiter.

Today, with a digital camera, people can zoom in on Jupiter and see its four "moons" for themselves. Using a high-zoom digital camera, we can see what Galileo saw. Here is an example of an amateur using a Nikon COOLPIX P1000 camera (125x optical zoom) to see Jupiter's moons (Fig. 42).

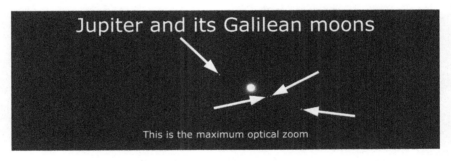

Fig. 42. Amateur capture of Jupiter (arrows added).

What did Galileo see? He saw points of light and claimed they were moons. The better question would be, "What could Galileo see?" *British Pathé*, a media archival website, has a short newsreel called *Through Galileo's Telescope* (1933). The newsreel will explain the importance of Galileo's discovery. Keep in mind the previous image of Jupiter's moons was taken with a 125x optical zoom with no digital enhancement (Fig.42). Galileo will use a 33x zoom telescope, which is comparable to a high-end CCTV security camera (Fig. 43). The newsreel from *British Pathé* reported:

Hearing that the Dutch spectacle maker Lippershey had invented an optic tube which made distant objects appear near, Galileo overnight invented and made one of his own ... crude as this telescope was, two simple lenses magnifying only 33x, it enabled him to verify certain of his beliefs and to disprove completely others essential to the Ptolemaic theory.[4]

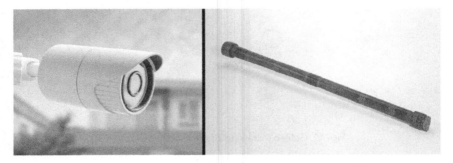

Fig. 43. Security camera and original Galileo telescope.

Galileo's telescope was only 33x (equivalent to a home security camera). There is even speculation if it was powerful or precise enough to make accurate observations. It is hard to verify Galileo's telescope since it has never been independently tested. Stillman Drake, a historian of science, wrote:

On 7 January 1610 Galileo first sighted satellites of Jupiter with his 'discoverer' – the most important event reported in his *Sidereus Nuncius* as printed at Venice on 12 March 1610. A few days before that famous book appeared, Galileo showed Sarpi an instrument that gave 30x magnification. That power was mentioned in the book, but I have found no evidence that Galileo used it in astronomical observation. Even in 1612, when he made his telescope an instrument of unprecented accuracy for angular measurement, he used telescopes of 18x and 20x, probably to have as great power as possible without excessively reducing the field of view.[5]

When using a modern camera with a 125x optical zoom, Jupiter and the "moons" are only seen as lights. The "moons" are only points of lights that are no different than any other star in the sky except smaller. Jupiter was known throughout history as a wandering star. Doug West wrote, "One of the bright 'wanderers' of the night sky is Jupiter, which is the fifth planet from the Sun."[6] What we call "planets" today, Mercury, Venus, Mars, Jupiter, and Saturn, were called wandering stars. Leah Crane wrote:

> For nearly all of recorded human history, people have ascribed special importance to planets. As Dr Jean-Luc Margot, an astronomer and professor at UCLA, put it, "For thousands of years, people have noticed that these planets are different. That may be why it's built into our culture that these objects are special. The sort of objects that, initially, we could see with our naked eye in the night sky, that behaved differently from the stars."[7]

Galileo's observations were crucial to Copernicus' heliocentric theory. No one knew of moons other than the earth's moon during Galileo's time. Galileo provided creditability to Copernicus' theory that "planets" orbit the sun and moons orbit their "planets." Even with Galileo's telescope, Copernicus still had not become entirely accepted. Galileo, who helped promote the heliocentric theory, now would have to reject Copernicus' theory to save his life.

In 1633, Galileo was ordered to stand trial before the Inquisition, a court for the Catholic church to fight heresies. After the Catholic church burned Giordano Bruno at the stake for promoting Copernicus' view of the "universe," Galileo thought it best to renounce his belief that the earth moves. Galileo wrote:

> But because I have been enjoined, by this Holy Office, altogether to abandon the false opinion which maintains that the Sun is the centre and immovable, and forbidden to hold, defend, or teach, the said false doctrine in any manner ...[8]

It has been reported that when Galileo was leaving his trial, he whispered, "And yet it moves." The first reference to this quote was over 120 years after Galileo's trial. Julie Mianecki, writing for the *Smithsonian Magazine*, stated:

> Legend has it that after he recanted his views, Galileo muttered, "And yet it moves," under his breath, but David DeVorkin, senior curator at the National Air and Space Museum, says there's no historical basis for that claim.[9]

Christian historians and scholars use Galileo's story to promote the heliocentric theory. They inform their readers that the "church" was wrong to condemn Galileo because of science. The *Oxford Dictionary of the Christian Church* reads, "'The 'Galileo Affair' has been a continuing leitmotif in accounts of the meeting of science and religion."[10] Galileo has been hailed as an example of how the church did not want to yield to new scientific discoveries. *Christian History Magazine* wrote, "None of these honors would have given Galileo as much satisfaction as the 1992 papal commission that formally acknowledged the church had erred in its treatment of the great Catholic astronomer."[11] *Christian History Magazine* also wrote "Despite Galileo's faithfulness to his church, he is most often portrayed today as a secular scientific hero who stood firm against religious bigotry. His loyalty to his faith is largely ignored."[12] Was Galileo a sincere and loyal Christian who believed in the Bible? No one can judge a man's heart, but we can review Galileo's position on God and the Bible using the words he wrote.

Galileo's reasoning for reversing his position on the moving earth had nothing to do with believing in God's word or the Catholic church. On January 15, 1633, three months before his trial, Galileo wrote a letter to his friend Ella Diodati. In his letter, Galileo will explain why we should not hold to God's word as infallible (incapable of error). Galileo believes that nature (the works of God) is the standard of truth, and the Bible needs to throwaway its claim regarding the sun and earth. Galileo wrote in his letter to Diodati:

> Whenever the works [nature] and the Word cannot be made to agree, we consider Holy Scripture as secondary, no harm will befall it, for it has often been modified to suit the masses and has frequently attributed false qualities to God. Therefore I must ask why it is that we insist that whenever it speaks of the Sun or of the Earth, Holy Scripture be considered as quite infallible?[13]

Galileo did not believe what the Bible said about the sun or the earth but chose to believe what Copernicus claimed about the sun and the earth. Despite Galileo's valiant attempt to anchor Copernicus' sun-centered theory as a scientific norm, people still did not fully accept it. Galileo's rejection of Copernicus' theory did not help the matter, but because of Galileo, people started to consider whether the earth was moving. John Freely wrote:

By the end of the century the heliocentric model of Copernicus had gained general acceptance and the geocentric model of Aristotle and Ptolemy had been discredited, principally through the efforts of Galileo Galilei (1564–1642), whose works opened the way for the new physics and astronomy of Newton.[14]

The last character that will help seal the deal would be Isaac Newton, the inventor of the force of gravity. The problem was that Newton did not know what gravity was. Newton would not even give his opinion on what he thought gravity was. William A. Wallace explains Newton's concept of gravity:

> Newton ran into problems, however, when his critics raised the question: how, specifically, does gravity cause this motion, or, better, what is the cause of gravity. ... Newton proposed the concept of attraction, but taken in a mathematical way and not as a physical cause. As to what the physical cause might be, he preferred to remain agnostic ... "*hypotheses non fingo*" ["I frame no hypotheses"] ... He knew that gravity exists in the universe, but he did not know the cause of gravity ... All he could do was invoke "attraction," an "occult quality," as it was characterized by critics, to explain it.[15]

It is hard to imagine that people would believe in the force of gravity when the inventor of gravity described it as, "that force, whatever it is."[16] Then again, people believe in gravity today even though it has never been proven. Today, no one knows what gravity is.

While Newton did release his unknown force of gravity theory, he was focused on other things. He was seeking "an original wisdom or knowledge in the ancients which had been mostly lost to mankind."[17] During the Renaissance, people, including Newton, sought the lost wisdom of the Egyptians through the writings of Hermes Trismegistus. Newton was interested in magic, which would give him the secrets of turning metal into gold and the ability to live forever. Miller explains Newton's fascination with magic:

> Newton was also obsessed with alchemy, an ancient philosophic and experimental practice related to the effort to change common substances into pure elements. In

Newton's day, alchemy included everything from manufacturing paint pigments and medicines to making fake precious stones. It also included trying to make the so-called philosopher's stone. This, alchemists believed, was a magical substance that would cure other substances of their impurities. It could turn lead into gold and cure humans of their illnesses. Newton practiced alchemy all his life. He often worked day and night conducting alchemical experiments in his laboratory. Historians who have studied Newton's alchemical notebooks believe he wanted to gain understanding of and power over nature rather than to gain wealth from his discoveries.[18]

Newton was interested in alchemy (magic), and there was no better teacher than Hermes Trismegistus. In order for Newton to create the philosopher's stone, Newton would have to bridge the natural and heavenly worlds. Then, Newton could control the elements of the earth to produce gold and the elixir of everlasting life. Newton would have to make the things below like the things above. In Newton's personal library, he had a book that he copied. The book read:

> Tis true without lying, certain & most true. That which is below is like that which is above & that which is above is like that which is below to do the miracles of one only thing. And as all things have been & arose from one by the mediation of one: so all things have their birth from this one thing by adaptation.[19]

The book Newton hand-copied was called the *Emerald Tablet* (Fig. 44). Newton would have found this book helpful. The *Emerald Tablet* was believed to be written by Hermes Trismegistus, the founder of the practice of alchemy (magic). Matteo Fornasier, Ca' Foscari University of Venice, Italy, wrote:

In the *Emerald Tablet*, attributed to the mythical founder of alchemy, Hermes Trismegistus, is written: "What is below resembles that which is above." "Below" is the sublunary world, saying it with Aristotelian words, and "above" is the celestial world. This is one of the fundamental teachings for the alchemist apprentice, because he had to understand the connections that go across the whole universe before being able to dominate its elements.[20]

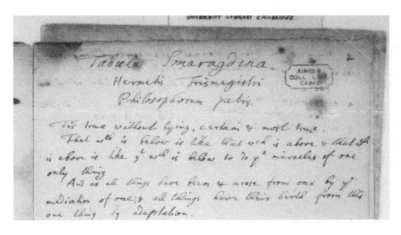

Fig. 44. Newton's copy of the *Emerald Tablet*.

When we hear the name Isaac Newton, people associate him with gravity, science, or genius. The fact is that Newton was interested in alchemy, the practice of magic taught by Hermes Trismegistus, also known as Thoth, the ancient Egyptian god. Michael M. Woolfson informs us that Newton spent his time "studying subjects which command little respect these days—astrology and alchemy."[21] As Betty J. T. Dobbs puts it, "Newton was not the first of the age of reason. He was the last of the magicians."[22]

Copernicus, Kepler, Galileo, and Newton all had a purpose. Their goal was to make the earth move. Once the earth began to move, the Bible would no longer be needed. People would have a new bible to follow, written in the language of "math" by men following their god, Hermes Trismegistus.

Chapter 28

Trouble in Paradise

Newton's law of gravity was in trouble as time passed, so another character was introduced over 200 years later, Albert Einstein. The role Einstein played was to save gravity. Einstein invented a new way of thinking about gravity, not as a force that no one could explain, but as the warping of space and time; the new fourth dimension was called spacetime. *Albert Einstein, the Human Side* reads:

> In Berlin in 1915, in the midst of World War I, Einstein completed his masterpiece, the general theory of relativity. It not only generalized his special theory of relativity but also provided a new theory of gravitation.[1]

In 1887, when the Michelson–Morley experiment proved the earth did not move, the scientific community had to act, and Einstein would help with their predicament. Instead of a force, gravity would now be understood as the bending of spacetime, affected by mass and energy. Tom Siegfried wrote:

> Gravity, said Einstein, actually moved matter along the curving pathways embodied in spacetime — paths imprinted by mass and energy themselves. As expressed decades later by the physicist John Archibald Wheeler, mass grips spacetime, telling it how to curve, and spacetime grips mass, telling it how to move.[2]

Einstein proposed a fourth dimension of spacetime but never had any proof. Tim Newcomb wrote, "Theoretical physicists believe math shows the possibilities of a fourth dimension, but there's no actual evidence—yet. Albert Einstein believed space and time made up a fourth dimension."[3] Gravity must be made true since our "solar system" depends on it.

The National Science Foundation held a press conference, announcing that the Laser Interferometer Gravitational-Wave Observatory (LIGO) was finally able to prove what Einstein believed about spacetime. LIGO explains gravitational waves:

Gravitational waves are 'ripples' in space-time caused by some of the most violent and energetic processes in the Universe. Albert Einstein predicted the existence of gravitational waves in 1916 in his general theory of relativity. … These cosmic ripples would travel at the speed of light, carrying with them information about their origins, as well as clues to the nature of gravity itself.[4]

Exactly one hundred years after Einstein theorized gravitational waves, a company designed to detect gravitational waves found gravitational waves. During the press conference on February 11, 2016, David Reitze, CEO of LIGO, would inform the audience what they discovered. Reitze said:

"Ladies and gentlemen, we have detected gravitational waves. We did it. I am so pleased to be able to tell you that. So, these gravitational waves were produced by two colliding black holes that came together, merged to form a single black hole about 1.3 billion years ago. … Let me start with what we saw … [we] recorded a signal … And, what was amazing about this signal is that it's exactly what you would expect, what Einstein's theory of general relativity would predict for two big, massive objects like black holes in-spiraling and merging together."[5]

Reitze will play a video during the press conference so the audience can see what he is talking about. Reitze said, "By the way, this is not a Hollywood production that I'm going to show you. It is actually a real computer simulation."[6] Reitze said he would show a real video, not a Hollywood movie. What Reitze showed them was a computer-generated (not real) simulation. Reitze could not show them a real video because they only recorded an audio signal.[7] The LIGO laboratory decided to call their audio recording gravitational waves from 1.3 billion years ago. How did LIGO determine that what they heard were gravitational waves? They just decided they were gravitational waves. They convinced themselves. David Reitze said:

"Now, it took us months of careful checking, re-checking, analysis, looking at every piece of data to make sure that what we saw was not something that wasn't a gravitational wave, but in fact, it was a gravitational wave, and we've convinced ourselves that's the case."[8]

Modern science needs gravity to be true. Modern science will convince itself that gravity works. Without gravity, the theory of evolution and the big bang both fail. If gravity fails, so does the "solar system" and "universe" since both are built on gravity.

Finding gravitational waves would confirm Einstein's version of gravity and prove there is a fourth dimension (spacetime). After Reitze said they discovered gravitational waves in 2016, Philip Perry wrote in 2018, "Mathematically, we can describe the 4th dimension, but we may never experience it in the physical realm."[9] Again, Newcomb wrote in 2020, "There's no actual evidence—yet."[10] In 2023, when Greene discussed the fourth dimension of spacetime, he said, "There is no experimental evidence for any of what I'm about to tell you."[11]

Modern science (theories from the Scientific Revolution) does not provide evidence for their claims. When modern science cannot prove its theories, it relies upon others to confirm their theories are true. When evidence is presented that proves the earth does not move (e.g., Airy, Morley, Hubble, NASA, etc.), modern science ignores the data and reaffirms the earth moves. Secular (non-religious) scholarship has stated that Greek philosophy of the "universe" started with Pythagoras (500 BC), was resurrected by Copernicus (1543), and is celebrated today with pictures and videos.

The "universe" was built upon pagan Greek philosophy, magic, and math. The "universe" was built upon the teachings of Hermes Trismegistus. Throughout history, people have put their trust in the false god named Hermes Trismegistus. Pythagoras believed him. Copernicus believed him. We believe in him. We believe what Hermes Trismegistus taught Pythagoras and Copernicus: the earth moves.

The Modern Christian World

Chapter 29

Rejecting God's Word

During the Prescientific Age (–600 BC), the Classical Era (600 BC–500), the Middle Ages (500–1300s), the Renaissance (1400s–1600s), the Age of Reason/Enlightenment (1700s–1800s), or the Modern Era (1900s–present), God has always had a remanent. There have always been people who held to His word and His commands. Even today, with the onslaught of gender wars, the secularization of the culture, the influx of misinformation, deception, and New Age practices, God still has a remanent who seeks Him and holds fast to His word.

Significant moments in history have impacted God's people. The Scientific Revolution would be one of those moments that changed the whole world, both inside and outside the church. Inside the church, Christians were becoming open to the idea that the earth was moving based on ancient teachings from Egypt. People knew the old words in Scripture would have to change to the new words of science. They knew that the literal reading of the Bible would now have to be reexamined and reinterpreted to match the newly established "universe."

The plot to change the truth found in God's word is nothing new. Our enemy has always conspired to cause us to misread and misinterpret God's word. If we do not understand or believe God's word, we are in danger of disobeying God's word. If we do not understand God's word, we are in danger of being "led astray from your sincere and pure devotion to Christ" (2 Corinthians 11:3).

The corruption and twisting of God's word is one of the schemes of our enemy. Our enemy knows that if he showed up at our front doors and invited us to join him for eternity in endless suffering in the lake of fire, we would decline his offer. Our enemy meticulously chips away at our faith until we do not recognize how far we have abandoned God's word. Christians who fall away do not even realize they have left their faith in Jesus, the Word of God (John 1:1). Jesus will tell a group of Christians who did fall away that they need to repent—a church who did good things and worked hard for the kingdom of God.

Revelation 2:5

[Jesus said,] "Consider how far you have fallen! Repent and do the things you did at first. If you do not repent, I will come to you and remove your lampstand from its place."

The word "repent | μετανοέω | *metanoeō*" means "to change one's way of life as the result of a complete change of thought and attitude with regard to sin and righteousness."[1] Jesus is not telling the church to ask for forgiveness to remove the offense of our sin and restore our innocence with God. When we do ask for forgiveness, Jesus promises to "purify us from all unrighteousness" (1 John 1:9). Repentance is a change of attitude and behavior from sin toward obedience to God. Jesus told this church that if they did not repent, they would not have "the right to eat from the tree of life" (Revelation 2:7).

Adam and Eve had the right to eat from the tree of life. Adam and Eve had the right to be in the presence of God (garden of Eden). Once they disobeyed God's command, they had to leave the garden, which meant they lost access to the tree of life. Having access to the tree of life meant they could "eat, and live forever" (Genesis 3:22). How did Adam and Eve lose access to the ability to live forever? They did not hold to God's word. God told Adam, "You must not eat from the tree of the knowledge of good and evil, for when you eat from it you will certainly die" (Genesis 2:17). Adam then passed on to Eve what God said since Eve was not created yet (Genesis 2:18). That is why the devil said, "Did God really say?" (Genesis 3:1). Eve did not hear God tell her not to eat from the tree. She only knew what God said because Adam passed on what he heard God say.

Today, we are in the same situation. God's word has been passed down to us. We were not there when God created the waters of the deep, the firmament, the land, the sun, the moon, and the stars. We have been passed down a story written nearly 3,500 years ago. Can we believe a pre-scientific account of the heavens and the earth? Can we trust the translations of the Bible that have been handed down to us from a culture entirely different than ours? Do we have the ability to know what the authors of the Bible wrote in a language we cannot speak? The answer is yes if we believe the Bible.

1 John 2:20, 27

But you have an anointing from the Holy One, and all of you know the truth. [27] As for you, the anointing you received from him remains in you, and you do not need anyone to teach you. But as his anointing teaches you about all things and as that anointing is real, not counterfeit—just as it has taught you, remain in him.

None of us witnessed what God spoke in the beginning. We must trust what Moses heard God say and what the Bible's authors heard God say. God's spoken words were gathered in a book called the Bible, which has been passed down to us. Our enemy knows we are putting our faith in a book that we declare "inspired by God" (1 Timothy 3:16, NSAB). A book that we believe is "the word of God" (1 Thessalonians 2:13). A book that we proclaim is "right and true" (Psalm 33:4). A book that we must not doubt when our enemy asks, "Did God really say?" (Genesis 3:1).

When God speaks, it is up to us to believe it or not, to accept it or not. God does not make conditional claims, cite untrue words, make cryptic speech, or cause deception. God's written word, the inspired text from His breath, is an account, declaration, and record of truth. It is up to us whether we believe it or not.

Our enemy knows that if we start to doubt what God said, we are susceptible to disobeying what God said. If we begin to mistrust what God says, then we are prone to disobey, willing to test our defiance towards the commands of God, which is exactly what Eve did. Eve knew what God said and even repeated it to the serpent. Eve said, "But God did say, 'You must not eat fruit from the tree that is in the middle of the garden, and you must not touch it, or you will die.'" (Genesis 3:3). Because Eve started to doubt God's word, contemplating her decision, thinking about what the serpent suggested, she ended up being deceived (2 Corinthians 11:3).

In the Old Testament, we see a pattern, over and over again, about the importance of obeying God's word. God told the people, "Keep my decrees and laws, for the person who obeys them will live by them. I am the LORD" (Leviticus 18:5). We learn in the New Testament that Jesus is the Word, walking among the people (John 1:14). What did Jesus, the living Word, tell us? Jesus said, "Very truly I tell you, whoever obeys my word will never see death" (John 8:51). Accepting or rejecting God's word is a serious choice we make.

When Samuel rebuked King Saul, it was not disobeying an order but the rejection of God's word that ended Saul's reign. Saul was told to destroy the Amalekites (1 Samuel 15:3). The Amalekites were defeated, but Saul ended up sparing Agag, the Amalekites' king and keeping all the best animals. When Samuel returns to Saul's camp, he hears the animals that were supposed to be destroyed. Samuel rebukes Saul and tells him that God has rejected him as king. Saul was not being punished because he disobeyed an order. Saul was being punished because he rejected God's word.

1 Samuel 15:23

[Samuel said to King Saul,] "For rebellion is like the sin of divination, and arrogance like the evil of idolatry. Because you have rejected the word of the LORD, he has rejected you as king."

The Bible does not give us many choices regarding God's word. We, believe it or not, obey it or not, accept it or not. If we choose to disbelieve, disobey, or dismiss God's word, we are simply rejecting God's word. The choice is up to us.

∅

When we reject God's word, we often fail to realize the extent of our fall (Revelation 2:5). We may not know when to seek forgiveness (Hebrews 8:12) or when to repent (Act 3:19). This is where grace comes in. When we accept Jesus Christ as our Lord, "we have all received grace" (John 1:16). The Bible assures us, "There is now no condemnation for those who are in Christ Jesus" (Romans 8:1) because Jesus, who "is faithful and just and will forgive us our sins and purify us from all unrighteousness" (1 John 1:9).

God declared David "a man after my own heart" (Acts 13:22), even though he committed adultery and murder. God could declare David innocent and righteous because David believed what God said. David believed God would not hold his mistakes against him when he asked for forgiveness.

Psalm 32:1–2
Blessed is the one whose transgressions are forgiven, whose sins are covered. [2] Blessed is the one whose sin the LORD does not count against them and in whose spirit is no deceit.

Forgiveness is one of the greatest gifts Jesus has given to the church. Forgiveness removes the offense of our sins, and because Jesus is faithful to His word, He makes us righteous and pure when we ask. The best way to keep from rejecting God's word is to remain close to Jesus, the one "full of grace" (John 1:14).

Ó

Rejecting God's word is a real danger. As Christians, we can fall for deception when we reject the truth. When we hold to things that are not true, the Bible tells us we can be led astray or, even worse, fall from the faith. Paul warned the church not to be deceived like Eve. Paul warned the church that their love for Christ was in danger if they fell for deception (2 Corinthians 11:3).

Paul knew the people in Corinth were easily led away from Jesus because they did not hold to the truth. When the church of Corinth heard a different message about Jesus or allowed a different spirit to enter the church, the people accepted it without hesitation. Paul knew when a counterfeit message was told to the church of Corinth, they would "put up with it easily enough" (2 Corinthians 11:4). The church of Corinth could not discern the truth from a lie. Paul knew they could not see the works of "false apostles, deceitful workers, masquerading as apostles of Christ" (2 Corinthians 11:13). Paul knew since they were led astray from the truth, they were easily deceived by Satan and his "servants of righteousness" (2 Corinthians 11:15).

2 Corinthians 11:14–15
And no wonder, for Satan himself masquerades as an angel of light. [15] It is not surprising, then, if his servants also masquerade as servants of righteousness. Their end will be what their actions deserve.

When we know something is authentic, genuine, or true, it is easy to see the counterfeit. We can easily discern things that are not real. The Bible tells us, "Do not believe every spirit, but test the spirits to see whether they are from God, because many false prophets have gone out into the world" (1 John 4:1). How are we able to test the spirits if we are not familiar with the Spirit of truth? The only counter we have for not falling into deception is to know the truth. Knowing the truth is the only way to avoid being led away from the truth. What happens when we do not see the truth? According to the Bible, we can be "led astray from your sincere and pure devotion to Christ" (2 Corinthians 11:3). Deception is not the end game; it is just the beginning. The final goal of deception is our denial and rejection of the truth, which eventually leads to our destruction, just like Eve.

Our enemy wants us to believe things that are not true for several reasons. First, we learn to listen to the devil's voice when we fall for deception. Jesus told us that lying is "his native language, for he is a liar and the father of lies" (John 8:44). Second, falling for deception prevents us from seeing the truth. The teachers of the Law and Pharisees knew the Old Testament. Still, they did not accept the one "who came from the Father, full of grace and truth" (John 1:14). Because they could not see the truth right in front of them, Jesus called them "blind fools" (Matthew 23:17). Third, when we fall for deception, it reduces our ability to discern the truth. If we are people of the Spirit, we will know the truth because the Holy Spirit is "the Spirit of truth" (John 16:13). If we fall for deception, we will not be able to make "judgments about all things" (1 Corinthians 2:15). Fourth, being deceived sets us in opposition to the truth. Either we are on the side of truth, or we are against the truth. Jesus said, "Whoever is not with me is against me" (Luke 11:23). When the people are against the truth, they want to destroy the truth. The Bible says, "From that day on they plotted to take his life" (John 11:53). Fifth, deception reduces the power of God in our lives. Our enemy knows that if we are deceived, we are less effective for the kingdom of God because we do not operate in the power of God.

Matthew 22:29

Jesus replied, "You are in error because you do not know the Scriptures or the power of God."

Jesus told the Sadducees they were in error because they did not know what the Old Testament said. Gary G. Porton wrote, "The Sadducees did not believe that the soul continued to exist after death or that people suffered punishments or received rewards after they died."[2] Walter A. Elwell and Barry J. Beitzel wrote, "For the Sadducees say that there is no resurrection, nor angel, nor spirit."[3] When the Sadducees tested Jesus on the final resurrection, Jesus told them they were deceived.

The word "error | πλανάω | *planaō*" means "to cause someone to hold a wrong view and thus be mistaken—'to mislead, to deceive, deception, to cause to be mistaken.'"[4] The word "error | πλανάω | *planaō*" means "'to lead astray' or 'to deceive.'"[5] The word "error | πλανάω | *planaō*" means "go astray, deceive, err, seduce, wander."[6] Jesus' words to the Sadducees are a warning to us all. When we are led astray from believing the truth found in Scripture, we put ourselves in a position to fall for deception, which could lead to our destruction.

Jesus warned the church in Ephesus because they had "forsaken the love [they] had at first" (Revelation 2:4). If we could ask the church in Ephesus if they loved Jesus, they would all say, "Yes." Jesus even told the church, "You have persevered and have endured hardships for my name, and have not grown weary" (Revelation 2:3). The church in Ephesus was being persecuted for their "love" and commitment to Christ. Why was the church warned about forsaking their love for Christ? We are not told the specific reasons for Jesus' warning. We are only told that the church has forsaken the love they had at first.

Love for who? Jesus. Who is Jesus? Jesus is "the truth" (John 14:6). The church was doing good things for Christ. Why was Jesus warning them? At some point, the church fell for deception. At some point, the church started to believe things that were not true. At some point, the church was blind to how far they were led away from Jesus. Paul told the church that deception could lead them "astray from [their] sincere and pure devotion to Christ" (2 Corinthians 11:3). Just as Paul warned the church in Corinth, Jesus warned the church in Ephesus. Jesus told the church, who had fallen so far from Him, to repent and return to their love for Him (the truth).

Revelation 2:5

[Jesus said,] "Consider how far you have fallen! Repent and do the things you did at first. If you do not repent, I will come to you and remove your lampstand from its place."

Chapter 30

The Framework of Creation

I wanted to provide a list comparing the claims of the Bible and modern science (Table 4). The list demonstrates the Bible's primary claims about the heavenly and earthly realms—claims opposite to modern science.

Bible	Modern Science
Start: God	Start: Gravity
Time: 144 hours (Day 1–6)	Time: 144 years (1543–1687)
Earth: Day 1	Earth: 4.54 billion years ago
Earth's Location: Below heaven	Earth's Location: Solar system
Water: Day 1	Water: 4.4 billion years ago
Firmament: Yes (solid dome barrier)	Firmament: No (vacuum of space)
Sea: Day 3	Sea: 4 billion years ago
Plants: Day 3	Plants: 600 million years ago
Sun: Day 4	Sun: 4.6 billion years ago
Moon: Light	Moon: Rock
Stars: Lights for earth	Stars: Ball of gas
Planets: 0	Planets: 21.6 sextillion*
Sun's Location: In firmament	Sun's Location: Milky Way Galaxy
Foundation: Yes	Foundation: No
Human: Day 6	Human: 300,000 years ago
People: God's image	People: Evolved from animals
Genders: 2	Genders: 112
Life: Because of God	Life: Because of sun
History: Genesis 1	History: big bang
Heaven: Yes	Heaven: No
Hell: Yes	Hell: No

*21,600,000,000,000,000,000,000,000

Table 4. Comparing the Bible and Modern Science.

As we look into Christian scholarship, it becomes evident that the Bible provides a fundamental framework for understanding the heavenly and earthly realms. This framework, based on God's word, sets the context for the authors of the Bible and forms the structure upon which Scripture is built. Understanding and working within this framework is essential when interpreting the Bible's claims about the natural world. It is important to remember that the Bible is not a human book but God's word. Every narrative, poetic verse, figurative passage, parable, and prophecy originated from God's breath. When we alter the meaning of the Bible's words, we are essentially altering God's message. Therefore, our beliefs should always align with the framework (context) of Scripture, as it is the unchanging word of God that is always "right and true" (Psalm 33:4).

Chapter 31

Alphabetizing Scripture

Things had to change for Biblical scholars once the earth was put into motion. Neil deGrasse Tyson, who is not a Christian, explains why and when Bible scholars had to change their interpretation of the Bible when dealing with scientific matters (the natural world). Tyson said:

> "So what happened was, when science discovers things, and you want to stay religious, or you want to continue to believe that the Bible is unerring, what you would do is you would say, 'Well, let me go back to the Bible and reinterpret it.' Then you'd say things like, 'Oh, well they didn't really mean that literally. They meant that figuratively.' So, this whole sort of reinterpretation of the, 'how figurative the poetic passages of the Bible are,' came after science showed that this is not how things unfolded. And so, the educated religious people are perfectly fine with that."[1]

Scholars changed their interpretation of Genesis because God's word did not work with the "discoveries" of modern science. Tyson was not the first one to recognize this. Galileo made the same argument in his letter to his friend, Ella Diodati. Galileo wrote, "Whenever the works [nature] and the Word cannot be made to agree, we consider Holy Scripture as secondary."[2] Tyson and Galileo make the same point. Whenever modern science tells the world its scientific "discoveries," the Bible must yield its truth to human knowledge. According to modern science, their words are the new standard of truth, and the Bible is always a second-class citizen.

Tyson's final point is that educated religious people are okay with reinterpreting Scripture to fit modern science's "universe." Educated by who? Educated by modern science who teaches the earth moves. Educated to accept modern science's theory of the sun-god-centered "solar system."

Because of modern science, Christian scholarship turned literal passages into symbolic, poetic, or mythological passages. As mentioned earlier, the literal reading of the Bible has been challenged throughout history. When did the Bible scholars and theologians begin to change their interpretation of the Bible? It was after the Scientific Revolution (1543–1687) that a new theory would form. The theory was called the JEDP theory, also known as the Documentary Hypothesis. Got Questions Ministries wrote:

> In brief, the JEDP theory states that the first five books of the Bible, Genesis, Exodus, Leviticus, Numbers, and Deuteronomy, were not written entirely by Moses, who died in the 1400s BC, but also by different authors/compliers after Moses. The theory is based on the fact that different names for God are used in different portions of the Pentateuch, and there are detectable differences in linguistic style. The letters of the JEDP theory stand for the four supposed authors: the author who uses *Jehovah* for God's name, the author who uses *Elohim* for God's name, the author of Deuteronomy, and the priestly author of Leviticus. The JEDP theory goes on to state that the different portions of the Pentateuch were likely compiled in the 4th Century B.C., possibly by Ezra.[3]

The JEDP theory started to analyze the Pentateuch's linguistic style. Scholars were beginning to notice different writing styles used in the Pentateuch (first five Old Testament books). From literary analysis, they concluded that the Pentateuch was compiled over many years. Josh McDowell wrote:

> Julius Wellhausen in 1895 added the finishing touches to a hypothesis prevalent in modern biblical circles and known as the documentary hypothesis (or JEDP hypothesis). Using literary criticism as its basis for argument, this hypothesis sets forth the theory that the Pentateuch (Genesis through Deuteronomy) was not written by Moses, as the Bible claims, but was completed years after Moses died. Those adhering to the documentary hypothesis teach that the first five books of the Bible were written close to one thousand years after Moses' death and were the result of a process of writing, rewriting, editing, and compiling by various editors or redactors.[4]

A new method of studying the Bible arose after the Scientific Revolution. Arthur G. Patzia and Anthony J. Petrotta tell us the history of the JEDP theory or Documentary Hypothesis:

A theory about the origins and composition of the Pentateuch. This hypothesis arose during the eighteenth century as a result of new methods for studying the texts (cf. source criticism).[5]

The JEDP theory created a new method of interpreting the Bible called source criticism. Patzia and Petrotta define source criticism as:

> An approach to texts that seeks to discover the literary sources of a document. The assumption is that certain biblical texts underwent a lengthy process of growth and composition, both oral and written. Source critics examine texts in order to discover evidence of sources on the basis of language and style, the use of divine names, doublets of stories and any discrepancies within or between passages.[6]

The newly formed way of approaching the text of Genesis assumed or guessed that the Pentateuch was written over a long period. Julius Wellhausen finally established the JEDP theory. This method was established after the Scientific Revolution. Ronald S. Hendel wrote:

> Since the beginnings of source criticism of the Pentateuch in the 17th and 18th centuries there has been much controversy over the sources of Genesis. There are several competing theories today, but the long-established identification of J (the Yahwist), E (the Elohist), and P (the Priestly source) still provides the most plausible model for the composition of Genesis.[7]

Hendel stated that source criticism of Genesis began after Copernicus said the earth moved. Historically speaking, source criticism is a modern approach to Genesis 1. Alan Cairns wrote:

> The hypothesis that these alleged sources were combined over a period of time to produce the Pentateuch as we have it was gradually developed in the 18th and 19th centuries. It commenced with the speculations of Jean Astruc in 1753 and culminated in Julius Wellhausen's definitive statement of it in 1876.[8]

Cairns tells us that Jean Astruc (1753) was the father of the JEDP theory, which began with his "speculations" about the first five books of the Bible. Cairns confirms that Julius Wellhausen finalized the JEDP theory. Astruc's initial speculation about Genesis developed an approach to the Bible that would soon question its history. Remember that this new theory happened after the visible god was placed at the center of modern science's new "solar system."

J. S. Wright and J. A. Thompson agree with Hendel and Cairns and state that scholars came up with theories about Genesis' structure starting in the 1700s. Wright and Thompson inform us that the JEDP theory began as a very different (radical) approach to Scripture and denied the history of the Book of Genesis. Wright and Thompson state:

> Since the days of Jean Astruc, in the 18th century, scholars have looked for various 'documents' in the Pentateuch. These for Genesis are J (which uses Yahweh for the divine name), E (which uses Elohim for the divine name) and P (which is concerned chiefly with religious matters). Early forms of this theory were extremely radical and denied historicity to a great deal in Genesis. More recently it has been argued that the 'documents' grew by the collection of ancient material until they reached their final shape; J in about the 10th or 9th century BC, E a little later and P in post-exilic times. Historicity is not necessarily denied in the more moderate forms of this theory.[9]

When the new JEDP theory about Genesis was being developed, the history of Genesis was being stripped away. Genesis was no longer viewed as a book that presented an accurate historical record. Genesis went from historical to mythological, from narrative to poetry, from Moses being the author to multiple authors. Thanks to a theory that started with an assumption by Jean Astruc (1753), God's word would take a secondary position to the JEDP theory. The JEDP theory only developed after Copernicus made the sun, a visible god, the center of the show.

The influence of the JEDP theory would continue to change how scholars viewed the historical narrative of Genesis. With the development of the JEDP theory, Genesis began to change from a historical narrative into a story based on mythological language. Herbert Edward Ryle wrote:

The early narratives of Genesis respecting the Creation, the Fall, and the Flood are based upon myths and traditions which the Israelites inherited in common with other branches of the Semitic family.[10]

Ryle argued that Genesis used myths and folklore to allow God to tell the truth about creation and counter other creation myths. Ryle will also reveal his approach to the Book of Genesis. Ryle continued:

The story of the beginnings of the world and of mankind is told, not with a scientific but with a religious purpose. The old-world myths, or tales of Semitic folklore, were employed for the purpose of setting forth in their true light—as discerned through the revealing spirit of J—the unchanging verities respecting the nature of God, of man, and of the created universe.[11]

Ryle, writing in a Bible dictionary from 1912, used the JEDP theory to form his understanding of the creation story. Ryle's opinion about the creation story came from a theory formed during the 18th and 19th centuries. Ryle indicates his approach by referencing the "J" material. The JEDP theory's impact still influences our interpretation of Genesis today. Allen Ross explains how myth is now an acceptable way of conveying truth:

Many writers describe the contents of Genesis as myth or attribute its origin to myth. Mythological literature seeks to explain the origins of things in symbolic forms. Myth records so-called 'sacred history' rather than actual history; it reports how reality came into existence through the deeds of gods and supernatural creatures. It purports to establish reality, the nature of the universe, the function of the state, and the values of life.[12]

Ross states that many people describe Genesis 1 as a myth and that it is no longer viewed as an actual historical event. The JEDP theory turned a special revelation from God into an ordinary piece of literature that talked about mythological or imaginary people. Cairns wrote:

> JEDP theory—the theory that the religion of Israel was not a special revelation, but developed naturally; that the patriarchs were not historical persons, but mythological characters; and that the Pentateuch is a patchwork of documents written by unknown men whose hand can be traced by their use of the divine names and other literary marks. Thus J used the name Jehovah, E used Elohim, D fused their work to produce Deuteronomy, and P was a very late priestly writer.[13]

Cairns states that the development of the JEDP theory changed historical people into imaginary characters that teach us "truth" but not real history. Anthony C. Thiselton and Gerald Sheppard will also explain why the understanding of Genesis changed after the Scientific Revolution. Thiselton and Sheppard will confirm what Neil deGrasse Tyson said about religious scholars trying to hold to the credibility of the Bible:

> Alongside the challenges confronted in the eighteenth century, the Christian search for the literal sense of Scripture in the nineteenth century faced an intensification of historical-critical methods, accompanied by a whole array of newer scientific, sociological, economic and psychological means of analysis.[14]

Thiselton and Sheppard said that Christians were searching for the meaning of the Bible because of new scientific data. The new methods for interpreting Genesis occurred after the Scientific Revolution, a revolution that taught the earth was moving and has influenced Christian scholars and theologians, past and present. As Galileo said, thanks to modern science, we now "consider Holy Scripture as secondary."[15]

Chapter 32

The Book of Genesis

This book lists the different perspectives of the Biblical, Greek, and Modern Christian worlds. The different worlds revolve around one story, Genesis 1's creation story. Since Genesis is the book that contains God's record of creation, it is necessary to discuss its genre and authorship.

Genre

What is a genre? Steven L. McKenzie defines genre as "categories of literature, as well as music, film, and the like."[1] What type of literature is Genesis? For most of history, Genesis was categorized as a narrative. What is a narrative? *Nelson's New Illustrated Bible Dictionary* defines it as "an orderly account that relates the details of a story."[2] Genesis 1 tells the detailed story of creation, which is a narrative genre. *How to Read the Bible for All Its Worth* wrote, "The following Old Testament books are largely or entirely composed of narrative material: Genesis ... "[3] Easley wrote:

> Although Genesis was "The First Book of the Law," it recorded relatively few divine commands (but see 2:16–27; 9:6–7). Genesis has preserved two historical narratives. Chapters 1–11 contain a selective history of the entire human race ... Chapters 12–50 tell the story of the direct ancestors of the Israelites.[4]

Genesis is a historical narrative that gives the details of creation. Genesis 1 is a factual and historical account of creation. Schaeffer wrote:

> [The] reason for taking the entire book of Genesis as historic is the external argument. The case may be put simply and concisely: Absolutely every place where the New Testament refers to the first half of Genesis, the New Testament assumes (and many times affirms) that Genesis is history and that it is to be read in normal fashion, with the common use of the words and syntax.[5]

Genesis 1 is a creation account set in the context of a historical narrative. The entire New Testament viewed the creation story as factual and accurate history. Jesus said, "At the beginning of creation God 'made them male and female'" (Mark 10:6). Jesus knew that after creation started, it would only be five days later when He would make Adam and Eve and not billions of years after the "universe" began.

According to Gareth Lee Cockerill, Genesis 1 is in "the primeval history found in Genesis 1–11."[6] The *ESV Study Bible* wrote:

> It is easy to see that Genesis aims to record actual events rather than mythical events … Further, the book is narrative prose, whose main function in the Bible is to recount history. The creation account, 1:1–2:3, is stylistically different from the rest of the book; it is exalted prose, and its historicity is assumed elsewhere in the Bible (e.g., Ps. 136:4–9).[7]

Genesis 1 is a historical account that the Old and New Testaments assume is a record of actual events. There is no evidence that the people in the Bible, from Genesis to Revelation, thought Genesis 1 was a symbolic, poetic, or mythical story. Steven Boyd, a specialist in the Hebrew language, was asked about the history of Genesis. Boyd responded:

> "It's an accurate historical account. The presentation is such, and the perspective of the writers, that they believed they were talking about real events. It's very obvious because of the way in which they insisted the next generation learn their history."[8]

Boyd was also asked about the meaning of "day." Del Tackett, the former Senior Vice President of Focus on the Family, mentioned that many people think Genesis is poetic and not an accurate historical account. Boyd responded:

> "First of all, it's not poetry. The world's greatest Hebraists all affirm that this is a narrative … One of the unique features of the Genesis accounts, of creation and the flood, is that they are narratives, because in the ancient near East, they are done in epic poetry, which is very different. And here we have a narrative to indicate that this is historical. What that means is that you should understand the words, the normal way in which those Hebrew words were understood."[9]

Genesis 1 is a detailed account of history. Modern scholars may label it poetic, figurative, symbolic, or mythological, but Genesis 1 was written to tell people about the factual, historical, and truthful account of creation. Today, it is hard to imagine people believing in a firmament, a solid dome barrier and a sun underneath the celestial water. Do you know who would think such a thing? Their names are Moses, David, Paul, and Jesus Christ. The people in the Bible believed Genesis 1 was a written historical record of what "God said" (Genesis 1:3, 6, 9, 11, 14, 20, 24, 26, 29).

Author

Who wrote the Book of Genesis? We would think that question would be settled since Jesus told us, "Everything must be fulfilled that is written about me in the Law of Moses, the Prophets and the Psalms" (Luke 24:44). William MacDonald wrote, "For Christians the fact that our Lord Himself accepted Mosaic authorship should settle the matter."[10] Jesus said that Moses gave them the Law, the Torah, which includes Genesis. Leon Morris commented on Jesus' words found in Luke 24:44:

> The solemn division of Scripture into the law of Moses and the prophets and the psalms (the three divisions of the Hebrew Bible) indicates that there is no part of Scripture that does not bear its witness to Jesus. This incidentally appears to be the only place in the New Testament where this threefold division is explicitly mentioned.[11]

The Hebrew Bible is divided into the Law of Moses, prophets, and "the Psalms" (Luke 24:44). Although the Hebrew Bible and the Christian Old Testament have the same books, they are divided and ordered differently into twenty-four and thirty-nine books, respectively. Both the Hebrew Bible and the Christian Old Testament start with Genesis.

Morris writes that Jesus credited Moses with writing the first five books of the Hebrew Bible, as the author of the Law (Genesis through Deuteronomy). Andrew Steinmann commented, "From antiquity, the first five books of the Old Testament, commonly called the Pentateuch or, in Hebrew, the Torah (i.e., 'the Teaching'), have been ascribed to Moses."[12] According to Steinmann, the belief that Moses wrote the first five books of the Bible was generally accepted since ancient times. The acceptance of Moses as the author of the Law has changed over the years. *The Eerdmans Companion to the Bible* wrote:

Genesis does not claim for itself a particular author or time of writing. The traditional view asserts that Moses authored Genesis, as well as Exodus through Deuteronomy (the "Five Books of Moses"), in the late 2nd millennium. Beginning in the 19th century A.D., scholars viewed Genesis as a compilation by three editors: the Yahwist (10th century B.C.), who used the name 'Yahweh' for God; the Elohist (9th century), who used the name 'Elohim' for God; and the Priestly writer (6th century), who added the 'priestly' or 'cultic' material.[13]

The traditional view was that Moses wrote Genesis 1. *The Eerdmans Companion to the Bible* tells us that authorship became an issue of debate only after the JEDP theory was introduced, beginning in the 1800s, which is after the Scientific Revolution (1543–1687).

Scholars started to debate Moses' authorship even though the Old Testament knew who wrote it. The Book of Joshua said, "Be very strong; be careful to obey all that is written in the Book of the Law of Moses" (Joshua 23:6). The New Testament knew who wrote Genesis. Paul's letter to Corinth said, "For it is written in the Law of Moses" (1 Corinthians 9:9). Scholars started to debate Moses' authorship even though Jesus knew who wrote it. Jesus said, "Everything must be fulfilled that is written about me in the Law of Moses" (Luke 24:44).

Summary

The Book of Genesis is a historical narrative that gives us a detailed account of the creation. According to the Old and New Testaments, Moses is the author. Genesis' genre and authorship are important since the JEDP theory (Documentary Hypothesis) has influenced the literal reading of the creation account. After the church started accepting a heliocentric (sun-god-centered) theory, Genesis went from a factual, historical, and truthful record into a mythological or poetic story.

Today, Genesis 1 is no longer accepted as a precise account of creation because we believe in an earth moving around the sun. How could we have a morning and evening on Day 1 if the sun was not created until Day 4? How could we believe in a solid dome barrier that holds water above the stars? The old Bible had to change when the heliocentric theory became the new standard of truth.

Since the 19th century, many theories about the creation story have been formed. There is the literal view, which holds to a six-day, 24-hour creation week (young earth).[14] The framework hypothesis divides the creation into realms (Days 1–3) and the filling of the realms (Days 4–6). The day-age theory believes that the days presented in Genesis are not actual 24-hour days but represent longer periods (old earth). There is the gap theory that inserts gaps of time in the first three verses of the Bible. There are many approaches to the creation story. Within each of these approaches, there are differences of opinion about the story's details. There is one common factor in all these theories. They all believe the earth moves.

It is essential to know that Genesis 1 teaches us the history God wants us to know. Genesis 1 is God's revealed history, which tells His(story). God chose to reveal creation to Moses, a prophet. The Bible said, "Since then, no prophet has risen in Israel like Moses, whom the LORD knew face to face" (Deuteronomy 34:10). Peter C. Craigie wrote, "Moses was a prophet."[15] J. A. Thompson wrote, "A final evaluation is now given of the character of Moses. He was the greatest of Israel's prophets."[16] Moses, the prophet, wrote Genesis 1 as a historical document.

Why do we need to know that the author of Genesis 1 was a prophet? It is important to know that Moses was a prophet because prophets wrote the words of God. Peter will tell us how prophets (e.g., Moses, David, Isaiah, Jeremiah, etc.) wrote the Bible.

2 Peter 1:20–21

Above all, you must understand that no prophecy of Scripture came about by the prophet's own interpretation of things. [21] For prophecy never had its origin in the human will, but prophets, though human, spoke from God as they were carried along by the Holy Spirit.

The apostle Peter wants us to know the origin of the prophet's words. Thomas R. Schreiner wrote, "The words the prophets spoke, however, ultimately came from God. They were inspired, or 'carried along,' by the Holy Spirit."[17] Daniel C. Arichea wrote, "It was God's Spirit that carried them along and enabled them to say what God wanted them to say."[18] Allen Black and Mark C. Black wrote, "It originated not 'in the will of man' but was rather 'from God,' through the agency of 'the Holy Spirit.'"[19] Moses, the prophet, did not write his own words or opinions. Moses wrote what the Holy Spirit inspired him to write.

Once the earth started moving, the authority of Scripture became secondary to modern science's word about the natural world. When the Scientific Revolution was complete, the contemporary Christian scholar had to reimagine and reinterpret the literal Bible to make it relevant to a changing culture influenced by pagan sun worship. Once the earth started to move, Genesis 1 no longer could be trusted to tell us the literal words that "God said" (Genesis 1:3, 6, 9, 11, 14, 20, 24, 26, 29).

Cosmogony or Cosmology

So far, most of this book has dealt with the subject of cosmogony. I have covered the origins and history of how our modern "universe" was created. *Encyclopedia* defines cosmogony as:

> The word cosmogony is derived from the combination of two Greek terms, *kosmos* and *genesis*. *Kosmos* refers to the order of the universe and/or the universe as an order. *Genesis* means the coming into being or the process or substantial change in the process, a birth. Cosmogony thus has to do with myths, stories, or theories regarding the birth or creation of the universe as an order or the description of the original order of the universe.[1]

Within the modern Christian world, I will be dealing more with cosmology. Today, most people use the word cosmology when talking about the subject of cosmogony. What is cosmology? NASA states:

> The scientific study of the large scale properties of the universe as a whole. The study of cosmology uses the scientific method to understand the origin, evolution and ultimate fate of the entire Universe. Like any field of science, cosmology involves the formation of theories or hypotheses about the universe which make specific predictions for phenomena that can be tested with observations. Depending on the outcome of the observations, the theories will need to be abandoned, revised or extended to accommodate the data. The prevailing theory about the origin and evolution of our Universe is the so-called "Big Bang" theory.[2]

Cosmogony and cosmology are words that are blended together. Since I have covered the myths and stories about the birth of modern science's "universe" (cosmogony), I want to focus on the structure and layout of the heavenly and earthly realms (cosmology). I will compare what the Bible claims and what modern science teaches about the function and nature of the "universe" and "solar system."

When comparing the Bible and modern science, there is a tendency for people to become defensive on their positions about scientific matters (e.g., the shape of the earth, movement of the earth, the layout of the "solar system," etc.). People can be swayed by logic and reasoning, but speaking about modern science is like talking to someone about faith. When a person sincerely holds to their religious beliefs, logic and reason will not easily persuade someone to change their trust in what they believe to be true. Here are two examples of people who believe their position about the movement of the earth is true and how they defend their beliefs.

Person 1: Earth Moves

A person who believes in an earth that moves would point out scientific arguments to prove their position (e.g., stellar parallax, lunar eclipses, retrograde motion of "planets," etc.). They would use specific passages in the Bible to claim their position as true. If confronted with a "non-moving earth" believer, they would dismiss that person as foolish, naïve, and simply uneducated for not trusting the facts: the earth moves.

Person 2: Earth Does Not Move

A person who believes in a non-moving earth would point out scientific arguments to prove their position (e.g., Pascal's law, properties of gas, line of sight, etc.). They would use specific passages in the Bible to claim their position as true. If confronted with a "moving earth" believer, they would consider that person as one who does not research or understand modern science's theories and is misguided for not seeing the truth: the earth does not move.

We always have the choice of what we want to believe. Eve had a choice to believe what God said about the tree. Noah had a choice to believe what God said about the ark. Moses had a choice to believe what God said at the burning bush. We have a choice to believe what God said about the layout of the heavenly and earthly realms.

I will present a choice between what God said and what modern science claims. I will compare the heavenly and earthly realms presented by the Bible and the "universe" promoted by modern science. There is no middle ground between the two. Either the earth is moving, or it is not. Either the earth is a sphere, or it is not. Either the earth is in a vacuum of space, or it is not. Either the Bible makes true claims about the heavenly and earthly realms, or it does not. We cannot have both.

Chapter 34

Faith and Stardust

There is an argument in favor of blending the Bible and modern science (theories from the Scientific Revolution). How can we merge the Bible and modern science when both say the opposite claims? At first, we may find compatibility, but we will always reach the same outcome. Here are the results of trying to blend the Bible and modern science.

(1) The Bible and modern science can find common ground on a particular subject (e.g., the earth's physical existence, water evaporation, etc.). (2) The Bible is modified to fit modern science (e.g., firmament, earth's foundation, etc.). (3) We ignore the fact that modern science does not recognize the Bible's claims (e.g., God's existence, hell's existence, etc.). (4) We pretend that the Bible and modern science are compatible by overlooking the foundation of modern science (e.g., Greek philosophy, gravity, etc.).

The fact is that modern science never changes because of the Bible. Even worse, modern science has changed our understanding of the Bible even though it does not recognize the Bible's author: God. We try to make the Bible and modern science work together even though modern science does not believe the very first verse of the Bible: "God created the heavens and the earth" (Genesis 1:1).

Can the Bible and science work together? Yes. As Menzies wrote, "True science and the Bible are not at odds."[1] Can the Bible and modern science work together? No. The two are contrasting by nature and state the opposite claims (Chapter 30: "The Framework of Creation." Table 4). The Bible says the earth is on a foundation and motionless with a solid dome barrier over us. Modern science says the earth rotates on its axis and orbits the sun in open space. The Bible says, as Jesus put it, "Your word is truth" (John 17:17). Modern science says, as Einstein put it, "I'd have to feel sorry for God, because the theory is correct."[2] The Bible and modern science cannot be merged without one of them compromising the statements it makes.

Some scientists have found Christ while working in the field of science. A famous example is Francis Collins. The *Scientific American* wrote:

> Collins was an atheist until 1978, when he underwent a conversion experience while hiking in the mountains and became a devout Christian. In his 2006 bestselling book

The Language of God, Collins declares that he sees no incompatibility between science and religion. "The God of the Bible is also the God of the genome," he wrote. "He can be worshipped in the cathedral or in the laboratory."[3]

Collins was an atheist and now is a Christian. I will never argue Collins' faith in Jesus Christ. I take him at his word. According to his testimony, we are brothers in Christ. What I will comment on is his view of Scripture. When a scientist becomes a Christian, this does not mean modern science is now validated as accurate or correct. The salvation of a scientist means they responded to the Holy Spirit, and everyone who "calls on the name of the Lord will be saved" (Romans 10:13).

Collins, even as a Christian does not believe what the Bible reads when it comes to the creation of mankind. During an interview on *Big Think*, Collins was asked about the influence genetics has had on his faith. Collins responded:

> "My study of genetics certainly tells me, incontrovertibly that Darwin was right about the nature of how living things have arrived on the scene, by descent from a common ancestor under the influence of natural selection over very long periods of time."[4]

Collins believes in the big bang and the theory of evolution, which are built upon the "universe" created by modern science. If we believe we came from a common ancestor like Collins believes, then we were created by the stars. Collins wrote:

> For the first million years after the Big Bang, the universe expanded, the temperature dropped, and nuclei and atoms began to form. Matter began to coalesce into galaxies under the force of gravity. It acquired rotational motion as it did so, ultimately resulting in the spiral shape of galaxies such as our own ... All of these steps in the formation of our solar system are now well described and unlikely to be revised on the basis of additional future information. Nearly all of the atoms in your body were once cooked in the nuclear furnace of an ancient supernova—you are truly made of Stardust.[5]

Collins, an atheist now turned Christian, believes the creation story in the Bible is the big bang. According to the big bang, mankind was not created by God but by the dying stars that brought life to the earth. Collins is no different than the atheist Lawrence Krauss, who teaches students to "forget Jesus, the stars died so that you could be here today."[6]

Collins trusts a man named Charles Darwin, who proposed his theory of evolution through natural selection (1859). Collins trusts Georges Lemaître, who proposed the big bang (1927). Darwin and Lemaître trusted a man named Nicolaus Copernicus, whose theory led to the creation of the "solar system." Copernicus trusted the god Hermes Trismegistus, who taught Copernicus what the sun was: a god. Copernicus wrote, "[Hermes] the Thrice Greatest labels it a visible god … Thus indeed, as though seated on a royal throne, the sun governs the family of planets revolving around it."[7] Copernicus trusted a god named Hermes Trismegistus, who taught people to worship the sun. Long wrote, "Hermetic writings [attributed to Hermes Trismegistus] pointed to sun worship and a Sun-centered universe."[8]

The mixing of faith and modern science is incompatible since the foundation of each origin story is in direct conflict with each other. Collins believes we came about because a supernova died and shed its stardust. Collins believes without a doubt (incontrovertibly) that "Darwin was right about the nature of how living things have arrived on the scene."[9] Collins believes the first man was created by a dying star that transformed dead rocks into living organisms (autogenesis). According to the Bible, the first man was made because the living God "breathed into his nostrils the breath of life, and the man became a living being" (Genesis 2:7). According to the Bible, Collins, who believes we came from stardust, is wrong.

In 2023, Disney released *Wish*. The *Internet Movie Database* (IMDb) summarizes the movie as follows: "A young girl named Asha wishes on a star and gets a more direct answer than she bargained for when a trouble-making star comes down from the sky to join her."[10] The movie is about a young girl who uses the power of magic from a star to defeat a powerful sorcerer through witchcraft and divination. Disney purposefully uses occult practices and suggestive themes. The movie shows Magnifico, the wizard, entering his secret room with Asha (Fig. 45). The sorcerer's secret room looks like a laboratory that a scientist would use.

Fig. 45. Magnifico's secret room.

During the Renaissance (1400s–1600s), the use of magic and science worked hand in hand. The magician or scientist would use "natural magic" to draw down understanding. Laura Sumrall, University of Sydney, Australia, wrote:

> [Natural magic] as the manipulation or application of higher (celestial) influences in the terrestrial world or as the active or applied aspect of natural philosophy, involving the knowledge and manipulation of occult properties, especially sympathetic correspondences in nature. Understood in this sense, natural magic can be seen to inform many diverse ideas and practices including chemistry, medicine, and mechanics.[11]

Magic was used to draw down the power of the stars (celestial [heavenly] influences) during the Scientific Revolution. Sumrall wrote, "Natural magic specifically was a crucial part of natural philosophy in the Renaissance, in particular for addressing insensible aspects of the physical world."[12] Sumrall wrote, "Fifteenth-century natural magic sought legitimacy in part from ancient authority, drawing not only from Greek philosophers such as Plotinus and the imagined Egyptian antiquity of Hermes Trismegistus."[13] Magic and modern science helped build the "solar system" today. When Disney showed Magnifico's secret room, they showed us the true history of modern science: magic.

Asha asks Magnifico for a favor, which ruins her chances of becoming his apprentice. Asha now seeks the help of the stars. A magical star comes down to help her. The star gets caught in a knitted garment and uses the yarn to make patterns in the trees. Asha, curious about this little star, asks, "What are you?" Disney then shows us what the star is (Fig. 46). Disney shows us a pentagram.

Fig. 46. "What are you?"

The star that Asha called down is a magical star—a pentagram (Fig. 47). The church of Satan teaches that the pentagram is the star of the magi. The church of Satan uses the term magi, which means "People who are believed to have expertise in interpreting the assumed influence of the stars, moon, and planets on human affairs."[14] The church of Satan also believes the pentagram is the symbol of demonic activity:

> The Pentagram, which in Gnostic schools is called the Blazing Star, is the sign of intellectual omnipotence and autocracy. It is the Star of the Magi ... it is Lucifer ... The pentagram or pentalpha is a symbol which has long been affiliated with demonic activity.[15]

Fig. 47. The pentagram with the Baphomet.

The pentagram is the star of the sorcerer. Asha's pentagram star shows its magical powers by sprinkling stardust, giving life to plants and speech to animals. Asha is still confused about how she was able to connect with a star. The animals help Asha understand that people and animals are not that different since we all come from the same stuff. The animals begin to sing:

> Have you ever wondered why
> You look up at the sky for answers? ...
> When it comes to the universe we're all shareholders
> Get that through your system, Solar! ...
> From supernovas now we've grown into our history...
> Your dust is my dust...
> We are our own origin story
> You don't have to look too hard
> It's all around and not too far,
> If you're try'na figure out just who you are,
> You're a star![16]

When children watch *Wish*, they are intentionally told that animals and humans are the same, meaning, they are being taught the theory of evolution. Children are also introduced to stardust, the magical power of a demonic pentagram star that enables people to be sorcerers. *Wish* may be labeled as a children's movie, but the concept it teaches to children and adults is New Age (a system to engage in satanism). *Wish* teaches that we have a divine spark or light inside each of us, giving us the power of the stars (Fig. 48). We are taught that everyone can possess the power to make our wishes come true.

Fig. 48. Power within each of us.

What Disney is teaching is nothing new. Satan, also known as Hermes Trismegistus, taught people their ability to harness power inside them. Coudert, Religious Studies, University of California, Davis, CA, told us what Hermes Trismegistus taught the people:

> See what power, what swiftness you possess ... Believe that nothing is impossible for you, think yourself immortal and capable of understanding all, all arts, all sciences, the nature of every living being.[17]

As Christians, we do have a light inside of us. His name is Jesus. The Bible tells us that "the true light that gives light to everyone was coming into the world" (John 1:9). When we accept Jesus as our Lord and Savior, we receive the "Spirit of Christ" (Romans 8:9). Because we belong to Christ, "the Spirit of him who raised Jesus from the dead is living in you" (Romans 8:11). The true light that came into this world now lives in us. We do not receive power from a fallen star but from the one who created the stars.

Disney teaches that everyone comes from stardust. Everyone includes the evil sorcerer Magnifico and the adored soon-to-be sorceress Asha. We have been taught magic and sorcery our whole life. *Doctor Strange in the Multiverse of Madness* (2022) is about Doctor Strange, a good sorcerer, recruiting the Scarlet Witch, an evil sorcerer, to save the world. *Star Wars: Episode IV – A New Hope* (1977) teaches us that the force has a good side, Luke Skywalker, and a dark side, Darth Vader. The movie's objective was not to defeat evil but to balance good and evil. It is also interesting to know that Luke and Anakin (Darth Vader) are called "Sky" walkers, like the prince whose kingdom is in the air (Ephesians 2:2). *Cinderella* (1950) teaches us about the wicked stepmother and her cat Lucifer, and the fairy godmother who is a respectable sorceress practicing witchcraft. Sorcery is demonic, but it has become cute, innocent, and fun thanks to movies, TV shows, and cartoons.

Deuteronomy 18:10–11

Let no one be found among you who sacrifices their son or daughter in the fire, who practices divination or sorcery, interprets omens, engages in witchcraft, [11] or casts spells, or who is a medium or spiritist or who consults the dead.

At the conclusion of *Wish*, the wicked sorcerer is defeated, and a new sorceress is created, Asha. The little star is leaving, but it gives Asha the magical power of the stars. The little star creates a magician's wand filled with the power of witchcraft and magic (Fig. 49). Now, Asha, the sorceress, has become the new fairy godmother who can make wishes come true.

Fig. 49. The new sorceress.

Ó

Francis Collins believes we came from stardust. Collins puts his trust in modern science's "universe," which was built during the time when people were seeking esoteric knowledge and magic from an ancient sage named Hermes Trismegistus, the one we know as the devil. Why were the scientists of the Scientific Revolution so interested in a false god's teachings? It was believed that the ones who mastered the power of the stars or the celestial gods would become gods. Christian H. Bull, University of Oslo, Norway, explains:

> The mythical account of the *Korê Kosmou* [Virgin of the World] is confusing, but it contains more information about Hermes Trismegistus and his associates than any other Hermetica. Even before mortals came into being, we are told, the creator of the universe instilled in Hermes and the other gods his love and his splendor, and the desire to seek after him. Hermes, after observing the universe, came to know the "mysteries of heaven," which he inscribed on stelae, and "in this way he ascended to the stars and flanked

his kindred gods"... Only after Hermes had discovered the mysteries of the universe and written them down for succeeding generations was he able to ascend and take his place as a celestial god.[18]

Hermes Trismegistus was gifted with the knowledge of the stars. Hermes Trismegistus would teach mankind this knowledge so people could become gods themselves. That is the very same lie that the serpent told Eve, "You will be like God" (Genesis 3:5). The teacher in Ecclesiastes was right, "What has been will be again, what has been done will be done again; there is nothing new under the sun" (Ecclesiastes 1:9). Hermes Trismegistus would teach the people how to become stars. In the writings of Hermes Trismegistus (*Korê Kosmou* [*Virgin of the World*]), the layout of the "universe" was revealed. From top to bottom was heaven, ether, air, and earth. It was in the ether where the sun and stars resided. In the *Korê Kosmou* [*Virgin of the World*], we learn what the stars really are. Hermes Trismegistus teaches, "The sun rules the stars (visible gods)."[19]

In Collins' book, *The Language of God: A Scientist Presents Evidence for Belief*, Collins' final words invite us to lay down our arms and agree. Collins believes faith and modern science can get along as we seek the truth. Collins wrote:

> It is time to call a truce in the escalating war between science and spirit. The war was never really necessary. Like so many earthly wars, this one has been initiated and intensified by extremists on both sides, sounding alarms that predict imminent ruin unless the other side is vanquished. Science is not threatened by God; it is enhanced. God is most certainly not threatened by science; He made it all possible. So let us together seek to reclaim the solid ground of an intellectually and spiritually satisfying synthesis of all great truths.[20]

Collins' call for unity is not about finding common ground or seeking the truth. Collins' plead for a truce is about God's word submitting to modern science. Let us see if we can find solid ground regarding modern science and God's word. Collins proclaims that Darwin's theory of evolution is how humans came into existence. Collins believes that Adam was the son of a chimpanzee, which ultimately came from stardust. The Bible said Adam was the "son of God" (Luke 3:38). According to the Bible, Adam did not inherit his life from any previous living organism. Collins' view of the Biblical account of the creation of people is secondary to the words of modern science. There is no middle, common, or solid ground for faith and modern science to agree on. God is always the one who must change His words when it comes to modern science.

Collins' call for a truce is not about finding the truth about the "solar system." Collins believes the big bang theory is true. Collins will credit God for being the supernatural force that made the big bang possible. Collins wrote:

> The Big Bang cries out for a divine explanation. It forces the conclusion that nature had a defined beginning. I cannot see how nature could have created itself. Only a supernatural force that is outside of space and time could have done that.[21]

Where is the common ground between the big bang and the creation story? Modern science tells us the sun started to shine over 9 billion years after the big bang occurred. *The Planetary Society* states, "4.55 billion years ago: Let there be light: The Sun begins fusing hydrogen into helium."[22] Then, the planets start to form. *The Planetary Society* states, "4.5 billion years ago: Mercury, Venus, Earth, and Mars form. A Mars-sized planet collides with Earth, and the debris forms the Moon."[23] After 50 million years of sunlight, the earth starts to form.

The Bible tells us that the earth existed before the sun was created on Day 4 (Genesis 1:16, 19). The Bible tells us that the heavens, the earth, waters of the deep, light (not the sun), the firmament holding water above it, the sky, the seas, land, and vegetation with seeds were all created before the sun started to shine in the sky. Where is the common ground? According to Collins, the Bible must yield its six-day creation story because our "universe" requires 13.8 billion years. Collins believes the science is settled and the big bang will never be proven wrong.

There is no common ground between faith and modern science. The Bible had to change once the "solar system" was established as the new standard of truth. God's word must be reinterpreted to make it work within modern science. Today, the sun is the very center of everything. The "solar system" cannot be questioned. The "solar system" cannot be touched, as *Wish* told us, "Get that through your system, Solar!"[24]

Chapter 35

Dealing with Flat Earth

Listing the incompatibility issues found between the Bible and modern science is a large subject. The purpose of this book is not to give us a detailed commentary on every scientific matter that could be argued. The most controversial subject for people is the shape of the earth. Of all the subjects that could be discussed, the earth's shape is an easy topic because it is a secondary issue.

People argue about the earth's shape as if it is the first and only issue. The Bible does not mention the earth's shape.[1] The Bible mentions a scientific claim that must be addressed first: the earth's motion. We must believe that either the earth moves or does not move. Once that choice is made, we must accept its ramifications. If we believe in a moving earth, modern science's "universe" will be our model, and the earth's shape requires it to be a sphere. If we believe in a motionless earth, modern science's "universe" does not work, including the globe. The shape of the earth is a secondary issue.

Ó

When dealing with the shape of the earth, the reason it is such a ridiculous topic for people is because a flat earth inserted into modern science's "universe" is ridiculous. Let me give you an example of how the earth's shape inserted into the wrong model causes problems. Here is an example of a globe showing a flight path from Doha, Qatar, to Chicago, Illinois (Fig. 50). The small circle is the city of Moscow, Russia.

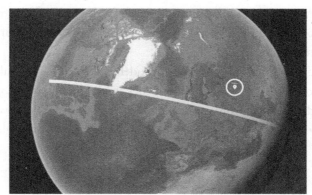

Fig. 50. Direct route from Doha to Chicago (Moscow highlighted).

Google Earth's route, when compared to the *Airportia* flight path from Doha to Chicago, displays the same route. *Google Earth* and *Airportia* show a path crossing Norway and Greenland (Fig. 51). Both *Google Earth* and *Airportia* use a spherical earth as their model.

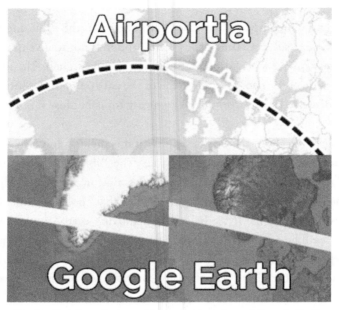

Fig. 51. Path from Doha to Chicago: *Airportia* and *Google Earth*.

In 2016, there was an emergency landing on flight QR725 from Doha to Chicago. A 14-year-old child went into a coma. *Airlive* reported, "A Boeing 777-300 flight QR725 from Doha to Chicago did an emergency landing today at Domodedovo airport in Moscow due to health state of 14-year-old child."[2] Britian's *Express* reported, "A Boeing 777-300 plane flying from Doha, Qatar to Chicago made an emergency landing today at Domodedovo airport in Moscow after a 14-year-old fell ill."[3] The direct flight from Doha to Chicago made an emergency landing in Moscow because of a serious medical emergency.

According to the spherical earth model, flight QR725 would have to travel out of its way to make an emergency landing. Moscow is outside the path of a direct flight from Doha to Chicago. *Airportia* and *Google Earth's* route show the same result: Moscow is outside the path of flight QR725 (Fig. 52).

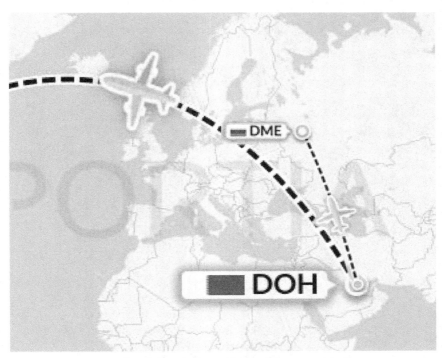

Fig. 52. Path from Doha to Chicago (Moscow added).

Flight QR725 needed to make an emergency landing due to a child going into a coma. The previous map displays a flight path over a globe from Doha to Chicago, showing us that Moscow is out of the way (Fig. 52). When a flight path is overlaid upon Gleason's New Standard Map of the World, the emergency stop in Moscow makes perfect sense (Fig. 53). The Gleason map is from 1892 and was labeled as "scientifically and practically correct, as 'it is.'"[4] The Gleason map provided numbers for major cities and was used to show an accurate line from Doha to Chicago. When flight QR725 needed to make an emergency landing, they chose a city directly on their flight path.

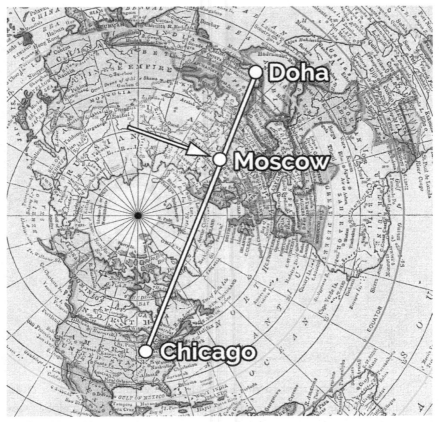

Fig. 53. Gleason's New Standard Map of the World (1892).

Ó

I have had multiple friends say to me, "Why can't I read certain Bible passages with my understanding, and you read it with your understanding?" I do not have a problem with that. The Bible has a problem with that. God's word puts us in a unique position. We either trust what God said or not. Can I read the Bible and claim that Jesus did not come in the flesh? No. The Bible does not allow for two interpretations. The apostle John told me that if I deny Jesus coming in the flesh, then I have "the spirit of the antichrist" (1 John 4:3).

I understand we may have different perspectives on different passages from the Bible. I know we can disagree on various topics, but I will also say this: every verse in the Bible is written to speak one truth. That truth may come through a narrative, poetic, or figurative passage, but the meaning of what the Bible is conveying to teach us is a single truth. The moment we change the Bible to fit our understanding or interpret passages to fit what we want to be true, we no longer hold to the literal meaning of the Bible. When we do not stick to the intended meaning of Scripture, we set ourselves up for deception by the enemy's craftiness, leading to our destruction (2 Corinthians 11:3).

In 2023, I was at a meeting with a group of pastors. During the meeting, we were invited to share a little about what was happening in our lives. I mentioned how I finished several books that year. One of the books I had written argued for a literal reading of Genesis 1. After the meeting, I offered my books to any pastors who wanted a copy. One pastor told me he was thankful that I took a literal approach to Genesis 1. He mentioned that he also believed in a literal reading of the creation story. I smiled and said, "That's great. It is nice to know that someone else believes the sun sits below water" (Genesis 1:7, 16–17; KJV). Surprised, he said, "I'll have to go back and read Genesis again."

While this pastor and I were talking, another pastor was listening to our conversation. He asked, "Are you a flat earther?" I responded, "No. I just don't believe in a globe made up by scientists seeking wisdom from false gods. I am a believer in an earth that does not move." Why did the pastor call me a "flat earther"? It is a typical response by people when their understanding of the "universe" is challenged.

Today, anyone who doubts that the earth is a globe is thrown into the category of "flat earther." When a person calls someone a "flat earther," it is a way to disregard the subject without providing evidence or reason for defending a spherical earth. When I speak about things contrary to what we have been taught in school, I am called a conspiracy theorist or a "flat earther."

I am not offended when someone calls me a "flat earther." I am not offended when someone tells me they believe in a globe. I know what I believe and why I believe it. My reasoning includes Biblical, scientific, historical, and observable problems with modern science's "universe." Since the history of modern science is hardly discussed, most people do not care, so it is easy to dismiss the problems of modern science's "universe" and "solar system" (e.g., water, gas pressure, line-of-sight, etc.).

There is a large and growing movement in our world with people who believe in a flat earth. People usually run across the idea on social media or hear it from a friend who thinks the earth is flat. "Flat earthers," Christians and non-Christians, are sincere in their rejection of the globe model. "Flat earthers" also have extreme groups, ranging from a scientific perspective to

New Age. If you ever meet a "flat earther," they are very passionate in their stance that the earth is flat.

If a person is curious and tries to investigate the topic of flat earth by searching the internet, their search results will tell them how much of an idiot they were for doubting the spherical earth. An internet search into flat earth will be filled with things that will lead people away from flat earth information and then promote modern science and a globe. The search results will be populated with critics who mock and condemn such foolishness (Fig. 54). If we find actual flat earth websites, the sites usually give misinformation or stupid ideas.

Fig. 54. Flat earth meme.

Google's search engine accounts for nearly 90% of the world's market for internet searches. Most people use Google to search for information. If a person uses Google Search and searches for "is the earth flat," the autofill will suggest that the earth is a sphere (Fig. 55). Even before a person hits the go button, Google informs their users, "The Earth is roughly a sphere."

Fig. 55. Google's search engine with suggested search queries.

If a person dares to ignore Google's suggestions and decides to search for "is the earth flat," the person will be told what Google wants them to know, regardless (Fig. 56). Google does not hesitate to say, "No, the earth is roughly a sphere."

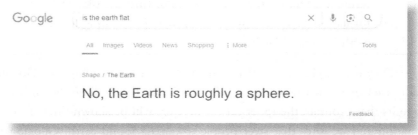

Fig. 56. Google's search engine results.

When we search for "is the earth flat," Google or other search engines will flood the results with anti-flat earth websites and videos that promote a moving, round earth. There is no free speech, open minds for debate, or civil dialogue regarding the earth's shape. According to Google, the only answer is "No, the earth is roughly a sphere."

Information on the earth is being suppressed from people who want to verify statements about the world. I am not talking about information when it comes to a spherical earth. I am talking about information that presents a non-spherical earth. I am talking about information that is being concealed from people. The concealing of information is a fact. This book is about a conspiracy and not a conspiracy theory. A conspiracy is a plan or scheme. A conspiracy theory is an idea with no evidence.

Information about the shape of the earth is being hidden on purpose. In 2018, a House Judiciary Committee met with representatives from Facebook, YouTube, and Twitter to discuss their role in filtering content on their social media platforms. Rep. Ted Deutch from Florida was concerned about spreading misinformation by conspiracy theorists, whom Deutch refers to as "truthers." Deutch asked the representative from Google, Juniper Downs, head of public policy for YouTube and Google Search, about how they address "conspiracy theories" on their platform. The context of Deutch's question was about social media that denied certain school shootings. Downs replied:

"The first way is by demoting low-quality content and promoting more authoritative content, and the second is by providing more transparency for users. So, we're introducing boxes that provide factual information at the top of results that have shown themselves to turn up a lot of information that is counterfactual, such as searching for the earth is flat on *YouTube*."[5]

Downs brought up the flat earth. Downs, a representative of Google, admitted that when people search for flat earth, they will be shown biased results that promote the spherical earth. They will be shown filtered information and websites that steer people towards a round earth. Google will even throw in Christian websites that speak negatively about the subject. After a while, people give up researching flat earth because it sounds ridiculous because of their filtered "authoritative content."

Filtering content and media is called propaganda. Propaganda means "Information, ideas, opinions, or images that give one part of an argument, which are broadcast, published, etc., in order to influence people's opinions."[6] Google is purposely influencing its users by withholding information and promoting the information they want us to know: "No, the earth is roughly a sphere."

My focus for this book is not on the earth's shape, which is a secondary issue. The first task is to resolve the movement of the earth. If the earth does not move, then a person will realize that everything else was just a deception, and the earth's shape would not be a difficult topic to discuss. In an interview with Alex Stein, Tucker Carlson, one of Fox News network's most-watched anchors, was asked about flat earth. *Rolling Stone* reported:

> Carlson was asked about the Flat Earth theory. "Well, I'm open to anything," [Carlson] replied. "How could I not be open to anything at this point? I mean, there's been so much deception that you can't trust your preconceptions."[7]

My focus is on what the Bible claims about the earth. Since the Bible does not explicitly tell us the earth is round or flat, it is not helpful to use verses that could be twisted to fit whatever narrative we want. The Bible does not say round or flat, but it does make statements that cannot work with a sphere.

The Bible claims, and the authors believed, that the earth is set upon a foundation and does not move. The Biblical model for the heavenly and earthly realms is incompatible with a sphere and would better suit an earth that was a flat plane. A flat and motionless earth is not a new model or idea. It is something that NASA assumes when it needs to make its technologies work.

NASA hired W. Frost and K. R. Reddy to study the effects of wind gusts when airplanes are landing. Frost and Reddy gave their analysis based on certain conditions that needed to be understood (Fig. 57). Frost and Reddy wrote, "The aircraft trajectory model employed in this study was derived based on the following assumptions: a) The earth is flat and non-rotating."[8] When studying the effects of wind on airplane landings, the earth is presumed to be flat and non-rotating.

TECH LIBRARY KAFB, NM

0061782

NASA Contractor Report 3073

Investigation of Aircraft Landing in Variable Wind Fields

Walter Frost and Kapuluru Ravikumar Reddy
The University of Tennessee Space Institute
Tullahoma, Tennessee

Prepared for
George C. Marshall Space Flight Center
under Contract NAS8-29584

National Aeronautics
and Space Administration

**Scientific and Technical
Information Office**

1978

Fig. 57. Investigation of Aircraft Landing in Variable Wind Fields.

NASA employed W. R. Sturgeon and J. D. Phillips to provide data so that the CH-53 helicopter could be tested in a simulator before actual test flights were taken (Fig. 58). Sturgeon and Phillips provided the data based on certain conditions that needed to be understood. Sturgeon and Phillips wrote, "The helicopter equations of motion are given in body axes with respect to a flat, nonrotating Earth."[9]

NASA Technical Memorandum 81238

(NASA-TM-81238)   A MATHEMATICAL MODEL OF THE   N81-12065
Cd-53 HELICOPTER (NASA)   60 p HC A04/MF A01
                                          CSCL 01C
                                                      Unclas
                                          G3/05   29424

A Mathematical Model of the CH-53 Helicopter

William R. Sturgeon
James D. Phillips, Ames Research Center, Moffett Field, California

National Aeronautics and
Space Administration

Ames Research Center
Moffett Field, California 94035

Fig. 58. A Mathematical Model of the CH-53 Helicopter.

NASA hired H. D. Edwards and A. J. Lineberger to assess the best equations to explain atmospheric oscillation (Fig. 59). Edwards and Lineberger state that the easiest solution is to use simplified equations based on a motionless flat earth. They wrote, "A model frequently used is that of a flat, nonrotating earth."[10]

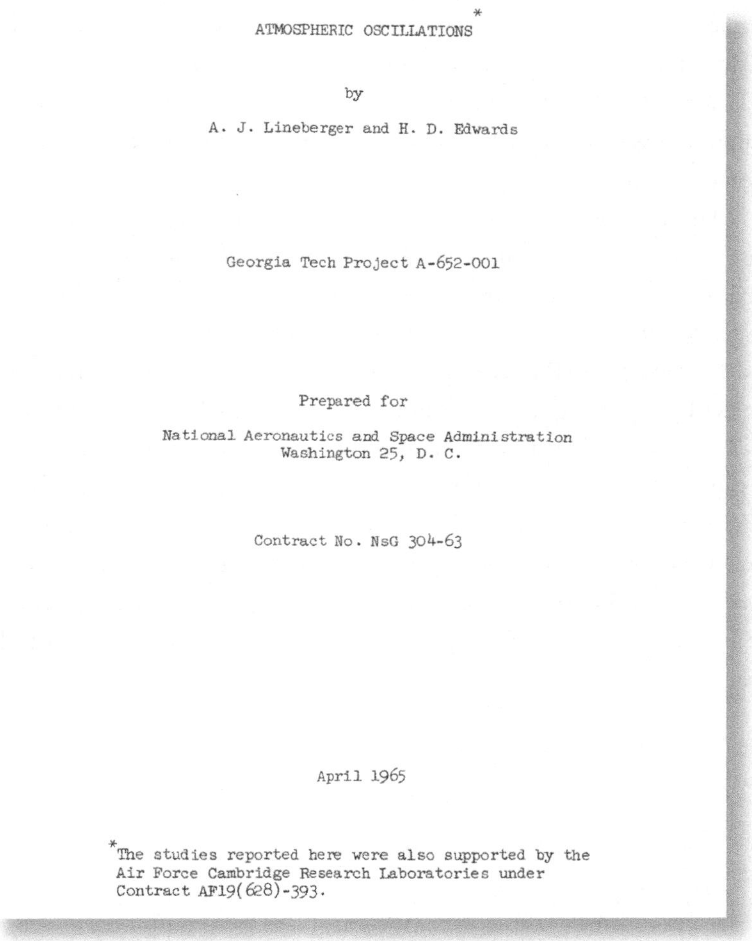

ATMOSPHERIC OSCILLATIONS[*]

by

A. J. Lineberger and H. D. Edwards

Georgia Tech Project A-652-001

Prepared for

National Aeronautics and Space Administration
Washington 25, D. C.

Contract No. NsG 304-63

April 1965

[*]The studies reported here were also supported by the
Air Force Cambridge Research Laboratories under
Contract AF19(628)-393.

Fig. 59. Atmospheric Oscillations.

I will get laughed at if I mention the earth is flat and nonrotating. When NASA accepts reports that state the earth is flat and nonrotating, they get more funding and are hailed as the experts of the "universe." If I mention the earth is flat, I get dismissed as a conspiracy theorist who has the IQ of an idiot. When NASA mentions that the earth is flat and nonrotating, it gets more funding to create pictures and animated videos. Why do the experts, people who teach at the Georgia Institute of Technology, GA, or the University of Tennessee Space Institute, TN, or employees at the NASA Ames Research Center Moffett Field, CA, get to claim the earth is flat and nonrotating? It is because the experts know that their technologies do not work on a rotating spherical earth.

Flat earth is a subject that cannot be discussed without ridicule by people who hold to a round earth. Christians and non-Christians instantly reject the idea without considering the reasons for their rejection. The Bible warns that if we do not take the time to make the right judgments, it could lead to deception (Proverbs 14:8). People believe they are rejecting a false subject by repeating what modern science has taught them. Still, people do not have any evidence or observations to back up their position. According to modern science, we cannot observe curvature from the earth unless a person is at least 40 miles above the earth's surface. According to modern science, we cannot observe any movement even though they tell us we are traveling at 1,367,017 mph.[11] The only thing people can claim as evidence for a spherical earth is counterintuitive theories that teach us not to believe what we see or feel.

Chapter 36

A Vision of Earth

Rick DuBose recently wrote a book called *In Jesus' Name: 5 Altars of Prayer That Move Heaven and Earth*. I attended a meeting where he discussed a vision that changed his understanding of prayer. I believe DuBose had a real vision, and the Lord accurately showed him how the Bible describes the earth. DuBose sees God's throne and twenty-four other thrones that made one large circle above the earth. Underneath the throne of God, the entire earth was visible all at once. DuBose wrote:

> One of the details I remember most clearly is what Scripture calls the sea of glass (see Revelation 4:6; 15:2). Within the ring of thrones was a massive surface that appeared like clear crystal. As I looked closer, however, beneath the glass was the earth stretched in such a way as to be entirely visible at once.[1]

DuBose knows there is a problem with the vision the Lord showed him because the vision conflicted with our modern understanding of a spherical earth. If the earth were a globe, only half would be visible to God. Some may argue that God is God, and He could see everyone and everything all at once if He wanted to. Yes, this is true. God could see everyone all at once if the earth was a globe. The problem is that if the earth were a globe, not every person would see Jesus if they lived on the opposite side of a spherical earth.

Revelation 1:7
"Look, he is coming with the clouds," and "every eye will see him, even those who pierced him"; and all peoples on earth "will mourn because of him." So shall it be! Amen.

When Jesus comes back, according to Revelation 1:7, everyone will see Him. Let us say that Jesus returns to Jerusalem. How will people in Mataura, located on the South Island of New Zealand, see Jesus? Mataura is the opposite of Jerusalem on a globe. When the people in Jerusalem look up to see Jesus, the people in Mataura will see nothing but the empty sky above them.

As I said, DuBose recognizes this problem with God's vision. DuBose knows having the entire earth visible all at once is impossible on a spherical earth. DuBose wrote, "We know that the earth is round. It rotates on an axis giving us light and shadow and it circles the sun in a sweeping annual orbit."[2] DuBose now injects his understanding into something that God revealed to him. I am not critical of DuBose, for I would have thought the same thing years ago. DuBose introduces ideas about the earth that cannot be found in Scripture. DuBose's position about the movement of the earth is opposite of what the Bible teaches. There is not one verse in the Bible that teaches the earth moves. The earth can be shaken, but the Bible is clear. God "set the earth on its foundations; it can never be moved" (Psalm 104:5).

How do we know the earth is round? It started with Pythagoras (500 BC), the Greek philosopher who worshiped false gods, believed in reincarnation, and just said the earth was a sphere without evidence. Thompson from the Ohio State University wrote, "Pythagoras proposed a spherical earth purely on aesthetic grounds."[3] To the Greek philosopher, the sphere was the perfect shape. Again, Henriksen wrote:

> Pythagoras (500 bc)—put forward the idea that the earth was round, but not on the basis of observation; rather he, like many ancient philosophers, believed that a sphere was the perfect shape and the gods would have therefore created the Earth in this form.[4]

We believe the earth was round because Greek philosophers told us it was round. Pythagoras, a pagan who sought magic and wisdom from the ancient Egyptian god Thoth, also taught that the earth moved around the sun. The earth moving around the sun did not originate from the Bible. Knight wrote:

> The heliocentric [earth moves] theory was held by the ancient Egyptians, and taught by them to Pythagoras. The theory did not flourish in Greece [until] ... it was eventually revived by Copernicus.[5]

The Bible warns us not to follow the teachings of Greek philosophers. The Bible states, "Do not deceive yourselves. If any of you think you are wise by the standards of this age, you should become 'fools' so that you may become wise" (1 Corinthians 3:18). The Bible tells us, "See to it that no one takes you captive through hollow and deceptive philosophy, which depends on human tradition and the elemental spiritual forces of this world rather than on Christ" (Colossians 2:8). We believe the earth is round and moves around the sun because of ancient Greek philosophers who the Bible warns to stay away from. Thompson said that for the Christians who did listen to Paul's advice, there was a "rejection of the 'pagan absurdity' of a spherical earth."[6]

DuBose wrote that we know the earth spins and travels around the sun. The truth is that we do not instinctively know this. We have been told this. We have been taught this. We have been shown this our entire life. DuBose continued:

> In this heavenly reality, though, all of it was visible and present at once. The whole earth was laid out before the throne of God ... the earth always before them.[7]

Are there different realities, one for God (heavenly) and one for people (earthly)? No. Jesus told us to pray, "Your kingdom come, your will be done, on earth as it is in heaven" (Matthew 6:10). Jesus wanted the reality of God's kingdom to manifest here on earth. Jesus said, "I will give you the keys of the kingdom of heaven; whatever you bind on earth will be bound in heaven, and whatever you loose on earth will be loosed in heaven" (Matthew 16:19). Is Jesus talking about two separate realities? No. There is only one reality. We may not see the heavenly reality with our physical eyes, but what is true in heaven is also true here on earth.

As stated, DuBose saw a correct vision. It really is a simple layout described in the Bible as the heavens, the earth, and the underworld. According to the Bible, the heavenly and earthly realms are a closed system where God is seated directly above the earth. Here is an example from 1906 (Fig. 60). This layout is based upon a literal reading of Scripture.

Fig. 60. Hebrew conception of the universe.

If the literal reading of Scripture were applied to the vision DuBose saw, it would work quite well. God would be seated above an earth that would be visible all at once. The earth would be a flat plane. The earth would be fixed and not moving. The problem with the spherical earth is that it does not work with Scripture.

For the majority of my life, I believed in a spherical earth. After researching the theories and history of modern science's "universe," I now believe what DuBose saw in the vision the Lord revealed to him. I believe the earth is always before Him, and God can see everyone all at once. I believe God's throne is above the earth, and the earth does not move. I believe heaven is located directly above the entire earth, just like Jesus said, "You are from below; I am from above" (John 8:23).

Chapter 37

Moon "Shine"

Regarding the Bible and modern science, some subjects seem debatable to people—for example, the moon. The Bible claims that God made two lights, and one of those lights was the moon (Genesis 1:16). If I said the moon was a light and not a rock, people could argue that the moon looks like a light, so in their minds, the Bible is correct, "it is a light." Both answers could work. The problem occurs when you talk about the moon in the larger framework of the Bible. The "moon reflects the sun's light, so it's a light" argument works only with a narrow focus on Scripture.

If a person accepts the Bible's claim, we must accept that the moon is a light placed in a solid dome barrier with water above it (Genesis 1:7, 16–17). Also, according to Jesus, the moon can shine independently of the sun. Jesus said the moon would "not give its light" (Matthew 24:29). According to the Revelation of Jesus, the moon, after the sun goes black, will still be seen as "blood red" (Revelation 6:12). According to modern science, if the sun does not shine, the moon will be black and unseen.

The "moon reflects the sun's light, so it's a light" argument requires us to believe in the complete "solar system" and "universe" that modern science presents. According to modern science, the moon was formed by a Mars-sized rock that collided with the earth and formed billions of years ago.[1] If we do not believe that, then another option is to say the moon is a solid rock (not a light) that was formed by *fiat* (God's speech; *fiat* is Latin for "let it be done"). No matter how or when the moon came about, if we believe the moon is only reflecting the sun's light, then we believe in modern science's "universe" and "solar system."

Modern science cannot explain the moon (e.g., formation, size, etc.). Is modern science open to the Bible's suggestion on how the moon came about? Absolutely not. They dismiss what the Bible claims about the moon or the creation story and view us as idiots. I am not talking about every day modern science believers. I am talking about the prophets and promoters of modern science.

In the secular world, most people do not discuss the theories that established the "universe." In the church world, most people do not discuss the creation story. When someone presents a different perspective from what we believe, we will fight for our beliefs and defend our position. We will shout,

"Gravity is proven," "Genesis is poetry," or "I just don't believe you." Let me show you how modern science feels about anyone who believes the Bible.

Bill Nye debated Ken Ham on February 4, 2014, at Ham's Creation Museum. Ham believes in modern science's "universe" and that God created everything in six days (young earth). After the debate, Nye wrote his book *Undeniable* (2014). Nye explains his view on Christians who hold to the creation story in any form. Nye wrote:

> In the case of creationism however, certain not-for-profit groups [Ken Ham's *Answers in Genesis*] set out to indoctrinate our science students in their central idea: that the first book of *The Bible's* assertion that Earth is only six or ten thousand years old (the exact number depends on their interpretation) is supported by scientific evidence. Such an idea is laughable ... In general, creationist groups do not accept evolution as the fact of life ... This attack on reason is an attack on all of us. Children who accept this ludicrous perspective will find themselves opposed to progress ... [Ken Ham] claims that his interpretation of *The Bible* is more valid than the basic facts of geology, astronomy, biology, physics, chemistry, mathematics, and especially evolution.[2]

According to Nye, it is pathetic, offensive, and absurd to believe in Genesis 1. Yes, they consider us who believe in the Bible as idiots. The promoters of modern science do not leave room for the creation story to be included in their theories about the "universe." The moment we try to blend the Bible and modern science, they reject it because it is an attack on their "truth." Nye said believing the creation story is laughable. After the debate, Nye summed up best how modern science feels about anyone who believes in the creation story, which includes the subject of the moon. Nye told Ham, "Your scientists and your staff, as respectful as I can be, are incompetent."[3]

According to modern science, no matter our spiritual status, Christian or non-Christian, the "universe" works the same for all people. So, what is the moon? Is it light, or is it a rock that reflects light? When Christians want to hold to the "moon reflects the sun's light, so it's a light" argument, they immediately side with modern science and must make God's word subordinate to the authority of modern science. Let me explain.

No modern scientist suggests the moon is a light. Dr. Eric Christian, NASA's senior research scientist and the lead scientist of the Energetic Particle Laboratory, wrote, "Light does not have mass."[4] If the moon were a light, then the moon would not have mass or material to reflect the sun's light. According to modern science, the moon is a solid rock that reflects the sun's light. For the moon to reflect light, the moon must orbit the earth to create the phases of the moon (Fig. 61). NASA writes:

> Like Earth, the Moon has a day side and a night side, which change as the Moon rotates. The Sun always illuminates half of the Moon while the other half remains dark, but how much we are able to see of that illuminated half changes as the Moon travels through its orbit.[5]

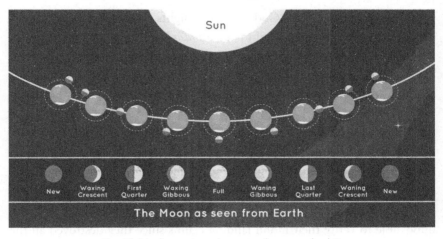

Fig. 61. Modern science's moon phases and orbit.

Modern science tells us that the moon's, earth's, and sun's position determine the moon's phases. If we believe this, we also accept that the sun is the sole reason the moon looks like a light. According to modern science, the sun is the only light the moon can reflect. NASA writes:

> In our entire solar system, the only object that shines with its own light is the Sun. That light always beams onto Earth and Moon from the direction of the Sun, illuminating half of our planet in its orbit and reflecting off the surface of the Moon to create moonlight.[6]

If we believe the moon reflects sunlight, which depends upon it being a rock and the sun's position, then we must also accept that the moon orbits the earth. What is the shape of that orbit? Spherical since the moon cannot orbit a flat plane. When we accept that the moon is solid and moving in a spherical orbit, we must now accept that the earth is a "planet." What is a "planet"? Bill Nye answers what a "planet" is for *WIRED*. Nye said, "You gotta have enough gravity to be a ball."[7]

What makes the moon orbit the spherical earth? According to modern science, it is gravity. Now that we accepted gravity, the moon can now orbit the earth, which means the earth can now orbit the sun. Now that we believe the earth moves, we now accept the sun is in the middle of the "solar system." We must accept quite a bit if we believe the "moon reflects the sun's light, so it's a light" argument.

The Bible tells us that God made two lights. The Hebrew language is easy to translate. The word "light | מָאוֹר | *mā'ôr*" means "light source, lights, luminary, i.e., that which gives out light."[8] According to the Bible, the moon does not reflect light but "gives out light." Let us assume the Bible is correct and God made the moon an actual light. The consequences of that statement are tremendous.

If the moon was an actual light, how did NASA land a ship on something that is not solid? Neil Armstrong would not have been able to step on "light." People question how NASA was able to stream live video, audio, sensor readings, and location information with a computer that had less power than the Texas Instruments' TI-73 calculator from 1998.[9] It is also impossible to verify their moon landing claims since they destroyed all the data. That is why modern science must destroy the authority of the Bible instead of people asking questions about their moon missions.

When Christian scholars address the "moon is a light" topic, they claim it is phenomenological language, meaning writing something the way it appears to a person's perspective. Brown et al. commented about God making the moon a light. Brown et al. wrote:

> The description bears plainly a phenomenal, not a scientific form: it is given from the position of an observer on the face of the earth, who records his observations according to the appearance of things.[10]

Commentators like to mention the moon looks like a light from our perspective. William David Reyburn and Euan McG. Fry wrote, "[The] great lights refers to their large size or great power, as no other celestial bodies compare with them from the point of view of the human eye."[11] H. D. M. Spence-Jones wrote over 100 years ago that Genesis was phenomenal. The word phenomenal means "known through the senses rather than through thought or intuition."[12] In 1909, Spence-Jones wrote that Moses was writing through his senses rather than with scientific thought. Spence-Jones wrote, "The Biblical narrative is geocentric and phenomenal, not heliocentric or scientific."[13] Spence-Jones also recognized that the Bible teaches a geocentric (motionless earth) model rather than the heliocentric (moving earth) theory.

Did Moses write Genesis using phenomenological language? No. For scholars to suggest that Moses wrote the moon was a light because that is how it appeared to him is to suggest that Moses was writing his own words. Creation is about what God said. The prophet Moses did not write his thoughts or interpretation of what God said. Moses, like all the prophets of the Bible, "though human, spoke from God as they were carried along by the Holy Spirit" (2 Peter 1:21).

If the moon was a rock, the Bible made an incorrect statement. A rock is not a light. The words found in Genesis are said to be "God-breathed" (2 Timothy 3:16). If the moon was a rock, then the Holy Spirit misled Moses to write a false claim. What did God make on Day 4? The Bible says God made two lights. For the modern Christian, we have learned to change the text and say that God made two lights, but one was really a rock. According to the Bible, the moon is a light independent of the sun because that is what "God said" (Genesis 1:14).

Chapter 38

Tiny Stars

The points of light that we see in the night sky are called stars. According to modern science, we see stars all the time. During the night they form constellations. During the day, the stars are still there, but the sun is too bright. What is a star? According to NASA, stars are just balls of gas. NASA writes:

> Stars are giant balls of hot gas – mostly hydrogen, with some helium and small amounts of other elements. Every star has its own life cycle, ranging from a few million to trillions of years, and its properties change as it ages.[1]

Modern science tells us that the stars are much larger than our local yellow dwarf star. According to modern science, the sun is 109 times larger than the earth. To get a visual, stand a nickel next to an average door; the sun would be the door, and the earth would be the nickel. Modern science teaches that the sun, compared to VY Canis Majoris, is only a dot next to modern science's stars (Fig. 62).

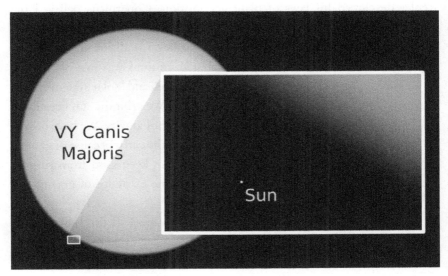

Fig. 62. The sun and VY Canis Majoris.

The stars create a problem between God's word and modern science. The Bible tells us that God made the stars. All points of light in the night sky are considered stars. There are no "planets" or other objects in the firmament, only the sun, moon, and stars.[2] Since many scholars and theologians believe in modern science's "universe," they read Genesis 1:16 and include other objects. For example, *Nelson's New Illustrated Bible Dictionary* wrote, "In the Bible the word 'star' is used as a generic term for all the heavenly bodies—including stars, planets, comets, and meteors—but excluding the sun and the moon."[3]

The Bible never mentions non-illuminating spherical objects that move in the night sky, like "planets." Remember, to be a "planet," we are forced to accept the theory of gravity even though it has never been proven, and nobody knows what it is today. The International Astronomical Union (IAU) states, to be a "planet" it has to be "big enough to have enough gravity to force it into a spherical shape."[4] Modern science does not know what gravity is, but they are positive that it makes a "planet" into a sphere.

The earth's shape may not be important to most people, but it is necessary to modern science. Causing people to accept "planets" makes people accept gravity. Without gravity, their invented "solar system" would come unhinged. Before Newton developed his theory, Kepler said the planets moved in an elliptical orbit that uses an imaginary point in space. Before Kepler developed his laws of planetary motion, Copernicus believed the planets orbited the sun on giant crystal balls. Omodeo wrote, "After the dissolution of the celestial spheres of the medieval tradition in the 1580s, the question about the causes of the celestial motions was raised."[5] Everything modern science believes about the "universe" and "solar system" needs gravity. We went to the moon because of gravity. We orbit the sun because of gravity. We have a breathable atmosphere because of gravity. We have oceans on the globe because of gravity. We do not fly off the earth because of gravity. As long as gravity is around, modern science can keep God from ruining their creation story. As Hawking said, "Given the existence of gravity, the universe can and will create itself from nothing."[6]

God's word made a specific claim about the stars. If the Bible, which God inspired, made a claim, that claim is either true or false. The Scripture claims that the stars will fall upon the earth.

Isaiah 34:4

All the stars in the sky will be dissolved and the heavens rolled up like a scroll; all the starry host will fall like withered leaves from the vine, like shriveled figs from the fig tree.

Mark 13:24–25

[Jesus said,] "But in those days, following that distress, " 'the sun will be darkened, and the moon will not give its light; [25] the stars will fall from the sky, and the heavenly bodies will be shaken.'"

Isaiah and Jesus Christ both claimed that the stars will fall. Fall from where? From the sky. Isaiah used the word "sky | שָׁמַיִם | šāmayim," which means "heaven, i.e., the realm of God where God abides, similar to the area of the sky, but with a focus of where God abides [or] … the area of the stars, skies, air, as a region above the earth including the horizon."[7] "Sky | שָׁמַיִם | šāmayim" can be translated to mean God's home, the firmament, or the atmosphere. Isaiah 34:4 references the firmament, which is called heaven. The Bible states, "And God called the firmament Heaven" (Genesis 1:8, KJV). The NIV translates the same word as "sky."

We know Isaiah is talking about the firmament because stars are not located with the clouds or in our atmosphere where the birds fly (Genesis 1:20). The stars are placed in the firmament. The Bible tells us, "God set them [sun, moon, and stars] in the vault (firmament) of the sky" (Genesis 1:17). Isaiah tells us that the stars are located above the earth, above our atmosphere, and will one day fall downward toward the earth.

Jesus makes the same statement as Isaiah concerning the stars falling to the earth, placing their location in the firmament. The word "sky | οὐρανός | ouranos" means "space above the earth, including the vault arching high over the earth from one horizon to another, as well as the sun, moon, and stars."[8] The *Greek-English Lexicon of the New Testament* describes the firmament as the solid dome barrier that sits over the earth (Genesis 1:6–8). The Bible places the location of the stars in the firmament (Genesis 1:17). According to *Theological Dictionary of the New Testament*, the word "sky | οὐρανός | ouranos" in the singular means "'heaven' either as the overarching firmament or as that which embraces all things."[9] Jesus made a claim that the stars, which are in the firmament, will fall upon the earth.

Did Jesus make a correct statement? Did Jesus mean the stars will fall upon the earth? According to modern science, the stars and our local sun are larger than the earth. The following image will compare the sun to other stars (Fig. 63). If one of modern science's stars or the sun would hit the earth, the earth would be destroyed entirely.

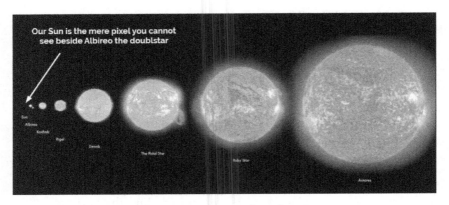

Fig. 63. The sun compared to other stars.

How large are the stars? According to modern science, our sun, a tiny star compared to other stars, would wipe out the earth. Did Jesus misspeak when He said the stars will fall to the earth? No. Jesus meant what He said because He knows what the stars are and where the stars are located. Allen Black commented on Mark 13:25. Black wrote, "It is difficult to decide whether to take Jesus literally or metaphorically. Since he is speaking of the second coming and the end of the world, it may be appropriate to take his language literally."[10] I agree with Black. Jesus meant what He said.

In Mark 13:25, Jesus was speaking privately to "Peter, James, John and Andrew" (Mark 13:3). We should take Jesus literally because "when he was alone with his own disciples, he explained everything" (Mark 4:34). Jesus was not talking in code about the end times. He was speaking in clear and precise language. Jesus told His disciples that the stars would fall from the firmament to the earth.

The stars taught to us by modern science are massive and their location is trillions and trillions of miles away. Since the stars are light years away, the Book of Revelation will take an eternity to come true.

Revelation 6:12–13

I watched as he opened the sixth seal. There was a great earthquake. The sun turned black like sackcloth made of goat hair, the whole moon turned blood red, [13] and the stars in the sky fell to earth, as figs drop from a fig tree when shaken by a strong wind.

Once again, Jesus claims that multiple stars will fall to the earth. The Book of Revelation is the "revelation from Jesus Christ" (Revelation 1:1). Jesus is telling John that the stars (plural) will fall to the earth. In Revelation 6, the tribulation begins, and the seals are being opened. After the sixth seal is opened, the world will have to wait until the first star can fall. The world will have to wait until the nearest star, Proxima Centauri, can arrive, which will have to travel 24,931,200,000,000 miles.

Jesus is the only eyewitness to creation that has ever walked the earth. Jesus made the stars. The Bible tells us, "All things have been created through him" (Colossians 1:16). Jesus created the stars on Day 4 and placed them in the firmament as revealed to Moses (Genesis 1:17). I believe Jesus, who is "the truth" (John 14:6), made an accurate statement about the stars falling from the firmament to the earth. Modern science wants us to believe in their balls of gas instead of believing in the one who made the stars.

John 1:1–3

In the beginning was the Word, and the Word was with God, and the Word was God. [2] He was with God in the beginning. [3] Through him all things were made; without him nothing was made that has been made.

Chapter 39

The Moving Sun

There is a natural conflict that occurs between God's word and modern science. What God said and what modern science claims is on the opposite ends of the spectrum. People may try to blend the two, but they are as compatible as oil and water. Victor P. Hamilton wrote:

> As far as the opening chapter of Genesis is concerned, the battle lines are drawn between the interpretation of the Creation story and scientific knowledge about the origin of the earth and mankind.[1]

Many Christians want to believe that modern science can confirm God's creation story or vice versa. That is not true. The reason modern science and the creation story will remain incompatible has to do with the sun. The sun is the most conflicting topic when it comes to the Bible and modern science. If we believe what the Bible says about the sun, then we would have to reject modern science's "solar system." If we accept our modern understanding of the "solar system," then we would have to abandon the plain and natural reading of Scripture.

I have witnessed a student at a Bible-based university who wanted to defend the literal reading of the creation story against modern science.[2] The student argued that the creation story was not poetic or mythological and spoke negatively against modern science. The professor rejected the paper. The student was allowed to resubmit another paper. The professor wanted the student to avoid addressing anything related to science when it came to Genesis. The professor wrote:

> Here is the fallacy in your conclusion: you have concluded that if Genesis 1 is read as poetry that it somehow lessens the power and authority of God's word, causing God's word to have an error; that is a horrible conclusion. ... Why do you feel so intent on attacking the science angle? ... Stick with the examination of Genesis 1 as being a literal event. ... One final suggestion, I think you need to abandon the idea of arguing Science versus the Bible. ... I still like your outline (with the science and universe stuff removed).

The professor wanted the student to refrain from bringing up the subject of science. Is it possible to read Genesis 1 without the influence of our modern scientific understanding? No. Today, it is impossible to read Genesis 1 without filtering it through modern science. We have all been taught the spherical earth spins in the vacuum of space and moves in orbit around the sun. We have all been taught to believe in the "solar system" created by modern science. We have all been taught to believe things that are opposite of what the Bible teaches. The professor wrote, "With reading Genesis 1, this is not a science debate." I agree. There is no reason to debate the creation story and modern science. The creation story found in Genesis 1 comes from a "God, who does not lie" (Titus 1:2). The creation of modern science's "universe" comes from "the father of lies" (John 8:44).

Could you read Genesis 1 as poetry? No. The poetry argument started after the Scientific Revolution (1543–1687). That is when the JEDP theory began to change Genesis from history into poetry. The poetic angle started when the earth began to move. Even if Genesis was written in poetry, it does not give us the right to make it say something different from what it intends to teach.

For example, the psalmist said that God will "cover you with his feathers" (Psalm 91:4). We do not believe that God has feathers, but the psalmist describes God in a poetic sense. Since Psalm 91:4 is poetry, it does not give us the right to say what we want the verse to say. We do not have the right to say that God does not care for us. We must understand what the author intends for us to know. The psalmist wants us to know about God's tender care. Jesus used the same metaphor when describing His care for people, "How often I have longed to gather your children together, as a hen gathers her chicks under her wings" (Matthew 23:37).

When the psalmist said, "He set the earth on its foundations; it can never be moved" (Psalm 104:5), it does not give us the right to say the earth is not on a foundation and it moves. That would be the opposite of what the psalmist is trying to teach us. When it comes to the creation of the sun on Day 4, scholars recognize the problem. How can we have mornings without the sun? Gordon J. Wenham wrote:

> There is no problem in conceiving of the creation of light
> before the heavenly bodies (vv 14–19). Their creation on
> the fourth day matches the creation of light on the first day
> of the week. But the existence of day and night (v 5) before
> the creation of the sun is more difficult to understand on a

purely chronological interpretation of this account of creation.[3]

Wenham believes in modern science. He may not believe in the big bang or evolution, but no matter how he interprets the creation story, Wenham believes the earth is moving and rotating around the sun. That is why he stated that the day/night cycle is difficult to understand.

Why is it problematic to say the sun was created on Day 4, as the Bible naturally reads? The problem, as Wenham states, is the day/night cycle. We have been taught that the only possible way a morning could happen is if the earth rotates and the sun provides its light. If the sun is not created until Day 4, how can the earth have morning and evening for three days? David Brown et al. wrote, "Besides, it has been shown on *v.* 1 that the sun, moon, and stars existed previously to the fourth day, being included in the original creation of the heavens."[4] Again, scholars are telling their readers not to believe in the literal translation of the creation story. Brown et al. states the sun was made on Day 1. Why would scholars encourage people to believe in something not stated in Scripture? Scholars believe in modern science's "solar system."

Professors, scholars, theologians, pastors, church members, and even the person making the coffee before church all believe the earth moves around the sun. Based on what? It is not based on anything found in the Bible. Our beliefs come from Greek philosophers who told us the earth is round and we are spinning on an axis as we orbit the sun. No one in the Bible ever claimed the earth moves.

Suppose a person searches online for Biblical evidence on a moving earth. The person will eventually find the *Open Bible's*, "What Does the Bible Say About the Earth Orbiting the Sun?"[5] The *Open Bible* lists one hundred verses dealing with the movement of the earth. I will list the first four.

The first verse listed is Job 26:7, "He stretches out the north over the void and hangs the earth on nothing" (ESV). In context, this is Job's opinion about the earth hanging or being suspended over empty space. Job never mentions that the earth moves but only hangs. In a few chapters, Job will be corrected and was told by God that the earth does not hang over nothing but is set upon a foundation that God Himself prepared (Job 38:4).

The second verse *Open Bible* gives is Isaiah 40:22, "It is he who sits above the circle of the earth, and its inhabitants are like grasshoppers; who stretches out the heavens like a curtain, and spreads them like a tent to dwell in" (ESV). This verse only speaks about the earth being directly below God's throne. Nowhere is the earth's movement mentioned. This verse is popular for people trying to prove the earth is round. This verse is also famous for stating the earth is flat. No one uses Isaiah 40:22 as proof of the earth's motion.

The third verse used to show proof that the earth moves is Psalm 104:5, "He set the earth on its foundations, so that it should never be moved" (ESV). The third verse on a list that "proves the earth moves" is a verse that states the earth does not move. Finding Biblical evidence that the earth moves is impossible. The Bible states that the earth can be shaken, but it does not teach that it moves. King David was a man who the "Spirit of the LORD spoke through" (2 Samuel 23:2). David was a man who loved to praise the Lord. David taught his men, "Tremble before him, all the earth! The world is firmly established; it cannot be moved" (1 Chronicles 16:30).

Open Bible's "What Does the Bible Say About the Earth Orbiting the Sun?" does not contain one verse that states the earth moves. *Open Bible* provides one hundred verses but none with a moving earth. The fourth verse used to "prove" that the earth moves is found in Joshua.

Joshua 10:13
So the sun stood still, and the moon stopped, till the nation avenged itself on its enemies, as it is written in the Book of Jashar. The sun stopped in the middle of the sky and delayed going down about a full day.

If we hold to the teachings of modern science, the account found in Joshua is wrong. According to modern science, the sun does not move; the earth does. David Guzik listed some different possibilities to explain the miracle of the sun standing still. Guzik wrote:

It could have been a slowing of the earth's rotation; it could have been a tilting of the earth's axis; it could have been a miracle of reflection of light; it could have been simply the presence of God manifested in light. Whatever it means, the result was clear. The sun seemed to stay still in the sky, and Israel was able to complete the victory[6]

Did Joshua record an untrue event? If the earth stopped spinning, then the Book of Joshua made a claim that was not scientifically correct. If the sun only appeared to remain visible, then the Book of Joshua is wrong. The only possibility for the accurate record to be told is if the sun and moon stopped in their motion. Maren H. Woudstra recognizes that if we believe the layout described in Genesis 1, we could interpret the Joshua account as literal. Woudstra wrote:

> In general it may be said that the biblical view of the world as created by God, who assigned to each heavenly body its place and function (Gen. 1:16), permits a rather literal view of the events reported here.[7]

The Joshua account is easily understood if we believe in the Biblical location of the sun and moon. The heavenly lights are located in the firmament, the solid dome barrier right above the air we breathe. According to the Bible, "The sun rises and the sun sets, and hurries back to where it rises" (Ecclesiastes 1:5). The word "rise | זָרַח | zāraḥ" means to "come forth."[8] The word "sets | בּוֹא | bô" means to "go."[9] In Ecclesiastes and Joshua, the movement is placed on the sun and not the earth. According to the Bible, the earth does not move. Stopping the sun works perfectly fine within the framework (context) of the Bible (Fig. 64). When we inject modern science into the text, things get complicated.

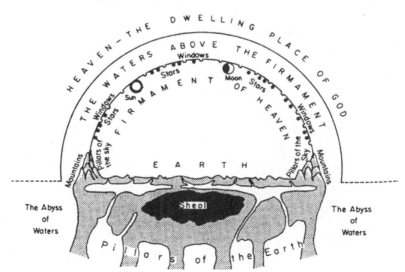

Fig. 64. Hebrew universe assumed by Old Testament writers.

It is hard to imagine the sun being close, let alone smaller than what we have been taught since childhood. We are told the sun is the center of our "solar system" over ninety million miles away. When scientists were trying to convince people about the distance and size of the sun, they were guessing how far the sun was. John Wesley (1703-1791), the preacher who co-founded the Methodist Church, knew not to trust astronomers and their theories about the sun. Wesley wrote:

> But the more I consider them, the more I doubt of all systems of astronomy. I doubt whether we can certainly know either the distance or magnitude of any star in the firmament. Else why do astronomers so immensely differ, even with regard to the distance of the sun from the earth? Some affirming it to be only three, others ninety, millions of miles![10]

When you start to compare images of the sun, it only gets even more confusing. When NASA releases a picture of the sun, it shows the sun with its nuclear fusion and surface covered with exploding activity. When an amateur takes a photo of the sun, it looks like a light, just like the Bible said it was. Here is a comparison of the sun according to NASA and an amateur (Fig. 65). The size of the sun is scaled to be the same.

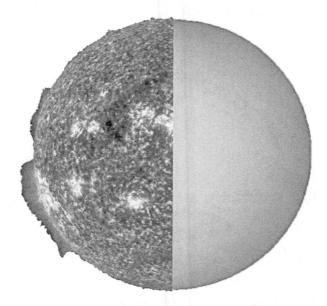

Fig. 65. Comparison of Sun.

To modern science, the sun is their creator. NOVA tells its audience, "The sun is a creator bringing together atoms forged in generations of ancient stars to create us ... We are the children of these stars."[11] Francis Collins, the Christian scientist, tells us, "The atoms in your body were once cooked in the nuclear furnace of an ancient supernova—you are truly made of Stardust."[12] According to Copernicus (1543), the father of the modern "solar system," the sun was a visible god as taught to him by Hermes Trismegistus, the ancient Egyptian god named Thoth. Ferris wrote, "In *De Revolutionibus* [Copernicus] invokes the authority of none other than Hermes Trismegistus ... who had become the patron saint of the new sun-worshipers: 'Trismegistus calls [the sun] a 'visible god.'"[13] The teachings of Hermes Trismegistus taught people to worship the sun. Long wrote, "[Hermes Trismegistus'] writings pointed to sun worship and a Sun-centered universe."[14]

The heliocentric (sun at rest; earth moves) theory was nothing more than sun worship that was taught to Pythagoras more than 2,500 years ago. Knight wrote, "The heliocentric theory was held by the ancient Egyptians, and taught by them to Pythagoras ... it was eventually revived by Copernicus."[15] The modern "solar system" is based on the heliocentric theory. Helios means "sun god." *Sol* is Latin for sun. Our modern "sol(sun) system" is about the sun god Helios being at the center, just like Copernicus told us nearly five hundred years ago (Fig. 66). Copernicus wrote, "Thus indeed, as though seated on a royal throne, the sun governs the family of planets revolving around it."[16]

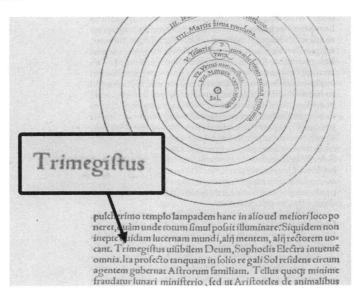

Fig. 66. *De revolutionibus* (Trismegistus highlight).

Attempt to Reject Paganism

While writing this book, I returned to an article from Creation Ministries International (CMI) called "Refuting Absolute Geocentrism." I previously read the article while researching the Christian perspective on the "universe."

The article was originally published on February 12, 2015. It was updated on January 1, 2024. CMI inserted a text frame into their original article. The title inside the text frame reads, "Was heliocentrism the result of Hermetic paganism?" CMI's original article received quite the pushback because even in 2015, people were questioning the movement and shape of the earth. Now, people are starting to learn about the pagan history of the ancient Greek philosophers during the Scientific Revolution (1543–1687), which prompted CMI to issue an update. Here is how CMI replied to the argument that a moving earth (heliocentric theory) is tied to pagan roots, as taught by the false god Hermes Trismegistus. Robert Carter and Jonathan Sarfati wrote:

> Some recent historians have tried to make the claim that Copernican theory was driven by some sort of Hermetic sun worship, but this is grossly anachronistic. By taking the 'perfect' sun and putting it at the center, instead of worshiping the sun, Copernicans were demoting it to the worst place.[1]

Carter and Sarfati tell us that Copernicus did not worship the sun but demoted it and placed it in the center, which, according to Carter and Sarfati, is the "worst place." According to Copernicus' own words, Carter and Sarfati are wrong. Where is the center that Carter and Sarfati are referencing? Carter and Sarfati believe the "solar system" is just a tiny little dot lost in the vastness of the Milky Way Galaxy. That is not how Copernicus saw things. Copernicus thought he was placing the sun at the center of the entire "universe." Owen Gingerich and James MacLachlan explain, "All the spheres encircle the sun, and therefore the center of the universe is near the sun."[2] Copernicus placed the sun in the center of the "universe" to light up everything. Placing the sun at the center was not a demotion.

Carter and Sarfati tell us Copernicus placed the sun in the center to avoid sun worship. Copernicus himself refutes their claim. Why did Copernicus put the sun in the center of everything? According to Copernicus, the sun was the "universe's" lantern, mind, ruler, visible god, and all-seeing. Copernicus believed the sun deserved to be seated on its throne like a king. Copernicus wrote, "At rest, however, in the middle of everything is the sun … Thus indeed, as though seated on a royal throne, the sun governs the family of planets revolving around it."[3] Copernicus believed only the sun, a god, deserves to have the "planets" circle its royal throne, located in the center of the "universe."

Copernicus believed the sun's throne was located in the temple of the "universe." Copernicus asked, "For in this most beautiful temple, who would place this lamp in another or better position than that from which it can light up the whole thing at the same time?"[4] Copernicus proposed a question to be answered, wondering if anything out there could light up the entire "universe" like the sun. Copernicus wanted the sun, the visible god, to sit on its throne. Placing the sun in the center was not a demotion, but it was honoring the ruler of the "universe."

Carter and Sarfati will then quote a Hermetic (writings of Hermes Trismegistus) text about heliocentrism (sun at rest; earth moving). Carter and Sarfati do not cite the passage they quote, but they use this reference to highlight, in their words, the "mystical nonsense" of Hermetic teachings:

> Since it is the visual ray itself, the sun shines all around the cosmos with the utmost brilliance, on the part above and on the part below. For the sun is situated in the center of the cosmos, wearing it like a crown. Like a good driver, it steadies the chariot of the cosmos and fastens the reins to itself to prevent the cosmos going out of control. And the reins are these: life and soul and spirit and immortality and becoming. The driver slackens the reins to let the cosmos go, not far away (to tell the truth) but along with him.[5]

I agree with Carter and Sarfati; the previous quote is "mythical nonsense." It was the same "mythical nonsense" the Renaissance humanistic movement sought. After the fall of Constantinople (1453), new Greek literature would become available, but people could only read Latin. Once Marsilio Ficino translated the *Corpus Hermeticum*, "mythical nonsense" would be sought after. The *Corpus Hermeticum* was a collection of writings attributed to Hermes Trismegistus, the ancient Egyptian god Thoth. What Copernicus presented was not new, but ancient Egyptian teachings. Hermes Trismegistus taught about the eight spheres that rotated around the sun. The *Corpus Hermeticum* reads:

> Around the Sun are the eight spheres, who depend on it; first is the sphere of the fixed stars, then the six of the planets and the one that encircles the earth.[6]

Copernicus released his theory with a diagram of the new "universe," described in the *Corpus Hermeticum*. The same "mythical nonsense" was taught to Pythagoras, who learned science, astronomy, and earth-measuring math from a pagan god. Here is Copernicus' diagram of the entire "universe" (Fig. 67). Copernicus' drawing includes eight spheres, as described in the *Corpus Hermeticum*. The first sphere (1) is the stars. The following six spheres are the "planets" (2–7). The eighth sphere circling the earth is the moon (8).

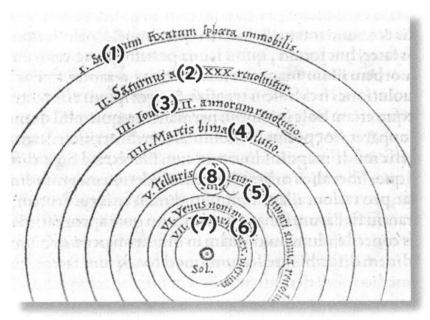

Fig. 67. *De revolutionibus with Corpus Hermeticum's* eight spheres.

Carter and Sarfati consider Hermeticism as senseless writings that are non-scientific. Their view is based upon their modern understanding of science. During the Renaissance, separating mysticism, magic, esoteric knowledge, and the occult from science was difficult. It was not until Francis Bacon (1561–1626) that scientists tried to separate magic and science. Bacon did not dismiss all magic but was among the first to suggest the separation of "mythical nonsense" and experimental science.

Copernicus did not discover anything new but repeated old theology that taught to elevate the sun into its royal position at the center of the entire "universe." Copernicus never mentioned worshiping the sun. When Giordano Bruno came along, he promoted Copernicus' theory as "sun worship." Carter and Sarfati wrote:

> So if any heliocentrist was influenced by Hermeticism, it was surely Giordano Bruno (1548–1600), a New-Agey non-scientist beloved of atheist Neil deGrasse Tyson.[7]

Carter and Sarfati make a true statement. Bruno did believe in sun worship because Hermetic writings were about sun worship. Pamela O. Long, a scholar in Renaissance Studies, wrote, "Hermetic writings pointed to sun worship and a Sun-centered universe."[8]

Carter and Sarfati will continue their disbelief that the writings of Hermes Trismegistus influenced Copernicus. They use the word "Hermitica," which is usually spelled as Hermetica. I have included their footnote, which explains they are speaking about Hermetica, also known as Hermetic or Hermeticism. Carter and Sarfati wrote:

> And even though the Hermitica[24] was widely read among the scholars of Copernicus' time (the Renaissance), we do not believe Copernicus was among the adherents. Copernicus had one passing mention of Hermes among other ancient writings.
>
> [24] Based on writings attributed to a mythical figure called Hermes Trismegistus (Greek *Hermēs ho Trismegistos* Ἑρμῆς ὁ Τρισμέγιστος, 'thrice-greatest Hermes'). The writings advocated an esoteric monotheism with reincarnation, and taught that man could control nature with rituals (theurgy), alchemy, and astrology.[9]

Carter and Sarfati claim that pagan influence during the Renaissance was a recent push by modern historians. Which historians? Carter and Sarfati never mention any Christian or secular scholars. Why would Christian scholars promote a false narrative about the influence of Hermetic writings that could easily be debunked by secular scholarship? What benefit would secular scholars have in promoting an occult philosophy steeped in magic, which would only undermine the creditability of Copernicus? Carter and Sarfati are wrong.

Carter and Sarfati claim that recent historians have imposed sun worship on Copernicus' theory. In this book, I have used books, journal articles, and reference materials that are sources approved by universities and research facilities. For example, George Grote wrote a twelve-volume series called *A History of Greece*. Here is what the Cambridge University said about *A History of Greece*:

> Cambridge Library Collection: Books of enduring scholarly value.
>
> Widely acknowledged as the most authoritative study of ancient Greece, George Grote's twelve-volume work ... established the shape of Greek history which still prevails in textbooks and popular accounts of the ancient world today.[10]

A History of Greece is held by scholarship as a premium source to know the culture and mindset of the Greek world. What does *A History of Greece* say about the happenings during the Renaissance (1400s–1600s)? *A History of Greece* said:

> The flight of Greek scholars to the West after the fall of Constantinople in 1453 gave impetus to the study of ancient Greek literature ... developments in textual criticism and linguistic analysis, and new ways of studying ancient societies, especially archaeology, led to renewed enthusiasm for the Classics.[11]

What were the "Classics" that *A History of Greece* is referencing? They were newly obtained literature from the west. Ancient literature that was believed to have been written by Hermes Trismegistus. Jason Kelly explains what "Classics" means. Kelly wrote:

> Renaissance classicism was an intellectual movement that sought to mimic the literature, rhetoric, art, and philosophy of the ancient world … Scholars, politicians, and philosophers looked to ancient literary and artistic models for inspiration, and in turn this love of the classical world is termed classicism.[12]

The classical literature of the Renaissance was the ancient writings from the east that came after the fall of Constantinople (1453). The philosophy of the ancient world was becoming the philosophy of the Renaissance, built upon magic and esoteric ancient teachings from Hermes Trismegistus.

Carter and Sarfati claim that modern historians are making up the narrative of a paganistic Renaissance influence on Copernicus. I used George Grote's *A History of Greece: Volume 4*, widely accepted as a valid resource for scholarly research because it was originally published in 1847. Grote, in 1847, wrote about Pythagoras and his visit to Egypt and his interest in mysticism and magic. Grote, in 1847, wrote about Pythagoras and his belief in reincarnation and an eyewitness account of Pythagoras claiming his friend's soul was living inside of a dog.

Another resource I used was *Knight's American Mechanical Encyclopedia*. Knight's encyclopedia told us that Pythagoras learned the heliocentric (sun at rest; earth moving) theory from the Egyptians. Knight also said that Copernicus would revive or renaissance (the French word for "rebirth") the ancient teachings that Pythagoras learned in Egypt by releasing his own version of a sun-centered "universe." Knight told us that Copernicus did not invent anything new but rebranded what Pythagoras learned in Egypt. Knight told us this in 1882.

Who taught Pythagoras, the Greek philosopher, about a sun-centered "universe"? It was the Egyptian god Thoth, who Egyptians claimed was the "All-knowing One." Patrick Boylan explained that Thoth was the one who taught all mankind about science, astronomy, geometry, and religion. Boylan told us this in 1922.

George T. Allen confirmed that the Egyptian god Thoth was one of the highest-ranking gods in Egypt. Allen also informed us about Thoth's influence in history. Allen let us know that Thoth would be known to the Greeks as Hermes. The Greek god Hermes would eventually turn into Hermes Trismegistus during the Renaissance, the author of the Hermetic or Hermetica writings that flooded Western Europe. Allen told us this in 1923.

Historians have long known about the Renaissance's demonic activities and its history of esoteric and occult practices. The Renaissance was about learning the new classics from the east, about esoteric wisdom and magic.

Carter and Sarfati make one more claim located in their text frame. They claim that the apostle Paul was just like Copernicus because Paul also referenced Greek pagans in his letters to the churches. Carter and Sarfati argue that since Paul used Greek pagans, we should not have a problem with Copernicus. Carter and Sarfati wrote:

> If this is a problem, then what about the Apostle Paul quoting pagan poets with approval: Aratus (Acts 17:28), Menander (1 Corinthians 15:33), and Epimenides (Titus 1:12)?

Paul did cite Greek pagan poets. In the Book of Acts, Paul cited Epimenides, "For in him we live and move and have our being" (Acts 17:28). Barclay Moon Newman and Eugene Albert Nida wrote, "The words alluded to by Paul in this verse are thought to have originated with Epimenides, a poet living in Crete in the sixth century B.C."[13] In the Book of Acts, Paul was talking with people who did not know about God or His Son, Jesus Christ. Paul spoke to people who worship "AN UNKNOWN GOD" (Acts 17:23). Paul distinguishes between the Greeks who worship known and unknown gods and our God, the Most High. Paul makes that distinction when alluding to Greek poets like Epimenides. Paul separates himself from Greek poets by saying, "As some of your own poets have said" (Acts 17:28).

Paul was leaving Titus in Crete, the home of the Greek poet Epimenides (Acts 17:28). Crete was a challenging place to build a church, so Paul wanted to give Titus some wisdom and advice. In Paul's letter to Titus, Paul warns about the dangers of Greek philosophers in Crete, including the false prophet Epimenides. Paul notifies Titus by quoting Epimenides himself, "Cretans are always liars" (Titus 1:12). Donald Guthrie wrote, "The lines quoted are from Epimenides, a sixth-century philosopher whom many of his countrymen had raised to mythical honours."[14] Paul told Titus not to trust Greek poets because they lie.

Copernicus is not Paul. Copernicus cited a false god. The apostle Paul rejected false gods. Paul did use words written by Greek poets. Today, many people believe "God moves in mysterious ways." People are not quoting Scripture but William Cowper who wrote a poem in 1773. Cowper's first line reads, "God moves in a mysterious way." Cowper did not write Scripture, but we can quote this phrase because it highlights the truth found in Scripture. God Himself said, "For my thoughts are not your thoughts, neither are your ways my ways" (Isaiah 55:8).

Paul did not have a problem using the words of men to highlight the truth in God's word. Paul had a problem with Greek philosophers who followed false gods. Paul knew that Greek philosophers introduced deceptive teachings designed to mislead the believer. Paul also knew that Greek philosophers depended upon the demonic forces of this world to gain their wisdom, just like Copernicus, who relied on the teachings of the false god Hermes Trismegistus. Paul said, "See to it that no one takes you captive through hollow and deceptive philosophy, which depends on human tradition and the elemental spiritual forces of this world rather than on Christ" (Colossians 2:8).

Carter and Sarfati close their text frame on Hermetica's influence by saying, "What we have to do is assess the evidence for and against absolute geocentrism and not resort to *ad hominem* distractions." Carter and Sarfati state that we should not be attacking Copernicus' character but should focus on the claims that Copernicus made. I disagree, and so does the Bible.

A person's character is a part of their motivation. Paul tells the church to "eagerly desire gifts of the Spirit" (1 Corinthians 14:1). Paul is telling this to people whose character is good. People who "Follow the way of love" (1 Corinthians 14:1). The people who should seek the gifts of the Spirit are people whose character is grounded in truth. The Bible says, "Love does not delight in evil but rejoices with the truth" (1 Corinthians 13:6). People with a bad character will only corrupt others with their evil desires. Even the Greek poet Menander knew this, "Do not be misled: 'Bad company corrupts good character'" (1 Corinthians 15:33).

Copernicus' character does matter. Character is the motivation behind our words and actions. Copernicus was motivated to draw what Hermes Trismegistus said in the *Corpus Hermeticum* (Fig. 67). Copernicus was motivated to place the "visible god" at the center of the "universe" because it was the lantern, mind, and ruler. Copernicus was motivated to promote the teachings of the Greek philosopher Pythagoras and his assumption of a spherical earth that was moving around the sun. As Africa wrote:

Copernicus was no revolutionary and fancied himself the restorer of ancient wisdom, rather than the discoverer of a new astronomy. Whatever his thesis meant to others, [Copernicus] saw it as the foundation of a Pythagorean Restoration.[15]

What was Paul's motivation for his audience? Paul wanted his readers to know Jesus. Paul wrote, "For Christ did not send me to baptize, but to preach the gospel—not with wisdom and eloquence, lest the cross of Christ be emptied of its power" (1 Corinthians 1:17). Paul was motivated to teach the wisdom that came from God. Paul knew the Greek philosophy was not true wisdom but only a lie. Paul wrote, "Where is the wise person? Where is the teacher of the law? Where is the philosopher of this age? Has not God made foolish the wisdom of the world?" (1 Corinthians 1:20). Paul knew the dangers of following liars like Pythagoras (500 BC). Paul knew that Greek philosophy was dishonest, deceitful, and devoid of anything of real value.

1 Corinthians 3:19–20
For the wisdom of this world is foolishness in God's sight. As it is written: "He catches the wise in their craftiness"; [20] and again, "The Lord knows that the thoughts of the wise are futile."

Choosing a World

Chapter 41

Movement, Water, and Gravity

We have only been taught a "universe" designed for a particular purpose. A "universe" that tells us we are nothing special. Many people do not care about the history of modern science because the earth is just an insignificant little dot in an enormous, ever-expanding "universe." As humans located on a tiny globe, ripping through the endless vacuum of space, our world is nothing special. That is known as the Copernican Principle. Ron Cowen wrote:

> The Copernican principle, a notion near and dear to the hearts of physicists and cosmologists … Named after the 16th century astronomer Nicolaus Copernicus, who made the then heretical proposal that Earth does not have a favored, central position in the solar system, the principle states that humans are not privileged observers in the universe, but have just as good — or bad — a vantage point as any other observer in the cosmos.[1]

When the Lord challenged my thoughts about the "universe," I went to look for evidence for the heliocentric theory. It was not there. The fabrication of the origin of our modern universe was a lie. When I tell people about the history of the "universe," it is usually followed with jeering, dismissal, or the common "I don't believe you." Let me give you an example of my dilemma when dealing with the Bible and modern science.

$\acute{O}$

Imagine a man named Jimmy who grew up in a traditional home. Jimmy had two parents who loved and raised him to the best of their abilities. Years later, Jimmy's last parent had passed away, and he was cleaning out their house. Sorting through old boxes, Jimmy discovered a box that revealed he had been adopted. Jimmy's first response was, "This can't be real." After going through the box, Jimmy realized that he was adopted and the parents that he loved, parents that he thought were his biological parents, were not his birth parents.

Jimmy decided to visit his friend. Jimmy told his friend, "My whole life was a lie. The people I thought were my biological parents are not my real biological parents. I loved them, but my mom lied to me when she said she gave birth to me." The friend replied, "I can't believe it. I knew your parents. They were good people. They would not lie to you." Jimmy replied, "Look. Here are my adoption papers. Here is the letter from the state and the new birth certificate."

The friend said, "Well, who are your real parents?" Jimmy replied, "I don't know. I just found out." The friend insisted, "Your parents would not lie to you. Do you think everyone at church was in on the lie? Do you think that everyone at work was in on the lie? Do you think I was in on the lie, also?" Jimmy said, "No. Everyone was not in on the lie. Everyone, including me, just believed what we were told." The friend replied, "Until you show me who your real parents are, I don't believe you."

Ó

The illustration of Jimmy and his friend is typical for people who discover that the "universe" is not what modern science has told us. People like Jimmy have found that what we thought was true (e.g., "universe," "solar system," gravity, etc.) was nothing more than just a lie told to us our whole life. When Jimmy tells his friend the truth, it is not accepted because the friend does not believe they fell for a lie. The friend does not believe even when Jimmy states the genuine truth and shows real evidence. The only response from the friend is, "I don't believe you." The denial of truth does not make a lie true.

What would our response be if we were told the earth does not move? Would we respond like the friend, "I don't believe you?" The response "I don't believe you" does not make something true that was never true. Like Jimmy, I discovered a lie. The lie: the earth moves. When a person responds, "I don't believe you," they are not addressing the issue presented but only dismissing the statement without giving reasons or evidence for their position.

Movement

I believe the earth does not move. A person may argue that my claim is not true, or they may say that the Bible does not mean the earth was set on a foundation. Let me be clear about the position that I take. The earth does not move. The earth is fixed to a position that does not rotate and is set upon a foundation. In making such a claim, the burden of proof is not on me to prove to people that the earth is not moving. I do not have to prove anything because the "earth not moving" is not my claim. It is God's claim found in the Bible. Does God have to prove what He inspired to be written in the Bible? No. God's word stands on its own.

The burden of proof is not on me to prove to Christians that the earth does not move. I do not have to provide any evidence for a statement made by a "God, who does not lie" (Titus 1:2). The burden of proof is on the Christian who does not accept what the Bible plainly states: "He set the earth on its foundations; it can never be moved" (Psalm 104:5). The burden of proof is on the Christian who believes the earth moves since the Bible teaches a fixed, non-moving earth that is set upon a foundation. *A Translator's Handbook on the Book of Psalms* describes how the audience reading Psalm 104:5 believed the earth to be:

> Yahweh placed the earth solidly on its foundations (see [Psalm] 24:2; 102:25a); this reflects the idea that the earth was a flat disk that rested on pillars under the ground, which reached down into the underworld. (Note the illustration [Fig. 68]).[2]

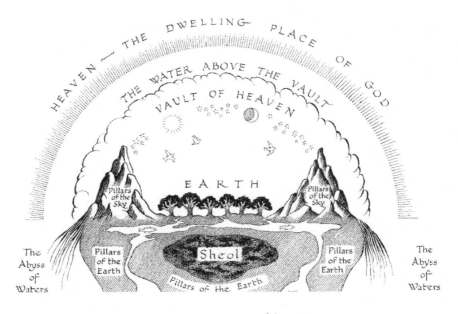

Fig. 68. An ancient concept of the universe.

What evidence would a person present to prove the earth moves? There is no observational evidence to prove the earth moves. When people argue for a moving earth, their statements are based on other people's theories that say the earth moves. We put our trust and faith in theories that make us think the opposite of what we experience. What evidence would a person present to prove the earth is round? Again, there is no observational evidence to prove the earth's curvature. Water alone makes it difficult to believe in a round earth.

Water

Water is level at any angle when we tilt a glass because we can observe it (Fig. 69). It is also level over great distances (Fig. 70). Because of our faith in theories from the Scientific Revolution, we think the opposite of what we see.

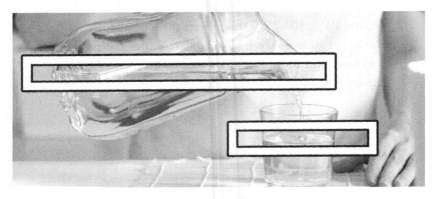

Fig. 69. Water remaining level in glass containers.

Fig. 70. Map of Suez Canal.

The Suez Canal is 120 miles long. It is a man-made canal without any locks. The Suez Canal Authority states, "The Suez Canal (In Arabic: Qanat as-Suways), is an artificial sea-level waterway running north to south across the Isthmus of Suez in Egypt to connect the Mediterranean Sea and the Red Sea."[3] There are no locks in the Suez Canal. *Encyclopedia Britannica* states, "The Suez Canal is an open cut, without locks, and, though extensive straight lengths occur, there are eight major bends."[4] A lock is only needed when the two endpoints are at different sea levels (Fig. 71). *Encyclopedia. com* wrote:

> To conserve water and to facilitate two-way travel, canals are built level. If there is a difference in elevation between the ends of a canal, the channel is built as a series of level sections linked by locks. A lock is a rectangular chamber with gates at both ends; with both gates closed, the water level within the lock can be adjusted to match the canal water level on either side.[5]

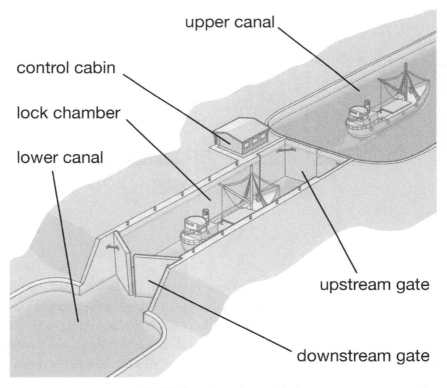

Fig. 71. Illustration of a canal lock.

The Suez Canal is level. The water must be level from the Mediterranean Sea to the Red Sea since there are no locks to adjust for a height difference. Canals only work on a flat plane. If water is poured on a surface that is not level, the water will flow down until it reaches a level area to rest. That is what Pascal's Law or principle teaches. *Wolfram Demonstrations Project* gives us an example of water remaining level even when poured into odd-shaped containers:

> The figure [Fig. 72] shows a set of interconnected tubes open at the top. Colored water is poured into one of them. The level of the liquid rises to the same level in all four tubes, regardless of their shape. This is a consequence of Pascal's principle, whereby pressure is uniformly transmitted throughout a liquid. In more familiar terms, "water seeks its own level."[6]

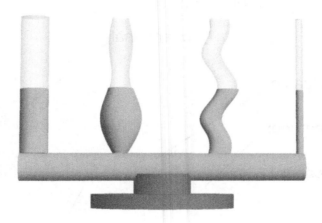

Fig. 72. Pascal's principal demonstration.

For the Suez Canal to work on a round earth, the canal's water would have to rest in a curved position. The Suez Canal is long enough to produce a curve with a height of nearly two miles. At 120 miles, according to *Omni Calculator*, a website that promotes a spherical earth, the earth's curve would be 9,583 feet (1.81 miles).[7] Water would have to rest, forming a curved surface nearly two miles high. Water does not work this way. How does modern science explain how a canal works on a spherical, non-flat surface? Gravity. Oceans, rivers, and canals do not work on a globe without a "force, whatever it is?"[8]

Gravity

Newton's gravity is the force that keeps water on the rotating earth. According to Einstein, gravity is not a force. Einstein said gravity was the bending of spacetime (Fig. 73). According to Einstein, gravity is not a force that pulls and pushes objects.

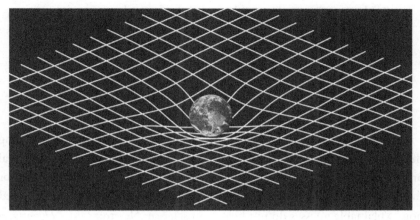

Fig. 73. Gravity illustrated through curved spacetime.

Which version of gravity will modern science use to explain how water can cling to a moving and spinning earth? Modern science will not use Einstein's new theory of gravity but will resurrect Newton's old theory. The force of gravity (Newton) keeps the water on the globe. NASA tells us, "Gravity is always uniformly pointed downward … which pulls the water due to the force of gravity."[9]

Should we believe in the force of gravity? No. According to Newton, the inventor of the force of gravity, if a person is intelligent, they should not believe in his theory. Newton wrote a personal letter to Richard Bentley. Newton was replying to Bentley's letter written on February 18, 1693. Bentley questioned Newton's gravity. Newton wrote:

> That gravity should be innate inherent & {essential} to matter so that one body may act upon another at a distance through a vacuum without the mediation of any thing else by & through which their action or force {may} be conveyed from one to another is to me so great an absurdity that I beleive [*sic*] no man who has in philosophical matters any competent faculty of thinking can ever fall into it.[10]

Newton could not explain "action at a distance," meaning the invisible force that pulls or pushes on objects without a physical connection. Newton said it was an absurdity to believe objects can affect each other without the mediation of something else. Newton wrote *General Scholium* as an appendix to the 2nd edition of the *Principia* (1713). Newton wrote:

> I have not as yet been able to deduce from phenomena the reason for these properties of gravity, and I do not *feign* hypotheses. For whatever is not deduced from the phenomena must be called a hypothesis; and hypotheses, whether metaphysical or physical, or based on occult qualities, or mechanical, have no place in experimental philosophy.[11]

Phenomena is the plural form of phenomenon, which means "something that exists and can be seen, felt, tasted, etc., especially something unusual or interesting."[12] According to Newton, if we cannot explain the reasons for the natural sensations, then it is only a guess (hypothesis). Newton believed non-explainable guesses do not belong in science. Newton said, "*Hypotheses non fingo*" (Latin for "I frame no hypotheses"). Since Newton did not form a hypothesis (guess) about the force, his assumptions could be taken as natural law. Newton wrote:

> And it is enough that gravity really exists and acts according to the laws that we have set forth and is sufficient to explain all the motions of the heavenly bodies and of our sea.[13]

Today, no one knows what gravity is because nearly 350 years ago, Newton did not know what gravity was. After Newton came, Einstein would try to complete the puzzle of gravity. Einstein gave us a new theory of gravity and said it was a spacetime distortion, not a force. Einstein's theory of gravity was incomplete, so now we have a new theory called quantum gravity. Of course, quantum gravity has never been proven, but modern science will continue to try to make gravity work because their "universe" will fall apart without it.

Chapter 42

Sun Worship

In the Book of Ezekiel, God will give Ezekiel a tour of the temple grounds. At the temple, the place where God's presence dwells, Ezekiel will be shown four different forms of pagan worship. God focuses Ezekiel's attention on the north gate. At the gate was an idol that "provokes to jealousy" (Ezekiel 8:3). Located on the temple grounds, where people were supposed to worship God, the people set up an idol, an image of a false god. God said that this act alone would drive God away from His people.

Ezekiel 8:5–6
Then he said to me, "Son of man, look toward the north." So I looked, and in the entrance north of the gate of the altar I saw this idol of jealousy. ⁶ And he said to me, "Son of man, do you see what they are doing—the utterly detestable things the Israelites are doing here, things that will drive me far from my sanctuary? But you will see things that are even more detestable."

God showed Ezekiel the awful worship of a pagan idol on the temple grounds. Now God is going to show him something even worse. The Bible tells us that Ezekiel was taken to a wall where he noticed a hole. God told him to dig, and Ezekiel started to dig into the wall and discovered a door. Inside this secret doorway, Ezekiel finds seventy elders of Israel worshiping "all kinds of crawling things and unclean animals and all the idols of Israel" (Ezekiel 8:10). They were using censers and offering fragrant offerings to these false idols. These men of Israel secretly did these detestable acts and believed that "The Lord does not see us" (Ezekiel 8:12).

How terrible it must have been for Ezekiel to see these detestable things. First the people set up an idol on sacred ground. Then, the leaders of Israel are worshiping false gods in secret. God reminds Ezekiel some practices are even worse.

Ezekiel 8:13
Again, he said, "You will see them doing things that are even more detestable."

Next, Ezekiel is taken to the entrance of the north gate to the temple, and he sees women mourning the god Tammuz. That is all the Old Testament says about this god. Tammuz was a Mesopotamian deity associated with an annual mourning ritual practiced by women. Knowing the background is interesting, but the main point is that this is the third item that God describes as "detestable." The people's worship of false idols and gods was no longer in secret but was now out in the open.

Ezekiel 8:15

He said to me, "Do you see this, son of man? You will see things that are even more detestable than this."

Finally, the Lord will show Ezekiel something worse than the three previous acts of idolatry. The Lord will bring Ezekiel to the temple entrance, revealing the final detestable thing the people were engaged in.

Ezekiel 8:16

He then brought me into the inner court of the house of the LORD, and there at the entrance to the temple, between the portico and the altar, were about twenty-five men. With their backs toward the temple of the LORD and their faces toward the east, they were bowing down to the sun in the east.

God considered one of the most detestable practices Israel could do was sun worship. The worship of the sun runs deep in the history of mankind. Sun worship has always been a part of our history.

Deuteronomy 4:19

And when you look up to the sky and see the sun, the moon and the stars—all the heavenly array—do not be enticed into bowing down to them and worshiping things the LORD your God has apportioned to all the nations under heaven.

From the Prescientific Age (–600 BC), to the Classical Era (600 BC–500), to the Middle Ages (500–1300s), to the Renaissance (1400s–1600s), to the Age of Reason/Enlightenment (1700s–1800s), and our Modern Era (1900s–present), sun worship still occurs. Modern science demands people's allegiance to Helios, the sun god at the center of heliocentrism. Modern science teaches us to follow the "solar calendar." Modern science pushes the use of "solar energy." Modern science ensures we know the doctrine (theories) that formed the "solar system." Sun worship is everywhere, except we have learned not to pay attention.

The 70s band Earth, Wind & Fire released a song called *Shining Star*, their first major hit. Growing up, I bobbed my head, tapped my foot, and sang *Shining Star*. I was singing about the worship of the sun. People may not think Earth, Wind & Fire was trying to trick me into sun worship. I would agree. Earth, Wind & Fire were not trying to mislead me, but their leader was. Earth, Wind & Fire sang:

> Born a man-child of the sun…
> You're a shining star,
> No matter who you are,
> Shining bright to see…
> What your life can truly be.[1]

Paul McCartney released a song called *Hosanna* in 2013 on his album called *NEW*. McCartney gave praise to the sun. The word hosanna in the New Testament is translated as "Save, I pray" but became equivalent to "Praise be to God." McCartney will also offer praise. McCartney sang:

> Do everything until we've got it done
> Then sing hosanna to the morning sun
> Hosanna, hosanna
> Sing hosanna to the morning sun.[2]

Sun worship is a part of our culture, language, and architecture. The Sree Padmanabhaswamy Temple in India is an ancient temple (Fig. 74). The date for the temple's construction is unknown, but it is believed to be hundreds of centuries old. During the equinox (daylight and night are equal; March and September), as the sun sets, the sun will display itself through each of the temple's center windows (Fig. 75). The sun is very important to the world outside the church.

Fig. 74. Sree Padmanabha Temple.

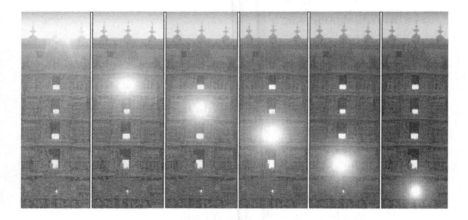

Fig. 75. Sree Padmanabha Temple during an equinox.

As Christians, we do not think like secular (non-religious) people. We have been "transformed by the renewing of your mind" (Romans 12:2). Our thoughts are not about the sun or the worship of false gods. The center of our world is God. Our thoughts are not about becoming a god or seeking the kingdoms of this world. The creator of our world is God. The psalmist knew who created the heavens and the earth. The psalmist knew not to worship the sun. The psalmist knew creation would always bow to its creator. The psalmist declared, "Praise him, sun and moon; praise him, all you shining star" (Psalm 148:3).

Sun worship is common outside of the church, but it is not called worship. It is called entertainment, modern science, or New Age. We hear the worship of the sun when Disney tells us, "You're a star."[3] We are taught the worship of the sun in astronomy. We see the worship of the sun in music videos (Fig. 76). Sun worship is all around us.

Fig. 76. Katy Perry and the Eye of Horus.

Katy Perry, a pop singer, was being interviewed by Ruby Rose on the *7 p.m. Project*. Rose, wearing upside-down cross earrings, mentioned that Perry was doing well now, but her first album was not received well. Perry admitted her first album, a Christian album, was not successful. Perry said, "It didn't work out, so I sold my soul to the devil."[4] Perry, in 2013, released her song called *Dark Horse*. In her music video, she is seen with the eye of Horus (Fig.76). The Egyptian god Horus would become known as Apollo. *Mysterium Academy* wrote, "The Greek equivalent of Horus the Egyptian god is Apollo, the god of sun, music, and plagues."[5] The Greek god Apollo is about sun worship. Ferris wrote, "Apollo the sun god."[6] Sun worship is still happening today.

During the Renaissance and the Scientific Revolution, the sun was not only viewed as the visible god but also, according to Copernicus, "the all-seeing."[7] Filippo Camerota, of Museo Galileo (formally named Institute and Museum of the History of Science), Italy, wrote, "The sun is at the same time both the seeing eye and the source of light."[8] The all-seeing eye, or the eye of Providence, was about the secrets of the sun:

> During the Renaissance, the all-seeing Eye gained popularity as a symbol of knowledge and enlightenment. It became a prominent feature in the works of many renowned artists and intellectuals of the time, including Leonardo da Vinci.[9]

People were not worshiping the sun because it was an object in the sky. People worship the sun because it represents the knowledge they need to become a god. Hermes Trismegistus taught his pupil Tat the benefits of knowing. Once the student learns the secrets of the "universe," they can ascend into the heavens to become god. Hanegraaff wrote:

> [Hermes Trismegistus explained to Tat:] Rise above the seven planetary spheres of the cosmos and reach the luminous spheres of the eight and the ninth, for "such is the happy end for those who have received gnosis: to become God."[10]

Our enemy has promised people they can become gods since the beginning. The serpent said to Eve, "For God knows that when you eat from it your eyes will be opened, and you will be like God" (Genesis 3:5). Today, that same lie is told to people who follow their father, the devil. I am not just talking about demon-possessed individuals or members of the church of Satan. I am talking about those who choose to follow the one who promises them "all the kingdoms of the world" (Luke 4:5).

Paul warned the church that the devil "masquerades as an angel of light" (2 Corinthians 11:14). It is the angel of light, Lucifer, the "morning star, son of the dawn" (Isaiah 14:12), that will deceive people into believing they can become a light themselves. David Spangler, a key figure in the New Age (a system to engage in satanism) movement, explained the purpose of finding Christ consciences. The purpose is not to discover Jesus Christ, the Son of God. The purpose is for people to realize they are a sun, and that knowledge comes only through the morning star, Lucifer. Through Lucifer, a person will discover, like Earth, Wind & Fire sang, "You're a shining star." Spangler wrote:

> Jesus said, "As the Christ, I am the way, the truth, and the life" … This is true … But the light that reveals to us the presence of the Christ, the light that reveals to us the path to the Christ comes from Lucifer. He is the light giver. He is aptly named the Morning Star … The true light of this great being can only be recognized when one's own eyes can see with the light of the Christ, the light of the inner sun … the Christ within me, as a star for you to place in the firmament of heaven. At some point each of us faces the presence of Lucifer.[11]

The world outside the church is very different from the world inside the church. It is a world that follows a god who has "blinded the minds of unbelievers, so that they cannot see the light of the gospel that displays the glory of Christ" (2 Corinthians 4:4). Unbelievers think they are following a light that will lead them to success, money, health, and fame. They cannot see that they are blinded and being led straight to hell.

Our enemy has created a bright "sun system" so people cannot see the truth. Our enemy has promised people they can be stars, little gods of their own. They are deceived. The only hope for them is to see the truth. That truth lives inside of us. His name is Jesus. Paul tells us that if we hold on to Jesus, "the word of life" (Philippians 2:16), we will be a witness to the unbeliever. Then people will see the truth in us because "you will shine among them like stars in the sky" (Philippians 2:15). We will not shine because we are little stars. We will shine because the Son of God who lives in us is the "bright Morning Star" (Revelation 22:16). It is Jesus, the true light that people will see (John 1:9). It is Jesus, the truth, that will set people free (John 8:32).

Chapter 43

Personal Note

In my first three books, I have covered the subject of Genesis 1, all or in part. I was finished writing about the creation story. In October 2023, I started to write on a different topic, *The Story of the Church*. When the influence of modern science is removed from the Bible, the church's story is remarkable. When modern science no longer impacts our interpretation of the Bible, subjects like predestination, Israel as God's people, Christians as God's people, New Jerusalem, etc., become easier to understand within the framework (context) of the Bible. I nearly completed the first draft when I stopped and started to write this book. After I get a chance to say hi to my family, Lord willing, I will finish *The Story of the Church*.

I knew God wanted me to write every book I have written. God asked me a question (*What if Genesis 1 was Correct?*). God woke me up and told me to write (*Proving the Bible Wrong*). God told me He meant what He said (*The Story of the Bible*). God said to write a book with my wife (*Parenting Handbook*). God always confirmed what I was doing with some sign at the beginning of the writing process. This book was different. I needed direction. I had no sign.

In January of 2024, I felt a burden to start writing this book. I began to write about the earth's foundation (Title: *Before Genesis 1*); I shelved it. I started a new document about modern science (Title: *History of the Universe*); I scrapped it. I started a new document about Christian scholarship (Title: *Interpreting the Bible*); I archived it. I was frustrated since I put many hours into each document without a clear direction. Then, in prayer, the Lord helped me see that I was writing about the Biblical, Greek, and Modern Christian worlds when it comes to understanding the creation story and the "universe." Still, no sign from the Lord.

Towards the end of writing this book, I had a dream. I do not dream, or at least I do not remember dreaming when I wake up. When I have a dream, I write it down since it is a rare occasion. I had a dream from the Lord, confirming why He wanted me to write this book. When I woke up, I was scared.

Ó

The Dream

My family and I were preparing to leave a home in a dangerous neighborhood. We were visiting friends, and it was time to go. We looked out the windows to make sure it was safe to head to the car. The path looked clear, and we quickly left the home and headed towards the car. As we were hurrying to get into our car, I turned around and saw the most peaceful scene imaginable.

The neighborhood went from a grey, rundown slum to a beautiful and peaceful place. People were all around, walking with their families, enjoying a perfect summer's day. Then, I saw a dog running away from the people in the distance. No one noticed the dog. As people were laughing and having a good time, I noticed a pack of dogs running away, still off in the distance.

When I saw the pack of dogs, I turned to my family and told them to get into the car. As beautiful as the neighborhood was, as happy as the people were, I sensed something was wrong. I knew we had to get out of there. Then, off in the distance, a dog stops and looks right at me. As I opened the car door, the pack of dogs stopped and started running towards us. I began to panic and told my family to hurry. As I turned to see where the dogs were, they were already there. Then I realized that they were not dogs but they were lions. The lions started to attack the people in the neighborhood, and I heard the most awful screams one could imagine. I yelled, "Get in!"

Ó

When I woke up, I started to pray for my family. I prayed for my wife, our marriage, my children, and myself. I prayed that God would watch over us and protect us from our enemy, who "prowls around like a roaring lion looking for someone to devour" (1 Peter 5:8). As I was praying, the Lord revealed to me that the dream was not about my family. The dream was about the people who could not see the danger they were in.

I am not a person who looks at things from a "doom and gloom" perspective. I know that "everyone who wants to live a godly life in Christ Jesus will be persecuted" (2 Timothy 3:12). I also know that no matter what we face, we "can do all this through him who gives me strength" (Philippians 4:13). I also understand that the church is facing a dangerous moment.

In our current times, the Bible is under assault from within and outside of the church. It may not seem like there is anything wrong. Our families are great, our jobs are successful, our churches are inspiring, our sports are fun, and our health is excellent. There is no reason to worry about something off in the distance that seems harmless, like the "universe."

The danger we face is deception. Deception is believing something that is not true. When we fall for deception, it makes us change the intended meaning of God's word. When we change God's word, we tell God that He is wrong and His words are untrue. We are informing God that He is wrong because His earth is orbiting the sun even though God's word said He "set the earth on its foundations" (Psalm 104:5). We are notifying God that His earth moves even though God's word claims that "it cannot be moved" (1 Chronicles 16:30).

The purpose of this book is to give people an opportunity to make an informed choice. We have three options: Biblical, Greek, or the Modern Christian World.

The Biblical World

(1) God does not lie (Numbers 23:19).

(2) The entire Bible is inspired (2 Timothy 3:16).

(3) The Holy Spirit will guide us into knowing God's word (John 16:13).

(4) The earth is on an actual foundation and does not move (Psalm 104:5).

The Greek World

(1) The "universe" was built by people seeking pagan gods and magic.

(2) The theories from the Scientific Revolution provided no experimental evidence.

(3) The round and moving earth are counterintuitive to our senses and observations.

(4) Gravity, that built the universe, is not real.

The Modern Christian World

(1) Modern science can inform us how to interpret the Bible.

(2) Poetry can be changed to mean the opposite of what it claims.

(3) We can only be guided into truth if we know history, culture, or ancient languages.

(4) As the Greek World has taught, the earth is not on a foundation and the earth moves.

Choosing a World

I made my choice. I chose to believe the Bible and the claims that it makes. The choice is up to you. What world will you believe in?

Please circle one:

A. The Biblical World

B. The Greek World

C. Modern Christian World

Copernicus' Heliocentric Theory

All quotes in Appendix A are taken from Copernicus'
De Revolutionibus (*On the Revolutions*) unless noted.[1]

I was asked by a friend to describe Nicholas Copernicus' best argument for his heliocentric theory (sun at rest; earth moving). According to Copernicus' theory, the world now believes the earth is moving. Copernicus' book, *De Revolutionibus* (*On the Revolutions*) is not well-known; many people have never read it. I will briefly cover Copernicus' **Declaration**, **Evidence**, **Reason**, and **Reality** with quotes from his book. Remember, this book is the foundation for modern science's solar system, even though Copernicus thought he was describing the entire universe consisting of transparent spheres that rotated around the sun.

When Copernicus released his book, he provided no experimental evidence to support his claims. He postulates that the earth was moving (Declaration). He also believed the earth was round because "the sun, moon, planets and stars are seen to be of this shape." Since everything looked spherical to Copernicus, the earth must be a sphere since "the sphere is the most perfect."

How did Copernicus prove his theory? The only proof (Evidence) he provided was observations of other objects moving. The movement of the sun, moon, and stars became his evidence for the earth's movement. Martin Luther best explains Copernicus' reasoning:

> [Copernicus] wants to prove that the earth moves and goes around instead of the sky, the sun, the moon, just as if somebody were moving in a carriage or ship might hold that he was sitting still and at rest while the earth and the trees walked and moved.[2]

Copernicus explains why he believes the sun should be at the center of the entire universe. His motivation (Reason) was based on his belief that the sun deserves to be "in the middle of everything" since the "visible god" should be "seated on a royal throne" with the earth "revolving around it."

In the end, Copernicus knew that his observations did not prove his theory (Reality). For centuries, people observed the movement of the sun, moon, and stars and concluded that the earth was motionless. Copernicus admitted that the observations he used to claim the earth was moving were the same observations that proved the earth did not move.

Declaration

"I ascribe certain motions to the terrestrial globe … against the traditional opinion of astronomers and almost against common sense."

Evidence

"PROOF OF THE EARTH'S TRIPLE MOTION *Chapter 11*"

The (1) day/night cycles ("the characteristic of a day plus a night"), the (2) annual motion around the sun ("the yearly motion of the center, which traces the ecliptic around the sun"), and the (3) precession of the equinoxes ("Inclination is consequently required. … also is a yearly revolution …").

Reason

"At rest, however, in the middle of everything is the sun. For in this most beautiful temple, who would place this lamp in another or better position than that from which it can light up the whole thing at the same time? For, the sun is not inappropriately called by some people the lantern of the universe, its mind by others, and its ruler by still others. [Hermes] the Thrice Greatest labels it a visible god, and Sophocles' Electra, the all-seeing. Thus indeed, as though seated on a royal throne, the sun governs the family of planets revolving around it."

Reality

"The motion of the sun and moon can be demonstrated, I admit, also with an earth that is stationary."[3]

Endnotes

Preface

1   Miller, Ron. *Recentering the Universe: The Radical Theories of Copernicus, Kepler, Galileo, and Newton.* Twenty-First Century Books, 2013, pp. 9-10.

2   "Philosophy." *Cambridge Dictionary*, 27 Mar. 2024, dictionary.cambridge.org/dictionary/english/philosophy.

3   Sgarbi, Marco. "Toward an Encyclopedia of Renaissance Philosophy." *Encyclopedia of Renaissance Philosophy*, edited by Marco Sgarbi, Springer, 2022, p. v.

4   Walton, John H., and J. Harvey Walton. *The Lost World of the Torah: Law as Covenant and Wisdom in Ancient Context.* InterVarsity Press, 2019, p. 9.

5   "Moon." *NASA Science*, accessed Mar. 2024, science.nasa.gov/moon.

6   "James Webb Space Telescope." *NASA Science*, accessed Mar. 2024, science.nasa.gov/mission/webb.

7   "Pseudoscience." *Bill Nye The Science Guy*, directed by Michael Gross and Darrel Suto, Buena Vista International, Inc., aired on 26 Jan. 1996 (03:32).

8   A book cited that does not include a page number was taken from an electronic edition, which can be searched to find the exact quote.

9   Siegel, Ethan. "How, Exactly, Does Planet Earth Move Through the Universe?" *Big Think*, 10 Jan. 2022, bigthink.com/starts-with-a-bang/earth-move-universe.

10 Greenwood, John D. *A Conceptual History of Psychology.* McGraw Hill, 2009, p. 1.

11 Boyd, Jeffrey H. "Biblical Psychology." *Encyclopedia of Psychology and Religion*, editors David A. Leeming, et al., Springer Science+Business Media, LLC, 2010, p. 102.

Chapter 1: Don't Talk About It

1   Estes, Daniel J. *Psalms 73-150.* Edited by E. Ray. Clendenen, vol. 13, B&H Publishing Group, 2019, p. 259.

2   Fausset, A. R. *A Commentary, Critical, Experimental, and Practical, on the Old and New Testaments: Job-Isaiah.* William Collins, Sons, & Company, Limited, accessed Mar. 2024, p. 320.

3   Warstler, Kevin R. "Psalms." *CSB Study Bible: Notes*, edited by Edwin A.

Blum and Trevin Wax, Holman Bible Publishers, 2017, p. 907.

4   Munyon, Timothy. "The Creation of the Universe and Humankind." *Systematic Theology: Revised Edition*, edited by Stanley M. Horton, Logion Press, 2007, pp. 233–34.

5   Fausset, A. R. *A Commentary, Critical, Experimental, and Practical, on the Old and New Testaments: Job-Isaiah*. William Collins, Sons, & Company, Limited, accessed Mar. 2024, p. 515.

6   Menzies, William W. *Bible Doctrines: A Pentecostal Perspective*. Edited by Stanley M. Horton, Logion Press, 1993, p. 78.

7   Munyon, Timothy. "The Creation of the Universe and Humankind." *Systematic Theology: Revised Edition*, edited by Stanley M. Horton, Logion Press, 2007, p. 234.

8   "Correct." *Cambridge Dictionary*, 13 Mar. 2024, dictionary.cambridge.org/dictionary/english/correct.

9   Menzies, William W. *Bible Doctrines: A Pentecostal Perspective*. Edited by Stanley M. Horton, Logion Press, 1993, p. 78.

10   Evolutionary science teaches autogenesis, the theory that living things come from nonliving materials. Evolutionary science believes humans came from monkeys, monkeys came from amoebas, amoebas came from rocks, and rocks came from exploding stars. Stars form because of gravity.

11   "Lawrence Krauss | ASU Search." *Arizona State University*, accessed Mar. 2024, search.asu.edu/profile/1249942.

12   Kreidler, Marc. "'A Universe From Nothing' by Lawrence Krauss, AAI 2009." *Richard Dawkins Foundation for Reason and Science*, 2 Feb. 2021 (17:09), richarddawkins.net/2009/10/a-universe-from-nothing-by-lawrence-krauss-aai-2009-2.

13   "Age of Stars." *NOVA Universe Revealed*, narrated by Talithia Williams, directed by Poppy Pinnock, PBS, 27 Oct. 2021 (36:38).

Chapter 2: Modern Times

1   Stenmark, Mikael. "What Is Scientism?" *Religious Studies*, vol. 33, no. 1, Cambridge University Press, 1997, p. 27.

2   "In Depth With Michio Kaku." *C-SPAN*, 3 Oct. 2010 (02:43), c-span.org/video/?295788-1/depth-michio-kaku.

3   Kaku, Michio. "A Universe in a Nutshell: The Physics of Everything, With Michio Kaku." *Big Think*, 30 Sep. 2021 (20:25), bigthink.com/videos/universe-in-a-nutshell-the-physics-of-everything-with-michio-kaku.

4   Greene, Brian. "This Is What the Fourth Dimension Looks Like." *Big Think*, 27 Jan. 2023 (2:41), bigthink.com/the-well/fourth-dimension.

5   Albelli, Alfred. "Radio Power will Revolutionize the World by Nikola Tesla." *Modern Mechanix and Inventions*, 1934, pp. 117-18.

6   Greene, Brian. "This Is What the Fourth Dimension Looks Like." *Big Think*, 27 Jan. 2023 (0:45), bigthink.com/the-well/fourth-dimension.

7   Siegel, Ethan. "Scientific Proof Is a Myth." *Forbes*, 22 Nov. 2017, forbes.com/sites/startswithabang/2017/11/22/scientific-proof-is-a-myth/?sh=37b62c6f2fb1.

8   "Scientific Proof Is a Myth." *Forbes*.

9   "What Causes the Seasons?" NASA Science for Kids, 22 Jul. 2021, spaceplace.nasa.gov/seasons/en.

10   Latitude 1° approx. 69 miles; Earth's circumference approx. 24,901.461 mi.

11   "What Causes the Seasons?" *NASA Science for Kids*.

12   Lennox, John C. *Seven Days That Divide the World: The Beginning According to Genesis and Science*. Zondervan, 2011.

13   Vermij, Rienk. "Cosmology in the Renaissance." *Encyclopedia of Renaissance Philosophy*, edited by Marco Sgarbi, Springer, 2022, p. 862.

14   Louw, Johannes P., and Eugene Albert Nida. *Greek-English Lexicon of the New Testament: Based on Semantic Domains*, Electronic ed. of the 2nd edition., vol. 1, United Bible Societies, 1996, p. 1.

15   Tate, Karl. "The Nearest Stars to Earth (Infographic)." *Space*, 28 Jan. 2022, space.com/18964-the-nearest-stars-to-earth-infographic.html.

16   Many historians have different names for an era/age and varying date ranges to when an era began or ended. I have chosen to list the consensus among historians for names and dates.

17   *Understanding Media and Culture: An Introduction to Mass Communication*. University of Minnesota Libraries Publishing, 2016, p. 35.

18   "Yuval Noah Harari | Speaker." *TED Talks*, 2016, ted.com/speakers/yuval_noah_harari.

19   Harari, Yuval Noah. *Sapiens: A Brief History of Humankind*. Signal, 2014.

20   Harari. *Sapiens*.

21   Harari, Yuval Noah. *21 Lessons for the 21st Century*. Random House, 2018.

22   Allen, Leslie C. *Psalms 101–150 (Revised)*. Word, Incorporated, 2002, p. 45.

23 Swanson, James. *Dictionary of Biblical Languages with Semantic Domains : Hebrew (Old Testament)*, Electronic ed., Logos Research Systems, Inc., 1997.

24 Swanson. *Dictionary of Biblical Languages with Semantic Domains.*

25 Allen. *Psalms 101–150 (Revised)*, p. 45.

Chapter 3: Extreme Nature

1 Mangum, Douglas. "Truth." *Lexham Theological Wordbook*, edited by Douglas Mangum et al., Lexham Press, 2014.

2 0-255 equals 256 values (0 is the first value; 255 is the last value); Black: RGB 0,0,0; Red: RGB 255,0,0; Green: RGB 0,255,0; Blue: 0,0,255; White: RGB 255,255,255.

3 Louw, Johannes P., and Eugene Albert Nida. *Greek-English Lexicon of the New Testament: Based on Semantic Domains,* Electronic ed. of the 2nd edition., vol. 1, United Bible Societies, 1996, p. 390.

4 Sundstrom, Ted. *Mathematical Reasoning: Writing and Proof. Version 1.1,* Grand Valley State University, 2014, p. 1.

5 Morris, Leon. *The Gospel according to John.* Wm. B. Eerdmans Publishing Co., 1995, p. 647.

Chapter 4: Binary Options

1 Baghramian, Maria and J. Adam Carter, "Relativism." *The Stanford Encyclopedia of Philosophy (Spring 2022 Edition)*, Edward N. Zalta (ed.), accessed Mar. 2024,
plato.stanford.edu/entries/relativism/.

2 Webster, Noah. *An American Dictionary of the English Language.* 1841, p. 563.

3 "Transgender Facts." *Mayo Clinic*, 14 Feb. 2023,
mayoclinic.org/healthy-lifestyle/adult-health/in-depth/transgender-facts/art-20266812.

4 "Understanding Transgender People, Gender Identity and Gender Expression." *American Psychological Association*, 6 June 2023,
apa.org/topics/lgbtq/transgender-people-gender-identity-gender-expression.

5 Kruse, Colin G. *The Letters of John.* W.B. Eerdmans Pub.; Apollos, 2000, p. 108.

6 Marshall, I. Howard. *The Epistles of John.* Wm. B. Eerdmans Publishing Co., 1978, p. 153.

Chapter 5: Trust, But Don't Verify

1   Wenham, Gordon J. *Genesis 1–15*. Word, Incorporated, 1987, p. xlvi.

2   "What Causes a Rainbow?" *NOAA SciJinks*, accessed Apr. 2024, scijinks.gov/rainbow.

3   Munyon, Timothy. "The Creation of the Universe and Humankind." *Systematic Theology: Revised Edition*, edited by Stanley M. Horton, Logion Press, 2007, p. 234.

4   Heritage Singers. *God Said It, I Believe It, That Settles It*. Chapel Records, 1975.

5   WIRED. "Astrophysicist Explains Gravity in 5 Levels of Difficulty." *YouTube*, 20 Dec. 2019 (0:08), youtube.com/watch?v=QcUey-DVYjk.

6   WIRED. "Astrophysicist Explains Gravity in 5 Levels of Difficulty," (10:03).

7   WIRED. "Astrophysicist Explains Gravity in 5 Levels of Difficulty," (13:07).

8   WIRED. "Astrophysicist Explains Gravity in 5 Levels of Difficulty," (21:18).

9   Fermilab. "Quantum Gravity." *YouTube*, 2 Feb. 2016 (6:57), youtube.com/watch?v=CbPWYjnQIO8.

10   WIRED. "Astrophysicist Explains Gravity in 5 Levels of Difficulty," (34:45).

11   WIRED. "Astrophysicist Explains Gravity in 5 Levels of Difficulty," (34:49).

12   Lincoln, Don. "Is Gravity a Force? It's Complicated." *Big Think*, 13 Oct. 2023, bigthink.com/hard-science/gravity-force-complicated.

13   "Forces." *NASA Science*, accessed Apr. 2024, science.nasa.gov/universe/overview/forces.

14   StarTalk. "Neil deGrasse Tyson and Janna Levin Answer Mind-Blowing Fan Questions." *YouTube*, 14 May 2024 (19:09), youtube.com/watch?v=kT7y1-clArQ.

15   Lincoln, Don. "Is Gravity a Force? It's Complicated." *Big Think*, 13 Oct. 2023, bigthink.com/hard-science/gravity-force-complicated.

Chapter 6: Before the Beginning

1   Rusten, E. Michael, and Sharon Rusten. *The Complete Book of When & Where in the Bible and throughout History*. Michael E Rusten, 2005, p. 17.

2   "Bible Timeline." *Bible Hub*, 2010, biblehub.com/timeline.

3   There is a debate about when the Book of Job was written. Due to literary criticism, dating Job is more complicated. Literary criticism developed

within the last few hundred years, changing the history of the Bible, including Genesis. Literary criticism will be covered in the section: The Modern Christian World.

4   Elwell, Walter A. and Barry J. Beitzel. "Job, Book Of." *Baker Encyclopedia of the Bible*, vol. 2, Baker Book House, 1988, p. 1169.

5   Ellison, H. L. "Job, Book Of." *New Bible Dictionary*, edited by D. R. W. Wood et al., 3rd ed., InterVarsity Press, 1996, p. 589.

6   Tsumura, David. *The First Book of Samuel*. Wm. B. Eerdmans Publishing Co., 2007, p. 148.

7   Klein, Ralph W. *1 Samuel*. Word, Incorporated, 1983, p. 14.

8   Baldwin, Joyce G. *1 and 2 Samuel: An Introduction and Commentary*. InterVarsity Press, 1988, p. 62.

9   Clines, David J. A., editor. *The Dictionary of Classical Hebrew, vol. 5*, Sheffield Academic Press; Sheffield Phoenix Press, 1993–2011, p. 449.

10   Clines. *The Dictionary of Classical Hebrew, vol. 5*, p. 449.

11   Swanson, James. *Dictionary of Biblical Languages with Semantic Domains : Hebrew (Old Testament)*, Electronic ed., Logos Research Systems, Inc., 1997.

12   Mounce, William D. *Mounce's Complete Expository Dictionary of Old & New Testament Words*, Zondervan, 2006, p. 982.

13   Clines. *The Dictionary of Classical Hebrew, vol. 5*, p. 449.

14   Hubbard, David A., et al. "Editorial Preface." *1 Chronicles*, vol. 14, Word, Incorporated, 1986, p. 193.

15   Strong, James. *Enhanced Strong's Lexicon*, Woodside Bible Fellowship, 1995.

Chapter 7: Learning from Job

1   Thomas Nelson Publishers. *Nelson's Complete Book of Bible Maps & Charts: Old and New Testaments*. Rev. and updated ed., Thomas Nelson, 1996.

2   Chapter 22: The Story of Access.

3   Swanson, James. *Dictionary of Biblical Languages with Semantic Domains : Hebrew (Old Testament)*, Electronic ed., Logos Research Systems, Inc., 1997.

4   John E. Hartley. *The Book of Job*. Wm. B. Eerdmans Publishing Co., 1988, p. 329.

5   William David Reyburn. *A Handbook on the Book of Job*. United Bible Societies, 1992, p. 418.

6   David J. Clines. A. *Job 21–37*. Thomas Nelson Publishers, 2006, p. 559.

7   Swanson. *Dictionary of Biblical Languages with Semantic Domains : Hebrew (Old Testament)*.

8   Benjamin M. Austin. "Afterlife." *Lexham Theological Wordbook*, edited by Douglas Mangum et al., Lexham Press, 2014.

9   William Lee Holladay and Ludwig Köhler. *A Concise Hebrew and Aramaic Lexicon of the Old Testament*, Brill, 2000, p. 5.

10   E. W. Maunder. "Astronomy." *The International Standard Bible Encyclopaedia*, edited by James Orr et al., vol. 1–5, The Howard-Severance Company, 1915, p. 308.

11   Fraser Cain. "Venus, the Morning Star and Evening Star." *Universe Today*, 25 Dec. 2015, universetoday.com/22570/venus-the-morning-star.

12   Swanson. *Dictionary of Biblical Languages with Semantic Domains : Hebrew (Old Testament)*.

13   Thomas, Robert L. *New American Standard Hebrew-Aramaic and Greek Dictionaries : Updated Edition*. Foundation Publications, Inc., 1998.

14   Hartley, John E. *The Book of Job*. Wm. B. Eerdmans Publishing Co., 1988, p. 94.

15   Alden, Robert L. *Job*. Broadman & Holman Publishers, 1993, p. 74.

16   Guzik, David. *Job*. David Guzik, 2007, p. Job 3:3–10.

17   Matthews, Victor Harold, et al. *The IVP Bible Background Commentary: Old Testament*. Electronic ed., InterVarsity Press, 2000, p. Job 3:8.

18   Swanson. *Dictionary of Biblical Languages with Semantic Domains : Hebrew (Old Testament)*.

19   Brown, Francis, et al. *Enhanced Brown-Driver-Briggs Hebrew and English Lexicon*, Clarendon Press, 1977, p. 1072.

20   Holladay, William Lee, and Ludwig Köhler. *A Concise Hebrew and Aramaic Lexicon of the Old Testament*, Brill, 2000, p. 392.

21   Thomas. *New American Standard Hebrew-Aramaic and Greek Dictionaries*.

22   Swanson. *Dictionary of Biblical Languages with Semantic Domains : Hebrew (Old Testament)*.

23   Brown et al. *Enhanced Brown-Driver-Briggs Hebrew and English Lexicon*, p. 531.

24   Holladay and Köhler. *A Concise Hebrew and Aramaic Lexicon of the Old Testament*, p. 174.

25   The original article is no longer available at Scholastic.com. I have includ-

ed the webpage as saved by Internet Archive's *Wayback Machine*.

26 "When Was the First Dinosaur Discovered?" *Scholastic*, posted by Internet Archive's Wayback Machine, accessed Mar. 2024, web.archive.org/web/20190123133506/https://www.scholastic.com/teachers/articles/teaching-content/when-was-first-dinosaur-discovered.

27 Brusatte, Stephen. "New Fossil Reveals Velociraptor Sported Feathers." *Scientific American*, originally published by The Conversation, 20 Feb. 2024, scientificamerican.com/article/new-fossil-reveals-velociraptor-sported-feathers.

28 "Is It a Bird? Is It a Dinosaur? No, It's a Fake." *The Guardian*, 6 Feb. 2000, theguardian.com/theguardian/2000/feb/07/features11.g22.

29 Black, Riley. "Why Birds Survived, and Dinosaurs Went Extinct, After an Asteroid Hit Earth." *Smithsonian Magazine*, 14 Sep. 2020, smithsonianmag.com/science-nature/why-birds-survived-and-dinosaurs-went-extinct-after-asteroid-hit-earth-180975801.

30 Hughes, Erin and Lita Sanders. "Creation for Kids: Did Dinosaurs and Man Live Together?" *Creation*, Jul. 2019, creation.com/cfk-dinosaurs-and-man.

Chapter 8: Statements Made In Job

1 Hooks, Stephen M. *Job*. College Press Pub., 2006, p. 310.

2 Hartley, John E. *The Book of Job*. Wm. B. Eerdmans Publishing Co., 1988, p. 482.

3 Clines, David J. A. *Job 1–20*. Word, Incorporated, 1989, p. 231.

4 Fausset, A. R. *A Commentary, Critical, Experimental, and Practical, on the Old and New Testaments: Job–Isaiah*. William Collins, Sons, & Company, Limited, accessed Mar. 2024, p. 607.

5 Swanson, James. *Dictionary of Biblical Languages with Semantic Domains : Hebrew (Old Testament)*, Electronic ed., Logos Research Systems, Inc., 1997.

6 Tyson, Neil deGrasse. *Death by Black Hole: And Other Cosmic Quandaries*. W. W. Norton and Company, 2007.

7 Tyson. *Death by Black Hole*.

8 Berry, Arthur. *A Short History of Astronomy*. Charles Scribner's Sons, 1899, p. 4.

9 Moyers & Company. "Neil deGrasse Tyson on Science, Religion and the Universe." Moyers, 14 Apr. 2016 (17:32), billmoyers.com/episode/neil-degrasse-tyson-on-science-religion-and-

the-universe.

10 Tyson. *Death by Black Hole.*

11 Tyson. *Death by Black Hole.*

12 Alden, Robert L. *Job.* Broadman & Holman Publishers, 1993, p. 259.

13 Hooks. *Job*, p. 309.

14 Guzik, David. *Job.* David Guzik, 2007, p. Job 26:5–13.

15 Barnes, Albert. *Notes on the Old Testament: Job.* Blackie & Son, 1847, p. 40.

16 Wiersbe, Warren W. *Be Patient.* Victor Books, 1996, p. 101.

17 Zuck, Roy B. "Job." *The Bible Knowledge Commentary: An Exposition of the Scriptures*, edited by J. F. Walvoord and R. B. Zuck, vol. 1, Victor Books, 1985, p. 749.

18 McGee, J. Vernon. *Thru the Bible Commentary.* Electronic ed., vol. 2, Thomas Nelson, 1997, p. 632.

19 Fausset. *Job–Isaiah*, p. 63.

20 Carroll, Sean. *Spacetime and Geometry: An Introduction to General Relativity.* Addison-Wesley, 2004, p. 1.

21 Siegel, Ethan. "This Is How, 100 Years Ago, a Solar Eclipse Proved Einstein Right and Newton Wrong." *Forbes*, 29 May 2019, forbes.com/sites/startswithabang/2019/05/29/this-is-how-100-years-ago-a-solar-eclipse-proved-einstein-right-and-newton-wrong/?sh=69bd-d1aa1610.

22 The Veritas Forum. "No One Knows What Gravity Is | John Lennox." *YouTube*, 28 Jul. 2020, youtube.com/watch?v=h3DO3PAFFX8.

23 Hartley. *The Book of Job*, p. 491.

24 Pietersma, Albert, and Benjamin G. Wright, editors. "Iob." *A New English Translation of the Septuagint (Primary Texts)*, translated by Claude E. Cox, Oxford University Press, 2007, p. Job 38:4.

25 Hartley. *The Book of Job*, pp. 494–95.

26 Andersen, Francis I. *Job: An Introduction and Commentary.* InterVarsity Press, 1976, pp. 295–96.

27 Swanson. *Dictionary of Biblical Languages with Semantic Domains.*

28 Hooks. *Job*, p. 427.

29 Alden. *Job*, p. 370.

30 Fausset. *Job–Isaiah*, p. 440.

31 Newton, Isaac. *Newton's Principia: The Mathematical Principles of Natural*

Philosophy. Translated by Andrew Motte, Daniel Adee, 1846, p. 73.

32   Newton. *Newton's Principia*, p. 73.

33   Panek, Richard. "Everything You Thought You Knew About Gravity Is Wrong." *Washington Post*, 4 Aug. 2019, washingtonpost.com/outlook/everything-you-thought-you-knew-about-gravity-is-wrong/2019/08/01/627f3696-a723-11e9-a3a6-ab670962db05_story.html.

34   "Copernicus: Facts, Model & Heliocentric Theory." *HISTORY*, 31 Jan. 2023, history.com/topics/inventions/nicolaus-copernicus.

35   "Oxford University Department for Continuing Education." *University of Oxford*, accessed Mar. 2024, conted.ox.ac.uk/tutors/3131.

36   Biography. "Sir Isaac Newton: Unhappy Scientific Genius." *YouTube*, 20 Nov. 2022 (29:51), youtube.com/watch?v=OK1bCqkn6Vk.

37   "Neil deGrasse Tyson: What Is Gravity?" *YouTube*, (00:09).

38   "Neil deGrasse Tyson: What Is Gravity?" *YouTube*, (00:12).

39   "A Teacher, a Student and a Church-State Dispute." *Neil deGrasse Tyson*, 21 Dec. 2006, neildegrassetyson.com/letters/2006-12-21-a-teacher-a-student-and-a-church-state-dispute.

40   "Religion Vs Science: Can the Two Coexist?" *YouTube*, 14 Apr. 2020 (08:05), youtube.com/watch?v=Xxz0W4OgG9k.

41   Hawking, Stephen, and Leonard Mlodinow. *The Grand Design*. Bantam, 2010.

42   Panek, Richard. *The Trouble With Gravity: Solving the Mystery Beneath Our Feet*. HarperCollins, 2019.

43   Hawking, Stephen, and Carl Sagan. *A Brief History of Time: From the Big Bang to Black Holes*. Bantam, 1988.

44   "How Much Water Is on Earth?" *Earth How*, 25 Sep. 2023, earthhow.com/how-much-water-is-on-earth.

Chapter 9: The Unreal Universe

1   "What Is the Universe? | What Is an Exoplanet? – Exoplanet Exploration: Planets Beyond Our Solar System." *NASA Exoplanets*, accessed Mar. 2024, exoplanets.nasa.gov/what-is-an-exoplanet/what-is-the-universe.

2   Wycliffe, John. *The Holy Bible, Containing the Old and New Testaments,*

with the Apocryphal Books: Early Version. Edited by Josiah Forshall and Frederic Madden, vol. I–IV, Oxford, at the University Press, 1850.

3 Tyndale, William. The 1536 Tyndale Bible New Testament, 1536.

4 Geneva Bible. Rovland Hall, 1560.

5 The Holy Bible: King James Version. Electronic ed. of the 1769 edition of the 1611 Authorized Version. Logos Research Systems, Inc., 1995.

6 Wesley, John. Explanatory Notes Upon the New Testament. 1755.

7 Cockerill, Gareth Lee. The Epistle to the Hebrews. William B. Eerdmans Publishing Company, 2012, pp. 523-24.

8 Lane, William L. Hebrews 9–13. Word, Incorporated, 1991, p. 331.

9 Allen, David L. Hebrews. B & H Publishing Group, 2010, p. 545.

10 Wenham, Gordon J. Genesis 1–15. Word, Incorporated, 1987, p. xlvi.

11 "Earth: By the Numbers." NASA Ames Research Center, accessed Mar. 2024, mobile.arc.nasa.gov/public/iexplore/missions/pages/solarsystem/earth-facts.html.

12 Nasa Goddard Space Flight Center. "Black Marble - Americas." Flickr, accessed Mar. 2024, flickr.com/photos/gsfc/8246896289/in/album-72157632172101342.

13 "City Lights of the Americas." NASA Earth Observatory, accessed Mar. 2024, earthobservatory.nasa.gov/images/79787/city-lights-of-the-americas.

14 NASA claims the upper left globe (Fig. 11) is an actual photo (not digital) from Apollo 17 (1972). The claim for the photo's authenticity is based on their "solar system" and the heliocentric (sun at rest; earth moving) theory.

15 Nasa Goddard Space Flight Center. "Most Amazing High Definition Image of Earth - Blue Marble 2012." Flickr, accessed Mar. 2024, flickr.com/photos/gsfc/6760135001/in/album-72157632172101342.

16 Micue, Fares. "What Is Composite Photography and How Can It Be Used?" Adobe Blog, 7 Jun. 2021, blog.adobe.com/en/publish/2021/06/07/what-is-composite-photogra-phy.

17 Nasa Goddard Space Flight Center. "Most Amazing High Definition Image of Earth - Blue Marble 2012." Flickr, accessed Mar. 2024, flickr.com/photos/gsfc/6760135001/in/album-72157632172101342.

18 "Most Amazing High Definition Image of Earth - Blue Marble 2012." Flickr.

19 "NPP NPOESS Preparatory Project: Building a Bridge to a New Era of Earth Observations." NASA, Oct. 2011, eospso.nasa.gov/sites/default/files/publications/NPP_MissionBrochure_

Color_508Compliant.pdf.

20 "Elegant Figures - Crafting the Blue Marble." *NASA Earth Observatory*, 6 Oct. 2011, earthobservatory.nasa.gov/blogs/elegantfigures/2011/10/06/crafting-the-blue-marble.

21 "Behind-the-Scenes View Shows How NASA Science Visualizer Creates Earth from Hundreds of Images." *Wayback Machine*. 28 Jun. 2010, web.archive.org/web/20100724165031/https://www.nasa.gov/topics/people/features/visualizer-creates-earth.html.

22 Moyers & Company. "Neil deGrasse Tyson on Science, Religion and the Universe." *Moyers*, 14 Apr. 2016 (16:59), billmoyers.com/episode/neil-degrasse-tyson-on-science-religion-and-the-universe.

23 Miller, Ron. *Recentering the Universe: The Radical Theories of Copernicus, Kepler, Galileo, and Newton*. Twenty-First Century Books, 2013, pp. 9-10.

24 Karttunen, Hannu, et al. *Fundamental Astronomy*. 5th edition, Springer Science+Business Media, 2007, p. 4.

25 Tyson, Neil deGrasse. *Death by Black Hole: And Other Cosmic Quandaries*. W. W. Norton and Company, 2007.

Chapter 10: Unseen Reality

1 Barton, Blanche. *The Secret Life of a Satanist: The Authorized Biography of Anton LaVey*. Feral House, 1992.

2 Lennox, John C. *Seven Days That Divide the World: The Beginning According to Genesis and Science*. Zondervan, 2011.

3 Lennox. *Seven Days That Divide the World*.

Chapter 11: Visible and Invisible

1 Paul Harvey was a radio commentator; "If I Were the Devil" originally aired on April 3, 1965.

2 "Paul Harvey - if I Were the Devil Radio Address." *American Rhetoric*, 23 Jan. 2022, americanrhetoric.com/speeches/paulharveyifiwerethedevil.htm.

3 "Paul Harvey - if I Were the Devil Radio Address." *American Rhetoric*.

Chapter 12: In the Beginning, Pythagoras Said

1 TED. "Militant Atheism | Richard Dawkins." *YouTube*, 15 Apr. 2008 (4:39), youtube.com/watch?v=VxGMqKCcN6A.

2 Henriksen, Janet. "An architectural paradigm." *Journal of Creation*, Vol. 24,

is. 1, spring 2010, p. 103.

3   Kingsley, Peter. *Ancient Philosophy, Mystery, and Magic: Empedocles and Pythagorean Tradition*. Oxford University Press, 1995, p. 333.

4   Long, Alex. *Death and Immortality in Ancient Philosophy*. Cambridge University Press, 2019, pp 21-2.

5   Wilson, K. S., and E. J. Dodson. "Michael Mark Woolfson. 9 January 1927–23 December 2019." *Biographical Memoirs of Fellows of the Royal Society*, vol. 71, Aug. 2021, pp. 529-53. https://doi.org/10.1098/rsbm.2021.0018.

6   Woolfson, Michael M. *The Origin and Evolution of the Solar System*. CRC Press, 2000, p. 111.

7   "Todd Thompson | Department of Astronomy." *Ohio State University*, accessed Apr. 2024, astronomy.osu.edu/people/thompson.1847.

8   "Pronouns." *LGBTQ at Ohio State*, accessed Apr. 2024, lgbtq.osu.edu/support/pronouns.

9   "Lecture 4: Measuring the Earth." *Ohio State University*, accessed Apr. 2024, astronomy.ohio-state.edu/thompson.1847/161/measearth.html.

10 Kingsley, Peter. *Ancient Philosophy, Mystery, and Magic: Empedocles and Pythagorean Tradition*. Oxford University Press, 1995, p. 342.

11 Kingsley. *Ancient Philosophy, Mystery, and Magic*, p. 342.

12 "Lecture 4: Measuring the Earth." *Ohio State University*.

Chapter 13: Trouble with the Curve

1   According to inflation theory (repulsive gravity), the universe took 10^{-38} (.00000000000000000000000000000000000001) of a second to start, while the rest of the big bang took 13.8 billion years.

2   "What Is a Planet?" *NASA Science*, accessed Apr. 2024, science.nasa.gov/solar-system/planets/what-is-a-planet/.

3   "First Pictures of Earth From 100 Miles in Space, 1947." *NASA*, 6 Mar. 2009, nasa.gov/image-article/first-pictures-of-earth-from-100-miles-space-1947.

4   Concepcion, Roel. "The Space Jump That Shook the World." *Red Bull*, 18 Feb. 2017, redbull.com/us-en/the-space-jump-that-shook-the-world.

5   SXSW. "A Conversation With Dr. Neil deGrasse Tyson (Full Session) | Interactive 2014 | SXSW." *YouTube*, 16 Apr. 2014 (38:58), youtube.com/watch?v=0FMGTVCIDbU.

6 McCrary, Eleanor. "Fact Check: Ample Evidence the Earth Is Round and Rotating, Contrary to Persistent Social Media Claims." *USA TODAY*, 17 Nov. 2022, usatoday.com/story/news/factcheck/2022/11/17/fact-check-ample-evidence-earth-round-and-rotating/8267678001.

7 Nye, Bill. Undeniable: *Evolution and the Science of Creation*. Macmillan, 2014.

8 Nye, Bill. "Pseudoscience." *Bill Nye*, 4 May 2018, billnye.com/the-science-guy/pseudoscience.

9 "Pseudoscience." *Bill Nye The Science Guy*, directed by Michael Gross and Darrel Suto, Buena Vista International, Inc., aired on 26 Jan. 1996 (02:42).

10 Schottlender, Moriel. "10 Ways You Can Tell the Earth Is Round." *Popular Science*, 1 May 2023, popsci.com/10-ways-you-can-prove-earth-is-round.

11 Munyon, Timothy. "The Creation of the Universe and Humankind." *Systematic Theology: Revised Edition*, edited by Stanley M. Horton, Logion Press, 2007, p. 234.

12 "Assemblies of God 16 Fundamental Truths." *Assemblies of God*, accessed Apr. 2024, ag.org/Beliefs/Statement-of-Fundamental-Truths#1.

13 Sproul, R. C. *Can I Trust the Bible?* Reformation Trust Publishing, 2009, p. 35.

14 Soanes, Catherine, and Angus Stevenson, editors. *Concise Oxford English Dictionary*, 11th ed., Logos Edition, Oxford University Press, 2004.

15 Evans, C. Stephen. *Pocket Dictionary of Apologetics & Philosophy of Religion*. InterVarsity Press, 2002, p. 60.

Chapter 14: Scientific Fortunetelling

1 According to modern science, faith is known as the "God of the gaps" theory; it is when people invoke God when they cannot explain a phenomenon with scientific data.

2 "About." *CERN*, 25 Mar. 2024, home.cern/about.

3 "Dark Matter." *CERN*, 25 Mar. 2024, home.cern/science/physics/dark-matter.

4 "In Depth With Michio Kaku." *C-SPAN*, 3 Oct. 2010 (02:54), c-span.org/video/?295788-1/depth-michio-kaku.

5 Newman, Barclay M., Jr., and Philip C. Stine. *A Handbook on Jeremiah*.

United Bible Societies, 2003, p. 655.

6   Youngblood, Ronald F., et al., Thomas Nelson Publishers, editors. *Nelson's New Illustrated Bible Dictionary*, Thomas Nelson, Inc., 1995.

7   Sullivan, Tim Mackie &. Aeron. "Genesis and Ancient Cosmic Geography." *BibleProject*, 7 Mar. 2024, bibleproject.com/articles/genesis-ancient-cosmic-geography.

8   Preisser, J. S. "Determination of Angles of Attack and Sideslip From Radar Data and a Roll-stabilized Platform." *NASA Technical Reports Server* (NTRS), 1 Mar. 1972, p. ii, ntrs.nasa.gov/citations/19720012071.

9   Youngblood et al. *Nelson's New Illustrated Bible Dictionary*, 1995.

10   Cartwright, Mark. "Claudius Ptolemy." *World History Encyclopedia*, 07 Sep. 2023, worldhistory.org/Claudius_Ptolemy.

11   Sagan, Carl. *Cosmos*. Ballantine Books, 2011.

12   "Quotations of Ptolemy" Maths History, School of Mathematics and Statistics, University of St Andrews, accessed Apr. 2024, mathshistory.st-andrews.ac.uk/Biographies/Ptolemy/quotations.

13   Kobe, D. H. "Copernicus and Martin Luther: An encounter between science and religion." *American Journal of Physics*, vol. 66, issue 3, 1 Mar. 1998, p. 191.

14   "Theoretical." *Cambridge Dictionary*, 27 Mar. 2024, dictionary.cambridge.org/dictionary/english/theoretical.

15   "Orbits and Kepler's Laws." *NASA Science*, accessed Apr. 2024, science.nasa.gov/resource/orbits-and-keplers-laws.

16   Wenham, Gordon J. *Genesis 1–15*. Word, Incorporated, 1987, p. xlvi.

17   Fowler, Lauren. "Prediction." *University of California, Berkeley*, 7 May 2022, undsci.berkeley.edu/glossary/prediction.

18   Sundstrom, Ted. *Mathematical Reasoning: Writing and Proof. Version 1.1*, Grand Valley State University, 2014, p. 1.

Chapter 15: Making the Earth Round

1   Sarfati, Jonathan and Lita Sanders. *Creation Astronomy for Kids*. Creation Book Publishers, 2023, p. 5.

2   Blakemore, Erin, and Erin Blakemore. "Christopher Columbus Never Set Out to Prove the Earth Was Round." *HISTORY*, 10 Aug. 2023, history.com/news/christopher-columbus-never-set-out-to-prove-the-earth-was-round.

3   Reuters Fact Check. "Fact Check: Humans knew Earth was round before

satellite imagery." *Reuters*, 14 Dec. 2023,
reuters.com/fact-check/humans-knew-earth-was-round-before-satellite-imagery-2023-12-14/.

4   Sagan, Carl. *Cosmos*. Ballantine Books, 2011.

5   Sagan. *Cosmos*.

6   Rawlins, Dennis. "Eratosthenes' Too-Big Earth and Too-Tiny Universe." *The International Journal of Scientific History*, vol. 14, Mar. 2008, p. 8.

7   Hannam, James. *The Globe: How the Earth Became Round*. Reaktion Books, 2023, p. 9, 12.

8   Hannam. *The Globe*, pp. 311-12.

9   Hannam. *The Globe*, p. 311.

10 "Earth: By the Numbers." *NASA Ames Research Center*, accessed Mar. 2024,
mobile.arc.nasa.gov/public/iexplore/missions/pages/solarsystem/earth-facts.html.

11 Hannam. *The Globe*, p. 98.

12 Sagan. *Cosmos*.

13 The original footage for Fig. 23 was a 25-hour timelapse video of the earth rotating in space without any clouds moving. After its initial release, many videos show clouds moving (Fig. 23). If searching, the original video is not easy to find, so I have included the link:
https://photojournal.jpl.nasa.gov/catalog/PIA00114.

14 StarTalk. "Neil Tyson Demonstrates Absurdity of 'Flat Earth.'" *YouTube*, 9 Mar. 2018 (04:35),
youtube.com/watch?v=hLPPE3_DVCw.

15 "Neil Tyson Demonstrates Absurdity of 'Flat Earth.'" *YouTube*, (05:14).

16 "School Children Join Forces to Recreate Eratosthenes' Experiment." *Kathimerini (English Edition)*, 30 Mar. 2021,
ekathimerini.com/society/1158142/school-children-join-forces-to-recre-ate-eratosthenes-experiment.

17 Tyson, Neil deGrasse. *Death by Black Hole: And Other Cosmic Quanda-ries*. W. W. Norton and Company, 2007.

18 "Lecture 4: Measuring the Earth." *Ohio State University*, accessed Apr. 2024,
astronomy.ohio-state.edu/thompson.1847/161/measearth.html.

19 "Lecture 4: Measuring the Earth." *Ohio State University*.

20 "Neil Tyson Demonstrates Absurdity of 'Flat Earth.'" *YouTube*, (05:45).

21 SXSW. "A Conversation With Dr. Neil deGrasse Tyson." *YouTube*, 16 Apr.

2014 (39:12),
youtube.com/watch?v=0FMGTVCIDbU.

22 Average distance to horizon if 6' tall standing at sea-level; Omni Calculator: www.omnicalculator.com/physics/distance-to-horizon.

23 "Longest Line of Sight on Earth Photographed." *Guinness World Records*,
16 Jul. 2016,
guinnessworldrecords.com/world-records/66661-longest-line-of-sight-
on-earth.

24 "Bloom, Influential Education Researcher." *University of Chicago Chronicle*, University of Chicago News Office, 23 Sep. 1999,
chronicle.uchicago.edu/990923/bloom.shtml.

25 Bloom, Benjamin S. *All Our Children Learning: A Primer for Parents, Teachers, and Other Educators*. McGraw-Hill Book Company, 1981, p. 180.

26 "Neil Tyson Demonstrates Absurdity of 'Flat Earth.'" *YouTube*, (06:56).

27 Cohen, Don. "Interview with Neil deGrasse Tyson." *Ask Magazine*, issue
31, NASA APPEL Knowledge Services, 1 Jun. 2008, p. 11.

28 Tyson. *Death by Black Hole*.

Chapter 16: Believe What You Don't See

1 Palen, Stacey. *Schaum's Outline of Astronomy*. McGraw Hill Professional,
2001, p. 122.

2 Athanasakis, Andreas. "Copernicus, Nicolaus." *Encyclopedia of Renaissance Philosophy*, edited by Marco Sgarbi, Springer, 2022, p. 851.

3 Omodeo, Pietro Daniel. "Copernicanism." *Encyclopedia of Renaissance
Philosophy*, edited by Marco Sgarbi, Springer, 2022, p. 844.

4 Lerner, Louise. "Noel M. Swerdlow (1941–2021)." *Bulletin of the AAS*, vol.
53, no. 2, Aug. 2021,
doi.org/10.3847/25c2cfeb.0f57765f.

5 Swerdlow, N. M. "Ptolemaic Astronomy." *Encyclopedia of the scientific
revolution: from Copernicus to Newton*, edited by Wilbur Applebaum,
Garland Publishing, Inc., 2005.

6 Hawking, Stephen, and Leonard Mlodinow. *The Grand Design*. Bantam,
2010.

7 Omodeo, Pietro Daniel "Geocentrism." *Encyclopedia of Renaissance Philosophy*, edited by Marco Sgarbi, Springer, 2022, p. 1355.

8 Walton, John H. *The Lost World of Adam and Eve: Genesis 2-3 and the
Human Origins Debate*. InterVarsity Press, 2015.

Chapter 17: Preparing the Way

1   Palen, Stacey. *Schaum's Outline of Astronomy*. McGraw Hill Professional, 2001, p. 225.

2   Omodeo, Pietro Daniel. "Astronomy." *Encyclopedia of Renaissance Philosophy*, edited by Marco Sgarbi, Springer, 2022, p. 244.

3   Grosholz, Emily. "Mathematics." *Encyclopedia of the Scientific Revolution from Copernicus to Newton*, edited by Wilbur Applebaum, Garland Publishing, Inc., 2005.

4   Pharr, Clyde. "The Interdiction of Magic in Roman Law." Originally quoted by Frazer (The Magic Art I [London, 1911], p. 426), *Transactions and Proceedings of the American Philological Association*, vol. 63, Johns Hopkins University Press, 1932, p. 269.

5   "Understanding Humanism." *Encyclopedia Britannica*, accessed Apr. 2024,
britannica.com/summary/humanism.

6   Wilde, Robert. "Key Dates in Renaissance Philosophy, Politics, Religion, and Science." *ThoughtCo*, 14 July 2019,
thoughtco.com/renaissance-timeline-4158077.

7   "CHRONOLOGY." *Encyclopedia of the Scientific Revolution from Copernicus to Newton*, edited by Wilbur Applebaum, Garland Publishing, Inc., 2005.

Chapter 18: Reading Ancient Greek

1   Robichaud, Denis J.-J. "Ficino, Marsilio" *Encyclopedia of Renaissance Philosophy*, edited by Marco Sgarbi, Springer, 2022, p. 1218.

2   Robichaud. *Encyclopedia of Renaissance Philosophy*, p. 1219.

3   Sumrall, Laura. "Natural Magic in Renaissance Science." *Encyclopedia of Renaissance Philosophy*, edited by Marco Sgarbi, Springer, 2022, p. 2301.

4   Lines, David A. "Action and Contemplation in Renaissance Philosophy." *Encyclopedia of Renaissance Philosophy*, edited by Marco Sgarbi, Springer, 2022, p. 49.

5   Kircher, Timothy. "Humanism" *Encyclopedia of Renaissance Philosophy*, edited by Marco Sgarbi, Springer, 2022, p. 1590.

6   Akopyan, Ovanes. "Causality, Renaissance." *Encyclopedia of Renaissance Philosophy*, edited by Marco Sgarbi, Springer, 2022, pp. 659-60.

7   Linden, Stanton J. *The Alchemy Reader: From Hermes Trismegistus to Isaac Newton*. Cambridge University Press, 2003, pp. 11-12.

8   Hanegraaff, Wouter J. "Hermes Trismegistus and Hermetism." *Encyclopedia of Renaissance Philosophy*, edited by Marco Sgarbi, Springer, 2022, p.

3220.

9   McKnight, Stephen A. "Prisca theologia." *Encyclopedia of the scientific revolution: from Copernicus to Newton*, edited by Wilbur Applebaum, Garland Publishing, Inc., 2005.

10   De Candia, Gianluca. "Theology, Renaissance." *Encyclopedia of Renaissance Philosophy*, edited by Marco Sgarbi, Springer, 2022, p. 3230.

11   Robichaud. *Encyclopedia of Renaissance Philosophy*, p. 1223.

12   "Copernicus on the Revolutions." *Dartmouth Department of Mathematics*, translation and commentary by Edward Rosen, The Johns Hopkins University Press, 1 Sep. 1999, math.dartmouth.edu/~matc/Readers/renaissance.astro/1.1.Revol.html.

13   Koestler, Arthur. *The Sleepwalkers: A History of Man's Changing Vision of the Universe*. The Macmillian Company, 1959, p. 192.

14   Gingerich, Owen. *The Book Nobody Read: Chasing the Revolutions of Nicolaus Copernicus*. Bloomsbury Publishing USA, 2009.

Chapter 19: Thrice Great

1   Hutchison, Keith. "Hermetism." *Encyclopedia of the Scientific Revolution from Copernicus to Newton*, edited by Wilbur Applebaum, Garland Publishing, Inc., 2005.

2   Hanegraaff, Wouter J. "Hermes Trismegistus and Hermetism." *Encyclopedia of Renaissance Philosophy*, edited by Marco Sgarbi, Springer, 2022, p. 1512.

3   Meroi, Fabrizio. "Bruno, Giordano." *Encyclopedia of Renaissance Philosophy*, edited by Marco Sgarbi, Springer, 2022, p. 517.

4   Merkel, Ingrid, and Allen G. Debus. *Hermeticism and the Renaissance: Intellectual History and the Occult in Early Modern Europe*. Associated University Presses, Inc., 1988, p. 21.

5   Salaman, Clement, et al. *The Way of Hermes: New Translations of The Corpus Hermeticum and The Definitions of Hermes Trismegistus to Asclepius*. Inner Traditions, 2000, p. 9.

6   Long, Pamela. "Humanism." *Encyclopedia of the Scientific Revolution from Copernicus to Newton*, edited by Wilbur Applebaum, Garland Publishing, Inc., 2005.

7   "Seeing in the Dark | About the Filmmakers." *PBS*, accessed Mar. 2024, pbs.org/seeinginthedark/about-the-film/about-the-filmmakers.html.

8   Ferris, Timothy. *Coming of Age in the Milky Way*. Harper Perennial, 2003.

9   Ferris. *Coming of Age in the Milky Way*.

10   Merkel and Debus. *Hermeticism and the Renaissance*, p. 21.

11 Salaman et al. *The Way of Hermes*, pp. 34–35.

12 "Copernicus on the Revolutions." *Dartmouth Department of Mathematics*, translation and commentary by Edward Rosen, The Johns Hopkins University Press, 1 Sep. 1999, math.dartmouth.edu/~matc/Readers/renaissance.astro/1.1.Revol.html.

13 Africa, Thomas W. "Copernicus' Relation to Aristarchus and Pythagoras." *Isis*, vol. 52, no. 3, The University of Chicago Press, Sep. 1961, p. 403.

14 Larson, Paul. "Occultism." *Encyclopedia of Psychology and Religion*, editors David A. Leeming, et al., Springer Science+Business Media, LLC, 2010, p. 638.

15 Larson. *Encyclopedia of Psychology and Religion*, p. 638.

Chapter 20: Fusion of Faith

1 Swanson, James. *Dictionary of Biblical Languages with Semantic Domains: Greek (New Testament)*, Electronic ed., Logos Research Systems, Inc., 1997.

2 Marshall, I. Howard. *Acts: An Introduction and Commentary*. InterVarsity Press, 1980, p. 330.

3 "Ovanes Akopyan." *University of Warwick*, accessed Apr. 2024, warwick.ac.uk/fac/arts/ren/prospective/alumni/akopyan.

4 Akopyan, Ovanes. "Francesco Patrizi da Cherso (1529–1597): new perspectives on a Renaissance philosopher." *Intellectual History Review*, vol. 29, num. 4, 2019, p. 542.

5 Hamblin, William. "What Is Prisca Theologia?" *Enigmatic Mirror*, 11 Mar. 2013, patheos.com/blogs/enigmaticmirror/2013/03/10/what-is-prisca-theologia.

6 "Astral." *Cambridge Dictionary*, 10 Apr. 2024, dictionary.cambridge.org/dictionary/english/astral.

7 De Carli, Manuel. "Renaissance Idea of Daimon." *Encyclopedia of Renaissance Philosophy*, edited by Marco Sgarbi, Springer, 2022, p. 943.

8 Geretto, Mattia, "Angels and Demons in the Renaissance." *Encyclopedia of Renaissance Philosophy*, edited by Marco Sgarbi, Springer, 2022, pp. 145–46.

9 Rabin, Shelia J. "Giovanni Pico della Mirandola (1463– 1494)." *Encyclopedia of the Scientific Revolution from Copernicus to Newton*, edited by Wilbur Applebaum, Garland Publishing, Inc., 2005.

10 McDonald, Grantley. "Censorship in the Renaissance." *Encyclopedia of Renaissance Philosophy*, edited by Marco Sgarbi, Springer, 2022, p. 678.

11 Louw, Johannes P., and Eugene Albert Nida. *Greek-English Lexicon of the New Testament: Based on Semantic Domains*, Electronic ed. of the 2nd edition., vol. 1, United Bible Societies, 1996, p. 544.

12 Brewster, David. *Memoirs of the Life, Writings, and Discoveries of Sir Isaac Newton*. vol. II, Edinburgh: Thomas Constable and Co., 1855, pp. 374–75.

13 The Editors of Encyclopedia Britannica. "Philosopher's Stone | History and Facts." *Encyclopedia Britannica*, 8 Mar. 2024, britannica.com/topic/philosophers-stone.

14 "Michael Maier, Symbola Aureae Mensae, 1617." *Cabinet*, accessed May 2024, cabinet.ox.ac.uk/michael-maier-symbola-aureae-mensae-1617.

15 Rusu, Doina-Cristina. "Bacon, Francis." *Encyclopedia of Renaissance Philosophy*, edited by Marco Sgarbi, Springer, 2022, p. 291.

16 "In Depth With Michio Kaku." *C-SPAN*, 3 Oct. 2010 (02:43), c-span.org/video/?295788-1/depth-michio-kaku.

17 Rusu. *Encyclopedia of Renaissance Philosophy*, p. 293.

18 Rusu. *Encyclopedia of Renaissance Philosophy*, p. 297.

19 Hessayon, Ariel. "Everard, John." *Encyclopedia of Renaissance Philosophy*, edited by Marco Sgarbi, Springer, 2022, p. 1172.

20 Coudert, Allison P. "Henry More, the Kabbalah, and the Quakers." *Philosophy, Science, and Religion in England 1640-1700*, edited by Richard Kroll et al., Cambridge University Press, 2008, p. 47.

21 Strazzoni, Andrea. "Henry More." *Encyclopedia of Renaissance Philosophy*, edited by Marco Sgarbi, Springer, 2022, p. 2243.

22 Levine, Joseph M. "Latitudinarians, neoplatonists, and the ancient wisdom." *Philosophy, Science, and Religion in England 1640-1700*, edited by Richard Kroll et al., Cambridge University Press, 2008. p. 95.

23 Coudert. *Philosophy, Science, and Religion in England 1640-1700*, p. 40.

24 Rossella Pescatori. "Renaissance Kabbalah." *Encyclopedia of Renaissance Philosophy*, edited by Marco Sgarbi, Springer, 2022, p. 1768-71.

25 Strazzoni, Andrea. "Heinrich Cornelius Agrippa." *Encyclopedia of Renaissance Philosophy*, edited by Marco Sgarbi, Springer, 2022, p. 71.

26 Strazzoni. *Encyclopedia of Renaissance Philosophy*, p. 71.

27 "Heinrich Cornelius Agrippa Von Nettesheim." *Stanford Encyclopedia of Philosophy*, 30 Mar. 2007, plato.stanford.edu/ARCHIVES/WIN2009/entries/agrippa-nettesheim.

Chapter 21: Greek Philosophy

1   "Andrew Dickson White | Office of the President." *Cornell University*, accessed Feb. 2024,
    president.cornell.edu/the-presidency/andrew-dickson-white.

2   White, Andrew Dickson. *A History of the Warfare of Science with Theology in Christendom*. Vol. 1, first published 1896, Cambridge University Press, 2009, pp. 15–16.

3   Wormald, Benjamin. "Religion and Science: A Timeline | Pew Research Center." *Pew Research Center's Religion & Public Life Project*, 26 Apr. 2022,
    pewresearch.org/religion/2009/11/05/religion-and-science-a-timeline.

4   Glaze, R. E. "Corinth." *Holman Illustrated Bible Dictionary*, edited by Chad Brand et al., Holman Bible Publishers, 2003, p. 343.

5   Ramsay, William M. "CORINTH." *A Dictionary of the Bible: Dealing with Its Language, Literature, and Contents Including the Biblical Theology*, edited by James Hastings et al., vol. 1, Charles Scribner's Sons; T. & T. Clark, 1912, p. 481.

6   Hoffe, Otfried. *Aristotle*. Ancient Greek Philosophy Series, edited by Anthony Preus, translated by Christine Salazar, State University of New York Press, 2003, p. 108.

7   Louw, Johannes P., and Eugene Albert Nida. *Greek-English Lexicon of the New Testament: Based on Semantic Domains*, Electronic ed. of the 2nd edition., vol. 1, United Bible Societies, 1996, p. 624.

8   Louw and Nida. *Greek-English Lexicon of the New Testament*, p. 770.

Chapter 22: The Bible Deceives

1   "Deceive." *Cambridge Dictionary*, 10 Apr. 2024,
    dictionary.cambridge.org/dictionary/english/deceive.

2   Louw, Johannes P., and Eugene Albert Nida. *Greek-English Lexicon of the New Testament: Based on Semantic Domains*, Electronic ed. of the 2nd edition., vol. 1, United Bible Societies, 1996, p. 759.

Chapter 23: The Moon Landing

1   Swanson, James. *Dictionary of Biblical Languages with Semantic Domains : Hebrew (Old Testament)*, Electronic ed., Logos Research Systems, Inc., 1997.

2   Holladay, William Lee, and Ludwig Köhler. *A Concise Hebrew and Aramaic Lexicon of the Old Testament*, Brill, 2000, p. 347.

3   Brown, Francis, et al. *Enhanced Brown-Driver-Briggs Hebrew and English Lexicon*, Clarendon Press, 1977, p. 956.

4 Reyburn, William David, and Euan McG. Fry. *A Handbook on Genesis.* United Bible Societies, 1998, p. 36.

5 Kissling, Paul J. *Genesis.* College Press Pub. Co., 2004, p. 102.

6 "What was the firmament in the Bible?" *Got Questions*, 4 Jan. 2022, gotquestions.org/firmament-Bible.html.

7 "The Apollo 11 Telemetry Data Recordings: A Final Report." *NASA*, 2009, nasa.gov/wp-content/uploads/static/history/alsj/a11/Apollo_11_TV_Tapes_Report.pdf.

8 Goddard Space Flight Center. "Proceedings of the Apollo Unified S-Band Conference." *NASA*, SP-87, Jul. 1965, p. 3.

9 "The Unified S-Band System." *Apollo Lunar Surface Journal*, 2005, nasa.gov/history/alsj/alsj-NASA-SP-87.html.

10 "Don Pettit, NASA" *BitChute*, 23 Jul. 2023 (0:01), bitchute.com/video/FgfsqNOesA30.

11 Clarkson, Chris, et al. "A General Test of the Copernican Principle." *Physical Review Letters*, vol. 101, article 011301, 2 Jul. 2008, p. 1.

12 Clarkson et al. *Physical Review Letters*, p. 3.

13 Clarkson et al. *Physical Review Letters*, p. 1.

14 Clarkson et al. *Physical Review Letters*, p. 1.

15 Hubble, Edwin. *The Observational Approach to Cosmology.* Oxford University Press, 1937, pp. 50–51, 58–59.

16 Hubble. *The Observational Approach to Cosmology*, p. 59.

17 "Overview - NASA Science." *NASA Science*, accessed Mar. 2024, science.nasa.gov/mission/webb/about-overview/.

18 Abiko, Seiya. "How I Created the Theory of Relativity." *Historical Studies in the Physical and Biological Sciences*, vol. 31, no. 1, University of California Press, 24 Sep. 2013, p. 13.

19 Fölsing, Albrecht. *Albert Einstein: A Biography.* Penguin (Non-Classics), 1998, p. 160.

20 Fölsing. *Albert Einstein*, p. 219.

21 Fölsing. *Albert Einstein*, p. 439.

22 Fölsing. *Albert Einstein*, p. 703.

23 Einstein, Albert, et al. *Albert Einstein, the Human Side: Glimpses from His Archives.* Edited by Helen Dukas and Banesh Hoffmann, Princeton University Press, 2013, p. 43.

24 Dawkins, Richard. *The God Delusion.* Houghton Mifflin Company, 2006.

25 Compton, Arthur H. "What is Light?" *The Scientific Monthly*, vol. 28, no. 4,

Apr. 1929, p. 289.

Chapter 24: Observation

1   "Earth: By the Numbers." *NASA*, accessed Mar. 2024,
    mobile.arc.nasa.gov/public/iexplore/missions/pages/solarsystem/earth-
    facts.html.

2   "Earth: By the Numbers." *NASA*.

3   Howell, Elizabeth and Doris Elin Urrutia. "How Fast Is Earth Moving?"
    Space, 19 Oct. 2023,
    space.com/33527-how-fast-is-earth-moving.html#sec-
    tion-how-fast-are-we-spinning.

4   "Sun: Facts." *NASA*, accessed Feb. 2024,
    science.nasa.gov/sun/facts.

5   Staveley-Smith, Lister. "Explainer: What Is the Great Attractor and Its Pull
    on Our Galaxy?" *The Conversation*, accessed Feb. 2024,
    theconversation.com/explainer-what-is-the-great-attractor-and-its-pull-
    on-our-galaxy-54558.

6   Karttunen, Hannu, et al. *Fundamental Astronomy*. 5th edition, Springer
    Science+Business Media, 2007, p. 4.

7   Harriman, David. *The Logical Leap: Induction in Physics*. Penguin, 2010.

8   Albelli, Alfred. "Radio Power will Revolutionize the World by Nikola Tesla."
    Modern Mechanix and Inventions, 1934, pp. 117-18.

9   "What Is a Planet?" *NASA Science*, accessed Mar. 2024,
    science.nasa.gov/solar-system/planets/what-is-a-planet.

10 "Planet." *Merriam-Webster Dictionary*, 10 Apr. 2024,
    merriam-webster.com/dictionary/planet.

11 Bury, Joshua. "Night Watch." *Flickr*, accessed Mar. 2024,
    flickr.com/photos/jbury/3874300109.

12 "Astronomy Picture of the Day." *NASA*, 9 Sep. 2009,
    apod.nasa.gov/apod/ap090909.html.

13 Long, Pamela. "Humanism." *Encyclopedia of the Scientific Revolution from
    Copernicus to Newton*, edited by Wilbur Applebaum, Garland Publishing,
    Inc., 2005.

14 Freely, John. *Celestial Revolutionary: Copernicus, the Man and His Uni-
    verse*. Bloomsbury Publishing, 2014, p. vii.

15 "Copernicus on the Revolutions." *Dartmouth Department of Mathematics*,
    translation and commentary by Edward Rosen, The Johns Hopkins Uni-
    versity Press, 1 Sep. 1999,
    math.dartmouth.edu/~matc/Readers/renaissance.astro/1.1.Revol.html.

16 Athanasakis, Andreas. "Copernicus, Nicolaus." *Encyclopedia of Renaissance Philosophy*, edited by Marco Sgarbi, Springer, 2022, p. 848.

17 Omodeo, Pietro Daniel. "Copernicanism." *Encyclopedia of Renaissance Philosophy*, edited by Marco Sgarbi, Springer, 2022, p. 844.

Chapter 25: Two Approaches to Astronomy

1 Omodeo, Pietro Daniel. "Copernicanism." *Encyclopedia of Renaissance Philosophy*, edited by Marco Sgarbi, Springer, 2022, p. 844.

2 Pogge, Richard. "Religious Objections to Copernicus." *Ohio State University*, Astronomy 161, 2 Jan. 2005, www.astronomy.ohio-state.edu/pogge.1/Ast161/Unit3/response.html.

3 Miller, Ron. *Recentering the Universe: The Radical Theories of Copernicus, Kepler, Galileo, and Newton*. Twenty-First Century Books, 2013, p. 28.

4 Lucas, E. C. "Some Scientific Issues Related to the Understanding of Genesis 1–3." *Themelios: Volume 12*, No. 2, January 1987, vol. 12, no. 2, The Gospel Coalition, 1987, p. 47.

5 Gingerich, Owen. "Did the Reformers Reject Copernicus?" *Christian History Magazine-Issue 76: The Christian Face of the Scientific Revolution*, Christianity Today, 2002.

6 Lucas. *Themelios: Volume 12*, p. 47.

Chapter 26: New Meets Old

1 Faulkner, Danny R. "The Copernican System & the Bible." *Answers in Genesis*, 19 Feb. 2024, answersingenesis.org/science/copernican-system-and-bible.

2 "Does the Bible teach geocentrism?" *Got Questions*, 4 Jan. 2022, gotquestions.org/geocentrism-Bible.html.

3 Galli, Mark, and Ted Olsen. "Introduction." *131 Christians Everyone Should Know*, Broadman & Holman Publishers, 2000, p. 347.

4 Feldmeth, Nathan P. *Pocket Dictionary of Church History: Over 300 Terms Clearly and Concisely Defined*, IVP Academic, 2008, p. 43.

5 Shedd, William Greenough Thayer. *Dogmatic Theology*. Edited by Alan W. Gomes, 3rd ed., P & R Pub., 2003, p. 123.

6 Hoffe, Otfried. *Aristotle*. Ancient Greek Philosophy Series, edited by Anthony Preus, translated by Christine Salazar, State University of New York Press, 2003, p. 70.

7 Knight, Edward H. *Knight's American Mechanical Encyclopedia. Vol. II GAS–REA*, H. O. Houghton and Company, 1882, pp. 1577–578.

8 Riedweg, Christoph. *Pythagoras: His Life, Teaching, and Influence*. Cornell

University Press, 2005, p. 7.

9   "Geometry." *Etymonline*, accessed Mar. 2024,
    etymonline.com/word/geometry.

10 Carabas, Markus. *Thoth: The History and Legacy of the Ancient Egyptian
    God Who Maintains the Universe*. Charles River Editors, 2018.

11 Boylan, Patrick. *Thoth the Hermes of Egypt: A Study of Some Aspects of
    Theological Thought in Ancient Egypt*. Oxford University Press, 1922, p.
    99.

12 Boylan. *Thoth the Hermes of Egypt*, p. 106.

13 Allen, George T. "The Egyptian God, Thoth." *The Journal of Religion*, vol.
    3, no. 2, The University of Chicago Press, Mar. 1923, p. 207.

14 Africa, Thomas W. "Copernicus' Relation to Aristarchus and Pythagoras."
    Isis, vol. 52, no. 3, The University of Chicago Press, Sep. 1961, p. 403.

15 Grote, George. *A History of Greece: Volume 4*. Cambridge University
    Press, 2010, p. 526.

16 Grote. A History of Greece: Volume 4, p. 526-27.

17 Aubrey Marcus Podcast. "Decoding the Principles of Hermetic Wisdom
    W/ Robert Edward Grant." *YouTube*, 14 Sep. 2022 (2:00:19),
    youtube.com/watch?v=pQ3fdRPh2sI.

Chapter 27: All For One and One For All

1   Omodeo, Pietro Daniel. "Astronomy." *Encyclopedia of Renaissance Philos-
    ophy*, edited by Marco Sgarbi, Springer, 2022, p. 246.

2   Voelkel, James R. *Johannes Kepler and the New Astronomy*. Oxford Uni-
    versity Press, 2001, p. 65.

3   Miller, Ron. *Recentering the Universe: The Radical Theories of Copernicus,
    Kepler, Galileo, and Newton*. Twenty-First Century Books, 2013, pp. 45-46.

4   "Through Galileo's Telescope." *British Pathé*, 24 Jul. 1933,
    britishpathe.com/asset/65012.

5   Drake, Stillman. *Galileo: Pioneer Scientist*. University of Toronto Press,
    1990, p. 134.

6   West, Doug. "Galileo Galilei Discovers the Moons of Jupiter and the
    Phases of Venus." *Owlcation*, 9 Sep. 2023,
    owlcation.com/stem/Galileo-Galilei-Discovers-the-Moons-of-Jupi-
    ter-and-the-Phase-of-Venus.

7   Crane, Leah. "Wandering Stars: A Brief History of Defining 'Planet'" *Lateral
    Magazine Physical Science*, Issue 9, 4 Apr. 2016,
    lateralmag.com/articles/issue-9/wandering-stars-a-brief-history-of-defin-
    ing-planet.

8   "Galileo's 'Confession.'" *Maths History*, School of Mathematics and Statistics, University of St Andrews, accessed Apr. 2024, mathshistory.st-andrews.ac.uk/Extras/Galileo_confession.

9   Mianecki, Julie. "378 Years Ago Today: Galileo Forced to Recant." *Smithsonian Magazine,* 16 Nov. 2013, smithsonianmag.com/smithsonian-institution/378-years-ago-today-galileo-forced-to-recant-18323485.

10 Cross, F. L., and Elizabeth A. Livingstone, editors. *The Oxford Dictionary of the Christian Church, 3rd ed. rev.*, Oxford University Press, 2005, p. 654.

11 Owens, Virginia. "Galileo and the Powers Above." *Christian History Magazine*, Issue 76: The Christian Face of the Scientific Revolution, Christianity Today, 2002.

12 Owens. Christian History Magazine.

13 "Galileo's 'Confession.'" *Maths History*.

14 Freely, John. *Celestial Revolutionary: Copernicus, the Man and His Universe*. Bloomsbury Publishing, 2014, p. 205.

15 Wallace, William A. "Causality." *Encyclopedia of the Scientific Revolution from Copernicus to Newton*, edited by Wilbur Applebaum, Garland Publishing, Inc., 2005.

16 Newton, Isaac. *Newton's Principia: The Mathematical Principles of Natural Philosophy*. Translated by Andrew Motte, Daniel Adee, 1846, p. 73.

17 Dobbs, Betty J. T. *The Foundations of Newton's Alchemy: The Hunting of the Green Lyon*. Cambridge University Press, 1975, p. 14.

18 Miller. *Recentering the Universe*, p. 53.

19 "Chymistry of Isaac Newton : Normalized Manuscript." *Indiana University*, accessed Mar. 2024, webapp1.dlib.indiana.edu/newton/mss/norm/ALCH00017.

20 Fornasier, Matteo. "Microcosm and Macrocosm in the Renaissance." *Encyclopedia of Renaissance Philosophy*, edited by Marco Sgarbi, Springer, 2022, p. 2186.

21 Woolfson, Michael M. *The Origin and Evolution of the Solar System*. CRC Press, 2000, p. 117.

22 Dobbs. *The Foundations of Newton's Alchemy*, p. 13.

Chapter 28: Trouble in Paradise

1   Einstein, Albert, et al. *Albert Einstein, the Human Side: Glimpses from His Archives*. Edited by Helen Dukas and Banesh Hoffmann, Princeton University Press, 2013, pp. 7–8.

2   Siegfried, Tom. "Einstein's Genius Changed Science's Perception of Gravi-

ty." *Science News*, 12 Mar. 2020,
sciencenews.org/article/einsteins-genius-changed-sciences-perception-gravity.

3   Newcomb, Tim. "Physicist Reveals What the Fourth Dimension Looks Like." *Popular Mechanics*, 21 Feb. 2024,
popularmechanics.com/science/environment/a42709141/what-the-fourth-dimension-looks-like.

4   "What Are Gravitational Waves?" *LIGO Caltech*, accessed Mar. 2024,
ligo.caltech.edu/page/what-are-gw.

5   National Science Foundation News. "Gravitational Waves Detected | LIGO (Laser Interferometer Gravitational Observatory)." *YouTube*, 11 Feb. 2016 (3:57),
youtube.com/watch?v=aEPIwEJmZyE.

6   "Gravitational Waves Detected." *YouTube*, (6:38).

7   LIGO Lab Caltech : MIT. "The Sound of Two Black Holes Colliding." *YouTube*, 11 Feb. 2016,
youtube.com/watch?v=QyDcTbR-kEA.

8   "Gravitational Waves Detected." *YouTube*, (5:26).

9   Perry, Philip. "Hints of the 4th Dimension Have Been Detected by Physicists." *Big Think*, 30 Sept. 2021,
bigthink.com/technology-innovation/hints-of-the-4th-dimension-have-been-detected-by-physicists.

10   "Physicist Reveals What the Fourth Dimension Looks Like." *Popular Mechanics*.

11   Greene, Brian. "This Is What the Fourth Dimension Looks Like." *Big Think*, 27 Jan. 2023 (0:45),
bigthink.com/the-well/fourth-dimension.

Chapter 29: Rejecting God's Word

1   Louw, Johannes P., and Eugene Albert Nida. *Greek-English Lexicon of the New Testament: Based on Semantic Domains*, Electronic ed. of the 2nd edition., vol. 1, United Bible Societies, 1996, p. 509.

2   Porton, Gary G. "Sadducees." *The Anchor Yale Bible Dictionary*, edited by David Noel Freedman, vol. 5, Doubleday, 1992, p. 892.

3   Elwell, Walter A., and Barry J. Beitzel. "Sadducees." *Baker Encyclopedia of the Bible*, vol. 2, Baker Book House, 1988, p. 1880.

4   Louw and Nida. *Greek-English Lexicon of the New Testament*, p. 366.

5   Kittel, Gerhard, et al. Theological Dictionary of the New Testament, Abridged in One Volume, W.B. Eerdmans, 1985, p. 858.

6   Strong, James. *A Concise Dictionary of the Words in the Greek Testament and The Hebrew Bible*, vol. 1, Logos Bible Software, 2009, p. 58.

Chapter 31: Alphabetizing Scripture

1   Moyers & Company. "Neil deGrasse Tyson on Science, Religion and the Universe." *Moyers*, 14 Apr. 2016 (18:28), billmoyers.com/episode/neil-degrasse-tyson-on-science-religion-and-the-universe.

2   "Galileo's 'Confession.'" *Maths History*, School of Mathematics and Statistics, University of St Andrews, accessed Apr. 2024, mathshistory.st-andrews.ac.uk/Extras/Galileo_confession.

3   "Got Questions? Bible Questions Answered." *Got Questions Ministries*. Logos Bible Software, 2002-2013.

4   McDowell, Josh. *Evidence for Christianity*. Thomas Nelson Publishers, 2006.

5   Patzia, Arthur G., and Anthony J. Petrotta. *Pocket Dictionary of Biblical Studies*. InterVarsity Press, 2002.

6   Patzia and Petrotta. *Pocket Dictionary of Biblical Studies*.

7   Hendel, Ronald S. "Genesis, Book of." *The Anchor Yale Bible Dictionary*, edited by David Noel Freedman, 2:933. New York: Doubleday, 1992.

8   Cairns, Alan. *Dictionary of Theological Terms*. Ambassador Emerald International, 2002.

9   Wright, J. S., and J. A. Thompson. "Genesis, Book of." *New Bible Dictionary*, edited by D. R. W. Wood et al., 3rd ed., InterVarsity Press, 1996.

10   Ryle, Herbert Edward. "GENESIS." *A Dictionary of the Bible: Dealing with Its Language, Literature, and Contents Including the Biblical Theology*, edited by James Hastings et al., vol. I-V, Charles Scribner's Sons; T. & T. Clark, 1911-1912.

11   Ryle. *A Dictionary of the Bible*.

12   Ross, Allen P. "Genesis." *The Bible Knowledge Commentary: An Exposition of the Scriptures*, edited by J. F. Walvoord and R. B. Zuck, 1:18. Wheaton, IL: Victor Books, 1985.

13   Cairns. *Dictionary of Theological Terms*.

14   Thiselton, Anthony C., and Gerald Sheppard. "Biblical Interpretation in the Eighteenth and Nineteenth Centuries." *Dictionary of Major Biblical Interpreters*, edited by Donald K. McKim, 58. Downers Grove, IL; Nottingham, England: InterVarsity Press, 2007.

15   "Galileo's 'Confession.'" *Maths History*.

Chapter 32: The Book of Genesis

1   McKenzie, Steven L. *Introduction to the Historical Books: Strategies for Reading*. Cambridge: William. B. Eerdmans Publishing Company, 2010.

2   Youngblood, Ronald F., et al., Thomas Nelson Publishers, editors. *Nelson's New Illustrated Bible Dictionary*, Thomas Nelson, Inc., 1995.

3   Fee, Gordon D., and Douglas Stuart. *How to Read the Bible for All Its Worth: Fourth Edition*. Zondervan Academic, 2014.

4   Easley, Kendell H. *Holman QuickSource Guide to Understanding the Bible*. Nashville, TN: Holman Bible Publishers, 2002.

5   Schaeffer, Francis A. *The Complete Works of Francis A. Schaeffer: A Christian Worldview*. Crossway Books, 1982.

6   Cockerill, Gareth Lee. *The Epistle to the Hebrews*. William B. Eerdmans Publishing Company, 2012.

7   "The ESV Study Bible." *Crossway Bibles*, Wheaton, IL: Crossway Bibles, 2008.

8   *Is Genesis 1 History?* Directed by Thomas Purifoy, narrated by Del Tackett, Compass Cinema, 2017 (18:36).

9   *Is Genesis 1 History?* (19:31).

10 MacDonald, William. *Believer's Bible Commentary: Old and New Testaments*. Edited by Arthur Farstad, Thomas Nelson, 1995.

11 Morris, Leon. *Luke: An Introduction and Commentary*. Vol. 3, InterVarsity Press, 1988.

12 Steinmann, Andrew E. *Genesis: An Introduction and Commentary*. Edited by David G. Firth, vol. 1, Inter-Varsity Press, 2019.

13 Fee, Gordon D., and Robert L. Hubbard Jr., editors. *The Eerdmans Companion to the Bible*. William B. Eerdmans Publishing Company, 2011.

14 The view is literal in that God created everything in six days (144 hours). There are many different opinions with the literal view about the details of the creation story.

15 Craigie, Peter C. *The Book of Deuteronomy*. Wm. B. Eerdmans Publishing Co., 1976, p. 406.

16 Thompson, J. A. *Deuteronomy: An Introduction and Commentary*. Inter-Varsity Press, 1974, pp. 348–49.

17 Schreiner, Thomas R. *1, 2 Peter, Jude*. Broadman & Holman Publishers, 2003, p. 324.

18 Arichea, Daniel C., and Howard Hatton. *A Handbook on the Letter from Jude and the Second Letter from Peter*. United Bible Societies, 1993, p. 100.

19   Black, Allen, and Mark C. Black. *1 & 2 Peter*. College Press Pub., 1998, p. 2 Pe 1:21.

Chapter 33: Cosmogony or Cosmology

1   "Cosmogony." *Encyclopedia*, 21 May 2018, encyclopedia.com/science-and-technology/astronomy-and-space-exploration/astronomy-general/cosmogony.

2   "Cosmology." *NASA's Wilkinson Microwave Anisotropy Probe* (WMAP), 10 Dec. 2010, map.gsfc.nasa.gov/cosmology/cosmology.html.

Chapter 34: Faith and Stardust

1   Menzies, William W. *Bible Doctrines: A Pentecostal Perspective*. Edited by Stanley M. Horton, Logion Press, 1993, p. 78.

2   Fölsing, Albrecht. *Albert Einstein: A Biography*. Penguin (Non-Classics), 1998, p. 439.

3   Horgan, John. "One of the World's Most Powerful Scientists Believes in Miracles." *Scientific American*, 20 Feb. 2024, scientificamerican.com/blog/cross-check/one-of-the-worlds-most-powerful-scientists-believes-in-miracles.

4   Big Think. "Why It's so Hard for Scientists to Believe in God? | Francis Collins." *YouTube*, 14 Jun. 2011 (2:41), youtube.com/watch?v=plNptKQYviQ.

5   Collins, Francis S. *The Language of God: A Scientist Presents Evidence for Belief*. Free Press, 2007, pp. 67– 68.

6   Richard Dawkins Foundation for Reason & Science. "'A Universe From Nothing' by Lawrence Krauss, AAI 2009." *YouTube*, 22 Oct. 2009 (17:18), youtube.com/watch?v=7ImvlS8PLIo.

7   "Copernicus on the Revolutions." *Dartmouth Department of Mathematics*, translation and commentary by Edward Rosen, The Johns Hopkins University Press, 1 Sep. 1999, math.dartmouth.edu/~matc/Readers/renaissance.astro/1.1.Revol.html.

8   Long, Pamela. "Humanism." *Encyclopedia of the Scientific Revolution from Copernicus to Newton*, edited by Wilbur Applebaum, Garland Publishing, Inc., 2005.

9   "Why It's so Hard for Scientists to Believe in God?" *YouTube*, (2:46).

10   "Wish." *IMDb*, 22 Nov. 2023, imdb.com/title/tt11304740.

11   Sumrall, Laura. "Natural Magic in Renaissance Science." *Encyclopedia*

of *Renaissance Philosophy*, edited by Marco Sgarbi, Springer, 2022, pp. 2298–299.

12 Sumrall. *Encyclopedia of Renaissance Philosophy*, p. 2299.

13 Sumrall. *Encyclopedia of Renaissance Philosophy*, p. 2301.

14 "Magi." *Dictionary*, accessed Apr. 2024, dictionary.com/browse/magi%2520.

15 "The History of the Origin of the Sigil of Baphomet and Its Use in the Church of Satan." *Church of Satan*, 3 Oct. 2018, churchofsatan.com/history-sigil-of-baphomet.

16 *I'm a Star*. Music by Julia Michaels and Benjamin Rice, Disney Music, 2023.

17 Coudert, Allison P. "Henry More, the Kabbalah, and the Quakers." edited by Richard Kroll et al. *Philosophy, Science, and Religion in England 1640–1700*. Cambridge University Press, 2008. p. 40.

18 Bull, Christian H. *The Tradition of Hermes Trismegistus: The Egyptian Priestly Figure as a Teacher of Hellenized Wisdom*. Brill, 2018, pp. 102–03.

19 Bull. *The Tradition of Hermes Trismegistus*, p. 116.

20 Collins. *The Language of God*, pp. 233–34.

21 Collins. *The Language of God*, p. 67.

22 "Solar System Timeline." *The Planetary Society*, 14 Jan. 2021, planetary.org/worlds/solar-system-timeline.

23 "Solar System Timeline." *The Planetary Society*.

24 *I'm a Star*, Disney Music.

Chapter 35: Dealing with Flat Earth

1 "Circle of the earth" (Isaiah 40:22): This verse, when taken in isolation, is often used to argue for a globe or a flat earth. However, it is crucial to interpret Isaiah 40:22 within the Bible's framework (context)—the earth is set on a foundation and is motionless.

2 "EMERGENCY Qatar #QR725 to Chicago Diverted to Moscow Today Due to a Teen Who Fell Into a Coma." *AIRLIVE*, 7 Apr. 2016, airlive.net/emergency/2016/04/07/emergency-qatar-qr725-to-chicago-diverted-to-moscow-today-due-to-a-teen-who-fell-into-a-coma.

3 Mowat, Laura. "Flight Diverted After Teen Falls Into a Coma." *Express*, 7 Apr. 2016, express.co.uk/news/world/659059/Qatar-Airways-flight-Chicago-diverted-Moscow-teen-coma.

4 "Gleason's New Standard Map of the World : On the Projection of J.S. Christopher, Modern College, Blackheath, England ; Scientifically and

Practically Correct ; as 'It Is.'" *Yale University Library*, accessed Apr. 2024, collections.library.yale.edu/catalog/15234639.

5   "Social Media Filtering." *C-SPAN*, 17 Jul. 2018 (1:43:19), c-span.org/video/?448566-1/social-media-filtering.

6   "Propaganda." *Cambridge Dictionary*, accessed Apr. 2024, dictionary.cambridge.org/dictionary/english/propaganda.

7   Kreps, Daniel. "Tucker Carlson Says He's 'Open' to the Flat Earth Theory." *Rolling Stone*, 16 Dec. 2023, rollingstone.com/politics/politics-news/tucker-carlson-flat-earth-theo-ry-1234931330.

8   Frost, W., and K. R. Reddy. "Investigation of Aircraft Landing in Variable Wind Fields." *NASA Technical Reports Server* (NTRS), 1 Dec. 1978, p. 6, ntrs.nasa.gov/citations/19790005472.

9   Sturgeon, W. R., and J. D. Phillips. "A Mathematical Model of the CH-53 Helicopter." *NASA Technical Reports Server* (NTRS), 1 Nov. 1980, p. 17, ntrs.nasa.gov/citations/19810003557.

10   Edwards, H. D., and A. J. Lineberger. "Atmospheric Oscillations." *NASA Technical Reports Server* (NTRS), 1 Apr. 1965, p. 10, ntrs.nasa.gov/citations/19650015408.

11   According to modern science, the speed of the Milky Way, which includes the sun and earth, is 1.4 million mph.

Chapter 36: A Vision of Earth

1   DuBose, Rick. *In Jesus' Name: 5 Altars of Prayer That Move Heaven and Earth*. Chosen Books, 2023, p. 19.

2   DuBose. *In Jesus' Name*, p. 19.

3   "Lecture 4: Measuring the Earth." *Ohio State University*, accessed Apr. 2024, astronomy.ohio-state.edu/thompson.1847/161/measearth.html.

4   Henriksen, Janet. "An architectural paradigm." *Journal of Creation*, Vol. 24, is. 1, spring 2010, pp. 99–105.

5   Knight, Edward H. *Knight's American Mechanical Encyclopedia. Vol. II GAS–REA*, H. O. Houghton and Company, 1882, pp. 1577–578.

6   "Lecture 4: Measuring the Earth." *Ohio State University*.

7   DuBose. *In Jesus' Name*, pp. 19–20.

Chapter 37: Moon "Shine"

1   Modern science has yet to learn how the moon formed. According to the Lunar and Planetary Institute (LPI) brochure for elementary students, "Sev-

eral models are proposed for how our Moon formed, but the theory that best explains the chemical evidence from Moon rocks and characteristic of the Moon's orbit around Earth is the 'giant impact theory'" (www.lpi. usra.edu/education/moonPosters/Poster1/Poster-1-frontfull-revised.pdf).

2   Nye, Bill. *Undeniable: Evolution and the Science of Creation*. Macmillan, 2014.

3   Answers in Genesis. "Most HEATED Moments From Bill Nye Debate With Ken Ham." *YouTube*, 28 Nov. 2016 (4:16), youtube.com/watch?v=V2t_bAg8Abo.

4   "Ask Us - General Physics - Properties of Matter." *NASA's Cosmicopia*, 29 Dec. 2006, cosmicopia.gsfc.nasa.gov/qa_gp_pr.html.

5   "Moon Phases." *NASA Science*, accessed Apr. 2024, science.nasa.gov/moon/moon-phases.

6   "Moon Phases." *NASA Science*.

7   WIRED. "Bill Nye Answers Science Questions From Twitter | Tech Support." *YouTube*, 19 Apr. 2017 (02:07), youtube.com/watch?v=gGaxo98yHuI.

8   Swanson, James. *Dictionary of Biblical Languages with Semantic Domains : Hebrew (Old Testament)*, Electronic ed., Logos Research Systems, Inc., 1997.

9   Kendall, Graham. "Your Mobile Phone vs. Apollo 11'S Guidance Computer." *RealClearScience*, 2019, realclearscience.com/articles/2019/07/02/your_mobile_phone_vs_apollo_11s_guidance_computer_111026.html.

10 Brown, David, et al. *A Commentary, Critical, Experimental, and Practical, on the Old and New Testaments: Genesis–Deuteronomy*. William Collins, Sons, & Company, Limited, accessed Apr. 2024, p. 7.

11 Reyburn, William David, and Euan McG. Fry. *A Handbook on Genesis*. United Bible Societies, 1998, p. 43.

12 "Phenomenal." *Merriam-Webster Dictionary*, 26 Apr. 2024, merriam-webster.com/dictionary/phenomenal.

13 Spence-Jones, H. D. M., editor. *Genesis*. Funk & Wagnalls Company, 1909, p. 21.

Chapter 38: Tiny Stars

1   "Stars." *NASA Science*, accessed Apr. 2024. science.nasa.gov/universe/stars.

2   The KJV uses the word "planet" (2 Kings 23:5). The underlying word in

Hebrew refers to stars. NIV, NASB, ESV, CSB, NLT, and NKJV translate "מַזָּלוֹת | mazzālôt" as "constellations."

3   Youngblood, Ronald F., et al., Thomas Nelson Publishers, editors. *Nelson's New Illustrated Bible Dictionary*, Thomas Nelson, Inc., 1995.

4   "What Is a Planet?" *NASA Science*, accessed Mar. 2024, science.nasa.gov/solar-system/planets/what-is-a-planet.

5   Omodeo, Pietro Daniel. "Astronomy." *Encyclopedia of Renaissance Philosophy*, edited by Marco Sgarbi, Springer, 2022, p. 246.

6   CNN Wire Staff. "Theology Unnecessary, Stephen Hawking Tells CNN." *CNN*. 11 Sep. 2010, cnn.com/2010/WORLD/europe/09/11/stephen.hawking.interview/index.html.

7   Swanson, James. *Dictionary of Biblical Languages with Semantic Domains : Hebrew (Old Testament)*, Electronic ed., Logos Research Systems, Inc., 1997.

8   Louw, Johannes P., and Eugene Albert Nida. *Greek-English Lexicon of the New Testament: Based on Semantic Domains*, Electronic ed. of the 2nd edition., vol. 1, United Bible Societies, 1996, p. 1.

9   Kittel, Gerhard, et al. *Theological Dictionary of the New Testament, Abridged in One Volume*, W.B. Eerdmans, 1985, p. 736.

10 Black, Allen. *Mark*. College Press, 1995, p. Mk 13:24–25.

Chapter 39: The Moving Sun

1   Hamilton, Victor P. *The Book of Genesis, Chapters 1–17*. Wm. B. Eerdmans Publishing Co., 1990, p. 53.

2   Identities are not necessary, but this situation was documented. The intent is to show the conflict between the literal approach to the creation story and modern science and not between a student and their professor.

3   Wenham, Gordon J. *Genesis 1–15*. Word, Incorporated, 1987, p. 18.

4   Brown, David, et al. *A Commentary, Critical, Experimental, and Practical, on the Old and New Testaments: Genesis–Deuteronomy*. William Collins, Sons, & Company, Limited, accessed on Mar 2024, p. 6.

5   "What Does the Bible Say About the Earth Orbiting the Sun?" *Open Bible*, 2001, openbible.info/topics/the_earth_orbiting_the_sun.

6   Guzik, David. *Joshua*. David Guzik, 2000, p. Jos 10:10–15.

7   Woudstra, Marten H. *The Book of Joshua*. Wm. B. Eerdmans Publishing Co., 1981, p. 176.

8   Brown, Francis, et al. *Enhanced Brown-Driver-Briggs Hebrew and English*

Lexicon, Clarendon Press, 1977, p. 280.

9 Swanson, James. *Dictionary of Biblical Languages with Semantic Domains : Hebrew (Old Testament)*, Electronic ed., Logos Research Systems, Inc., 1997.

10 Wesley, John. *The Works of John Wesley*. Third Edition, vol. 2, Wesleyan Methodist Book Room, 1872, p. 392.

11 "Age of Stars." Narrated by Talithia Williams, directed by Poppy Pinnock, *NOVA Universe Revealed*, PBS, 27 Oct. 2021 (36:38).

12 Collins, Francis S. *The Language of God: A Scientist Presents Evidence for Belief*. Free Press, 2007, pp. 67–68.

13 Ferris, Timothy. *Coming of Age in the Milky Way*. Harper Perennial, 2003.

14 Long, Pamela. "Humanism." *Encyclopedia of the Scientific Revolution from Copernicus to Newton*, edited by Wilbur Applebaum, Garland Publishing, Inc., 2005.

15 Knight, Edward H. *Knight's American Mechanical Encyclopedia*. Vol. II GAS–REA, H. O. Houghton and Company, 1882, pp. 1577–578.

16 "Copernicus on the Revolutions." *Dartmouth Department of Mathematics*, translation and commentary by Edward Rosen, The Johns Hopkins University Press, 1 Sep. 1999, math.dartmouth.edu/~matc/Readers/renaissance.astro/1.1.Revol.html.

Chapter 40: Attempt to Reject Paganism

1 Carter, Robert and Jonathan Sarfati. "Refuting Absolute Geocentrism." *Creation*, 1 Jan. 2024, creation.com/refuting-absolute-geocentrism.

2 Gingerich, Owen, and James MacLachlan. *Nicolaus Copernicus: Making the Earth a Planet*. Oxford University Press, 2005, p. 67.

3 Carter and Sarfati. *Creation*.

4 Carter and Sarfati. *Creation*.

5 Carter and Sarfati. *Creation*.

6 Salaman, Clement, et al. *The Way of Hermes: New Translations of The Corpus Hermeticum and The Definitions of Hermes Trismegistus to Asclepius*. Book 16, Healing Arts Press, 2000, p. 77.

7 Carter and Sarfati. *Creation*.

8 Long, Pamela. "Humanism." *Encyclopedia of the Scientific Revolution from Copernicus to Newton*, edited by Wilbur Applebaum, Garland Publishing, Inc., 2005.

9 Carter and Sarfati. *Creation*.

10   Grote, George. *A History of Greece: Volume 4.* Cambridge University Press, 2010, p. C2.

11   Grote. *A History of Greece: Volume 4*, p. C2.

12   Kelly, Jason M. "The Evolution of Renaissance Classicism." *World History Encyclopedia.* ABC-CLIO, 2011.

13   Newman, Barclay Moon, and Eugene Albert Nida. *A Handbook on the Acts of the Apostles.* United Bible Societies, 1972, p. 342.

14   Guthrie, Donald. *Pastoral Epistles: An Introduction and Commentary.* InterVarsity Press, 1990, p. 209.

15   Africa, Thomas W. "Copernicus' Relation to Aristarchus and Pythagoras." *Isis*, vol. 52, no. 3, The University of Chicago Press, Sep. 1961, p. 403.

Chapter 41: Movement, Water, and Gravity

1   Cowen, Ron. "Atom & Cosmos: A special place in the universe: Scientists propose tests of Copernican principle." *Science News*, vol. 173, no. 18, 7 Jun. 2008, p. 12.

2   Bratcher, Robert G., and William David Reyburn. *A Translator's Handbook on the Book of Psalms.* United Bible Societies, 1991, p. 880.

3   "SCA - about Suez Canal." *Suez Canal Authority*, 2019, suezcanal.gov.eg/English/About/SuezCanal/Pages/AboutSuezCanal. aspx.

4   Fisher, William B., and Charles Gordon Smith. "Suez Canal | History, Map, Importance, Length, Depth, and Facts." *Encyclopedia Britannica*, 15 Apr. 2024, britannica.com/topic/Suez-Canal.

5   "Canal and Lock." *Encyclopedia*, accessed Apr. 2024, encyclopedia.com/manufacturing/news-wires-white-papers-and-books/ canal-and-lock.

6   "Pascal's Principle." *Wolfram Demonstrations Project*, accessed Apr. 2024, demonstrations.wolfram.com/PascalsPrinciple.

7   Borchia, Davide. *Earth Curvature Calculator*. 12 Jul. 2022, calctool.org/astrophysics/earth-curvature.

8   Newton, Isaac. *Newton's Principia: The Mathematical Principles of Natural Philosophy.* Translated by Andrew Motte, Daniel Adee, 1846, p. 73

9   "Sea Level 101: What Determines the Level of the Sea?" *NASA Science*, 3 Jun. 2020, science.nasa.gov/earth/climate-change/sea-level-101-what-determines- the-level-of-the-sea.

10   "Original Letter From Isaac Newton to Richard Bentley (Normalized)."

Trinity College Library, Oct. 2007,
newtonproject.ox.ac.uk/view/texts/normalized/THEM00258.

11 Newton, Isaac. *The Principia: Mathematical Principles of Natural Philoso-phy.* Translation by I. Bernard Cohen and Anne Whitman, assisted by Julia Budenz, University of California Press, 1999, p. 943.

12 "Phenomenon." *Cambridge Dictionary*, accessed Apr. 2024, dictionary.cambridge.org/dictionary/english/phenomenon.

13 Newton. *The Principia*, p. 943.

Chapter 42: Sun Worship

1 *Shining Star.* Earth, Wind & Fire, produced by Charles Stepney and Maurice White, Sony Music Studios, 1975.

2 *Hosanna.* Paul McCartney, produced by Ethan Johns, AIR Studios and Abbey Road Studios, 2013.

3 *I'm a Star.* Music by Julia Michaels and Benjamin Rice, Disney Music, 2023.

4 7pmProject. "The 7pm Project - Ruby Rose Interviews Katy Perry." *You-Tube*, 20 Aug. 2009 (1:37), youtube.com/watch?v=N8056a6jhjU.

5 Dee, Everet, et al. "Apollo: The Greek Equivalent of Horus." *Mysterium Academy*, 20 Apr. 2023, mysteriumacademy.com/apollo-the-greek-equivalent-of-horus.

6 Ferris, Timothy. *Coming of Age in the Milky Way.* Harper Perennial, 2003.

7 Carter, Robert and Jonathan Sarfati. "Refuting Absolute Geocentrism." *Creation*.com, 1 Jan. 2024, creation.com/refuting-absolute-geocentrism.

8 Camerota, Filippo. "Perspective in Renaissance Philosophy." *Encyclopedia of Renaissance Philosophy*, edited by Marco Sgarbi, Springer, 2022, p. 2493.

9 "The All-Seeing Eye: Exploring the Symbolism and Hidden Meanings." *Medium*, 12 Feb. 2024, medium.com/@systementcorp/the-all-seeing-eye-exploring-the-symbol-ism-and-hidden-meanings-25157aa92cbd.

10 Hanegraaff, Wouter J. "Hermes Trismegistus and Hermetism." *Encyclope-dia of Renaissance Philosophy*, edited by Marco Sgarbi, Springer, 2022, p. 1514.

11 Spangler, David. *Reflections on the Christ.* Findhorn Foundation, 1978. pp. 43-44.

Appendix A

1   Copernicus, Nicolaus. *De revolutionibus orbium coelestium*, 1543.

2   Pogge, Richard. "Religious Objections to Copernicus." *Ohio State University*, Astronomy 161, 2 Jan. 2005,
www.astronomy.ohio-state.edu/pogge.1/Ast161/Unit3/response.html.

3   This deleted material, which was not printed in the first four editions of the Revolutions (1543, 1566, 1617, 1854), but was incorporated in those published after the recovery of Copernicus' autograph (1873, 1949, 1972). Jackson School of Geosciences. "Full text - Nicolaus Copernicus. 'De revolutionibus (On the Revolutions),' 1543 C.E." *University of Texas at Austin,* 30 Nov. 2008,
https://www.geo.utexas.edu/courses/302d/Fall_2011/Full%20text%20
-%20Nicholas%20Copernicus,%20_De%20Revolutionibus%20(On%20
the%20Revolutions),_%201.pdf.

Figure Credits

Fig. 1   Miller, Ron. *Recentering the Universe: The Radical Theories of Copernicus, Kepler, Galileo, and Newton*. Twenty-First Century Books, 2013, p. 10.

Fig. 2   Kaku, Michio. "A Universe in a Nutshell: The Physics of Everything, With Michio Kaku." *Big Think*, 30 Sep. 2021 (20:37), bigthink.com/videos/universe-in-a-nutshell-the-physics-of-everything-with-michio-kaku.

Fig. 3   "What Causes the Seasons?" *NASA Space Place*, accessed Arp. 2024, spaceplace.nasa.gov/seasons/en.

Fig. 4   "What Is a Planet?" NASA Space Place, 27 Jun. 2024, spaceplace.nasa.gov/planet-what-is/en.

Fig. 5   Sengupta, Argha. "Which Has a Higher Gravitational Pull, a Stationary or a Rotating Object? Why?" *Science ABC*, 19 Oct. 2023, scienceabc.com/pure-sciences/which-has-a-higher-gravitational-pull-a-stationary-or-a-rotating-object-why.html.

Fig. 6   Ortega, Pete. "Illustration of items used to create a Megalosaurus dinosaur." *What if Genesis 1 was Correct?* Pete Ortega, 2022, p. 214.

Fig. 7   "Megalosaurus | Jurassic Period, Carnivore, Reptile." Encyclopedia Britannica, 29 Apr. 2024, britannica.com/animal/Megalosaurus.

Fig. 8   Nigg, Joseph. "The Sea Serpent." *Sea Monsters: A Voyage Around the World's Most Beguiling Map*, The University of Chicago Press, 2013, p. 114.

Fig. 9   "GW Orionis in the Constellation of Orion." European Southern Observatory, 3 Sep. 2020, eso.org/public/images/eso2014d.

Fig. 10   NASA Goddard Space Flight Center. "Most Amazing High Definition Image of Earth - Blue Marble 2012." *Flickr*, 25 Jan. 2012, flickr.com/photos/gsfc/6760135001/in/album-72157632172101342.

Fig. 11   NASA Goddard Space Flight Center. "What Is Your favorite...Old, New, Aqua, Blue, White or Black Marble?" *Flickr*, 6 Dec. 2012, flickr.com/photos/gsfc/8250779068/in/album-72157632172101342.

Fig. 12   *See Fig. 10*

Fig. 13   "Worldview: Explore Your Dynamic Planet." *Worldview*, 1 Mar. 2024, worldview.earthdata.nasa.gov.

Fig. 14   NASA Goddard Space Flight Center. "Black Marble - Americas." *Flickr*, 5 Dec. 2012 flickr.com/photos/gsfc/8246896289/in/album-72157632172101342.

Fig. 15. BBC Studios. "Jumping From Space! – Red Bull Space Dive – BBC." *YouTube*, 17 Mar. 2016 (1:54), youtube.com/watch?v=E9oKEJ1pXPw.

Fig. 16. *The Boy Mayor*. Directed by Henry McRae, Universal Film MFG. Co., 15 Dec. 1914.

Fig. 17 "Space Jump." *Red Bull*, 2 May 2024 (25:52), redbull.com/int-en/films/space-jump-stratos.

Fig. 18 Preisser, J. S. "Determination of Angles of Attack and Sideslip From Radar Data and a Roll-stabilized Platform." *NASA Technical Reports Server* (NTRS), 1 Mar. 1972, ntrs.nasa.gov/api/citations/19720012071/downloads/19720012071.pdf.

Fig. 19 Moebs, William, et al. 13.5 "Kepler's Laws Of Planetary Motion - University Physics Volume 1." *OpenStax*, 19 Sep. 2016, openstax.org/books/university-physics-volume-1/pages/13-5-keplers-laws-of-planetary-motion.

Fig. 20 "Eratosthenes | Biography, Discoveries, Sieve, and Facts." *Encyclopedia Britannica*, 20 July 1998, britannica.com/biography/Eratosthenes.

Fig. 21 Pogge, Richard W. "Aristarchus and Eratosthenes." *Ohio State University*, 2014, astronomy.ohio-state.edu/thompson.1847/161/measearth.html.

Fig. 22 "Solar Eclipse Guide: What They Are and How to Watch Safely." *Natural History Museum*, 26 May 2021, nhm.ac.uk/discover/solar-eclipse-guide.html.

Fig 23 Mitchell, Horace. "Earth Rotation From Galileo Imagery: 3600 X Real-Time." *NASA Scientific Visualization Studio*, 1 Sep. 1998, svs.gsfc.nasa.gov/1375.

Fig. 24 StarTalk. "Neil Tyson Demonstrates Absurdity of 'Flat Earth.'" *YouTube*, 9 Mar. 2018 (03:04), youtube.com/watch?v=hLPPE3_DVCw.

Fig. 25 *See Fig. 24*, (04:55).

Fig. 26 *See Fig. 24*, (05:03).

Fig. 27 *See Fig. 24*, (05:23).

Fig. 28 Ortega, Pete. *Proving the Bible Wrong: The attempt to undermine the authority of God's word with science*. Pete Ortega, 2023, p. 217.

Fig. 29 *See Fig. 24*, (05:48).

Fig. 30 Public Domain.

Fig. 31   *The Last Judgment*. Michelangelo, 1536–41, Sistine Chapel, Vatican City, Public Domain.

Fig. 32   Copernicus, Nicolaus. *De revolutionibus orbium coelestium*, 1543.

Fig. 33   Original version of coexistence image created by Piotr Młodożeniec, Warsaw, Poland, 2000.

Fig. 34   Maier, Michael. "Hermes Trismegistus." *Symbola aureae mensae*, 1617.

Fig. 35   Eurythmics. "Sweet Dreams (Are Made of This) (Official Video)." *YouTube*, 25 Oct. 2009 (0:07), youtube.com/watch?v=qeMFqkcPYcg.

Fig. 36   *See Fig 35*, (0:11).

Fig. 37   "Astronomy Picture of the Day." *NASA*, 9 Sep. 2009, apod.nasa.gov/apod/ap090909.html.

Fig. 38   *See Fig. 32*.

Fig. 39   Dee, Everet, et al. "Thoth the Immortal God of Atlantis, Egypt and Greece." *Mysterium Academy*, 4 Feb. 2023, mysteriumacademy.com/thoth.

Fig. 40   Voelkel, James R. *Johannes Kepler and the New Astronomy*, Oxford University Press, 2001, p. 65.

Fig. 41   West, Doug. "Galileo Galilei Discovers the Moons of Jupiter and the Phases of Venus." Owlcation, 9 Sep. 2023, owlcation.com/stem/Galileo-Galilei-Discovers-the-Moons-of-Jupiter-and-the-Phase-of-Venus.

Fig. 42   Mr SuperMole. "Zooming Jupiter With Only a Camera! Nikon P1000 - Super Zoom!!" *YouTube*, 1 Oct. 2020 (0:31), youtube.com/watch?v=d6C1b2_1W0Q.

Fig. 43   Right: Public Domain / Left: "Galileo's Telescope." Museo Galileo, accessed Mar. 2024, catalogue.museogalileo.it/object/GalileosTelescope_n01.html.

Fig. 44   "Chymistry of Isaac Newton : Normalized Manuscript." *University of Indiana*, image: <2r> Page, accessed Mar. 2024, webapp1.dlib.indiana.edu/newton/mss/norm/ALCH00017.

Fig. 45   *Wish*. Directed by Chris Buck and Fawn Veerasunthorn, Walt Disney Pictures, 2023 (14:24).

Fig. 46   *See Fig. 45*, (31:33).

Fig. 47   Beyer, Catherine. "Pentagrams Meaning." *Learn Religions*, 24 Sep. 2018, learnreligions.com/pentagrams-4123031.

Fig. 48   *See Fig. 45*, (1:20:36).

Fig. 49   *See Fig. 45*, (1:25:10).

Fig. 50   *Google Earth*. Accessed Apr. 2024,
earth.google.com/web.

Fig. 51   Top: *See Fig. 52*; Bottom: *See Fig. 50*.

Fig. 52   "QR725 Flight Status Qatar Airways: Doha to Chicago." *Airportia*,
accessed Apr. 2024,
airportia.com/flights/qr725/doha/chicago/.

Fig. 53   "Gleason's New Standard Map of the World : On the Projection of
J.S. Christopher, Modern College, Blackheath, England ; Scientifically
and Practically Correct ; as 'It Is.'" *Yale University Library*, accessed
Apr. 2024,
collections.library.yale.edu/catalog/15234639.

Fig. 54   Flat Earth meme, Public Domain.

Fig. 55   Screen capture of Google's auto suggestion, accessed Apr. 2024,
google.com.

Fig. 56   Screen capture of Google search results, accessed Apr. 2024,
google.com.

Fig. 57   Frost, W., and K. R. Reddy. "Investigation of Aircraft Landing in
Variable Wind Fields." *NASA Technical Reports Server* (NTRS), 1 Dec.
1978,
ntrs.nasa.gov/api/citations/19790005472/downloads/19790005472.
pdf.

Fig. 58   Sturgeon, W. R., and J. D. Phillips. "A Mathematical Model of the CH-
53 Helicopter." *NASA Technical Reports Server* (NTRS), 1 Nov. 1980,
ntrs.nasa.gov/api/citations/19810003557/downloads/19810003557.
pdf.

Fig. 59   Edwards, H. D., and A. J. Lineberger. "Atmospheric Oscillations."
NASA Technical Reports Server (NTRS), 1 Apr. 1965, p. 10,
ntrs.nasa.gov/api/citations/19650015408/downloads/19650015408.
pdf.

Fig. 60   Robinson, George L. "Leaders of Israel: A Brief History of the Hebrews." *The International Committee of Young Men's Christian Associations*, New York, 1906, p. 2.

Fig. 61   "Moon Phases." *NASA Science*, accessed Apr. 2024,
science.nasa.gov/moon/moon-phases.

Fig. 62   Villanueva, John Carl. "VY Canis Majoris." *Universe Today*, 25 Dec.
2015,
universetoday.com/39472/vy-canis-majoris.

Fig. 63   Cain, Fraser. "What Are the Different Types of Stars?" *Universe Today*,
13 Nov. 2019,

universetoday.com/24299/types-of-stars.

Fig. 64   Christian, James L. "Hebrew cosmos assumed by Old Testament writ-ers." *Philosophy: An Introduction to the Art of Wondering*. Cengage Learning, 2008, p. 526.

Fig. 65   Ortega, Pete. *The Story of the Bible: Understanding the Bible from within the world God created*. Pete Ortega, 2023, p. 258.

Fig. 66   *See Fig. 32.*

Fig. 67   *See Fig. 32.*

Fig. 68   Bratcher, Robert G., and William David Reyburn. *A Translator's Hand-book on the Book of Psalms*. United Bible Societies, 1991, p. 879.

Fig. 69   Ryazanova, Oksana. *Getty Images*. ID: 1432014682, 14, Oct. 2022.

Fig. 70   "About." *Suez Canal Authority*, 2019, suezcanal.gov.eg/English/About/SuezCanal/Pages/AboutSuezCanal.aspx.

Fig. 71   "Canals and Inland Waterways." *Encyclopedia Britannica*, 9 May 2024, britannica.com/technology/canal-waterway/Locks.

Fig. 72   "Pascal's Principle." Wolfram Demonstrations Project, accessed Apr. 2024, demonstrations.wolfram.com/PascalsPrinciple.

Fig. 73   "100 Years of General Relativity." *NASA Goddard Space Flight Center*, 25 Nov. 2015, asd.gsfc.nasa.gov/blueshift/index.php/2015/11/25/100-years-of-gen-eral-relativity.

Fig. 74   Dobson, Jim. "A One Trillion Dollar Hidden Treasure Chamber Is Dis-covered at India's Sree Padmanabhaswamy Temple." *Forbes*, 9 Dec. 2021, www.forbes.com/sites/jimdobson/2015/11/13/a-one-trillion-dol-lar-hidden-treasure-chamber-is-discovered-at-indias-sree-pad-manabhaswam-temple/?sh=49de41481ba6.

Fig. 75   "World's Richest Temple During Equinox." *YouTube*, 21 Nov. 2017 (starting at 2:51), youtube.com/watch?v=NaLTdL9CEzQ.

Fig. 76   Perry, Katy. "Katy Perry - Dark Horse (Official) Ft. Juicy J." *YouTube*, 20 Feb. 2014, youtube.com/watch?v=0KSOMA3QBU0.

Works Cited

Alden, Robert L. *Job*. Broadman & Holman Publishers, 1993.

Allen, David L. *Hebrews*. B & H Publishing Group, 2010.

Allen, Leslie C. *Psalms 101–150 (Revised)*. Word, Incorporated, 2002.

Andersen, Francis I. *Job: An Introduction and Commentary*. InterVarsity Press, 1976.

Applebaum, Wilbur. *Encyclopedia of the scientific revolution: from Copernicus to Newton*. Garland Publishing, Inc., 2005.

Arichea, Daniel C., and Howard Hatton. *A Handbook on the Letter from Jude and the Second Letter from Peter*. United Bible Societies, 1993.

Baldwin, Joyce G. *1 and 2 Samuel: An Introduction and Commentary*. InterVarsity Press, 1988.

Barnes, Albert. *Notes on the Old Testament: Job*. Blackie & Son, 1847.

Barton, Blanche. *The Secret Life of a Satanist: The Authorized Biography of Anton LaVey*. Feral House, 1992.

Berry, Arthur. *A Short History of Astronomy*. Charles Scribner's Sons, 1899.

Black, Allen. *Mark*. College Press, 1995.

Black, Allen, and Mark C. Black. *1 & 2 Peter*. College Press Pub., 1998.

Bloom, Benjamin S. *All Our Children Learning: A Primer for Parents, Teachers, and Other Educators*. McGraw-Hill Book Company, 1981.

Boylan, Patrick. *Thoth the Hermes of Egypt: A Study of Some Aspects of Theological Thought in Ancient Egypt*. Oxford University Press, 1922.

Brand, Chad, et al., editors. *Holman Illustrated Bible Dictionary*. Holman Bible Publishers, 2003.

Bratcher, Robert G., and William David Reyburn. *A Translator's Handbook on the Book of Psalms*. United Bible Societies, 1991.

Braun, Roddy L. *1 Chronicles*. Word, Incorporated, 1986.

Brewster, David. *Memoirs of the Life, Writings, and Discoveries of Sir Isaac Newton*. Vol. II, Edinburgh: Thomas Constable and Co., 1855.

Brown, David, et al. *A Commentary, Critical, Experimental, and Practical, on the Old and New Testaments: Genesis–Deuteronomy*. William Collins, Sons, & Company, Limited, n.d.

Brown, Francis, et al. *Enhanced Brown-Driver-Briggs Hebrew and English Lexicon*. Clarendon Press, 1977.

Bull, Christian H. *The Tradition of Hermes Trismegistus: The Egyptian Priestly Figure as a Teacher of Hellenized Wisdom*. Brill, 2018.

Cairns, Alan. *Dictionary of Theological Terms*. Ambassador Emerald International, 2002.

Carabas, Markus. *Thoth: The History and Legacy of the Ancient Egyptian God Who Maintains the Universe*. Charles River Editors, 2018.

Carroll, Sean. *Spacetime and Geometry: An Introduction to General Relativity*. Addison-Wesley, 2004.

Clines, David J. A., editor. *The Dictionary of Classical Hebrew, vol. 5*, Sheffield Academic Press; Sheffield Phoenix Press, 1993–2011.

---. *Job 21–37*. Thomas Nelson Publishers, 2006.

Cockerill, Gareth Lee. *The Epistle to the Hebrews*. William B. Eerdmans Publishing Company, 2012.

Collins, Francis S. *The Language of God: A Scientist Presents Evidence for Belief*. Free Press, 2007.

Craigie, Peter C. *The Book of Deuteronomy*. Wm. B. Eerdmans Publishing Co., 1976.

Cross, F. L., and Elizabeth A. Livingstone, editors. *The Oxford Dictionary of the Christian Church*. 3rd ed. rev., Oxford University Press, 2005.

Dobbs, Betty J. T. *The Foundations of Newton's Alchemy: The Hunting of the Green Lyon*. Cambridge University Press, 1975.

Drake, Stillman. *Galileo: Pioneer Scientist*. University of Toronto Press, 1990.

DuBose, Rick. *In Jesus' Name: 5 Altars of Prayer That Move Heaven and Earth*. Chosen Books, 2023.

Easley, Kendell H. *Holman QuickSource Guide to Understanding the Bible*. Nashville, TN: Holman Bible Publishers, 2002.

Einstein, Albert, et al. *Albert Einstein, the Human Side: Glimpses from His Archives*. Edited by Helen Dukas and Banesh Hoffmann, Princeton University Press, 2013.

Elwell, Walter A. *Baker Encyclopedia of the Bible*. Vol. 2, Baker Book House, 1988.

Estes, Daniel J. *Psalms 73–150*. Edited by E. Ray. Clendenen, vol. 13, B&H Publishing Group, 2019.

Evans, C. Stephen. *Pocket Dictionary of Apologetics & Philosophy of Religion*.

InterVarsity Press, 2002.

Fausset, A. R. *A Commentary, Critical, Experimental, and Practical, on the Old and New Testaments: Job–Isaiah*. William Collins, Sons, & Company, Limited, n.d.

Fee, Gordon D., and Douglas Stuart. *How to Read the Bible for All Its Worth: Fourth Edition*. Zondervan Academic, 2014.

Fee, Gordon D., and Robert L. Hubbard Jr., editors. *The Eerdmans Companion to the Bible*. William B. Eerdmans Publishing Company, 2011.

Feldmeth, Nathan P. *Pocket Dictionary of Church History: Over 300 Terms Clearly and Concisely Defined*. IVP Academic, 2008.

Ferris, Timothy. *Coming of Age in the Milky Way*. Harper Perennial, 2003.

Fölsing, Albrecht. *Albert Einstein: A Biography*. Penguin (Non-Classics), 1998.

Freedman, David Noel, Gary A. Herion, et al., editors. *The Anchor Yale Bible Dictionary*, Doubleday, 1992.

Freely, John. *Celestial Revolutionary: Copernicus, the Man and His Universe*. Bloomsbury Publishing, 2014.

Galli, Mark, and Ted Olsen. *131 Christians Everyone Should Know*. Broadman & Holman Publishers, 2000.

Gingerich, Owen. *The Book Nobody Read: Chasing the Revolutions of Nicolaus Copernicus*. Bloomsbury Publishing USA, 2009.

Greenwood, John D. *A Conceptual History of Psychology*. McGraw Hill, 2009.

Grote, George. *A History of Greece: Volume 4*. Cambridge University Press, 2010.

Guthrie, Donald. *Pastoral Epistles: An Introduction and Commentary*. InterVarsity Press, 1990.

Guzik, David. *Job*. David Guzik, 2007.

---. *Joshua*. David Guzik, 2000.

Hamilton, Victor P. *The Book of Genesis, Chapters 1–17*. Wm. B. Eerdmans Publishing Co., 1990.

Hannam, James. *The Globe: How the Earth Became Round*. Reaktion Books, 2023.

Harari, Yuval Noah. *21 Lessons for the 21st Century*. Random House, 2018.

---. Sapiens: *A Brief History of Humankind*. Signal, 2014.

Hartley, John E. *The Book of Job*. Wm. B. Eerdmans Publishing Co., 1988.

Harriman, David. *The Logical Leap: Induction in Physics*. Penguin, 2010.

Hastings, James, et al., editors. *A Dictionary of the Bible: Dealing with Its Language, Literature, and Contents Including the Biblical Theology*. vol. I–V, Charles Scribner's Sons; T. & T. Clark, 1911–1912.

Hawking, Stephen, and Carl Sagan. *A Brief History of Time: From the Big Bang to Black Holes*. Bantam, 1988.

Hawking, Stephen, and Leonard Mlodinow. *The Grand Design*. Bantam, 2010.

Hoffe, Otfried. *Aristotle*. Ancient Greek Philosophy Series, edited by Anthony Preus, translated by Christine Salazar, State University of New York Press, 2003.

Holladay, William Lee and Ludwig Köhler. *A Concise Hebrew and Aramaic Lexicon of the Old Testament*. Brill, 2000.

Hooks, Stephen M. *Job*. College Press Pub., 2006.

Horton, Stanley M. *Systematic Theology: Revised Edition*. Logion Press, 2007.

Hubble, Edwin. *The Observational Approach to Cosmology*. Oxford University Press, 1937.

Karttunen, Hannu, et al. *Fundamental Astronomy*. 5th edition, Springer Science+Business Media, 2007.

Kingsley, Peter. *Ancient Philosophy, Mystery, and Magic: Empedocles and Pythagorean Tradition*. Oxford University Press, 1995.

Kissling, Paul J. *Genesis*. College Press Pub. Co., 2004.

Kittel, Gerhard, et al. *Theological Dictionary of the New Testament, Abridged in One Volume*. W.B. Eerdmans, 1985.

Klein, Ralph W. *1 Samuel*. Word, Incorporated, 1983.

Knight, Edward H. *Knight's American Mechanical Encyclopedia*. Vol. II GAS–REA, H. O. Houghton and Company, 1882.

Koestler, Arthur. The Sleepwalkers: *A History of Man's Changing Vision of the Universe*. The Macmillian Company, 1959.

Kroll, Richard et al. *Philosophy, Science, and Religion in England 1640-1700*. Cambridge University Press, 2008.

Kruse, Colin G. *The Letters of John*. W.B. Eerdmans Pub.; Apollos, 2000.

Lane, William L. *Hebrews 9–13*. Word, Incorporated, 1991.

Leeming, David A. et al. *Encyclopedia of Psychology and Religion*. Springer Science+Business Media, LLC, 2010.

Lennox, John C. *Seven Days That Divide the World: The Beginning According to Genesis and Science.* Zondervan, 2011.

Linden, Stanton J. *The Alchemy Reader: From Hermes Trismegistus to Isaac Newton.* Cambridge University Press, 2003.

Long, Alex. *Death and Immortality in Ancient Philosophy.* Cambridge University Press, 2019.

Louw, Johannes P., and Eugene Albert Nida. *Greek-English Lexicon of the New Testament: Based on Semantic Domains.* Electronic ed. of the 2nd edition., vol. 1, United Bible Societies, 1996.

MacDonald, William. *Believer's Bible Commentary: Old and New Testaments.* Edited by Arthur Farstad, Thomas Nelson, 1995.

Mangum, Douglas, et al., editors. *Lexham Theological Wordbook.* Lexham Press, 2014.

Marshall, I. Howard. *Acts: An Introduction and Commentary.* InterVarsity Press, 1980.

---. *The Epistles of John.* Wm. B. Eerdmans Publishing Co., 1978.

Matthews, Victor Harold, et al. *The IVP Bible Background Commentary: Old Testament.* Electronic ed., InterVarsity Press, 2000.

McDowell, Josh. *Evidence for Christianity.* Thomas Nelson Publishers, 2006.

McGee, J. Vernon. *Thru the Bible Commentary.* Electronic ed., vol. 2, Thomas Nelson, 1997.

McKenzie, Steven L. *Introduction to the Historical Books: Strategies for Reading.* Cambridge: William. B. Eerdmans Publishing Company, 2010.

McKim, Donald K., editor. *Dictionary of Major Biblical Interpreters.* InterVarsity Press, 2007.

Menzies, William W. *Bible Doctrines: A Pentecostal Perspective.* Edited by Stanley M. Horton, Logion Press, 1993.

Merkel, Ingrid, and Allen G. Debus. *Hermeticism and the Renaissance: Intellectual History and the Occult in Early Modern Europe.* Associated University Presses, Inc., 1988.

Miller, Ron. *Recentering the Universe: The Radical Theories of Copernicus, Kepler, Galileo, and Newton.* Twenty-First Century Books, 2013.

Morris, Leon. *Luke: An Introduction and Commentary.* Vol. 3, InterVarsity Press, 1988.

---. *The Gospel according to John.* Wm. B. Eerdmans Publishing Co., 1995.

Mounce, William D. *Mounce's Complete Expository Dictionary of Old & New Testament Words*. Zondervan, 2006.

Newman, Barclay M., Jr., and Philip C. Stine. *A Handbook on Jeremiah*. United Bible Societies, 2003.

Newman, Barclay Moon, and Eugene Albert Nida. *A Handbook on the Acts of the Apostles*. United Bible Societies, 1972.

Newton, Isaac. *Newton's Principia: The Mathematical Principles of Natural Philosophy*. Translated by Andrew Motte, Daniel Adee, 1846.

---. *The Principia: Mathematical Principles of Natural Philosophy*. Translation by I. Bernard Cohen and Anne Whitman, assisted by Julia Budenz, University of California Press, 1999.

Nye, Bill. *Undeniable: Evolution and the Science of Creation*. Macmillan, 2014.

Orr, James, et al., editors. *The International Standard Bible Encyclopaedia*. Vol. 1-5, The Howard-Severance Company, 1915.

Palen, Stacey. *Schaum's Outline of Astronomy*. McGraw Hill Professional, 2001.

Panek, Richard. *The Trouble With Gravity: Solving the Mystery Beneath Our Feet*. HarperCollins, 2019.

Patzia, Arthur G., and Anthony J. Petrotta. *Pocket Dictionary of Biblical Studies*. InterVarsity Press, 2002.

Pietersma, Albert, and Benjamin G. Wright, editors. *A New English Translation of the Septuagint (Primary Texts)*. Oxford University Press, 2007.

Reyburn, William David. *A Handbook on the Book of Job*. United Bible Societies, 1992.

Reyburn, William David, and Euan McG. Fry. *A Handbook on Genesis*. United Bible Societies, 1998.

Riedweg, Christoph. *Pythagoras: His Life, Teaching, and Influence*. Cornell University Press, 2005.

Rusten, E. Michael, and Sharon Rusten. *The Complete Book of When & Where in the Bible and throughout History*. Michael E Rusten, 2005.

Sagan, Carl. *Cosmos*. Ballantine Books, 2011.

Salaman, Clement, et al. *The Way of Hermes: New Translations of The Corpus Hermeticum and The Definitions of Hermes Trismegistus to Asclepius*. Inner Traditions, 2000.

Sarfati, Jonathan and Lita Sanders. *Creation Astronomy for Kids*. Creation Book Publishers, 2023.

Schaeffer, Francis A. *The Complete Works of Francis A. Schaeffer: A Christian Worldview*. Crossway Books, 1982.

Schreiner, Thomas R. *1, 2 Peter, Jude*. Broadman & Holman Publishers, 2003.

Sgarbi, Marco. *Encyclopedia of Renaissance Philosophy*. Springer, 2022.

Shedd, William Greenough Thayer. *Dogmatic Theology*. Edited by Alan W. Gomes, 3rd ed., P & R Pub., 2003.

Spangler, David. *Reflections on the Christ*. Findhorn Foundation, 1978.

Spence-Jones, H. D. M., editor. *Genesis*. Funk & Wagnalls Company, 1909.

Sproul, R. C. *Can I Trust the Bible?* Reformation Trust Publishing, 2009.

Steinmann, Andrew E. *Genesis: An Introduction and Commentary*. Edited by David G. Firth, vol. 1, Inter-Varsity Press, 2019.

Sundstrom, Ted. *Mathematical Reasoning: Writing and Proof*. Version 1.1, Grand Valley State University, 2014.

Swanson, James. *Dictionary of Biblical Languages with Semantic Domains : Hebrew (Old Testament)*. Electronic ed., Logos Research Systems, Inc., 1997.

Thomas Nelson Publishers. *Nelson's Complete Book of Bible Maps & Charts: Old and New Testaments*. Rev. and updated ed., Thomas Nelson, 1996.

Thomas, Robert L. *New American Standard Hebrew-Aramaic and Greek Dictionaries : Updated Edition*. Foundation Publications, Inc., 1998.

Thompson, J. A. *Deuteronomy: An Introduction and Commentary*. InterVarsity Press, 1974.

Tsumura, David. *The First Book of Samuel*. Wm. B. Eerdmans Publishing Co., 2007.

Tyson, Neil deGrasse. *Death by Black Hole: And Other Cosmic Quandaries*. W. W. Norton and Company, 2007.

Voelkel, James R. *Johannes Kepler and the New Astronomy*. Oxford University Press, 2001.

Walton, John H. *The Lost World of Adam and Eve: Genesis 2-3 and the Human Origins Debate*. InterVarsity Press, 2015.

Walton, John H., and J. Harvey Walton. *The Lost World of the Torah: Law as Covenant and Wisdom in Ancient Context*. InterVarsity Press, 2019.

Walvoord, John F., and Roy B. Zuck, Dallas Theological Seminary. *The Bible Knowledge Commentary: An Exposition of the Scriptures*. Victor Books, 1985.

Warstler, Kevin R. *"Psalms."* CSB Study Bible: Notes, edited by Edwin A. Blum and Trevin Wax, Holman Bible Publishers, 2017.

Webster, Noah. *An American Dictionary of the English Language*. 1841.

Wenham, Gordon J. *Genesis 1-15*. Word, Incorporated, 1987.

Wesley, John. *The Works of John Wesley*. Third Edition, vol. 2, Wesleyan Methodist Book Room, 1872.

White, Andrew Dickson. *A History of the Warfare of Science with Theology in Christendom*. Vol. 1, first published 1896, Cambridge University Press, 2009.

Wiersbe, Warren W. *Be Patient*. Victor Books, 1996.

Wood, D. R. W., and I. Howard Marshall. *New Bible Dictionary, 3rd ed*. InterVarsity Press, 1996.

Woolfson, Michael M. *The Origin and Evolution of the Solar System*. CRC Press, 2000.

Woudstra, Marten H. *The Book of Joshua*. Wm. B. Eerdmans Publishing Co., 1981.

Understanding Media and Culture: An Introduction to Mass Communication. Author's Name Unpublished, University of Minnesota Libraries Publishing, 2016.

Youngblood, Ronald F., et al., Thomas Nelson Publishers, editors. *Nelson's New Illustrated Bible Dictionary*. Thomas Nelson, Inc., 1995.

Books by Author

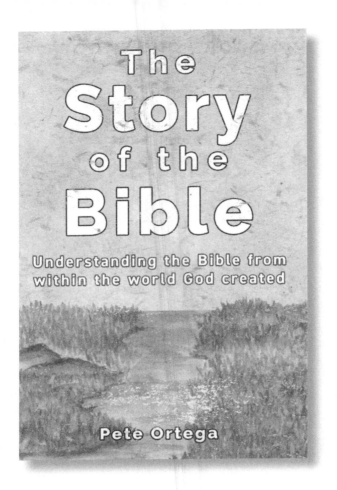

The Story of the Bible

Do you know it? The Story of the Heavens. The Story of Land. The Story of Images. The Story of the gods. The Story of the Soul. The Story of Bloodlines. The Story of Power. It is a beautiful story that works within the system that God created. If you ignore the structure and purpose of the heavenly and earthly realms, you will miss one of the greatest stories ever told.

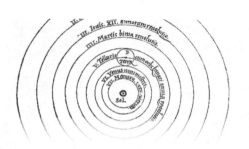

Proving the
B I B L E
Wrong

The attempt to undermine the
authority of God's word with science.

Pete Ortega

Everything you believe about the universe has a beginning. You did not discover the universe on your own. You were told how it began. The Bible informed you "In the beginning," and you believed it. You believed it because the Bible is God's word. Thanks to science, you have been taught to believe the very opposite of what the Bible teaches. It was no accident. It was by design, all from a brief moment in history. This book is about the pursuit of science in *Proving the Bible Wrong.*

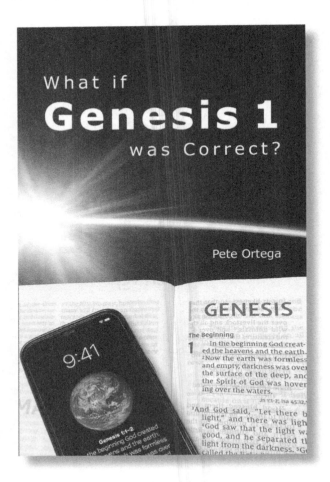

The way we currently understand the world and the layout of the universe, is it possible to believe the Creation Story as written in the Bible? Can we trust what the Bible tells us? Many would argue that the Bible is not a book of science. I believe it is. And so much more. This book is my story about hearing God's voice and how I came to deal with the question, *"What if Genesis 1 was Correct?"*

There is no such thing as a perfect family. There is also no reason why you cannot be great parents and raise loving, polite, and well-behaved children. No matter the size of your family, the number of parents, or the age of your children, you can start becoming a great family. From bedtime to dealing with pornography, there is a solution. Our method is based on simple principles and practical things. We invite you into our family to see how parenting is easier than you think if you are willing to work for it.

About the Author

Pete Ortega lives in Southern Minnesota. He enjoys research, writing, and family. He has written several books including a parenting book with his wife. He can be reached at the following email address.

Contact

info@ortegalife.com